How the Canyon

Became Grand

Books by Stephen J. Pyne

GRAND CANYON SUITE

How the Canyon Became Grand: A Short History

Grove Karl Gilbert

Fire on the Rim: A Firefighter's Season at the Grand Canyon

CYCLE OF FIRE

World Fire: The Culture of Fire on Earth

Vestal Fire: An Environmental History, Told Through Fire,
of Europe and Europe's Encounter with the World

Fire in America: A Cultural History of
Wildland and Rural Fire

Burning Bush: A Fire History of Australia

The Ice: A Journey to Antarctica

OTHER FIRE STUDIES

Introduction to Wildland Fire

America's Fires: Management in Wildlands and Forests

A SHORT HISTORY

Stephen J. Pyne

HOW

THE

CANYON

BECAME GRAND

VIKING

VIKING
Published by the Penguin Group
Penguin Putnam Inc., 375 Hudson Street,
New York, New York 10014, U.S.A.
Penguin Books Ltd, 27 Wrights Lane, London W8 5TZ, England
Penguin Books Australia Ltd, Ringwood, Victoria, Australia
Penguin Books Canada Ltd, 10 Alcorn Avenue,
Toronto, Ontario, Canada M4V 3B2
Penguin Books (N.Z.) Ltd, 182–190 Wairau Road,
Auckland 10, New Zealand
Penguin India, 210 Chiranjiv Tower, 43 Nehru Place,
New Delhi 11009, India

Penguin Books Ltd, Registered Offices:
Harmondsworth, Middlesex, England

First published in 1998 by Viking Penguin,
a member of Penguin Putnam Inc.

10 9 8 7 6 5 4 3 2 1

Illustration credits appear on page 201.

LIBRARY OF CONGRESS CATALOGING-IN-PUBLICATION DATA
Pyne, Stephen J., date.
How the Canyon became Grand : a short history / Stephen J. Pyne.
p.   cm.
Includes bibliographical references and index.
ISBN 0-670-88110-4
1. Grand Canyon (Ariz.)—History.   I. Title.
F788.P97   1998
979.1'32—dc21   98-20094

This book is printed on acid-free paper.
∞

Printed in the United States of America
Set in Simoncini Garamond
Designed by Kathryn Parise
Topographic map pages viii–ix by L. Kubinyi

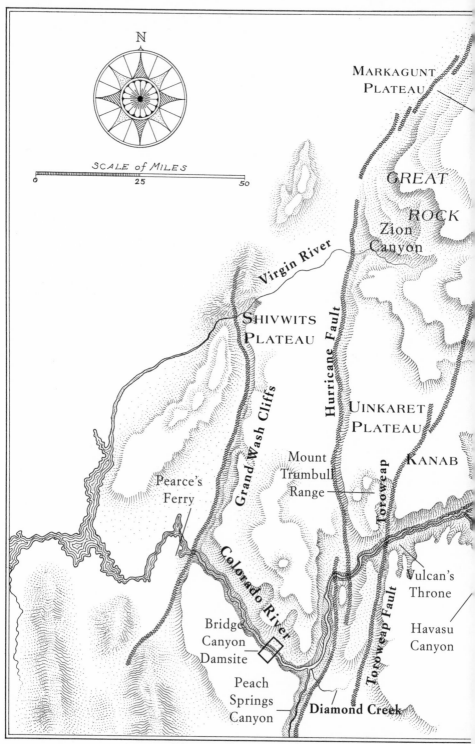

N

SCALE of MILES

0   25   50

MARKAGUNT
PLATEAU

GREAT

ROCK

Zion
Canyon

Virgin River

SHIVWITS
PLATEAU

Hurricane Fault

UINKARET
PLATEAU

KANAB

Mount
Trumbull
Range

Toroweap

Pearce's
Ferry

Grand Wash Cliffs

Vulcan's
Throne

Colorado River

Havasu
Canyon

Bridge
Canyon
Damsite

Toroweap Fault

Peach
Springs
Canyon

Diamond Creek

WESTERN CANYON

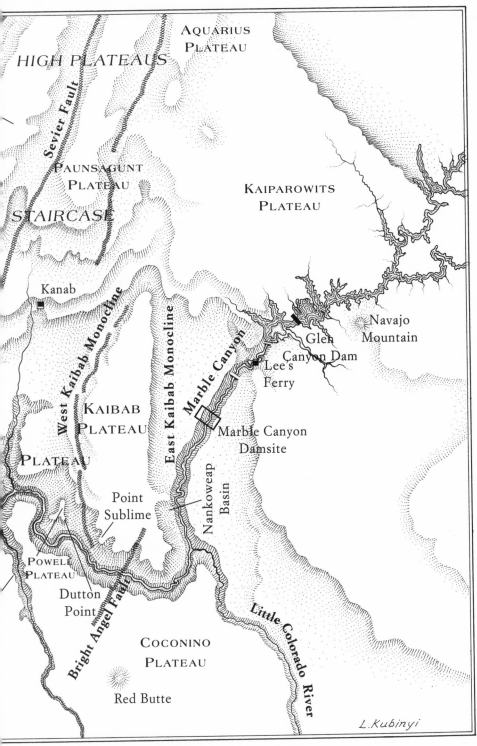

HIGH PLATEAUS

Sevier Fault

AQUARIUS
PLATEAU

PAUNSAGUNT
PLATEAU

STAIRCASE

KAIPAROWITS
PLATEAU

Kanab

West Kaibab Monocline

East Kaibab Monocline

Marble Canyon

Navajo
Mountain

Glen

Canyon Dam

Lee's
Ferry

KAIBAB
PLATEAU

Marble Canyon
Damsite

PLATEAU

Point
Sublime

Nankoweap
Basin

POWELL
PLATEAU

Dutton
Point

Bright Angel Fault

Little Colorado River

COCONINO
PLATEAU

Red Butte

L. Kubinyi

EASTERN CANYON

OVERLOOK:

THE VIEW FROM DUTTON POINT

Even for a landscape known for its uniqueness, this place is special. At Powell Plateau, an isolated mesa, the natural and human history of the Canyon distill into one compact monument. The mesa trails west like a pennant flapping in the winds of geologic time. A thick peninsula, concluding in Dutton Point, anchors that stony banner not only to the Canyon's gorge but also to the American civilization that claimed it. Stand at Dutton Point and see the features that make this landscape what it is.

All the geologic processes that have shaped the Canyon converge to sculpt a Canyon in miniature. The Muav fracture zone to the east separates the eastern and western Canyons and testifies to the forces that had pushed the plateaus to their great heights. An entrenched Colorado River arcing to the south and west shows the counterforce of erosion that turned a lithic hump into a hole. To the north there are more faults, spring-fed gorges, terraced strata, and the relentless recession of rock-wasting cliffs. Taken together they define the mesa's borders and document the events and processes large and small that have sculpted it. Even so, a perspective on the place is hard to maintain. By itself Powell Plateau stands taller than any peak east of the Rocky Mountains. Set within the Canyon, its dimensions are dwarfed and its distinctiveness compromised.

More important, the scene distills another Canyon, the one that most visitors actually see, a cultural Canyon, the Grand Canyon as a place with meaning. This landscape has been shaped by ideas, words, images, and experiences. Instead of faults, rivers, and mass wasting, the processes at work involved geopolitical upheavals and the swell of empires, the flow of art, literature, science, and philosophy, the chisel of mind against matter. These determined the shape of Canyon meaning. As they converged in place and time, they distinguished the Canyon from among hundreds of other, competing landscapes.

All this too is apparent from Dutton Point. Look southeast and see where Captain García López Cárdenas, equipped with odd baggage from the Renaissance, first peered over the South Rim searching for a river of empire. Look southwest and observe where Padre Francisco Tomás Garcés, carrying the continued burdens of the Counter-Reformation, entered the gorge through Cataract Canyon in a search for souls. Then came fur trappers and freebooters and agricultural colonizers. They peered and probed and, unable to discover much of value, let the gorges sink back into obscurity. Its size did not make the Canyon significant. Its physical geography alone could not establish meaning.

Look now about Powell Plateau itself. In one crowded throng of place-names, the mesa tells another story, a sudden outpouring of discovery and fevered interrogation as distinctive and separate as the mesa's physical presence. Its points all bear the names of Canyon explorers, from military commanders like Lieutenants Joseph C. Ives and George M. Wheeler to scientists like John Strong Newberry, John Wesley Powell, and Clarence Edward Dutton. One after another the major personalities of Canyon history had come to its brink. Here is where Powell directed Thomas Moran to the rim, and here the *Chasm of the Colorado* acquired its focal lens on the river. Here Dutton and William Henry Holmes came and looked east to the peninsula they named Point Sublime, bas-reliefs of geologic antiquity. They made rocky rims beckon instead of frighten, shaped limestone-fractured peninsulas into focal points for a perspective of earth time instead of overlooks to voids, and allowed yellow, red, and mauve stone to radiate its own appreciated brilliance instead of merely betraying the absence of floral greenery. They elevated a ride down and through the gorge into the status of a national rite of passage. Until such transformations—until, in brief, the Canyon became a national monument as rich with cultivated meaning as a St. Peter's Basilica or a Crystal Palace—it was shunned. But once endowed with significance, like a rough diamond cut and placed under light, it dazzled, and America declared it beyond price.

The creation of Canyon meaning was as arduous and dramatic as the excavation of its great gorges. The process required a flow of ideas as vigorous as the Colorado River, and much as the scale of the Canyon depended on the height and mass of the excavated Kaibab Plateau, so the texture of understanding derived from the immense bulk of American civilization. The outcome was especially sweeping because for the Grand Canyon that interaction occurred between landscape and an educated elite—call it America's high culture—to large themes and high styles. No ancient folk resided between rims. No centuries-long tradition of utilization bound a peasantry to the place and shaped meaning with the slow patience of water dripping on a stone. Those who interpreted the Canyon would never live within it. They met it suddenly, and they could afford to see the gorges and mesas and sunbleached terraces in idealistic and cosmopolitan terms.

Without that act of imagination the Canyon would likely have joined the throngs of forgotten and dismissed landscapes that litter the surfaces of the earth, a geographic freak, a landscape curiosity rather than a cultural oracle. But the improbable happened. Since the mid-nineteenth century, the Canyon has been explored and appreciated, and for the better part of a century it has been a central emblem, a profound truth, for many major American intellectuals and, through them, for American culture at large. In the from which they later immortalized the Canyon, in words and panoramas, as a Grand Ensemble. Here Uncle Jim Owens escorted Teddy Roosevelt to hunt mountain lions. At Dutton Point the Canyon's heroic age, figuratively and often literally, gathered to look and comment. Even amid the panoramic sweep of American society this overlook offered a special vision. Here a great civilization encountered a great natural phenomenon. Neither was the same afterward.

Why did they come and what did they see? At the heart of every Canyon overlook there lies the paradox that while indescribable, the scene is not incomprehensible. It has meaning, and that meaning depends less on the scene's physical geography than on the ideas through which it can be viewed and imagined. Those ideas are not something added to Canyon scenery, like a coat of paint, or taken from it, like a snapshot, any more than the river was something added to a prefabricated gorge. They have actively shaped the Canyon's meaning, without which it could hardly exist as a cultural spectacle.

The Grand Canyon was not so much revealed as created. More than once the Canyon was missed entirely or seen and dismissed. Then, with the suddenness of a summer storm, American society in the mid-nineteenth century mustered the capacity and the will to match its discovered opportunity and transformed land into place and place into symbol. The outcome was neither obvious nor inevitable. Popular instincts argued that river-dashed gorges were hazards, not adventures, and that immense chasms were geographic gaps, not gorgeous panoramas. A generation of intellectuals labored to instruct the public otherwise. They interpreted erosion-molded buttes as natural architecture and sculpture, as the coliseums, temples, and statuary of an inspired nature; they made folded blocks of crust into notebooks from the experimental laboratories of the earth; they rendered the etched strata of hard sandstone and friable shale into landscape frescoes and end, the Grand Canyon cut a swath through the landscape of American history no less unique and grandiloquent than that which the Colorado River had excavated out of the Colorado Plateau. Indeed, the dramatic abruptness of the Canyon's brink matches the suddenness of that historic moment in which a Colorado canyon and American civilization met. How rim and river intersected remains a geologic mystery; how the place and its poets came together endures as something of an intellectual miracle.

No single vantage point captures all the Canyon. The panorama is too vast; the details of its evolution are too demanding. But the cultural Canyon did have its heroic age, during which it underwent a cultural chrysalis, and more than most the task of interpretation fell to—or rather was seized by—a curious polymath, Clarence Edward Dutton, captain of ordnance in the U.S. Army, geologist, raconteur, explorer, landscape critic, and author of that most comprehensive of Canyon books, *Tertiary History of the Grand Cañon District*. It was Dutton who argued that the Grand Canyon was a "great innovation in our modern ideas of scenery," that like all such innovations, it had to be understood before it could be appreciated, and cultivated before it could be understood. Then he showed how to do it.

So return to Powell Plateau and especially to that anchoring overlook that peers into the Canyon's core. Probably its scenic panorama is more comprehensive than majestic, the view more instructive than inspiring. It is a place not easily reached nor commonly visited nor readily appreciated. Its importance, in fact, lies less as a place than as a perspective; and for this it is unexcelled. Ultimately, Dutton's Point proposes a point of view, a positioning of the intellect to refract a whole culture, breaking like a sunset through prisms of sculpted rock and gilt-edged sky. So Clarence Dutton had argued; and so through Dutton can we refract the history of Canyon meaning. Stand at Dutton's Point and see how the Canyon became Grand.

CONTENTS

How the Canyon

Became Grand

TWO NEW
WORLDS

I have heard rumors of visitors who were disappointed. The
same people will be disappointed at the Day of Judgment. In
fact, the Grand Canyon is a sort of landscape Day of Judgment.
It is not a show place, a beauty spot, but a revelation.

—J. B. PRIESTLEY

From the top they could make out, apart from the canyon, some
small boulders which seemed to be as high as a man. Those who
went down and who reached them swore that they were taller
than the great tower of Seville.

—PEDRO DE CASTEÑADA,
WITH THE CORONADO EXPEDITION

The gorges of the Colorado Plateau are remarkably elusive.
Even so pronounced a landform as the Grand Canyon—
prominent on satellite photos hundreds of miles aloft—is virtually
invisible until one stands on the rim. It is possible to pass within a
score of miles, or sometimes of meters, from that rim and never
see the gorge, and more than one traveler has done just that.
There is no measured transition: the plateau instantly ends; the
canyon instantly begins. The rim is an edge, a weld between

incommensurate landscapes. The river is more a barrier than a conduit. The Canyon suddenly is.

No impression of the place is more constantly invoked than the abruptness of its vision, a perspective almost wholly formed upon first view. The grand-manner tourist hotels erected along its rims exploited this fact, gave not a hint of the Canyon to motorists or train travelers until, as they passed through the foyer, the full spectacle burst upon them. A common query at the national park is the disarmingly perceptive, Where is the Grand Canyon? Few people have stumbled on to the Canyon; they had to set out with deliberation to find it. And to search it out, they needed an adequate reason.

The contrast with other landscapes is profound. Unlike a mountain's flank, the Canyon rim is defined with a geologic razor, and within its borders the Canyon is completely contained. A mountain may be seen from afar, its nature appreciated long before it is climbed, and for Western civilization the cultivation of mountain scenery had centuries behind it. So also rivers could be assessed from their tributaries, and traversed by them, one current feeding with measured flow into the other. So in other commanding landscapes known to Western civilization one feature led by gradation to another. But nothing led to the Canyon. It came as a phenomenon, an idea, and an aesthetic almost wholly without precedent. The Canyon suddenly was.

There was no evolved aesthetic or science for canyons as there was for mountains and waterfalls and other monuments of nature. For a defile on the scale of the Grand Canyon there was almost no prior preparation. The vision came—all of it, in all of its complexity and stunning uniqueness—as an instantaneous revelation. For those sixteenth-century Europeans who first encountered it, for whom the Renaissance was still aglow, the Grand Canyon was as unexpected an intellectual as it was a geographic enigma. They arrived more or less by accident.

But while the place remained, the civilization moved on. Those who came three hundred years later followed a scientific revolu-

tion in natural history, a Romantic revolution in art and consciousness, and a wave of democratic political revolutions. For them the
Canyon called, and the abruptness of Canyon scenery became a
tenet of its appreciation, part of an aesthetic canon of Canyon
mannerisms, and the abruptness of its rims, an illustration of the
erosive mechanics that had sculpted the region. That transformation in appreciation came, when it finally appeared, with a suddenness and completeness that seem peculiarly appropriate.

CANYON, FOUND AND LOST

No one knows what significance the Canyon held for the peoples
who came and went and for periods of decades or centuries lived
around the region over the ten thousand inhabited years before
Europeans arrived. Paleo hunters pursued bighorn sheep and
deer and left split-twig figurines in caves. In later times foragers
and farmers constructed stone dwellings along the rims and built
runoff terraces on Walhalla Plateau and grew beans, squash, and
maize around even inner Canyon springs and the Nankoweap and
Chuar deltas and laid out trails from rim to river.

What the place meant cognitively is unknown, or how each of
the handful or hundreds of peoples who saw it refracted the scene
through the prism of their aesthetic sensibilities or repositioned it
within their own moral geographies. Its magnitude alone demanded explanation and probably attracted some mythic significance commensurate with its physical dimensions and utilization.
Probably each people believed the space theirs, and themselves
chosen. The Hopi located the *sipapu,* the orifice through which
they emerged from the earth, near the junction of the Little Colorado with the Canyon. For the Havasupai, who farmed in the
well-watered Havasu Canyon, a tributary to the Colorado, and
hunted and foraged on the plateau's rim, the greater Canyon was
the border to where they lived.

But what other peoples believed about the site they kept to

themselves. Every society, after all, has its own sacred places. The Canyon became transnationally grand only after far-voyaging Europeans peered into it and then only after a much-metamorphosed European culture created a metaphoric matrix by which to interpret it.

Renaissance Europe encountered two new worlds, one of learning, another of geographic discovery. They were not always or necessarily fused. Scholars who constructed gorgeous *mappae mundi* with Jerusalem squarely in the center of the world had little in common with pilots who kept rutters and consulted empirically drawn portolan charts. That is why the Canyon was discovered quickly after the Great Voyages and why it was immediately forgotten.

The Canyon was, in fact, among the earliest of North America's natural wonders to be visited. Spanish conquistadors came to the South Rim in 1540, earlier by 138 years to Father Hennepin's sighting of Niagara Falls, by 167 years to John Colter's encounter with the Yellowstone, by almost 300 years to Joseph Reddeford Walker's discovery of Yosemite Valley. The Colorado River was identified and mapped long before the St. Lawrence, the Columbia, the Hudson, or even the Mississippi. Yet the Canyon was among the last of these wonders to be assimilated, much less celebrated. As far as Spain and the rest of Europe were concerned, the discovered Canyon quickly became a lost Canyon. While the sails of European expansion had swiftly reached the Colorado River, the Renaissance died on the voyages upstream and the overland *entradas* across its chromatic rocks.

The reason was in good measure due to the peculiar character of exploration in the sixteenth century. Beginning with the African coasting inspired by Henry the Navigator in the fifteenth century and concluding roughly with a revival of circumnavigations during the eighteenth century, well symbolized by the voyages of Captain James Cook, Europe had launched a great age of discovery, but one that was predominantly maritime. Leaving its inland seas, the Mediterranean and the Baltic, voyagers from Europe had sailed across the global ocean. The era's greatest discovery was the unity of the world sea; its grand gesture, a circumnavigation of that expanse; its outstanding achievement, a *mappa mundi* of the world's shorelines. Hammered for centuries from the Eurasian landmass, peninsular Europe had turned to the sea, and by stitching together, with the threads of its long-voyaging expeditions, previously segregated maritime regions, it produced a common quilt of the world ocean, the beginning of a truly global imperium. Newly discovered islands assisted that enterprise, but continents as often as not impeded it and provoked an endless search for straits, portages, or other passages around, over, or through them. For the Great Voyages the ship was the means, and the sea the end.

Europe's experiments in conquest, colonization, and commerce clung like ship's barnacles to the littoral of the world ocean or sought out offshore islands surrounded by sea moats. Everywhere outposts were founded on the coasts, and even the conquests of Mexico and Peru were preceded by the establishment of port cities, Veracruz and Lima. For the most part, penetration inland came by following major rivers that connected ports to the interior, or by crossing inland seas like the Great Lakes, or in a few exceptional instances by traversing overland.

Among the latter, however, were several *entradas* of epic proportion, and two of the greatest, those of Hernando de Soto and Francisco Vásquez de Coronado, set out in 1539 and 1540 respectively. Each had as its goal fabulous city-states, new Tenochitláns and Cuzcos, reputedly located somewhere in the interior, in Quivira. De Soto approached from Florida, Coronado from Mexico. Yet even the Coronado Expedition, at least in its conception, dared not abandon a maritime lifeline. While the main party probed northward into the American Southwest, another party under Melchior Díaz sought to rendezvous with ships commanded by Hernando de Alarcón moving up the Sea of Cortés to its rumored confluence with a great river. That rendezvous failed, but in an effort to reestablish such a waterway and during a time when "no other commissions pressed upon him," Pedro Álvarez de Tovar dispatched a party under García López de Cárdenas to investigate the rumor of a great river to the west of their winter camp at Zuñi. Such a river might be the same as that Alarcón was probing. It was worth investigating.[1]

With Indian guides from Tuzán to lead them, the Cárdenas party advanced to the Canyon's rim, probably near present-day Desert View. The site was cold and arid, covered with low-growing piñon and juniper. Proper perspective was impossible. The canyon looked like an outsize arroyo, the river little more than a fathom wide, boulders within the gorge no larger than a man. For three days, cold and thirsty, they probed for a way down. At last three members led by Captain Pablos de Melgosa attempted to scramble down at a place that "seemed less difficult." They returned that afternoon, having failed to reach the bottom, exclaiming that the Indians had been right, that the canyon was immense, that the river was broader than the Tagus and the perceived boulders taller "than the great tower of Seville." Of the chromatic view they said nothing. The river they could see but not reach. They had no means.[2]

With the wind biting, water scarce, and descent difficult, the Spaniards withdrew in disappointment. Intent on the discovery of civilizations, and with them gold to plunder and souls to convert, or on geographic discoveries that would lead to such conquests, the Spanish conquistador had little to say of the Grand Canyon. Only two chroniclers mention the foray; even Cárdenas says nothing in his *Relación*. Canyon geography proved to be little more than a false lead in the geopolitics of conquest, and an account of its exploration not much more than an aside in the narrative of an epic but politically futile trek. The Colorado River soon appeared on European maps by mid-century. It dominates North America on the Gastaldi map of 1546. But there is no indication of a great arroyo along the river's inland channel.

This indifference betrays something more than the steely soul of a conquistador. Coming three years before Copernicus published *De revolutionibus*, the symbolic prolegomenon to the scientific revolution, only twenty years after Magellan's fleet first circumnavigated the globe, and nearly thirty years before Mercator synthesized the known geography of the *terra nova orbis* with his famous projection, the Spanish had little context for the revelation of the Canyon. There were no scientists among the entourage, nor any artists; priests or personal secretaries doubled as chroniclers. Not for three hundred years would science even acquire its modern name. Granada, the last Moorish stronghold in Spain, had fallen to Spanish arms only in 1492, the year Columbus made landfall in the New World. Like Russia slowly sloughing off the Mongol yoke, Spain, in driving out the Moorish overlords, found itself curiously skewed to Western culture, an amalgam of Europe and North Africa as Russia was of Europe and Central Asia.

Where Spain had once led Europe's revival of learning, it now began to lag. The thirteenth century had experienced a renaissance of scholarship, culminating in the theological synthesis of Thomas Aquinas, that had derived in no small way from the recovery and translation of ancient texts. In this restoration Spain had been both center and conduit. It had prompted a reconciliation of Christianity with ancient learning. But the greater Renaissance that flourished in the fifteenth and sixteenth centuries passed over Spain without reaching, as it did elsewhere, the scientific revolution of the seventeenth.

Spain came hesitatingly to the experimental empiricism, the mechanical philosophy, and the secularism that increasingly informed Western thought. Renaissance yielded to a revival of religious orthodoxy, not modern science. By the time of Coronado's expedition Spain had become a stronghold of the Counter-Reformation; its scholars continued to meditate on the old texts and dismiss many of the new. Probably no European country was prepared to appreciate a phenomenon like the Canyon, but Spain was intellectually among the least receptive. While, in much of Europe, the Book of Nature joined Scripture as a testimony to the Creator, Spain proscribed it. That book proposed a different philosophy and demanded a different dialectic from that used to translate Arab-transmitted texts from antiquity. There were no Grand Canyons in the Aristotelian classics or the prophetic books of Holy Scripture.

Ironically, although Spain was perhaps the most advanced nation of Europe in its ability to mount expeditions and establish colonies, it was among the most retarded in its capacity to absorb its discoveries within the context of the new ideas and new sensibility that raged across the rest of Europe. Its interest in natural history focused largely on the question of native populations, a topic of supreme political, economic, and theological significance. Spanish rationalism was directed, in a dauntless rearguard action, toward the preservation of scholasticism. Five years after Captain Cárdenas halted on the Canyon rim, the Council of Trent began its counterattack against both Renaissance humanism and the practice of the new natural philosophy; eight years after Captain Melgosa clambered over the South Rim, there was born the greatest of Spanish philosophers, Francisco Suárez, a man whose twenty-six volumes consolidated Spanish metaphysics and theology on a thoroughly Thomistic basis.

In 1540 Spain demonstrated its imperial talents by expeditions of conquest, like those of Coronado and de Soto; by reforms in colonial administration, like the new Law of the Indies; and by the founding of the Jesuit order by a former soldier, Ignatius of Loyola. That the Cárdenas party could only liken Canyon features to those of Seville, the point of departure for Spain's overseas imperium, suggested both the power and the limitations of Spanish discovery. Its conquistadors were knights-errant, not savants. Yet Spain hardly stood alone. Decades were to pass before other nations began to penetrate the New World, and centuries were to unfold before European civilization could cope with what its explorers found.

The apparatus for valorizing such phenomena did not exist. Even had there been scientists with Cárdenas, there was hardly yet a cosmology suitable for interpreting a landscape as peculiar as the Canyon. The earth was believed to have commenced a few thousand years before, its great natural features shaped by the Noachian Flood. The invention of mathematical perspective was barely a century old. Cartographic projections, even those based on such methods, concentrated on the coastlines and oceans, not on the interiors. Had there been artists, they would have possessed few techniques on their palettes by which to convey the Canyon's immensity, awesomeness, and complex matrix of color and structure. Perspective had entered Spanish art only a handful of years before Coronado began his march; the conventions of modern landscape as formulated by Claude Lorrain were still a century in the future. Not for another 250 years would the calculation of longitude become more or less routine, would natural historians coin the word *geology,* would an educated elite begin to attach the word *sublime* to distinctive landscapes. With regard to learning sixteenth-century Spain was no worse off—was probably more advanced—than its European or Islamic rivals.

The celebration of natural monuments in and of themselves was alien to them all. Great arroyos held no value, not political, not economic, not intellectual, not aesthetic. None had any means by which to triangulate such a spectacle into a vision even remotely resembling the modern one. The Grand Canyon as a landscape fact attracted less attention than did geographic fables like Quivira, the Strait of Anian, or the Río Buenaventura. It was, after all, the fabulous but well-traveled yarns of Fray Marcos de Niza that had set the Coronado *entrada* into motion. That Spanish adventurers and missionaries made it to the Canyon rim is one of the marvels of Western history; that they failed to appreciate what they saw, one of its lesser mysteries. The Spanish mind was prepared to understand, and Spanish political economy prepared to assimilate, the discovery of Golden Cíbolas, not Grand Canyons.

For 256 years after Cárdenas no subsequent expedition

ventured to the Canyon's brink, and then the encounter was accidental to the search for heathen souls. To Spain, the Canyon remained a barrier, one of many along a daunting river that refused to behave as a new Guadalquivir or Plata. The Grand Canyon was an impenetrable tangle of *cañones,* mesas, and rapids, uninhabited, inaccessible, peripheral, not a presence so much as an absence, a place to be avoided. And so it was.

Still, the New Worlds of discovered geography did not remain independent from the new worlds of learning. Each complemented (and challenged) the other, and together they questioned the inherited worldview. The doubling in size of the known globe, like the multiplication of ancient texts and critics, helped shatter the authority of antiquity and antiquated methodology. The breakdown of Ptolemaic astronomy, symbolized by the sixteenth-century Copernican revolution, had its parallel in the disintegration of Ptolemaic geography under the blows of successive voyages. The intellectual challenge to inherited cosmology involved both data and theory. Telescopes and explorers discredited the presumed completeness of the synthesis recovered from the ancients; mathematics, its theoretical organization; and the new metaphysics of natural philosophy, its epistemology. Astronomers discovered new moons unknown to the *Almagest.* Adventurers unveiled immense new lands, populated with civilizations wholly unsuspected by the *Geographia.* Humanist scholars found in newly recovered texts from antiquity other geographies, unlike that of Ptolomeaus and the Alexandrian school. Not only were new data added, but over the centuries old errors were expunged.

The expanding imperium was intellectual as much as geopolitical, and exploration served both purposes. The Great Voyages became a model for empirical inquiry, a dramatic and intensely practical manifestation of a *novum organon* in which the tested reality of nature would substitute for the revelations of inherited texts. Captains and their pilots to the New World had little to

learn from Herodotus, Lucretius, or Pliny the Elder. Their lives depended on understanding, as best they could, the shoals and currents and tides they actually encountered. So would modern scholarship. Francis Bacon captured that spirit nicely when he used as a frontispiece to his *Great Instauration* a picture of ships sailing beyond the Pillars of Hercules. In leaving the Mediterranean for America, European civilization was also venturing beyond antiquity's dominion of understanding.

Yet the two often ran in parallel, like a stream beside hills, the main currents of thought draining from and trimming the heights of land. The rush of the Renaissance passed. Overseas colonies claimed islands and clung to coasts, like seal rookeries. Exploration devolved into trade; piracy and poaching brought more rewards than sponsored discovery. Even the scientific revolution stalled. Having gathered momentum and inspiration over the seventeenth century from mathematics and experimentation, it reached a dazzling crescendo with Isaac Newton's synthesis of natural philosophy. That example of exalted reason radiated throughout European culture. The light of the new learning flooded into dark corners of superstition and ignorance; the Greater Enlightenment acquired its master metaphor. Then, after this wild burst of genius, exhaustion set in, an era of intellectual housekeeping. Scholars sought to illuminate inherited lore in the light of reason. They preferred to consolidate and codify existing knowledge and practices rather than seek out bold new philosophies. Metaphysical speculators and naive travelers became an object of ridicule, as in Jonathan Swift's *Gulliver's Travels*; squabbles over existing trade routes replaced the daring discovery of new ones; the importation and invention of new worlds gave way to dictionaries, and of imagined worlds to practical knowledge. Enlightenment scholars pored over windy texts and hypothetical maps through the sharpened vision that practical inventions like bifocals made possible.

Then the pace quickened again. By the mid-eighteenth century political rivalries and intellectual curiosity revived. Together

empire and enlightenment began to stun geographic exploration out of its institutional fibrillation.

SECOND AGE, SECOND CHANCE

The motivations spanned European culture. There was a renewal of extraterritorial expansion for which geopolitical rivalries were both cause and consequence. Russia commenced its imperial traverse of Eurasia; Britain and France inaugurated a new hundred years' war, this time sparring from India to Canada to the Antilles; the Netherlands poached Portuguese trade routes and even settlements from Brazil to the East Indies. Circumnavigation became the rage, and every nation aspiring to civilized status sponsored prolonged voyages of discovery. Every thrust brought European powers into conflict with one another as much as with indigenes. Coastal colonies in the Americas, Africa, and Australasia, drafting tens of millions of European émigrés, swept inland in a fantastic surge. By the early twentieth century Europe enjoyed political and economic hegemony over most of the planet. And from empire, exploration was never far removed.

Nor was learning. The Enlightenment spread first by applying new methods and perspectives to the existing canon. Scholars reworked inherited texts with the zeal of Renaissance humanists, this time not merely to translate but to rationalize. John Dryden rewrote Shakespeare to prune away fanciful language and excess. Alexander Pope translated Homer into heroic couplets. Everywhere savants sought to codify according to more modern criteria. Linnaeus proposed a *Systema naturae* by which to organize the flora and later the fauna of the world. Samuel Johnson assembled the first English dictionary. Denis Diderot oversaw the modern *Encyclopédie*, and Montesquieu, an annotated digest of the law. The age honored "practical" knowledge much as it sought a "plain" style.

Everywhere architects of Enlightenment tried to discover, or

where they deemed necessary sought to impose, a reformed order based on their perception of Reason. But if the texts of the old authorities lay like broken idols, the concept of authority itself endured. The Enlightenment substituted and secularized; Nature replaced Scripture as a source of general authority; natural philosophy succeeded theology as the exemplar of knowledge. Newton's universe was as absolute in its structure as Aquinas's, though it removed dialectical logic for experimentation and allegory for mathematics. A full-blown relativity had to wait for modernism. The break with religion, however, at least helped quiet the era's politics. Europeans no longer slaughtered one another over minute differences between Newtonian and Leibnitzian calculus or among various models of gravity as they had over the mysteries of transsubstantiation and the practices of full- or partial-immersion baptism.

More important, the Enlightenment's momentum carried it beyond the status of a secular Renaissance. Its agenda had proposed a diffusion of learning—empirical, secular, mathematical, experimental where possible—that promised to penetrate every field of inquiry. It was inevitable that a period of consolidation and reconstruction should follow. But experimental science, unlike text-based scholasticism, could not long pause, nor long thrive with endless glosses; it needed more data, novel experiences, new worlds; and modern science (call it Newtonian after its greatest symbol) fueled the Enlightenment's engines. Natural science rested long enough to regroup, then it pushed on. It no more halted at putative frontiers than had Europe's adventurers. Its practitioners sought out new fields for study as eagerly as Clives and La Salles had new lands for claims and conquest. One dynamic, in fact, fed the other. Inevitably the imperial ambitions of Enlightenment learning fused with the imperial fervor of European expansion to yield both a new kind of explorer and a new era of exploration.

What William Goetzmann has termed the Second Great Age of Discovery, a revival of exploration that gathered force in the mid-eighteenth century, had many tributaries. As trade followed the flag, so did learning. The need to validate Newtonian mechanics, that exemplar of Enlightenment scholarship, could best be addressed by paired expeditions to the poles and equator, the famed surveys of Pierre-Louis Moreau de Maupertuis to Lapland and Charles-Marie de la Condamine to the Andes in the 1730s. The need to calibrate the Newtonian solar system, specifically to measure the distance between the earth and the sun, inspired a much-vaster enterprise in which in 1761 and again, on a larger scale, in 1769, astronomers surveyed the transit of Venus at sites around the world, from Philadelphia to Tomsk, from St. Helena to Tahiti. Meanwhile, Enlightenment science moved briskly from natural philosophy to natural history. By mid-century Carl von Linné had pioneered the natural history excursion, field-testing it on a series of traverses throughout Sweden and then, by means of his "apostles," twelve students he dispatched on foreign expeditions, throughout most of the European imperium, there to undertake an inventory of each region's biota.

Political and intellectual purposes soon converged. Probably nothing so characterized the transition as Captain James Cook's first voyage, a circumnavigation in which he traveled to Tahiti to survey the transit of Venus; carried one of Linnaeus's apostles, Daniel Solander; discovered New Zealand and eastern Australia, the sites of subsequent British colonization; and introduced Joseph Banks, one of the age's great naturalists and a founder and patron of the African Society and president of the Royal Society. "Every blockhead does that," Banks replied contemptuously of the social elite that traveled Europe; "my Grand Tour shall be one round the whole globe." Even enlightened despots sponsored analogous expeditions much as they did academies of science, as a symbol and instrument of the modernizing state. So Catherine II had sent Peter Pallas and a corps of savants to the land of Sibir (1768–74). From those studies came theories of importance to the cosmology of the earth—to geology, then a science without a name. Cook repeated his circumnagivation twice more before dying, a martyr to Enlightenment learning, on the third.[3]

But if Cook's circumnavigations effectively displayed the alliance of modern science with imperial ambitions, the final mapping of the world ocean's littoral, the extinction of the fabled Northwest Passage, and the abolition of a *Terra Australis* luxuriating in tropical splendor at the South Pole, the breakthrough came with the transfer of such methods to the continents. The Second Age would ride the wave of Europe's sweep over the earth's landmasses. Its grand gesture would be a traverse across a continent, a cross section of natural history. Its data, stories, and images would fill portfolios, stuff atlasses, line libraries with published personal narratives, stock the shelves of freshly endowed museums, and force the invention of new sciences like geology and of new genres of scholarship like anthropology. Moreover, much of what the First Age had discovered, the Second rediscovered. On the basis of his travels to South America, resulting in an encyclopedic survey of natural history, Alexander von Humboldt was popularly hailed as a "second Columbus."

That designation—applied to a foreign scientist, traversing the cores of Spain's New World empire—showed how far behind Spain had fallen as an intellectual power. Looking more imperious than imperial, Spain had for long decades stood outside the Enlightenment. Still equipped with the Inquisition and the Index, it remained wary of a secularizing rationalism, a transnational science, and an enthusiasm for overseas adventures that, it surmised, would likely come at its expense. Instead it closed its borders and fought the new learning with the same zeal it had the Reformation. And for so long as Spain remained beyond the reach of the Enlightenment, the Grand Canyon, nominally under the dominion of New Spain, would remain outside the Second Great Age of Discovery.

Eventually Spain, both peninsular and colonial, could no longer resist. Reform commenced with the ascendancy of Carlos III in 1759, effectively announcing a Spanish Enlightenment. The resulting reformation engulfed both empire and exploration. Northern New Spain, in particular, seemed threatened. For two centuries, valley by valley, tribe by tribe, the mission system had advanced northward, steadily bringing more land under the control of the crown. But in the eighteenth century the system faltered. By the 1760s, especially after a chastised France had been removed as an imperial contestant in 1763, New Spain undertook a general rehabilitation of its northern frontier. There were threats beyond the border from the British and the Russians, serious troubles within the *provincias* from the Apache, and vexing problems with the fabric of colonial administration itself. Provincial reformation proposed new routes of communication, projected a stronger cordon of presidios, mobilized the Royal Corps of Engineers, and substituted Franciscans for the Jesuits expelled in 1767.

It took longer, however, for field parties to gear up to Enlightenment standards. Pre-Bourbon Spain had tolerated the La Condamine expedition to Ecuador, though only after insisting that two reliable Spaniards accompany the corps to report on the suspected spies. It had also allowed one of the Linnaean apostles, Pehr Löfling, to visit Spain (1751) and accompany a foray to Venezuela (1754). With Carlos III, however, the crown endowed institutions of science—museums, botanical gardens, observatories—at which to train scholars to participate in the expeditions, particularly those within colonial possessions, that were becoming de rigueur for European powers. With the crown's sanction a Franco-Spanish team observed the transit of Venus from Baja California. A decade later the crown dispatched a botanical survey under Hipólito Ruiz and José Antonio Pavón to Peru and Chile, then granted permission to José Celestino Mutis to survey Nueva Granada (1783). The momentum provided by Carlos III even survived his death as Spain mounted two Cook-inspired enterprises:

the Royal Scientific Expedition to New Spain (1785–1800) and the Alejandro Malaspina Expedition to the Pacific (1789–94). But these were in style as much as setting light-years away from the *entradas* that passed along the Colorado canyons.

The first missed altogether, or avoided, the great gorge. While Juan Bautista de Anza pioneered an overland route from Monterey to Alta California, erecting missions and presidios, two priests, Father Silvestre Vélez de Escalante and Father Francisco Domínguez, accompanied by Captain Bernardo de Miera y Pacheco, a retired military engineer, trekked across much of the land that would become the Old Spanish Trail. The Escalante-Domínguez Expedition, it was hoped, would blaze an overland route between the Spanish settlements long established at Santa Fe with the new ones being developed in California. It was during this surge of Spanish interest in the region that the canyons of the Colorado River again entered the archives of Western civilization.

The party passed to the north of the Grand Canyon proper, made no attempt to inspect it, found a ford across the river (the Crossing of the Fathers), and reported on the character of the tribes and of the lands through which they passed. Though they failed in their larger objective, they successfully traversed much of the Colorado Plateau and, thanks to Miera's cartographic talents, gave a reasonably complete (though far from geodetically accurate) representation of the hydrography of the Colorado River system. They had no reason to visit the Canyon—had in fact every reason to shun it—and became as peripheral to its historiography as the Canyon was to their agenda.

Father Francisco Tomás Garcés, however, did see it. An old hand around the lands of Sonora, Garcés detached himself from the Anza Expedition, and under the direction of Indian guides pushed up the Colorado River to the Río Jabesua. This was the travertine-laden stream through Havasu Canyon, inhabited by the Havasupai Indians, a tribe linguistically related to the Yuman people who had served as guides.

From Havasu, Garcés evidently first encountered the western

Grand Canyon. Of the eastern Canyon to which Cárdenas had ridden, he witnessed nothing until he passed near the rim on a journey to the Hopi villages in June 1776. The Canyon he referred to as the Puerto de Bucareli, a gap by which the river passed through the sierra, and he referred to the river as the Río Colorado, sustaining the long-held Spanish belief that this river was continuous with that which empties into the Sea of Cortés. Because he brushed it only twice, and episodically, he missed completely or just misrepresented, as did Escalante and Domínguez, the great bend of the river—the central fact and mystery of its geography, the Colorado's east-west flow across the Kaibab Plateau—that had made the Canyon possible. But this lapse was of no consequence to the mission.

Of the setting, Garcés remarked only that he was "astonished at the roughness of this country, and at the barrier which nature had fixed" and, showing an inability to fathom the size of the phenomenon, thought "to all appearances would not seem to be very great the difficulty of reaching" the river. Only the size of the side canyons persuaded him otherwise. Evidently he was ignorant of the Coronado *relaciones*. Returning from the Hopi pueblos, Garcés again alluded to the gorge, this time as a "prison of cliffs and canyons." Probably his native guides steered him clear; his own cultural compass also pointed him elsewhere. He retired to missionary labors along the lower Colorado. Five years later he died during the Yuman uprising.[4]

Though Garcés visited the Canyon, it is obvious that it was not the object of his journeys. He traveled as part of a larger Spanish ambition to better integrate its frontier. Garcés, in particular, came to inspect the indigenous tribes along the Río Colorado, the most far-flung of which were the Havasupai, and when there were no longer any people, he left the river. He visited Havasu Canyon to size up its inhabitants and their agriculture; he cruised the rim of the Canyon only because it was, from Havasu, the most direct route to the well-known Hopi (Moqui) villages. The Canyon was an aside to his real purpose, and even then not one that especially interested him. Like Cárdenas, he saw nothing special about it except its superior ruggedness. Had the Havasupai not been present, he would not have made the trek at all. Hurrying directly to Moqui, he would have had no inkling that anything like the Canyon existed, even a league away, on the horizon.

The Canyon remained invisible. Between them the two expeditions had all but circumnavigated the Canyon, and while they continue to elicit admiration for the endurance and determination of their individual participants, they remain collectively irrelevant to the larger agenda of Enlightenment exploration. Even as their diaries, maps, and *relaciones* traveled to the authorities, their collective reconnaissance must have seemed like a heroic anachronism. But that was true, overall, for the Spanish Enlightenment itself. Spain's contributions to the Second Age of Discovery ended with explorer notes lost, unedited, and unpublished and its monumental expeditions in disarray. Once more geographic data were not broadcast as the common knowledge of transnational science, but hoarded, like other New World treasures, by the Spanish state. The Spanish Enlightenment imploded. What Carlos IV failed to resanction, the Napoleonic Wars terminated. Spain had dispatched Malaspina too late to the Cook-surveyed North Pacific and had failed to mount a natural history survey to places that might have rewarded the venture. It is as though a reinvigorated stream had veered out into a closed basin and dried into a salt playa.

The Canyon accounts more resemble the Jesuit *Relations* than the encyclopedic tomes characteristic of the new scholarship in natural history. Even as Escalante, Domínguez, and Garcés sent off their diaries and Miera his report and remarkable map, Peter Pallas was publishing the results of his expedition to Sibir and Captain James Cook's crew was returning, as melancholy heroes, from the last of the great voyager's circumnavigations. Pallas and Cook were the harbingers of a new style of discovery; Escalante, Domínguez, and Garcés resuscitated the old pattern of the *entrada* and the errant padre, the almost picaresque travels of the quixotic missionary guided from village to village by native Sancho Panzas.

Thus at a time when Pallas and the Linnaean apostles were promulgating a new mode of exploration, whose data virtually demanded a new science; when Georg Forster was publishing his *Voyage Round the World*, which helped established a new genre of literary travelogue and was to inflame the young Alexander von Humboldt; when William Bartram was completing his celebrated travels to the southeastern United States, the account of which was to inspire a generation of literary Romantics from Chateaubriand to Rousseau; when Britain's cultured elite considered a grand tour a necessary vehicle for eduction; when, in brief, new forms of art and science were evolving to describe nature's wonders, the Spanish explorers to the Grand Canyon are remarkable for their conservatism, their silence, their stubborn incuriosity about anything outside their prescribed agenda.

Their European and American counterparts were beginning to see even old scenes with new eyes. It is impossible to imagine Cook or Pallas, Linnaeus, Joseph Banks, or Daniel Solander before the scientific revolutions of the seventeenth and eighteenth centuries, or Forster and Bartram before the sensibilities of the later Enlightenment, yet it is easy so to imagine Escalante, Domínguez, and Garcés. There was no sense that what they saw required a new genre of literature or new ideas of physical science, or that the landscape they traversed represented a new metaphysic or aesthetic, or that, God willing, it was even worth a second look. Even that crowning achievement of Spanish exploration in the borderlands, Miera's map, shone because of its extensiveness, a triumph of practical empiricism, not because it was a new kind of map or a new way of looking at landscapes. It is as though Enlightenment physicians still read Galen or Newtonian physicists analyzed the solar system with the geometry of Eratosthenes.

As expeditions these sorties are almost completely interchangeable with Spanish surveys of a century (or two) before. As contributors to the history of ideas they are revealing in that they show a trend toward secularization and empiricism, but they neither derive from nor contribute to the revolution in scholarship exfoliating around them. Like the Spain that sponsored them, the motive behind the expeditions was conservative, defensive, and so was their interpretation. On the eve of the American Revolution, Spain sought to strengthen its colonial borders, and at the outset of an intellectual revolution, Spanish rationalism likewise strove to rebuild its frontiers, finding novelty somehow intrinsically threatening.

So in this latest round of reconnaissance, the Spanish carefully recorded oases of native tribes that they encountered, but not the natural splendors they saw. Certainly there was nothing in Garcés's account to give the impression that the Puerto de Bucareli was at all unique, much less that it required special language or new ideas, though far lesser scenes were beginning to inflame the imagination of European intellectuals. Even Thomas Jefferson was waxing wondrous about so prosaic a phenomenon as Virginia's Natural Bridge, and moody Britons on their grand tours swooned over fallen ruins and painters romanticized rustic Italy and literati hungry for the old and the exotic invented Highland epics like the saga of Ossian. Instead Spanish interest in the Colorado River, like Garcés himself, retired to its more accessible and populous lower stretches and there died.

When Alexander von Humboldt drew up his compendium of borderlands geography from Spanish (Mexican) sources in 1811, the Canyon appeared only as the Puerto de Bucareli, located at the junction of the Río Colorado and the Río Jaquesila (Little Colorado). The Colorado River was presented as running north and south, without the defining bend it makes through the Kaibab Plateau to form the Grand Canyon, thus eliminating the complex interaction of river and plateau that is the region's essence. Similarly, where Miera's map had been almost cluttered with ethnographic notes, Humboldt's meticulous compilation was sparse, employing the latest in cartographic technique and voiding the primary source of Spanish interest in the area, the Havasupai. Ironically it was Humboldt, a German geographer writing in French from Spanish sources, and Humboldt's *Map of the Kingdom of New Spain*, a part of his *Political Essay on the Kingdom of New Spain*, that finally introduced the region to the intellectual culture of Europe. The map became in turn the principal conduit for formal American knowledge about the region prior to the Mexican War.

The glamour of Spanish exploration came later, after European Romantics had transformed Spain into a tableau of the picturesque, and after similarly inclined historians like William Prescott had done for Old Mexico what Francis Parkman had done for New France. It was only later, after the Canyon had been publicized and its marvels extolled, that the Spanish contribution was recognized. Paradoxically it was not the Spanish accounts that helped make the Grand Canyon into an important emblem for Western civilization, but the Canyon, when once valorized, that gave meaning to the search for a cultural genealogy, that conveyed a value to Spanish travels not apparent at the time.

The encounter of Cárdenas with the Canyon in particular has become invested with a scholarship and significance out of all proportion to what seemed important to the *entrada*'s participants. Only two of the numerous *relaciones* bother to mention the episode at all, and only one of those expended more than two sentences in what the twentieth century has come to regard as a defining moment. Of all the events of that curious quest, its casual contact with the Canyon has become perhaps the most celebrated. For that Cárdenas and Coronado can thank the uninviting gorge they dismissed in their forlorn search for Quivira.

CONVERGENCE

The Canyon remained hidden until geopolitics met geopoetry; that synthesis required almost another century. By then imperial contests had transferred the region from an old and defensive Spain to a new and aggressive United States. Those same years, however, had witnessed a no less astonishing evolution and redefinition of cultural values that focused art, science, literature, philosophy, and nationalism on the acquired landscapes. The more majestic the scene, the more celebrated it became; the more singular, the more valued. That suited precisely the remote and peculiar canyons of the Colorado.

The threat to the Spanish colonies was real, but it came by revolution from within rather than invasion from without. From 1810 to 1821 Mexico, like much of New Spain, remained in revolt, eventually achieving independence. Where Spain had pursued a garrison policy along the frontier, sealing it off from inquisitive foreigners, Mexico quickly liberalized its policy of cross-border trade. In 1821, as the Ashley-Henry party pushed up the Missouri to inaugurate America's Rocky Mountain fur trade, other groups probed toward the Southwest, blazing the Santa Fe Trail. Fur trappers were prominent among the entrepreneurs of both expeditions; they turned Taos, especially, into a base of operations. Within a few years, if his *Personal Narrative* may be both believed and interpreted correctly, one such Taos trapper, James Ohio Pattie, passed around or through the Canyon.

During its heyday the fur trade revealed most of the scenic wonders of the Far West, though it often didn't identify them as such and left them with folk names like Colter's Hell and Brown's Hole. Parties of trappers exposed the Yellowstone, the Yosemite, the redwoods, the peaks and basins of the Rockies, the Great Salt Lake, and if they did not similarly dramatize the Grand Canyon, they apparently knew of its existence. The trapper had already become a stock character of American literature ever since John Filson had memorialized Daniel Boone in the late eighteenth century; by 1827 James Fenimore Cooper could make the Old

Trapper the center of adventure and moral drama in *The Prairie*. Often ghostwritten by professional literati, trapper accounts were surprisingly abundant, though frequently of doubtful reliability.

Pattie's *Personal Narrative* was one such piece of literature, and an especially problematic one at that. It was recorded by Timothy Flint, already renowned for biographies of Boone and others. Like all such narrators, Pattie (through Flint) claimed that he spoke only from plain facts, but again, like the rest, the story was embellished with common set pieces. The facts seem to be that Pattie was among the original group of trappers to the Southwest, that he traveled widely, that he visited the lower Colorado and Gila, and that he was imprisoned for a time by suspicious Mexican authorities.

Among his wanderings, however, he claimed in 1823 to have ascended the Colorado River to a place where "horrid mountains" shut in the river for nearly three hundred miles and prevented any descent. A rather nebulous, even feverish description gives only an impression of desolation. His allusion to the prisonlike feature of the gorge recalls Garcés and may reflect information Pattie picked up from the Mexicans during his captivity. His *Narrative*, moreover, proceeds as a series of burials and imprisonments, and his account of a similarly incarcerated river and canyon-buried trapper fits suspiciously well with that motif.[5]

Whether Pattie's *Personal Narrative* really describes the Grand Canyon or not, it does apparently give an accurate rendition of what from their travels Southwest trappers knew of the canyon country. They knew its general locale, that it was big, that it was desolate and impassable. Unlike his role with regard to so many other scenic highlights of the acquired West, the trapper for the most part worked to obscure the Canyon, not to reveal it. Antoine Leroux, for example, advised the Sitgreaves Expedition in 1851 not to continue along the drainage of the Little Colorado, for that would only bring it to a hopeless maze of rugged gorges. With other trappers as scouts, the Whipple Expedition a few years later passed by and named Red Butte, only a handful of miles from the

South Rim, but failed to approach the Canyon, even across terrain that offered not the slightest impediment to travel. The Coconino Plateau, which rises to the South Rim, was no more rugged than the swells of the Great Plains. Even the intrepid Jedediah Strong Smith, the Odysseus of the fur trade, missed the Canyon, following the Virgin River to the Colorado. His objective was the Old Spanish Trail, California, and beaver, not impassable gorges. The massacre of his party by Mohaves did nothing to improve the interest of the fur trade in this beaver-barren region.

In the end the American adventurers resembled nothing so much as secular padres, Franciscans of the fur trade, pursuing pelts rather than souls and as eager as missionaries for paths, not barriers. Certainly trappers said little about the landscape as a scenic or nationalist wonder. Yet there were stories—tales and folk fables not unlike those that circulated about Colter's Hell in the Yellowstone. When an Army expedition finally did proceed, with deliberation, to the region, its organizers already knew it by the name Big Cañon, likely a trapper sobriquet, and they knew "the accounts of one or two trappers, who professed to have seen the cañon, and propagated among their prairie companions incredible accounts of the stupendous character of the formation. . . ." Such reports "magnified" for the savants who followed "the marvellous story of Cárdenas," and if there were no trappers among the Ives Expedition to guide it to that scene, those yarns had the power to inspire to them, much as the tall tales of Fray Marcos de Niza had set Coronado on the path to Cibola. Before it became grand, the Canyon became fabulous.[6]

Meanwhile other forces were at work in the greater Southwest. In 1848 the Treaty of Guadalupe Hidalgo ceded most of the Spanish borderlands to the United States, and in 1853 the Gadsden Purchase added the lands of present-day Arizona south of the Gila River. The Canyon country found itself in the middle of a vast geopolitical realignment that would compel, eventually, an intellectual no less than a political assimilation. No longer was it part of an indigestible geography on a remote frontier of Spain or Mexico. It was instead a prominent natural feature of the major river of the Southwest, an American Nile, well within the heartland of Manifest Destiny. From the north came Mormon guides and colonists; from the east and south came traders up the Colorado and Army explorers searching for transportation routes. When the two processes finally met, they did so at the gateway to the western Grand Canyon.

Like their predecessors, Mormon frontiersmen were the tentacles of empire, and like them, the scouts mapped a practical geography, in this case of townsites and roads. Driven from Nauvoo, Illinois, in 1846, the Mormon hegira had resettled the Latter Day Saints on the shores of the Great Salt Lake. Joseph Smith, the martyred Mormon prophet, resembled nothing so much as the Emersonian poet-seer, arising like an avatar along the frontier, and the gathering of Mormon Zion in the Great Basin was a defining event in the geopolitics of western expansion. Powered by conversions and eager to expand Zion into the political state of Deseret, the Mormon state began to swell its territory by systematic colonization, especially to the south along the Wasatch Range and the fault valleys of the High Plateaus. Guides would investigate potential sites, and on the basis of their reports, whole communities could be "called" to settle the area. By 1851 towns, like Cedar City, hugging the western perimeter of the Colorado Plateau had been founded; by 1870, Kanab, at the foot of the plateau's Great Rock Staircase.

Perhaps the most celebrated of Mormon frontiersmen, Jacob Hamblin, had already circumambulated the Canyon region by 1862 and, like nearly every other visitor to the region, had found visits to the Hopi pueblos irresistible. But he avoided the Canyon proper, and so did Deseret. Mormon colonization veered to Lee's Ferry, where the Paria River joins the Colorado. Settlement then followed the Little Colorado south to a country of high meadows and forested mountains and eventually extended to the Mexican border. Another thrust fashioned a corridor to the sea along the Old Spanish Trail by way of Las Vegas and Los Angeles. Colonization grew around and incorporated the Canyon the way injured muscle might grow around an embedded arrowhead. What mattered were the Colorado's fords—Lee's Ferry, the Crossing of the Fathers, Pierce's Ferry—not gorges that could swallow Salt Lake City with hardly a trace.

The genius of Mormonism was for administration and religion: it created a new church and the machinery of empire, not a great literature, art, or science. New testaments to supplement the Bible, novel social institutions, a system of coinage, even an experimental alphabet—the cultural inventiveness was great, but it served an imagination intent on settling communities in an agriculturally forbidding landscape. No one concerned with irrigating crops in an arid land or searching out suitable timber, pasture, or townsites had the time or inclination to contemplate landscapes that offered little enough of any such things. The remembered sagas of settlement—the ordeal of the Muddy Mission, the intrepid trek to Hole-in-the-Rock—emphasized a social order that struggled against a formidable land. The land valorized their efforts by challenging the basis for their physical survival.

Nothing in their Scripture, not in the Old or New Testaments or in the plates buried by the prophet Moroni, said anything of revelatory canyons. Mormon imagination could interpret the deserts, mountains, and the salt lakes of the eastern Great Basin by analogy to the landscape of the Holy Land. Their chosen place thus complemented their creation story, the Exodus that had carried them across the Sinai of the Great American Desert. The promised land was a new Zion, a place to reclaim, not a picturesque Nature worthy of sublime awe and genteel contemplation or a secular text full of the lessons of natural philosophy and ready for explication by Gentile science. The Colorado canyons, in particular, were places to avoid or to ford.

While his acumen in political economics made Brigham Young one of the great captains of American industry, the probes he ordered to survey the landscape surrounding Deseret carried with them few of the instruments of high culture and shipped few such soundings back. Mormon settlers occupied such scenic marvels as Bryce Canyon, Canyonlands, Capitol Reef, Arches, and, with a rare gush of poetic enthusiasm, Zion Canyon. All framed riverine communities. Settlers along the Virgin River in particular could, with relative ease, enter and engage Zion's excavated valley and could allude to it as a kind of sandstone Yosemite. But of the Grand Canyon they said nothing. Within settled Deseret the Grand Canyon was as much wasteland as the salt playas of Sevier.

Yet even as Deseret swelled beyond the Great Basin, the Second Great Age of Discovery was overrunning the earth. The era's geopolitical sagas—the pursuit of a Passage to India, the rivalry between France and Britain over the South Seas, the westward Course of Empire across the North America, Britain and Russia's Great Game in Central Asia, Europe's unseemly Scramble for Africa—all were boulders rolled over imperial cliffs that scattered before them rockslides of exploring expeditions, sojourners, savants, and adventurers, a tumbling scree of the curious and the obsessed that constantly reshaped the topography of thought and the cultural contours of Western civilization.

In truth, geographic expansion was as much a cultural as a political process. The information the Second Age shipped back in bulging sea chests and personal narratives and steamer trunks of pressed plants, animal pelts, and artifacts of exotic indigenes forced a phase change in the Greater Enlightenment. Existing systems of scholarship could no longer cope with the rising flood of artifacts, impressions, weather recordings, logs, journals, specimens, barometric readings, drawings—the sheer volume of intellectual production that swelled over and ruptured the levees of inherited categories. By mid-century the floodcrest of the Second Age was reaching its high-water mark. Its emissaries were trekking across whole continents.

It was, accordingly, a great era of natural history for which Alexander von Humboldt serves as both promulgator and symbol. What Beethoven was to the music of the Romantic period, what Napoleon was to its politics, Humboldt was to its science. More than anyone else Humboldt transferred the apparatus of Cook-style exploration to the natural history of continents. Appropriately, Humboldt had been born in 1769, the year of Cook's transit of Venus voyage; he had taken inspiration from Georg Forster, the ethnographer with Cook's second voyage; and he was to dine with Thomas Jefferson the same month the Corps of Discovery under Captains Meriwether Lewis and William Clark departed from St. Louis on their epic journey across North America.

Lewis and Clark were beginning what Humboldt was already completing. His five-year expedition (1799–1804) to South America had pioneered a new genre of exploration. Even more, his exploits riveted the attention of Europe; his letters to his sister Caroline and brother Wilhelm, published as they arrived, made him a frontline journalist of discovery and a celebrity of geographic science. He had paddled up tropical rivers like the Orinoco, scaled peaks like Chimborazo, sketched the ruins of lost civilizations, experimented with electric eels, watched fruit-eating bats and carnivorous alligators, measured latitudes and mountain slopes, and obsessively collected, more than sixty thousand specimens in all. From landfall near Cumaná he wrote his brother Wilhelm that he and Aimé Bonpland, his traveling companion, were "like a couple of mad things. . . . Bonpland keeps telling me that he'll go out of his mind if the wonders don't cease soon." Here was the naturalist as Promethean hero. The contrast with the chroniclers of Coronado, with Escalante, Domínguez, and Garcés could hardly be greater.[7]

More than merely experiencing, however, Humboldt labored to bring the discovered new world of natural history into formal learning. His *Personal Narrative*, a partial rendering of his five-year travels through South America, expanded the model of his mentor, Forster, and established a literary genre for the scientific discovery of the exotic and the sublime. His fifty-four-volume *Voyage to the Equinoctial Regions of the New World* created an exemplar by which to appreciate and understand other newly discovered or rediscovered continents then entering European consciousness. In the process he helped invent modern geography and outfitted it with a methodology of comparative analysis and such organizing techniques as isothermals. His Thomistic *Cosmos*, first conceived in 1834, attempted to summarize, in vivid and popular language, both the new impressions and the expanded knowledge of nature freighted back by the science of his age. Here was the French *Encyclopédie* fused with German *Naturphilosophie*. Here incarnate was Tennyson's Ulysses, determined "to follow knowledge like a sinking star." Here, in the Humboldtean explorer, was the means by which to search out and peer over the Canyon rim.

Humboldt exercised special appeal to Americans and was a model explorer for a nation pushing into a western wilderness. An ardent democrat, he expressed vast hopes for the young Republic, and Young America responded enthusiastically. Emerson called him "a universal man, . . . one of those wonders of the world, like Aristotle." Walt Whitman, the self-styled "poet of the cosmos," attempted to synthesize with verse ensembles what Humboldt did with geographic science. Edgar Allan Poe dedicated his metaphysical prose poem *Eureka* to this giant of scientific discovery. The officers of the Army Corps of Topographic Engineers, the principal organ of government exploration, took him for a polestar; John Charles Frémont corresponded regularly. Louis Agassiz, professor at Harvard's Museum of Comparative Zoology, sought to synthesize North American natural history as Humboldt had South American. John Lloyd Stephens traveled to the Yucatán to rediscover the American Egypt that Humboldt had done so much to popularize; Federick Church, doyen of American landscape artists, trekked to South America to paint the grand scenes of Humboldt's adventures; and at the age of seventy-six, John Muir realized a lifelong ambition when he journeyed to the headwaters of the Amazon to find the flowers and trees Humboldt had described. When Americans rediscovered the Grand Canyon, they did so as Humboldteans.

They were almost too late. Humboldt had pioneered new intellectual ground, not only by proposing ideas but by inventing techniques with which to make sense of the Second Age's embarrassment of intellectual riches. Along with his contemporary Karl Ritter, he developed modern geography, integrating the thousands of newly discovered species, strata, and human artifacts through physical principles of geography; organizing them into ensembles of plants, suites of rocks, and communities of human settlement; analyzing them by systematic comparison. To the Great Chain of Being, Humboldt effectively added another dimension, cross-weaving its many parallel chains into a maplike grid. Yet the data continued to pour in, and the Humboldtean floodplain, however broad, could no longer hold it. By mid-century the Humboldtean explorer, like Humboldtean science, was already becoming a glorious anachronism.

Too much was revealed to be stuffed into the domain of geographic space alone, even into a cosmos like Humboldt's. Humboldt the geographer had tried to organize a progressively more complex universe through "laws" of space, while most metaphysically inclined thinkers were increasingly following Georg Wilhelm Friedrich Hegel's appeal to laws of time. More and more, intellectuals became natural *historians*. Behind that impulse, like a flood pushing against saturated levees, pressed the mounting evidence of exploration. The discovery of new lands was matched by the exhumation of landscapes lost in time. Fossils supplemented surface ruins; mastodons and dinosaurs, denizens of past epochs, added to the exotica of nature; ancient geologic empires were found in metamorphosed strata much as forgotten civilizations were dug out of desert sands and hacked from jungle vines. They could not be explained except by appeal to history.

The antiquity of the earth mattered. Whether the universe followed chance or design; whether humans had evolved from other life-forms or experienced a separate creation; whether time was a presence or a principle—all depended on how old the earth really was and how its history was organized. The Humboldtean became a Darwinian, broadly defined. With eerie timing, the aged Humboldt, born the year Captain Cook set out to measure the transit of Venus, died with *Cosmos* still—inevitably—incomplete in 1859, the year Charles Darwin published *On the Origin of Species*, the outgrowth of his own five-year voyage of discovery.

So they came together: the Greater Enlightenment, the Second Age, the colonization of continental interiors, the unprecedented terrains of America's Far West. The compound exploded Western civilization's horizons of geography, history, and perception. Nowhere were its shock waves felt more powerfully than in the United States, a self-consciously new nation as eager for a past as for a future, for which nature often substituted for culture and the westward migration of which coincided precisely with the broader parameters of European expansion.

Natural history and national history proceeded in sync, a cultural fugue to Manifest Destiny. A new people shaped by colonization, democratic revolution, and industrialization found particular confidence in the idea of progress, for which nature's evolution seemed to furnish both precedent and precondition. The national creation story commemorated the encounter of Old World civilization with New World wilderness; the contest for empire and its westward expansion was the national saga, the American *Aeneid*; history interpenetrated geography to make this a march into the future. The frontiersman, forged along this border, close to nature, became the putative wellspring of American virtue. The explorer served as guide, an almost Moses-like figure.

The national epic found its monuments, as often as not, in the American landscape. Nature, which America had in abundance, replaced the built environments that it lacked. Niagara Falls mocked the fall line of Europe's overshot water mills and even more the contrived fountains of Versailles or Bernini's Fountain of the Four Rivers in the Piazza Navona. The Rockies dwarfed the Alps. The majestic Mississippi lorded over a quaint Rhine. The Great Lakes reduced Europe's waterscapes to ponds. Redwoods defied Europe's hoary oaks, grizzly bears its domesticated farmyard fauna, Yellowstone's geysers the lapdog hot springs of European spas. The natural, the big, the distinctive—all challenged the artifice of ancient and aristocratic societies, while arguing strenuously for a republic of native, once-and-future virtue.

The unveiled spectacles begged to be seen and drew artists like bees to clover. Some inventoried the lands with the zeal of Linnaean apostles. Mark Catesby tabulated flora and fauna; John Jacob Audubon recorded birds and quadrupeds; George Catlin feverishly documented (and idealized) the indigenous peoples before they passed away forever. But the same fervor soon applied to landscapes, and landscape quickly became America's dominant art form, certainly its most popular. The moral didacticism that had previously been invested in grand-manner history paintings now infused the scenes of natural history. A genre pioneered by isolated artists like Thomas Cole rapidly blossomed into regional and national stature like the Hudson River school and went international. Frederick Church, the outstanding American artist of mid-century, carried the landscape beyond Niagara Falls and the Adirondacks—American wilds, removed from rural gentility—to the South American vistas popularized by Humboldt and even to Greenland. Germany's Düsseldorf school formalized practice with theory and elevated landscape into the grandest of arts, the opera of painting. Americans like Albert Bierstadt compounded both, studying at Düsseldorf and then journeying to the Rockies and the Sierra Nevada. Artists thus sought out the remote, the sublime, the monumental, and the distinctive and often exploring expeditions that could take them to such places.

Thus the historical tributaries all converged, like the three forks of the Missouri, to make a pathway into the interior. Expansion had acquired new, seemingly vacant lands; modern science turned its attention precisely to such landscapes, pushing natural history into exponential growth, reinventing sciences like geography and biology, spawning new sciences like geology and anthropology by rapid fission; the arts celebrated landscape as its highest expression; literature thrived on travelogues and personal narratives of adventuring expeditions; nationalism demanded new monuments and found them in the landscape-sculpted Far West; Romanticism in the arts and philosophy celebrated the natural over the artificial and the new over the inherited. All these currents converged into the exploring expedition, and as the American empire surged westward, the federal government endowed, as its official organ of discovery, the Army Corps of Topographical Engineers. It is estimated that the U.S. government invested as much as 25 percent of its antebellum budgets in just such exploration.

The corps conducted a series of expeditions that far surpassed its political charge to record transportation routes and survey boundaries. It was in fact an institution of the Second Age, and it oversaw a "great reconnaissance," as Edward Wallace and William Goetzmann have aptly termed it, that was both a consequence of and a stimulant to the revolutions in science and sensibility that gave the age its dynamism and color. Educated at West Point, a professional engineer as well as a soldier, conversant with the scientific and artistic luminaries of the day, often with European travel as well as western exploration behind him, the topographic engineer "considered himself by schooling and profession one of a company of savants." He became an agent of cultural no less than political expansion. When the corps was authorized in 1838, it postdated by only two years Ralph Waldo Emerson's transcendentalist manifesto *Nature* and Thomas Cole's inaugural landscape *The Oxbow*. When Lieutenant G. K. Warren summarized the corps's collective discoveries in cartographic form, the map preceded by two years the first edition of Charles Darwin's *Origin of Species*. It was an era that looked to nature for inspiration as well as information; the corps was a prime vehicle of that inquiry.[8]

The corps's exploration of the canyon country spanned the 1850s. There came, first, the Sitgreaves Expedition (1851), searching for wagon roads across northern Arizona; then the Whipple Expedition (1853), plotting out a potential route for a transcontinental railroad; then Beale's Expedition (1858), improbably crossing the Great American Desert by camel; and finally, a culmination, the supreme achievement of two decades of dedicated exploration, the Ives Expedition (1857–58), hopefully paddling up the Colorado River by steamboat and recording, for the first time since Garcés, an encounter with the Canyon.

The stimulant was a collision of political ambitions that pitted Mormon Deseret against the United States at a time when Bleeding Kansas and sectional divisiveness in general threatened the integrity of the Republic altogether. The so-called Utah War is best known for the Mountain Meadows Massacre and the occupation of Salt Lake City by federal troops under Albert Sidney Johnston. But the Ives Expedition, nominally a search for transportation and supply routes to Utah, an uncanny echo of the Coronado and Alarcón missions, may be its most enduring legacy. The final result, not fully realized until the Civil War ended sectional secessionism, was the integration of the region into the United States, not into a quasi-autonomous Deseret, and into the cultural— indeed moral—geography of the Second Age. Mormon exploration was intensely practical, a search for sites that could replicate and sustain the plat of Zion that formed the basis for communities called to colonize. The Canyon held nothing of value, was in fact repugnant, to such purposes. The corps brought with it different ambitions. It was eager for the exotic, the spectacular, the scientifically instructive, the curiously picturesque.

Consequently, although Mormon scouts probably preceded the Army and while some scouts certainly shadowed Army parties as they worked through river and gorges, it was the corps, with its cartographers, naturalists, and foreign eccentrics, that penetrated the western Grand Canyon, that began the assimilation of the Canyon into American political institutions and intellectual traditions, that allowed the rapids of the Colorado River to enter the mainstream of American ideas. The Ives Expedition commemorated two encounters, that between Deseret and the Army of the United States and that between the Second Great Age of Discovery and the Grand Canyon.

Stream and hill, process and place, so long in parallel, closed. American civilization in all its snarled currents and swirling exuberance converged on a landscape uniquely its own. The revelation of the Canyon—the Canyon itself as a kind of revealed knowledge—finally followed when that cultural river deepened and turned and the mountain rose to meet it. The two new worlds merged at last.

RIM AND RIVER

Nowhere on the earth's surface, so far as we know, are the secrets of its structure revealed as here.

—JOHN STRONG NEWBERRY

If any of these stupendous creations had been planted upon the plains of central Europe, it would have influenced modern art as profoundly as Fusiyama has influenced the decorative art of Japan.

—CLARENCE EDWARD DUTTON

Before 1857 the Canyon was an incidental landform, concealed amid scores of exotic western scenes, no more distinguished than the ancient shorelines of the Great Basin or the glaciated summit of Mount Shasta. Hell's Canyon on the Snake River was deeper. The channeled scablands of the Columbia were more savagely eroded. The Colorado River itself had excavated a dozen other canyons, through strata more singular and monumental. The Far West abounded in geographic marvels. Zion Canyon, Arches, and Monument Valley—all on the Colorado Plateau— exhibited land sculpturing on a more humanly impressive scale.

But the Canyon gradually transcended them all. From 1869 to

1882 it went from the status of a legendary giant suck to the subject of two classic works of American letters, from a place shunned even by professional pathfinders to one sought out by scholars and tourists with evangelical zeal and to which, at considerable inconvenience, the 1893 International Geological Congress would be directed. A peripheral landscape without cultural precedent—a scene as alien to Western civilization as the plains of Mars or the craters of Mercury—had seized the center and become an exemplar of geology, an epitome of historicism, a talisman of landscape art, and an icon of American nationalism. In 1903 Teddy Roosevelt, then president of the United States, rode a train along a specially constructed spur track to the opulent El Tovar Hotel on the South Rim and proclaimed to reporters of the *New York Sun* that the landscape before them was one of the "great sights every American should see."[1]

In roughly forty years the Canyon had become Grand.

LONELY AND MAJESTIC WAY: BIG CAÑON

The Colorado Exploring Expedition (1857–58) under Lieutenant Joseph Christmas Ives was among the last of the antebellum surveys directed by the Army Corps of Topographic Engineers and was in many respects its apex. It had all of the strengths of the Humboldtean mode, and most of its weaknesses. Almost immediately upon its completion America's exploratory and imperial impulses experienced a profound redefinition. *Report upon the Colorado River of the West*, published in 1861, appeared at the outbreak of the Civil War and two years before the formal dissolution of the corps. No less significantly, it occurred amid a major reorientation in natural science and social theory, aptly timed with the debate over Darwin's theory of evolution by natural selection. Symbolically, the vehicle for Ives's expedition, the steamboat *Ex-*

plorer, slammed into submerged rocks at the entry to Black Canyon while its crew were "eagerly gazing into the mysterious depths beyond. . . ." One might say the same for the Romantic haze through which latter-day Humboldtean exploration tried to proceed.[2]

The expedition's specific charge was to determine the limit of navigation to the Colorado River. But its ranks were staffed with a sampling of the era's educated elite, not only the military engineer and explorer Ives but a physician-naturalist, John Strong Newberry; a German artist, H. B. Möllhausen; and a Prussian-born cartographer, Baron F. W. von Egloffstein, all veterans of Army exploration in the Far West, all fellow travelers of the Second Age. More than an experiment in hydrography, the expedition proposed a full-bore survey of natural history. With the *Explorer* beached for repairs, Ives satisfied their formal charge by piloting a skiff up Black Canyon and, with the water low, the gorge deep, and the rapids frequent, determined that here indeed was the Ultima Thule of river transport. To meet the expedition's second, grander purpose, he divided his command, sending half back downstream and organizing the remainder, including his scientists and artists, and marched overland to the east.

With native guides, hence along roughly the traditional routes of human traffic, Ives recapitulated (and elaborated) Garcés's itinerary. Ives's principal innovation, the one on which the expedition's reputation was to rest, was to descend down Peach Springs Canyon to the inner gorge of the western Grand Canyon, where Diamond Creek joins the Colorado. It was an easy route, down a tributary canyon wide enough to accommodate a wagon had Ives chosen to force one. There, at the junction, the corps of discovery remained for several days, contemplating, sketching, musing, until finally deserted by their guides. The party then resurfaced, moved east, and reentered the Canyon at Cataract Canyon (Havasu) before again retiring, this time for good. The expedition followed existing trails and corps-blazed wagon roads to Fort Defiance, New Mexico, where it mustered out.

The expedition missed as much as it found. Of the eastern Grand Canyon or of the confluence between the Colorado and the Little Colorado, it saw nothing, and its published map reflected this ignorance. It extended the Big Cañon westward to include Black Canyon and confused the relationship between mainstream and tributary, making the Little Colorado River into the main branch, and it diverted the Colorado proper into Kanab Canyon to the inaccessible north. For all the topographic care invested in its cartography, the expedition's hydrography was worse than Miera's nearly two centuries before. But its descent down Diamond Creek marked the first journey from rim to river, and with that passage the expedition carted the Second Great Age of Discovery face-to-face with perhaps the most fantastic of the innumerable landscapes that era would confront. Its collective contribution far exceeded the perspective of a lieutenant enamored with the prospects of literary fame and harassed by unreliable guides and perpetual shortages of drinking water.

Joseph Ives was a Yale man, a West Pointer, and a veteran of the Whipple Expedition that had traversed northern Arizona in 1853 as part of the Pacific Railroad surveys. He knew the accounts of Cárdenas and Escalante and knew, probably from trapper stories, about the Big Cañon somewhere up the Colorado. He could envision himself as a Humboldtean knight-errant and could appreciate the exploration of the mysterious Big Cañon as a quest. "He talked of the Colorado expedition," as even one critic admitted, "as 'the event of his life,' destined to make fame for his children." In that judgment he was right. So was his assessment that as military transport routes the landscape and river were useless, and as sites for agriculture or settlement, hopeless. Unfortunately in other judgments he erred, sometimes spectacularly.[3]

The central narrative for the *Report* was Ives's. Most of his prose was charming rather than overwrought, and his eye for the picturesque rested most often on the natives, like the irascible Mohave chief Ireteba, who accompanied the party for long weeks. Yet the idea of the sublime—more convention than concept, no longer infusing awe with terror—was never far from his pen. He surveyed the scenes with "wondering delight," citing particularly those prolific examples of its most picturesque forms: its "gigantic chasms," like a "vast ruin"; "isolated mountains," like natural pyramids; fissures "so profound that the eye cannot penetrate their depths"; spires "that seem to be tottering upon their bases," rising thousands of feet like Egyptian obelisks. At times it seemed that the Colorado Exploring Expedition had metamorphosed into the Institut d'Égypte sent to the Nile by Napoleon. Within the Canyon a Gothic gloom pervaded Ives's field of vision, as though the passage down Diamond Creek had been an Odyssean descent to the underworld.[4]

Then he indulged in a rhetorical flourish that made his narrative more or less notorious in Canyon history. "The region is, of course, altogether valueless," he concluded. "It can be approached only from the south, and after entering it there is nothing to do but leave. Ours has been the first, and will doubtless be the last, party of whites to visit this profitless locality. It seems intended by nature that the Colorado River, along the greater portion of its lonely and majestic way, shall be forever unvisited and undisturbed." Ives meant that as a kind of compliment, and it was a fine expression of literary melancholy from an era of Romantic discovery whose agents had rediscovered the Alps and climbed the Andes, probed the Khyber and Bolan passes, uncovered ruins from the jungles of the Yucatán and stood, echoing Shelly's Ozymandias, as they overlooked civilizations submerged by desert sands. At the Big Cañon, nature itself lay in sublime ruin.[5]

But in the light of what was to follow, and even in the context of what his colleagues on the expedition were discovering, Ives could not have been more wrong. The Big Cañon was not a

sphinx, obscuring in gloomy veils and gaping fissures nature's past, but a revelation, exposing the lost secrets of natural history. Melancholic, perhaps, but undoubtedly sublime. While Ives struggled to convey both sentiments, the very aesthetic and literary conventions that enhanced his appreciation also constricted his judgment. He could not envision a meaning beyond grotesque sculpturings, Gothic atmospherics, and picturesque prose.

Curiously the breakdown began at Black Canyon. Once they were beyond the head of navigation, prose and illustrations lost a sense of reality. Without having to measure, map, and test the river for utility as a transportation route, the Romantic imagination roamed unchecked by the imperatives of practical engineering. Almost everyone, from Ives down, indulged in it to some degree. Their points of reference were those predecessors who had blazed routes to the south, trails they left reluctantly and to which they eagerly returned. The head of navigation was also, it seems, the limit of critical perspective. After the expedition Ives's judgment seemingly worsened, to the further declension of his reputation. The ambitious lad from New Haven married into southern society and the Confederacy, served as aide-de-camp to Jefferson Davis, and was eventually buried in Oxford, Mississippi.

A similar intellectual schizophrenia afflicted the expedition's two artists, H. B. Möllhausen and Baron F. W. von Egloffstein, both Germans, both Humboldteans, and both veterans of the Pacific Railroad surveys, and both compromised between the landscape they saw and the one they were equipped (and avid) to express. Between them they introduced the Canyon to Western art. Their sketched and painted landscapes were visual cognates to Ives's Romanticized prose, and their judgment echoed his.

This was Heinrich Balduin Möllhausen's third expedition to the American West and his second to the Colorado River. In 1851 he had joined the excursion of Duke Paul of Württemberg to the Rocky Mountains, an adventure in Humboldtean natural history.

From 1853 to 1854 he served the Whipple Expedition across northern Arizona in the capacity of topographer. There he met Ives, another member. A return to Germany introduced him to the illustrious Humboldt himself. He proceeded to marry the daughter of the old explorer's personal secretary and returned with letters of introduction, a personal benediction, from the Second Age's éminence grise. "Mr. Möllhausen," Humboldt concluded, "dreams of nothing but of the happiness to be attached once more to an American expedition." His aspirations and Ives's coincided. The lieutenant hired him as "artist and collector in natural history."[6]

Möllhausen kept a journal and, as the expedition's official artist, sketched a visual log of what the party saw: flora, fauna, natives, expedition members, landscapes, above all the river, which Möllhausen assessed artistically as Ives did hydrographically. His personal narrative Möllhausen published in German, *Reisen in de Felsengebirge Nord Amerikas* [*Journey to the Rocky Mountains of North America*]; his sketches, suitably engraved, entered into Ives's official *Report* and, reworked into watercolors, Möllhausen retained as his "most precious treasure."[7]

Whipple remarked sourly that the only thing Möllhausen had painted accurately was a Navajo blanket. But most of his sketches for Ives are recognizable, if not strictly representational. Like Ives, Möllhausen succumbed to Romantic reverie, imagined in the chasm's "peculiar formations," for example, "the well preserved ruins of an Indian city," and heavily salted his formal compositions with the conventions of European art and German *Naturphilosophie*. The odd mix of the precise detail and the grand impression so characteristic of the Humboldtean enthusiast suffused the Möllhausen oeuvre. His *Dead Mountain, Mojave Valley* includes a snow-summited peak that exists nowhere along the flanks of the Colorado's floodplain but echoes Humboldt's iconic Chimborazo. That the *Report*'s engraver exaggerated some features recorded on Möllhausen's sketches hardly alters the outcome. What Ives wrote, Möllhausen drew. They even agreed in

their prophecies. "With awe I imagined a picture of the rocky canyon of the 'Colorado of the West,' which perhaps for coming centuries will remain a secret to mankind."[8]

But he would make no secret of his western adventures. Returned to Germany, Möllhausen began to shed his acquired roles as naturalist and artist and inaugurated a remarkable career as a writer of romances, a pioneer in the genre of the western. His *Das Halbindianer* [*The Half-Breed*] appeared the same year as the Ives *Report*. His future lay with his wildly popular prose. He settled comfortably at Potsdam, painting in his leisure but writing romances as a career. Along with Karl Friederich May he helped stamp the American West into German Romanticism. Much as James Fenimore Cooper had become the "American Scot," so Möllhausen became the "German Cooper." And while perhaps a minor figure in the American assimilation of the West—sharing the fate of the Ives enterprise overall, its impact shattered by the Civil War—Möllhausen did much to shape European conceptions. America's West, he proved, was also Europe's.

The visual revolution passed to his comrade in arts, F. W. von Egloffstein. Another veteran of the Pacific Railroad surveys, Baron von Egloffstein was more willing to experiment, saw keenly the need for new modes of expression to convey the region's bizarre land sculpture, and carried both poles of the Humboldtean vision to extremes. The schizophrenia between Ives the hydrographic engineer and Ives the literary poseur widened. While the accuracy of Egloffstein's maps increased, the representational quality of his drawings dissipated into Gothic gloom.

A master draftsman, later credited with inventing halftones, Egloffstein had himself engraved Frémont's map of 1853, Beckwith's of 1854, and much of Warren's master map of 1857. Egloffstein the cartographer confronted the radically molded landscapes of the Southwest by inventing clever techniques for depicting the shape of landforms on a map, a system of molding land features by shading that was a useful anticipation of contour mapping.

Yet when Egloffstein the artist examined the same landscape,

he gave way almost entirely to the conventions of Gothic illustration. The Canyon became grotesquely exaggerated, a manifesto of Romanticism. In *Big Cañon at the Foot of the Diamond River*, the human figures appear like insects amid gargantuan masses rising to all sides, suggesting, as William Goetzmann has observed, the imaginative engravings of Gustave Doré. Ives alluded to the Canyon as a gateway to the underworld; Egloffstein reinforced that allusion by visually recalling Doré's illustrations to Dante's *Inferno*. Panoramas from the rim show an almost fabulous lack of correlation to any tangible features. Subsequent sketches lose themselves not in a geographic tangle of knotted lines but in a vague dreaminess, almost hallucinatory. A later picture, *Big Cañon*, hedges into phenomenological fantasy. Any objective references, even to diminutive figures, are gone.[9]

It is easy to lampoon Egloffstein's exaggeration, and perhaps he deserves it. But like other Germans of his generation awash in the aspirations of *Naturphilosophie*, Egloffstein could paint impressions with wild hyperbole while simultaneously recording facts in minute, faithful detail. On the Ives Expedition those tendencies finally fissioned, the cartographic science proceeding one way, the landscape art another, with hardly a vestige of their common point of departure.

Yet his art could tap a richer range of associations than the Tower of Seville suggested by the Cárdenas party. There was the literary tradition of a descent to a netherworld, the topographic illustrations and personal narratives of the Second Age, the figurative allusions of Doré, a sanctioned landscape art, especially a landscape art for the Alps. Romantic art and aesthetics had come to emphasize the ascent to light, symbolized by Alpine scenery. The mountain summit was a feature of transcendence, its snow and mist an index of the soul's radiance.

But the Canyon reversed this sense, and Egloffstein struggled to invert not only the aesthetics but the techniques. Alpine conventions forced the eye away from canyon gloom to mountain glory. There is no sublime descent to darkness, no way to celebrate the abyss except as a negation. The thrust is to the summit, and the sooner an exaggerated gorge can carry the eye upward, the better. Oddly, the painting thus looks away from its real subject. The gorge is sealed. On the rim not even this act of inversion was possible; the foreground simply gives way to empty space. There is nothing—no icons, no conventions, no figures—with which to fill it.

Perhaps one can say that the Canyon overwhelmed artistic language. More probably, without input from any contrasting sources of information or the necessity of empirical representation, conventions of art and philosophies of nature overwhelmed the Canyon. Each genre, even in the hands of a common practitioner, went its separate way, splitting as did the Ives Expedition itself. Egloffstein, like Ives, like the expedition, could cope with the river more easily than with the rim. They could share a tradition of explorers plunging through geographic portals into Dark Depths Beyond. They could see the gorge as an inverted summit. There was no equivalent for the rim.

Big Cañon at the Foot of the Diamond River, for all its troubled hyperbole and aesthetic evasiveness, nevertheless remains the first great picture of the Grand Canyon. (Möllhausen's watercolors from Diamond Creek were not published with the report.) It shows what the expedition expected to find, shows the spirit that for better or worse first brought intellectuals to the Canyon, shows how they in turn brought the Canyon into the art of Western civilization. In the end the distortions are less surprising perhaps than the fact that they found any value to the scene at all.

There was no such uneasy compromise for the expedition's chief scientist, John Strong Newberry. The fantastic erosion that had stalled travel and bewildered Alpine art was, for a geologist, a vast commentary on the Book of Nature. Newberry appreciated what the canyons of the Colorado meant, and it was his genius to reconcile their lessons with the larger questions of the age. The Big Cañon moved from freak to exemplar.

Newberry had taken a common path from physician to professor of natural history. Educated at Case Western College, then at Cleveland Medical School, with further studies in France, he field-tested his training with the Williamson-Abbot Expedition in the Northwest, part of the Pacific Railroad surveys. When the Ives Expedition called for his services, he had already established ties with the Smithsonian Institution and George Washington University, part of what was to evolve into a federal science establishment. When his tour with Ives ended at Fort Defiance, Newberry continued on to Kansas. A year later he joined the Macomb Expedition from Santa Fe to the junction of the Green and Grand (Colorado) rivers, elaborating the stratigraphy and erosional mechanics he had witnessed in the western Canyon. During the Civil War he served with the influential U.S. Sanitary Commission. But all this was only a prelude for a man who became one of the patriarchs of American geology. From personal knowledge Newberry could construct a gigantic geologic cross section through North America, and with his expertise Newberry went on to a distinguished career at the Columbia School of Mines, to the directorship of the Geological Survey of Ohio, and to an important role behind the scenes in the politics of national science.

It was Newberry who, more than anyone else, demonstrated that science—historical geology, in particular—was the means by which to incorporate what he referred to as the "Great Cañon of the Colorado" within the canons of intellectual culture. His contribution to mapping Canyon geology is inestimable. He produced the first geologic column of Canyon strata and one of the most important ever drawn, that through which he descended to Diamond Creek. He was the first to intuit the vastness of erosion in the province, an erosion of such magnitude that the Grand Canyon itself was only a minor epilogue. Between his tours with Ives and Macomb, Newberry knew more about the geology of the

Colorado Plateau (which he named) than anyone in the country. He passed this wisdom, along with his maps, to his protégé Grove Karl Gilbert, probably the greatest of American geologists, and from Gilbert, who went back to the Canyon with the Army's Wheeler Expedition in 1871, they became amalgamated with original and borrowed ideas that were to make up the contributions of the Powell Survey during the 1870s and those of its successor, the U.S. Geological Survey after 1879.

"Dr. Newberry" knew the value of what he witnessed, knew that European conventions, even of science, were inadequate to describe it. Boldly he proclaimed that "though valueless to the agriculturalist, dreaded and shunned by the emigrant, the miner, and even the adventurous trapper, the Colorado Plateau is to the geologist a paradise." To one who believed that geology was founded on stratigraphy, the "most splendid exposure of stratified rocks that there is in the world"—as Newberry wrote of the Canyon—was far from worthless, and his account of what he saw there far transcended the picturesque impressions of a traveler's journal or artist's sketchbook. The Big Cañon was a revelation.[10]

His scientific insights had two parts. One concerned fluvial erosion and was specific to geology, although it quickly acquired nationalist overtones. Newberry concluded unequivocally that the plateau's magnificent land sculpturings, both its gorges and its residual monadnocks, *"belong to a vast system of erosion, and are wholly due to the action of water. Probably nowhere in the world has the action of this agent produced results so surprising as regards their magnitude and their peculiar character."* In contrast with reigning thought, on the authority of Lyell, that erosional terraces were the product of marine activity or, following Hopkins, that they were the result of structural catastrophes, Newberry supported and enriched a tradition of fluvialism that argued for the power of rivers as geologic agents, as something more than flumes to move water and debris. Rivers had shaped the land, not merely the landscape its rivers.[11]

There was a nationalist bias to this declaration, for Americans had proclaimed the fluvialist argument most strenuously. James Dwight Dana, a professorial counterpart at Yale and a fellow traveler of the Second Age thanks to the Wilkes Expedition, had argued for the power of fluvial erosion from his observations on South Seas islands. A nation that had several centuries of experience with Niagara Falls needed little urging that rivers could be powerful agents of erosion, but the heartland of geology, Europe, did. That encouragement Newberry supplied magnificently by his contribution to the Ives *Report*, which, significantly, appeared the same year as the monumental tome by Henry Abbot and A. A. Humphreys for the Army Corps of Engineers, *The Physics and Hydraulics of the Mississippi River*. Rivers mattered as much to science as they did to commerce. Almost immediately, thanks to Newberry, the Colorado River became one of the scientifically great rivers of the world, and its canyon not merely an indescribable and impassable tangle of gorges but a textbook case of American fluvialism. The river—not only a Colorado gorged with runoff and spring flood, but that deeper, inexorable flow of geologic time—had made the rim possible.

The question of fluvialism, however, was only a subtext to the larger debate about the antiquity of the earth. If rivers were competent agents of erosion, they succeeded because time was on their side. Conversely, a dramatic demonstration that fluvial erosion had proceeded on an immense scale was an argument for a very old earth. This was Newberry's second achievement. It was no accident that Darwin published the *Origin of Species* the same year Newberry journeyed to the junction of the Green and the Grand, where the great canyons of the Colorado River proper commence. By the time Newberry published for the Ives *Report* two years later, that vision of earth history was not lost on the professor or his readers. Subsequently Newberry assumed a leading role in the reconciliation of Darwinian evolution with theology. In a presidential address to the American Association for the Advancement of Science in 1869, he outlined the terms of compromise, sketching a new version of the argument from Design, this one based on historicism and the belief that "fossils . . . are labels written by the Creator on all the fossiliferous rocks." That same year John Wesley Powell made the first descent of the Colorado's canyons.[12]

The age of the earth mattered to this society, for the Second Age had forced an intellectual crisis. The torrent of discovered organisms, rocks, ruins, peoples, and places demanded an order that geography alone could not impose. Instead the culture turned to history and the belief that time itself obeyed grand patterns. The idea of progress, a ubiquitous organic metaphor that relied on growth, not merely expansion, the sheer immensity of revealed time, all converged on the belief that causality was temporal, the design of the world historical, and the surest explanation one that arranged itself as a successive unfolding of events, stage by providential stage. Increasingly historicism became the common soil of cultivated discourse.

No field of inquiry escaped untouched. In biology, historicism came in the form of theories of development: of the individual, as a pattern of growth and aging; of the species, as evolution; and of the two in syncopation, as proposed by Ernst Haeckel's biogenetic law in which ontogeny reputedly recapitulated phylogeny. It appeared in philosophy, through the dialectic of Hegel; in physical science, with the second law of thermodynamics; and in positivistic social science, by a belief in the laws of progress. Time's arrow, to use Arthur Eddington's striking phrase, was apparently as evident in the physical universe as in the biological and as inevitable in the social world as in the natural. But behind those metaphors and models lay the hard rock of geology, the ground truth of earth time.

The earth sciences shared in this crisis of thought, in fact helped precipitate it and, in the end, helped resolve it. The greatest *terra nova* of the Second Age was geological time—as vast as astronomical space, patient, inexorable, sublime. Like the subtle ether of classical physics, geologic time saturated the natural world from the tiniest crystal to the span of nebulae. Between the late eighteenth century and the mid-twentieth, the known age of the earth increased a millionfold, from less than 6,000 years to more than 4.6 billion. The determination of the exact scale of geologic time and how to organize its unfathomable domain remained the particular province of geology. Upon its conclusions rested the mechanics of organic evolution, and upon those mechanics depended the program of social progress. The age of the earth decided whether Darwinian evolution by natural selection, with its immense drafts of time, was possible. The debate over models of organic evolution informed discussions over moral progress and the future of civilizations.

What the discovery of geologic time had disoriented, the invention of geology helped reorganize. It necessarily did so by appeal to historical methods—created, in fact, methods that became models for other fields of inquiry. The critical breakthrough involved the invention of two types of conceptual chronometer. Both provided a means by which to measure, define, and organize the otherwise unbounded landscapes of time. Both lashed geologic concepts to major scientific themes, a larger universe of philosophical and social discourse. One, the entropy clock, joined geology to the physical sciences through the emerging laws of thermodynamics; the other, the evolutionary fossil, connected geology to the life cycle concepts of the biological sciences, a metaphor that saturated prevailing thought like indigo dye.

The entropy clock treated the earth as a closed physical system. Geologically no new energies would enter, and none would exit. Like the turn of a steam engine, or a bowl of soup placed in a box, energy would flow one way, from a hot core to a cool perimeter. The process was irreversible; each event drove the whole system in one direction; and in the end the earth, or one by one its separate parts, would die an inevitable heat death and survive as a cold, inert slab of stone. Useful work would cease. Energy would exist as entropy. But what gave this melancholy specter promise was that it was possible to measure the flow of loss, which is what an entropy clock could do, and to organize its declination, as natural philosophers and geologists promptly did.

The earth was in fact full of entropy clocks. The progressive cooling ("secular refrigeration") of an originally molten earth, tidal retardation resulting from the friction of the oceans, the decay of solar radiation, the loss of thermal reserves in the earth because of volcanic activity, and so on—all were examples. The most fundamental, however, was the thermal contraction of the planet; to this phenomenon, physical geology could relate all its important topics, especially the evolution of mountains and basins, continents and oceans. For measurements, the infinitesimal calculus was an ideal tool. Like geologic time, it would be unspeakably tiny at any instant of differentiation and suitably vast when integrated over longer intervals. The ultimate entropy clock arrived with the discovery of radioactive decay because this provided both a universal process and an absolute chronology.

The second set of theoretical timepieces relied on another ruling concept of the nineteenth century, evolution. The timeless links on the Great Chain of Being became fossil steps on an evolutionary ladder. Historicizing the Great Chain in this way made paleontology into a reliable and scientifically respectable chronometer. Paleontology became the mathematics of geology, and stratigraphy, the first specifically geologic subject to be organized by fossils, became its mechanics. Just as physics had proceeded by discovering new areas of nature to mechanize, so geology advanced by revealing new strata of the earth, however remote, that it could assimilate into historical chronologies and by discovering new varieties of fossil equivalents in the earth that it could order on the same principles as it had stratigraphy. The earth abounded in preserved relics of its past. By their shape, for example, landforms were believed to reveal a particular stage of development; their forms rendered a kind of geomorphic fossil. So also planetary motions expressed "dynamic vestiges," fossils of the earth's astrophysical origin. Its orbital path, its rotation, its precessional wobble—all testified to the earth's historic evolution as surely as if they were brachipods from a Permian sea or the feathered fossils of *Archeopteryx*.

The various chronometers were themselves similarly scaled and synchronized. Just as the thermodynamic cycle of geophysics could be manifest on a macro and micro scale, so also the evolutionary cycle of biology had its macro and micro versions, from the life cycle of an individual to that of a species—or indeed to the evolution of life itself. Further, the biological and physical conceptions of time could combine. The contraction of the earth by secular refrigeration made for progressively more complex geologic environments; these in turn provided more ecological niches, a prerequisite for progressively more complicated biological evolution; and this additionally made possible the vista of cultural, spiritual, and moral evolution by humans and their institutions. It was simple to project from an evolutionary past to an evolutionary future.

Few of the landscapes penetrated by the Second Age offered so much to geologists so quickly as did the American West. Agricultural wastelands could be scientific and scenic wonderlands. Even beyond enriching its data base, the western experience allowed the earth sciences to intersect the Romantic syndrome of the age. Geology discovered lost earth empires, like ancient mountains worn to oblivion by desert sands in the Triassic or overgrown by fossil jungles of the Carboniferous It exhumed vanished creatures from the Pleistocene and Cretaceous, the forgotten civilizations of natural history buried amid the melancholy rubble of time. It could turn tales of scientific discovery into grand sagas of frontier adventure. It gave the New World natural wonders to compete with decaying castles and lofty cathedrals so fundamental to the cultural adornment of the Old World.

This shared vision of natural and cultural history did not appear instantaneously but emerged piecemeal, as inherited ideas worked through new information and as the new information reworked those ideas. *Geology* did not become a name until the

1780s, and it did not resolve the informing question of the earth's age until the 1950s. But between the time Ives mustered out his troop and worked his reports into print, Darwin published, and Western civilization accelerated a great debate about the character of the natural world and humanity's place within it.

By the early twentieth century so rapidly had geology advanced in the West that an American school of earth science had become the premier of American sciences, its accomplishment recognized through the world. By organizing the realm of geologic time according to certain kinds of historical principles, the American school offered a comprehensive vision of the earth from its microcosm, the mineral, to its macrocosm, the solar system. By focusing especially on landforms, American geology fused philosophy with the practical questions of settlement. Along that sculpted surface earth and humanity met, and with geomorphology the American school made its greatest contributions to science. Nothing, however, epitomized these lessons and this unique experience so fully as did the Colorado Plateau and the illuminated text of the Grand Canyon.

The Ives Expedition journeyed close to the symbolic and geographic center of the Second Age. A complex process finally reached a place commensurate to its ideas and ambitions.

The new explorers to the Canyon saw the scene differently from their predecessors. They had different expectations and the means to satisfy them. In particular, the scientific revolution ensured that the new vision did not merely recycle old perspectives but evolved beyond them. A civilization that pondered the age of the earth would not blink past the Big Cañon, could not dismiss it as strictly the scene for adventurous exploits, or regard it as just another of the West's oversized terrains. The gorge was a trench through geologic time, a place so close to the foundations of earth history that it became axiomatic.

In truth the Canyon was not merely a landscape of time; it was a landscape whose time had come.

INTO THE GREAT UNKNOWN: GRAND CANYON

The political dynamics that made the Ives Expedition possible did not survive the Civil War. Ives joined the Confederacy, Newberry and Egloffstein served the cause of Union, and Möllhausen retired to Potsdam and a shelf of potboiler *Romans*. The Army Corps of Topographic Engineers dissolved in 1863, its members redirected from western rivers and wagon routes to the Little Round Tops and Chickamauga Ridges of the nation's battlefields. Western exploration retired to California, where gold gave geology a reason for state support of the Whitney Survey and where the breadth of a continent intervened between the intrusions of war. The Army never recovered its antebellum preeminence as an exploring institution.

The Second Age, its summit reached, commenced a slow decline. It quickly concluded its most spectacular transcontinental traverses. By 1869 a railroad spanned North America. Between 1867 and 1879 four Great Surveys sprawled across the Far West. The Geographical Survey of the Territories under F. V. Hayden and the Geographical and Geological Survey of the Rocky Mountain Region under John Wesley Powell were civilian, as was the Geological Survey of the 40th Parallel under Clarence King, though it remained nominally attached to the Army Corps of Engineers; only the later Geographical Survey West of the 100th Meridian, directed by Lieutenant George Wheeler of the corps attempted to recapture in full the old style of Army reconnaissance. The postwar surveys were often staffed by college men, frequently graduates of the new scientific schools like Hooper at Harvard and Sheffield at Yale, or of German universities, not by all-purpose naturalists and physicians. By 1879, when the U.S. Geological Survey forced the Great Surveys into consolidation, Henry Stanley had plunged through the Congo, John Forrest and Ernest Giles had crossed Western Australia, and on every continent exploring expeditions of grand reconnaissance surrendered pride of place to routine scientific surveys. Exploration crowded along the surveyed boundaries of Dark Africa's multiplying colonies. For pure discovery only the poles remained.

What did survive, though altered, were the era's intellectual drivers. Darwinian evolution succeeded Humboldtean geography as a model of exploration science. On Newberry's example, history superseded space as an organizing principle, and geology, geography. The age of the earth and the principles by which earth time was organized endured as issues of broad significance. By the year the golden spike was hammered at Promontory Point, Asa Gray and Louis Agassiz had publicly debated both the science and the implied theology of Darwinism, while O. C. Marsh had stepped off a train in Nebraska, uncovered the bones of *Eohippus* from exposed shale, and provided the missing fossil link for the evolution of the horse, a paradigm for organic design. Historical geology based on similar evolutionary principles was not far behind, and that meant that the Grand Canyon, after a ten-year hiatus, would not long stay unvisited.

The lacuna between the Ives Expedition and the Powell and Wheeler surveys was surely not total. Even before Ives a good bit of geographic lore about the canyons along with a dose of rumor and fabrication had circulated among old Southwest hands. At least some trappers knew the region, steamboats had plied the lower Colorado River for at least six years before Ives arrived, and one operator had preceded Ives to Black Canyon by a couple of months. Mormon scouts traveled widely around the region. In 1867 Mormon colonists at Callville, Nevada, rescued a half-dead man on a raft from the river. Whether James White, as he later

claimed, had really descended the length of the Canyon or not, he had certainly not intended to if he had, and apart from injecting controversy into the inevitable disputes over priority for the first descent through the Canyon, he contributed nothing to its understanding.

By 1868 the name Grand Canyon had appeared on a railroad survey report by General William Jackson Palmer, Samuel Bowles had confessed that the "great mocking mystery of our geography is the Grand Canyon of the Colorado," and Major John Wesley Powell in outlining his ambitions about descending the river by boat had given as his reason that "the Grand Canyon of the Colorado will give the best geological section on the continent." Certainly something had been added since Ives. The domain of this "mocking mystery" formally began at Lee's Ferry and ended outside Grand Wash Cliffs, with some samplings at Diamond Creek, at Havasu Canyon, and perhaps at a few overlooks on the South Rim. No one had systematically traversed the whole. No one place-name commanded consensus. No dominant image fixed the scene in the public imagination. The eastern Canyon remained terra incognita.[13]

Or it was until Powell penetrated the Canyon twice—once in 1869 and again (to Kanab Creek) in 1871–72. His insight was to float (or bob, row, race, splash, line, and otherwise descend) down the currents instead of fighting them upstream, which demanded steam power. But it was no coincidence that he set his specially modified dories into water at Green River, Wyoming, because here the Union Pacific Railroad intersected the watershed of the Colorado. Between railroad and river, the episodes encapsulated precisely the transition of exploration that would follow.

More than anyone else Powell made the Colorado and its canyons a part of Americana. His personal narrative created the classic expression of the view from the river, the words by which his generation appreciated its revelation, the images by which tourists throughout the twentieth century have understood it. Confronted with the deepening gorges and dark granites of the Grand Canyon proper, Powell announced: "We have an unknown distance yet to run; an unknown river yet to explore. What falls there are, we know not; what rocks beset the channel, we know not; what walls rise over the river, we know not." But ready Powell and his crew were to plunge ahead "down the Great Unknown." These were not the words of literary naturalism or hard science, though they echoed almost exactly Humboldt's pause on his ascent of the Orinoco. "Beyond the Great Cataracts," the young explorer had declared gravely, "an unknown land begins." And in truth Powell's was a final gesture of the Humboldtean adventurer, and his account belongs with Samuel Baker's ascent up the Nile, Henry Bates's travels up the Amazon, and David Livingstone's passage along the Zambezi.[14]

It seemed as if he had uncovered a lost world. Though Newberry had already been to the confluence of the Green and Grand that commenced the Colorado and to the river's debouchment through Grand Wash Cliffs, the stunning bravura of Powell's ambition and his charged, spellbinding prose—filled with commands and heightened by his use of the historical present—made his own voyage of discovery appear unique. A new personality had burst onto the American scene in intimate association with a new landscape. The Major, as he preferred to be called, had deliberately reinforced these impressions by rendering one account out of his two voyages. The *Exploration of the Colorado River of the West*, his official account of the voyages, was finally published under the auspices of the Smithsonian Institution in 1875 after earlier versions had appeared in *Scribner's*.

In terms of securing publicity for a further reconnaissance of the region, the technique was shrewd. A Civil War veteran who had lost his right arm at Shiloh, the Major returned to civilization with the acclaim normally reserved for war heroes or, in a later age, for Mercury astronauts. The Geographical and Geological Survey of the Rocky Mountain Region, based out of Kanab, Utah, became a reality, cobbled together from congressional funds, War Department rations (courtesy of U. S. Grant), and Smithsonian oversight. By the summer of 1872 Powell and others were traveling to the Canyon from Kanab, the first contact for the North Rim. Survey parties explored the High Plateaus, discovered the Henry Mountains, worked out the hydrographic history of the Great Salt Lake, and laid an empirical foundation for later political reform of the public lands.

Publicity and politics were mutually reinforcing. The geology was an open book. Erosion exposed geologic structures as cleanly as dinosaur bones. Strata spread out like illuminated parchments. What Newberry had suggested, Powell confirmed. But Powell the politician recognized that art could reach a larger audience than science and arranged for Thomas Moran, fresh from his triumphs with the Hayden Survey at Yellowstone, to join him. Riding popular acclaim as he did the Colorado rapids, Powell acquired a prominence sufficient to eventually become director of both the Bureau of American Ethnology and the U.S. Geological Survey.

Yet in many respects Powell's celebrated account, like Powell himself, was an anachronism. Powell the explorer was a throwback to the Humboldtean tradition of the personal narrative and the explorer as Romantic hero, much as Powell the politician was a throwback to the agrarian philosophy of the Jacksonian era and its reformist enthusiasms. His report was a journal, though one helped mightily by the character of the river on whose powerful current the narrative could travel. It segregated its science from that story as much as Ives had. Powell's party had consisted largely of adventurers—Civil War veterans, displaced mountaineers, relatives—and they were led by a self-taught naturalist, though he made himself into one of the great scientific amateurs of the nineteenth century. The original Powell Survey and its immediate successors were a far cry from the sophisticated corps fielded by Clarence King or the armada of naturalists brought west by Ferdinand Hayden or even the cartographic expertise exemplified by Lieutenant Wheeler and his Army engineers. Powell's literary characterization of the Canyon was largely of a piece with that of Ives, or Pattie, or even Garcés. The gorge was confining; Powell referred to it as "our granite prison."[15]

In reality there was little science in the *Exploration,* and a good deal of stunt, and of melodrama, and of rhetoric. The science came later, after Wheeler had brought his party up by river to Diamond Creek and after G. K. Gilbert, the crown jewel of Wheeler's scientific contingent, had begun a close, lifelong exchange with Powell. The science appeared in the 1875 edition of the *Exploration* and, even more, in the companion *Geology of the Uinta Mountains* published a year later—the same year, in fact, as Newberry's long-withheld report for the Macomb Expedition. Curiously, the Major's insights into the structural geology of the region came from the dramatic intersection of the Uintas with the Green River, like a melon cut in half, not from the complex passage of the Colorado through the Kaibab.

The process was not dissimilar, however, and its description was Powell's great service to geology. In both cases the river had plunged through an upward-swelling earth, cutting a deep canyon, a process that Powell labeled "antecedence" because the river was antecedent to the mountain and a process that with his gift for homely analogies, he likened to the action of a log (the mountain) being raised into a buzz saw (the river). It was a position entirely in keeping with American fluvialism and one that a later Powell associate, Clarence Dutton, formalized into the law of the persistence of rivers. It was the river that excited Powell's imagination, and it was rivers—or more properly their water—that animated his subsequent career as a geologist and administrator of the Geological Survey.

The law of the persistence of rivers. The phrase might as well apply to Powell's *Exploration*, for it not only permanently forged the perspective of the Grand Canyon from the river but confirmed that the river was the Canyon's essence. The flow of one provided the narrative structure for the other. In fact, Powell's account speaks little of the Canyon and much about the prisonlike defile down which his group labored. The Grand Canyon was noteworthy for having the worst rapids, not the best scenery. Powell said as much. "All around me are interesting geological records. The book is open, and I can read as I run. All about me are grand views, for the clouds are playing again in the gorges. But somehow I think of the nine days' rations, and the bad river, and the lesson of the rocks and the glory of the scene is but half seen."[16]

Only much later, after he had resigned under pressure from the directorship of the Geological Survey, after he had helped conduct an International Geological Congress to the South Rim, after he had undertaken to expand and revise the *Exploration*, did Powell climb out of that confining gorge and survey the rim and declare the scene "the most sublime spectacle on the earth." By then he had the advantage of others' aesthetics, as he did their science. "A year," he announced, "scarcely suffices to see it all." But "if strength and courage are sufficient for the task, by a year's toil a concept of sublimity can be obtained never again to be equaled on the hither side of Paradise."[17]

John Wesley Powell rode the rapids of the Colorado to prominence. His voyage became as much a saga of American discovery as Lewis and Clark ascending the upper Missouri or Jedediah Strong Smith circumnavigating the Trans-Mississippi West. His vision remained fixed to the river and through it to the power of fluvial erosion as a geologic force and, more broadly, to water as a social force in western settlement.

In Canyon historiography, Powell has remained the prime mover. What the river gave, he returned. Once invested with power, Powell ensured that the Grand Canyon would share his prominence as a kind of monument to America's westward destiny. Without him, it is unlikely that the Army would have sent

G. M. Wheeler to recapitulate the Ives Expedition, that Thomas Moran and William Holmes would have drawn and painted their Canyon panoramas, that Clarence Dutton and Grove Karl Gilbert would have amplified the legacy of Newberry and interrogated the geomorphology of the Colorado Plateau, that the Grand Canyon would have become preeminent among American landscapes.

Without Homer the Trojan War would have disappeared amid the endless, unrecorded conflicts of ancient history, and the sack of Troy would be indistinguishable among the thousand-year strata of rubble and ash that layer its site. Without Homer there would have been no Achilles, Agamemnon, Helen, or Odysseus; no *Aeneid* to transfer the epic elsewhere; no Heinrich Schliemann to search out and exhume its artifacts. So it was with John Wesley Powell and the Canyon: the Colorado River and its gorges had found their poet laureate, and an American bard, the saga he would sing for his career.[18]

AGAINST THE CURRENTS: RETURN TO BIG CAÑON

By the time Powell readied his second voyage down the Colorado rapids, the Army Corps of Engineers was organizing for a second trip up. Lieutenant George M. Wheeler raised again the banner of the Army explorer. After two seasons in the field with modest parties, the Geographical Survey West of the 100th Meridian expanded in personnel and ambitions. In 1871 it logged more than six thousand miles through the Great Basin and the Southwest in a furious effort to reclaim Army preeminence. Not surprisingly that revival began where Ives left off. This time the Army engineers transported their boats through the gorges from Black Canyon to Diamond Creek.

Ultimately the Wheeler Expedition succeeded in sailing, poling, and dragging three boats from Camp Mojave to Diamond

Creek, where they rendezvoused with the memory of Ives and departed. Wheeler asserted that he had finally answered the riddle of the Colorado River's limit of navigation—not that anyone doubted that it ended at the great canyons of the plateau. And then, echoing Ives's misjudgments, he studiously slighted Powell and pontificated that "the exploration of the Colorado River may now be considered complete." That proclamation was as flawed as Ives's.[19]

Yet the expedition had some impressive achievements. For a photographer Wheeler had the services of Timothy O'Sullivan, a Mathew Brady protégé and a veteran of the King Survey, recently returned from the Navy's Darien Survey Expedition to Panama. Wrestling heavy cameras and glass negatives, commandeering the services of a whole boat, O'Sullivan produced the first photographs of the Canyon. For geologists the expedition had men like Archibald Marvine and G. K. Gilbert. For artists, regrettably, the Wheeler Survey had none, and for its narrator, even more regrettably, it had only Wheeler himself. Wheeler's clumsy prose, crimped vision, and political posturing made even his survey's best work look flaccid and sometimes fatuous. Its accomplishments failed to match its promise.

The survey's real coup was Gilbert, a figure destined for geologic glory. The 1871 expedition was his introduction to western exploration. With two years' apprenticeship under Newberry behind him—both in Ohio fieldwork and as a kind of aide-de-camp for the professor's winters at Columbia—Gilbert came with his old boss's insights in his head and his maps in his hands. To Gilbert belongs the formal naming of the Colorado Plateau and the Basin-Range Province and the first systematic delineation of their unique features. He added other names to Newberry's stratigraphic column—the Redwall limestone, for instance. He worked out the basic mechanics behind the structural geology and volcanics of the region. In 1872 he surveyed the region from out of

Kanab, visiting the North Rim and descending Kanab Creek to the river. Later in Salt Lake City, he met Powell, and they began their great collaboration—"swapping lies," as Gilbert put it. In 1875, irritated by Army methods of reconnaissance and mapping that subordinated geology to topography, Gilbert transferred to the Powell Survey, where, ironically, he spent his first field seasons remapping areas that Powell's amataeurs had bungled.[20]

Powell reaped what Wheeler had fecklessly sown. Gilbert's thoughts on the structural geology of the plateaus, on rivers, on rainfall and lake levels in the Great Basin—all programs that had begun under the Wheeler Survey—were released under Powell's rubric and to Powell's fame. Gilbert's final report for the Wheeler Survey was published in 1875, though its ideas had been expressed in progress reports as early as 1872. For Powell he summarized important ideas on the structural geology of the plateaus and the mechanics of fluvial erosion in the classic *Report on the Geology of the Henry Mountains* (1877), and he supplied most of the scientific research behind Powell's manifesto for land reform, *Report on the Lands of the Arid Region of the United States* (1878). Gilbert continued many of the Powell Survey themes as director of the Division of the Great Basin after the U.S. Geological Survey was established. Under Powell's regime at the Geological Survey (1881–94), he faithfully surrendered original research for administrative chores, eventually becoming chief geologist. Only with Powell's resignation from the survey did Gilbert return to the field, and curiously only after Powell's death in 1902 did he revive the brilliance of his early years. The executor to Powell's will and his boss's first memoirist, Gilbert apparently found it necessary to lay the patriarch to rest before he could return to his own special studies.

In his science too Gilbert organized, rationalized, cleaned up after the charismatic and often careless Powell. Though Powell dramatized the concept of antecedence, it was Gilbert who systematically translated fluvial erosion into Newtonian mechanics. Where Powell turned the river's gorge into a purple-prosed prison, Gilbert defined it as a gigantic flume engaged in the business of moving debris. Where Powell likened river and Uinta Mountains to a buzz saw and log, at the Henry Mountains Gilbert compared the laccolith (a mountain type he named and first described) to a hydraulic piston and applied some elementary mathematics to the forces involved. It was Gilbert, not Powell, who consolidated the American fluvialist position, Gilbert who translated river silt and sand into equations, Gilbert who wrote a Euclidean treatise on erosion and structure that served as the *Elements* of the American school. Though he had to wait more than thirty-five years after the Wheeler Expedition to do it, and though they would be based on mining debris in the Sacramento rather than silt in the Colorado, Gilbert's flume experiments on the University of California campus marked the beginning of experimental sedimentology and the scientific investigation of debris transport by streams. Conceptually the Colorado River Gilbert entered at Fort Mojave ultimately debouched over the tidal bar outside San Francisco's Golden Gate.

Its experience with Gilbert was in many ways typical of the Wheeler Survey at large. Time and again, the lieutenant found himself outranked by the Major. Devoted to the Army and the tradition of the military explorer, egged on by the combative chief of the Army engineers, A. A. Humphreys himself, Wheeler searched eagerly for a spectacle that would put his survey in the public eye. Powell had the Colorado canyons, Hayden the Yellowstone, King the Sierra Nevada. With a mixture of boldness and temerity, Wheeler sent field parties to all those areas—too late to claim priority, yet early enough to be charged with duplication.

His grand gestures always fell short. When he labored up a mountain in the Sierra Ancha and satisfied himself that no white man had ever been there before, no white man seemed to care either. A July traverse across Death Valley ended in sunstroke and ridicule. His expedition up the Colorado River in 1871, clearly intended to challenge Powell's presumption and to recapture the glory days of the corps, instead left him fighting against the currents of popular opinion. Wheeler was traveling the wrong way. His Canyon experience is surely the least remembered (or valued) of any of the era.

Though more solid work came out of his survey than out of Powell's, that fact hardly mattered. Powell was a master of prose and politics who brought his work to the public; Wheeler's tomes struggled to make it from government files to library shelves. No one mapped more of the West than Wheeler, and with the possible exception of the King Survey, no one mapped it with more skill. But his turgid prose and prosaic straining for effect looked florid, even silly, next to Powell's taut narratives and dramatic simplifications. Of the Colorado canyons Wheeler declaimed in 1889, "They stand without a known rival upon the face of the globe, and must always remain one of the wonders, and will, as circumstances of transportation permit, attract the denizens of all quarters of the world who in their travels delight to gaze upon the intricacies of nature." They would indeed come to the Canyon, but not on the strength of Wheeler's numbing prose.[21]

After 1879, broken in health and granted a disability discharge from the Army, embittered over rivalries with "scientific filibusters" like Powell, his beloved survey abolished in favor of the civilian U.S. Geological Survey, Wheeler retired into anonymity, laboring for another decade over his accounts. By the time his *Geographical Report* appeared in 1889, few people cared about the survey or even remembered it. His work in the Canyon was completely overshadowed by that of Powell; even Gilbert's monograph *Geology* is the least well known of all Gilbert's writings. Instead Gilbert's ideas—and those of Wheeler's 1871 expedition—were absorbed into the corpus of the Powell Survey and the works of John Wesley Powell himself.

* * *

have been its most heroic creation because it was the strangest of its encountered scenes. Meaning requires a cultural context; none existed for so unprecedented a place. Such a context, moreover, requires continuities. But logic and language strained against features so bizarre and unexpected.

Yet the deed was done. Powell positioned the Canyon squarely in the vogue of the Humboldtean explorer and the context of a Civil War veteran, feverishly pursuing the dark unknowns of the West, breaching plateaus with the élan of an assault against the fortifications at Cold Harbor. Gilbert fused the region to natural science. He established its significance through close analogies from known to unknown, solving its geologic puzzles with almost algebraic rigor. The Colorado Plateau became not merely a textbook demonstration but a source of exemplars and first principles. It remained to Clarence Dutton, however, to close the cultural triangle by bonding the Canyon to art. What the graphic artists of the Powell Survey did with pencil, paint, and wet plate, Dutton did with words. The Canyon became a place where the great themes of the age found monumental expression.

More than the others, Dutton appreciated the core problem, the oddity of the place. He understood that the Canyon was a grand ensemble whose effect was greater than the sum of its parts. And he discovered a means by which to celebrate that strangeness and to hold those pieces together. The *Tertiary History of the Grand Cañon District*, which Dutton published in 1882, was itself an extraordinary ensemble of the science, aesthetics, cartography, painting, photography, illustration, and ideas that had animated the intellectual and imperial expansion of America.

Dutton created an aesthetics without a popular substrate, without historical antecedents or cultural transitions, and he did it from the rim, without the narrative flow that a river trip intrinsically imposes. From the rim the perspective is more diffuse; there is no obvious focus because no central figure dominates and the eye sweeps across a vast horizon, almost an inversion of typical perspective; a narrative of the panorama has no intrinsic structure. Instead Dutton discovered in the flow of geologic time, in eras of deposition and erosion, an equivalent to the river's pools and rapids, and in the organization of time that preoccupied so much of the nineteenth century's intellectual elite, he discovered an informing conceit for an epic history of the earth.

He accepted the essential strangeness of the scene. Instead of feeble allusions or forced analogies, a soothing similitude to contemporary tastes, Dutton boldly asserted the peculiarity of the place, its unblinking uniqueness. There was really nothing else like it anywhere. It might have come from another planet or another existence. Had it been sculpted in central Europe, it would have shaped European aesthetics as much as the Alps. But it wasn't, and it didn't, and instead it stood outside virtually every convention of perception and understanding that millennia of Western art and philosophy had nurtured. John Muir, no amateur at cultivating landscapes, observed that "no matter how far you have wandered hitherto, or how many famous gorges and valleys you have seen, this one, the Grand Cañon of the Colorado, will seem as novel to you, as unearthly in the color and grandeur and quantity of its architecture, as if you have found it after death, on some other star. . . ."[24]

Dutton appreciated precisely the problem. "Great innovations, whether in art or literature, in science or in nature, seldom take the world by storm," he explained. "They must be understood before they can be estimated, and must be cultivated before they can be understood." No one has stated the fundamental issue better; probably no one ever will. By the time Dutton finished his inquiry, the Grand Canyon, essentially unknown twenty years before, utterly outside canons of art, literature, and science, had become an inextricable part of all and in fact became itself an exemplar of landscape aesthetics.[25]

Dutton's was the great innovation, the view from the rim. He put ideas behind the imagery. If, in Canyon historiography, Powell is the indispensable man, Dutton is the indispensable mind. For Powell the Grand was one of many canyons, and had it been absent, his river adventure—and the attendant geology and drama— could have continued and carried him to fame on the revelations from the Canyon of Lodore and Glen Canyon and the drama of Separation Rapids. For Dutton, however, Grand Canyon was a climax, without which the other landscape parts had no defining presence, no informing narrative. The *Exploration* took its narrative flow and rhythms effortlessly from the river. The rim offered no equivalent order. It was Dutton's insight to find that requisite flow in the passage of geologic time and to order it by an evolutionary progression of landforms. A Canyon panorama was not a confusion of lithic shapes and an empty sky. It told a story; it had a structure by which the mind could organize the eye; its geomorphic profligacy constituted in fact an aesthetic ensemble.

Wallace Stegner observed that Dutton has become "almost as much the *genius loci* of the Grand Canyon as Muir is of Yosemite." With few exceptions, those who came to the Canyon saw it, as Dutton did, from the rim. Those who followed Powell down the river (like Robert Brewster Stanton), or put their own voyages before the public (as did Frederick Dellenbaugh), or who tried to compete with Powell's narrative (as did Wheeler) wrote too late and, for all their labors, added too little. The river's narrative drive was powerful but singular in its effects, limited to one tale, and for long decades inaccessible in its popular recreation. For nearly a century after Powell's feat, the American public connected to the Canyon through its overlooks, not its rapids. The Santa Fe Railroad brought tourists and pilgrims to the South Rim, not to the Inner Gorge. Accordingly, as Stegner concluded, "although it is Powell's memorial to which the tourists walk after dinner to watch the sunset from the South Rim, it is with Dutton's eyes, as often as not, that they see."[26]

* * *

Who was Dutton, and how did he come to see what others had overlooked? The unorthodoxy of his vision reflected that of his career.

Clarence Edward Dutton was a Yale man (class of 1860); an athlete (he rowed crew); a litterateur, who had won the literary prize as a senior; an enthusiastic scientist, attracted to mathematics and chemistry and through them to geology; a Civil War veteran, brother to a West Point engineer, a volunteer who made the Army his career, despite some "pretty rough service," as he put it; an accomplished conversationalist, who could lecture extemporaneously on the silver question or on South Seas ethnography with equal relish; and an agnostic, who after spending two weeks at the Yale Divinity School, in his words, left before he was thrown out. He had a soldier's bearing and a scientist's mind. He was, in brief, the epitome of that great transition in American exploration between the Army engineer-explorer and the civilian scientist. He was both.[27]

A congenital polymath—he once described himself as "omnibiblical"—Dutton combined concentration with versatility. He loved cerebral games, especially chess, although eventually he abandoned the game because the sleepless nights he spent puzzling over it threatened to undermine his health. Instead he transferred that intellectual passion to other subjects with their own riddles: ordnance, chemistry, and geology. His memory was prodigious. He composed most of his manuscripts in his head, then wrote them down or dictated them in marathon sessions during which he stalked back and forth across a room, alternately speaking and puffing on an omnipresent cigar. In one such session he dictated eleven thousand words, of which two minor corrections were made in later revisions. No doubt this procedure helps account for the exceptional grace and conversational tone of his writings.

During the war he transferred from the Connecticut Volunteers to the Ordnance Corps of the regular Army, only one of three to pass the examinations. When the war ended, he remained as a

FIRST IMPRESSIONS

Two visions from the Ives
Expedition: At left, F. W.
Egloffstein's *Big Cañon at
Mouth of Diamond River*,
redrawn by J. J. Young, and
below, Balduin Möllhausen's
*Mouth of Diamond Creek,
Colorado River, View from the
South.* Since Möllhausen's
watercolor was not published
with the official report,
Egloffstein's *Big Cañon*
begame the primary source of
visual appreciation.

THE SECOND AGE GOES WEST

The Ives Expedition's celebrated steamboat, *The Explorer,* as recorded by Möll-hausen (above) is a curious blend of American genre painting and German *Naturphilosophie*—with noble savages in the foreground, improbable land-scapes to the background, and the crew rather resembling George Bingham's merry flatboatmen on the Mississippi. *Dead Mountain, Mojave Valley* by Möll-hausen, and redrawn by J. J. Young (opposite, top), shows an improbable feature of the Colorado River region, but one that echoes the iconography of the Humboldtean explorer, as recorded in this F. G. Weitsch painting (opposite, bottom) of Humboldt, every inch the European savant, bringing the light of modern learning to Ecuador with a radiant Mount Chimborazo in the background.

Canyon Columns: Science and Sentiment

Egloffstein recorded the western Canyon as a Gothic spire (*Big Cañon*, left), while John Strong Newberry recorded the features as geologic strata in one of the most famous stratigraphies from the Grand Reconnaissance (below). Ives himself considered Newberry's report the "most interesting and valuable result of the explorations."

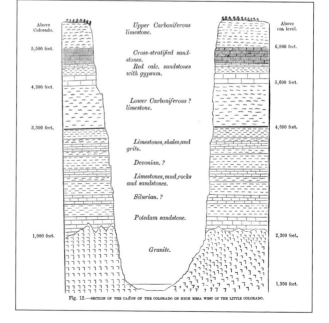

Above Colorado.	Upper Carboniferous limestone.		Above sea level.
5,500 feet.	Cross-stratified sandstones. Red calc. sandstones with gypsum.		6,800 feet.
4,300 feet.	Lower Carboniferous ? limestone.		5,600 feet.
3,300 feet.	Limestones, shales, and grits.		4,600 feet.
	Devonian. ?		
	Limestones, mud, rocks and sandstones.		
	Silurian. ?		
	Potsdam sandstone.		
1,000 feet.	Granite.		2,300 feet.
			1,300 feet.

Fig. 12.—SECTION OF THE CAÑON OF THE COLORADO ON HIGH MESA WEST OF THE LITTLE COLORADO.

GEOLOGISTS IN THE GORGE

The critical personalities in the transition from geographic reconnaissance to geological science: John Strong Newberry (above left), John Wesley Powell (above right), and the link between them, Grove Karl Gilbert (below), studying rocks while others sleep.

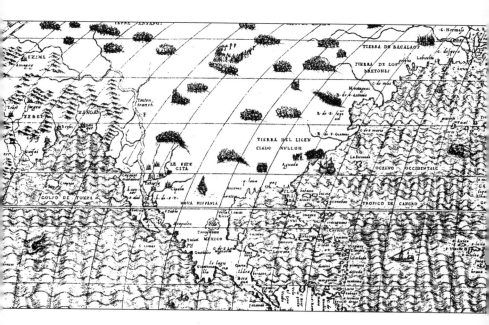

THE CARTOGRAPHIC CANYON I: CAÑON AND QUIVIRA

ABOVE: The Gastaldi map of 1546 (detail), one of the greatest of early New World maps, with the Colorado River dominating the known terrain of North America.

OPPOSITE, TOP: The Miera map of 1777, summarizing the cartography of the Dominguez-Escalante expedition. Miera obscures the main region of the Canyon, which the expedition bypassed, though he refers to Marble Canyon as *mui escarpada* and shows the Little Colorado. Like most maps of the period, its basic information is hydrographic and ethnographic.

OPPOSITE, BOTTOM: Garcés's map of his journey to the Moqui (1776–77). The map accurately portrays the major drainage of the Colorado River, though—because Garcés did not follow the river continuously but leap-frogged from settlement to settlement—it misses the great bend above Black Canyon and the rivers to the north. It does, however, show two streams entering from the south into what Garcés called the Puerto de Bucareli, surely Diamond Creek and Havasu Creek. Garcés named the Puerto after Antonia Maria Bucareli, Viceroy of New Spain.

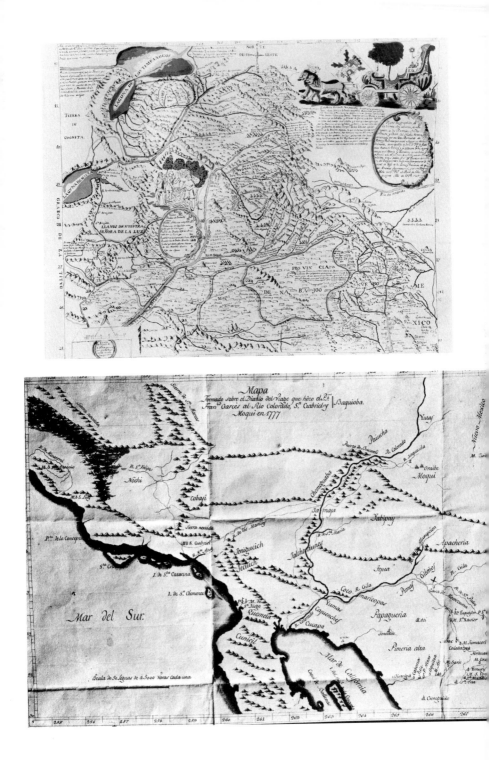

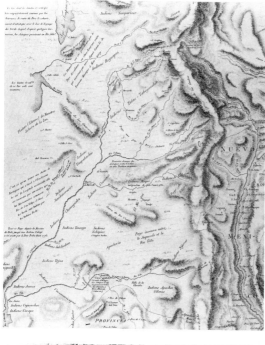

THE CARTOGRAPHIC CANYON II: GRAND RECONNAISSANCE

LEFT: Humboldt eyes the Canyon—the 1811 map (detail). Humboldt collated Spanish sources into a great map of New Spain. Through it he popularized the cartographic device of hachures as a means of indicating mountains, one of his many innovations. The Puerto de Bucareli is kept, probably on the basis of the Garcés map, but its location has shifted from the Colorado River to the Little Colorado.

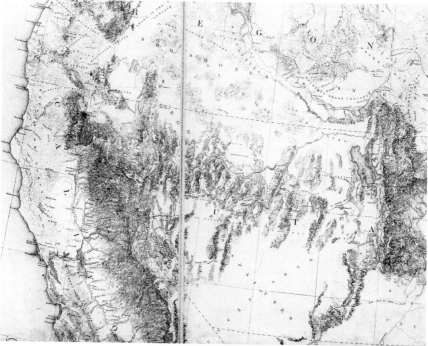

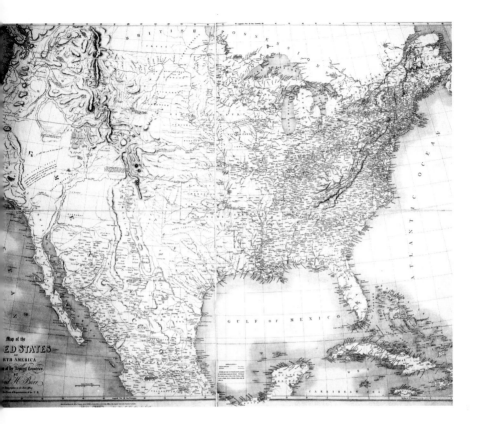

OPPOSITE, BOTTOM: The David H. Burr map of 1839 (detail). Relying on information generated by the fur trade, the map is reasonably complete for the Rocky Mountains and northwest; but, except for Jedediah Smith's trek along the Old Spanish Trail, the southwest is a void. Until official surveys that followed the Mexican War, Humboldt's map remained the primary reference for high culture.

ABOVE: G. K. Warren's map of 1857. Consolidating the Pacific Railroad Surveys of the 1850s with previous information, Warren's map shows with some accuracy the country traversed by the proposed transcontinental railroad routes and of course the Old Spanish Trail. The Colorado River is sketched very lightly; its east-west transit is recognized and the Little Colorado is located correctly, but nothing identifies the Canyon. Still, this sophisticated map shows major advances in scientific cartography. Within its format the context clearly exists for a landscape feature like the Canyon, devoid of ethnographic identity or commerical hydrographic significance.

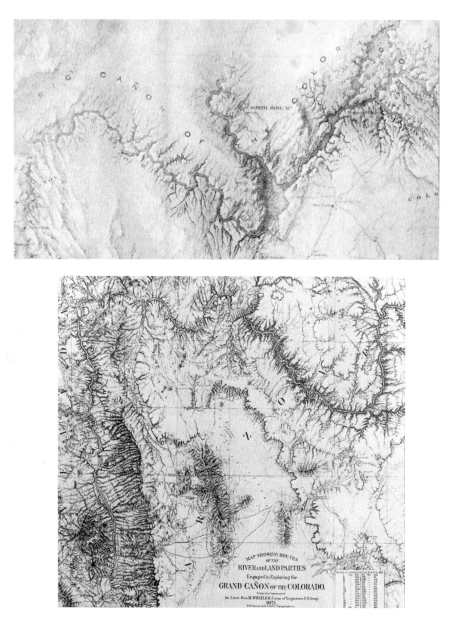

THE CARTOGRAPHIC CANYON III: HEROIC AGE

TOP: Egloffstein's magnificent map for the Ives Expedition, 1861 (detail). The map marvelously captures the serpentine river and its gorges, though the overall hydrography is flawed by confusing tributaries with the main Colorado. The contrast with Egloffstein's landscape art is striking.

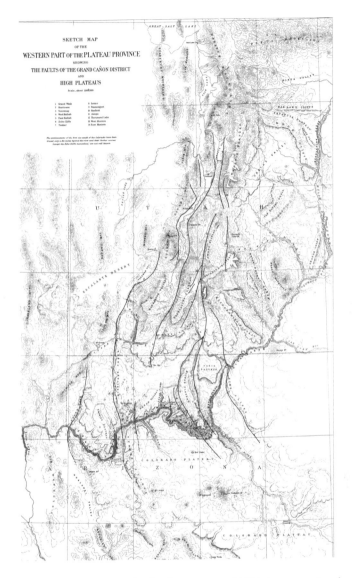

OPPOSITE, BOTTOM: The Wheeler Survey map of 1871, incorporating the 1871 Canyon expedition. Though much is still missing, the larger hydrography of the Canyon is at last accurately represented, thanks especially to the two Powell surveys.

ABOVE: Clarence Dutton's map of the High Plateaus and Grand Cañon district, showing clearly the main landscape feature and the geologic structures that define them. Canyon cartography is beginning to incorporate Canyon time.

SCIENTIFIC SUBLIMITY: THE PANORAMIC CANYON OF WILLIAM HOLMES

ABOVE: *The Temples and Towers of the Virgen*

OPPOSITE, TOP: *The Grand Cañon at the Foot of the Toroweap*

OPPOSITE, BOTTOM: *Panorama from Point Sublime, Looking East*

Superb examples of topographic art, and perhaps the finest landscapes ever made of the Grand Canyon region, east and west.

Captain Clarence E. Dutton

William Henry Holmes

THE GRAND ENSEMBLE:
A GREAT INNOVATION AND ITS INNOVATORS

Thomas Moran

rather than mechanical
ial studies of the Colo-
s, was a commanding
sensibility.31

red of three mono-
n; a common sub-
istry of geologic
Plateaus of Utah
sances for the
ajor cause for
erwise devas-
s. In the last
86), Dutton
ndated by
t only the
ain, like
In both
s—not
cenes
geo-

ory
a-
e

problems
ry made Du
and geophysi-

orado Plateau
t was twofold.
ught the strange
sas, and fabulous
tion. Together they
hat became the basis
whereas Newberry an-
ert reduced to Euclidean
ation. He cultivated a criti-
geography that lacked refer-
rcome what he considered the
brought in new descriptive terms
ative Hawaiian, and scrapped stock
ng allusions to architectural forms,
ent. The geological significance of the
Newberry had proclaimed with a strati-
n matched with an aesthetic canon, a stele

e brink of the Aquarius Plateau, Dutton ex-
scene should be described "in blank verse and
vas," for here "the geologist finds himself a poet."
ajor, he did not command nature to stand front and
cajoled it with reason, arranged it with a keen sense for
ness, and critiqued its artful outcomes. His prose was
firm and varied, full of suppleness and infinitely varied
ms, an ideal medium for a landscape full of exotic shapes
d surprises yet comprehensible. He differed from Powell too in
nat he saw the morphology of scenery by analogy to art rather
than to paleontology. He found an aesthetic meaning where Powell promoted a taxonomic order. He differed from Gilbert in that
he measured the landscape with figures of speech rather than with

bers and reached for architectural
metaphors. But what organized his influen
rado Plateau, as with his other investigatio
sense of history, one suffused with a literary

Dutton's survey of the Colorado Plateau consis
graphs. Each work had a common theme, erosio
ject, vulcanism; and a common sensibility, the a
time. In the *Report on the Geology of the High*
(1879–80), which consolidated Dutton's reconnar
Powell Survey, vulcanism dominates. In fact, a m
the elevation of the plateaus amid a landscape oth
tated by erosion was precisely their thick volcanic ca
of the triptych, *Mount Taylor and the Zuñi Plateau* (18
portrays an inverse scene. Here a region formerly inv
volcanic extrusions has so wasted away from erosion tha
vents and conduits that brought basalt to the surface rer
broken ruins or toppled idols left from a vanished empire.
studies Dutton presents his material in the form of journey
strict itineraries, but an imaginative recasting of events and
so that in the course of the journey one travels through the
logic history of the region.

Between these two studies lies the masterpiece, *Tertiary His*
of the Grand Cañon District (1882). Vulcanism is a secondary f
ture, a decorative vignette to the great text of earth time. Her
erosion and uplift exist in magnificent equilibrium; the Grand
Canyon is their dynamic outcome. Remove the river, and only a
plateau would remain. Remove the plateau, and there would exist
only an undistinguished river valley. The two had to cross to produce rim and river. That dialectic was aptly expressed in the geologic history of the larger region.

But what made the Grand Canyon a "great innovation in our
modern ideas of scenery," as Dutton declares, was another inter-

action, that of science with art. The sense of gigantic proportion displayed, the remarkable clarity of forms, the almost baroque splendor carved out of grand symmetries went beyond the explanatory models by which cliffs receded and rivers carved; they express the aesthetics of erosion. River and Canyon worked against each other like chisel and marble, brush and canvas. Nature was artist as well as engineer. For Dutton, unlike the members of the Ives Expedition, the scenic cliff and the geologic cliff were the same cliff. Both could be understood by similar acts of critical imagination, and one could be used to reinforce the other. The shape of the land involved mind as well as rock, reason together with impression.[32]

So journeys proceed not only through geologic time, as revealed through the stratigraphic column, but through a hierarchy of aesthetic effects, as manifest by the Canyon country's many features. Typically, a chapter of science alternates with a chapter of art. In a way, Dutton's construction of imaginary journeys by which to arrange the significant facts is not so different from Thomas Moran's invention of imaginary vantage points from which to assemble assorted features into a proper impression. With Moran, however, art in all its painterly excesses can run rampant into a glorious chromolithograph of Emerson's "transparent eyeball." With Dutton science disciplines the art so that each counters the other.

And so that, equally, each enhances the other. Aesthetics amplifies the often inadequate geology. "I have in many places departed from the severe ascetic style which has become conventional in scientific monographs," Dutton confesses. "Perhaps no apology is called for. Under ordinary circumstances the ascetic discipline is necessary. Give the imagination an inch and it is apt to take an ell, and the fundamental requirement of scientific method—accuracy of statement—is imperiled. But in the Grand Cañon district there is no such danger. The stimulants which are demoralizing elsewhere are necessary here to exalt the mind sufficiently to comprehend the sublimity of the subjects." The Grand Canyon was a scenic innovation. It required a new eye, a new voice, and a new perspective.[33]

That perspective begins on the summit of the Great Rock Staircase, the stepped cliffs that form the receding flank of the High Plateaus. The *Tertiary History* thus opens where the *High Plateaus* concludes. Here Dutton's persona surveys the scene, establishes its boundaries, sketches the whole into which each particular must fit. As Dutton's quest proceeds, journey by journey, to its climax, those individual phenomena will become more heavily laden with meaning, richer in complexity, and animated by the geographic and historical ensemble of which they are a part. But first the proportions, first the standards by which to understand and appreciate: Dutton's descent down the Great Rock Staircase to Kanab defines a stratigraphy of the landscape, a standard by which to measure both geology and aesthetics. Just as it functioned as a baseline for the Powell Survey's cartography, so Kanab serves as a kind of narrative referent for the journeys to follow.

This first traverse also introduces the informing process for the whole of the Grand Cañon district, erosion. Two images of erosion frame the text, one current, one buried in the geologic past. The first is what Dutton calls the Great Denudation. At one time the High Plateaus had extended far south, covering even the Canyon in thousands of feet of rock. Then, like a receding shore, the plateaus had ebbed to their present conditions. The reason is erosion, erosion on so vast a scale that it beggars the imagination, and with it Dutton commences the *Tertiary History*. A second, complementary image, the Great Unconformity, will conclude the monograph. Buried in the depths of the Inner Gorge, the Great Unconformity records a dramatic break in the rock record where Precambrian mountains—two ranges, one after the other—had worn away like mastodon molars to their roots, yielding a plain as level as a lake. The great stratigraphic column visible in the Canyon then arose layer by layer upon this scoured surface. Thus between them these two events define the borders of the Canyon's

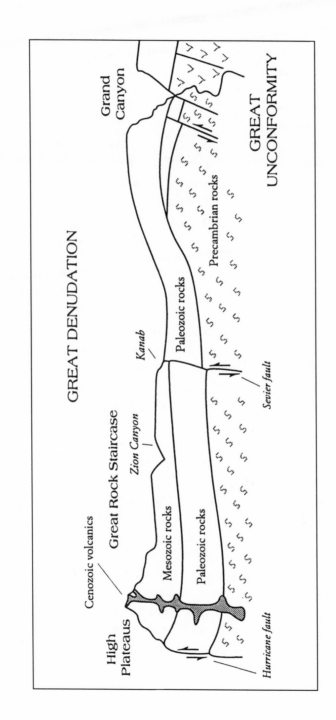

geologic history, the one its basement, the other its roof. They provide the historical heads and tails that Dutton demanded, as the regional panorama from the Aquarius Plateau and the Canyon panorama from Point Sublime furnish geographic boundaries. They define the whole.

In comparison with such events the excavation of the Grand Canyon proper is almost trivial. The Canyon appears magnificent only because it has occurred at a time when water and rock, downcutting and uplift, are balanced, after the river has carved and begun widening its gorge but before new layers of rock can be stripped away to empty sky. The middle displays what the extremes have eliminated. At the Canyon's temporal borders geologic time has abolished geologic history. Within the Canyon itself, however, the record is writ large on lithic parchment with the quill of erosion.

From Kanab, Dutton conducts three imaginary journeys. Each highlights a geologic process and a scenic phenomenon characteristic of the canyon country. Each merits double chapters, one of science, another of aesthetics. Each builds upon the other. Each concludes with a climactic illustration in the form of a synthetic panorama, coming as though to the end of an imaginative syllogism. En route Dutton accents certain facts of special importance, scrutinizes "type" formations and features, and constantly relocates his position within the larger scope of the region. Amid a landscape of such sweeping vistas and chaos of exotic forms, such a typology acts to focus attention, a necessary organizing technique to provide something for the eye and mind to rest upon. The narrative never loses shape by the sheer accumulation of fact or overstrains itself searching for perspective. Science and art are not hopelessly homogenized, as in the worst of German Romanticism, or diluted of presence, as in much of American transcendentalism. Instead aesthetics and science, impression and fact—a chapter of one followed by chapter of the other—develop in calculated counterpoint.

The first journey travels to Zion Canyon and the Valley of the

Marx, Herbert Spencer, to name a few. In America the century boasted William Prescott, Francis Parkman, Henry Adams, Frederick Jackson Turner, and Lewis Henry Morgan, to cite some of Dutton's more prominent contemporaries, all of whom credited history as an explanatory method and a medium of immense synthesis.

Into their ranks, on the strength of his heroic biography of the Grand Canyon, came Clarence Dutton. In an age that tried to cast its thoughts into evolutionary sequences, directed by single principles, and synthesized in grand teleological climaxes, Dutton did precisely that in the *Tertiary History*. The Grand Canyon symbolized earth history as nowhere else on the planet, dramatized the temporal ether that suffused every event, and elucidated the principles by which such a universe might be comprehended. An era that invented geology, that was in fact obsessed with the larger questions that the discovery of earth and time had exhumed like dinosaur bones found in the Grand Canyon an eloquent emblem of that mystery and in the *Tertiary History* an epic retelling of its story. The *Tertiary History of the Grand Cañon District* created the view from the rim. Together with Powell's river-defining *Exploration*, it made the Canyon truly Grand.

It was a timely no less than time-synthesizing book. First published as part of the Geological Survey's 1881 *Annual Report*, it was republished, complete with a chromatic *Atlas* in 1882, as the first of the USGS's distinguished series of monographs, the inaugural big book of arguably the most significant scientific bureau of nineteenth-century America. While mining engineer Samuel Emmons might grumble that he started Dutton's book "but came to the conclusion that life was too short," reviewers like Archibald Geikie in Britain and James Dwight Dana at Yale University received it enthusiastically. It quickly established itself as a model of modern natural history.[35]

The *Tertiary History* was received in fact much like Osmond Fischer's first synthesis of the planet's natural philosophy, *Physics of the Earth's Crust*, which was published contemporaneously with it, which quoted Dutton frequently, and which Dutton reviewed in the *American Journal of Science*. Fischer's text was an attempt to relate geophysical topics to the evolution of the globe made possible by the contractional hypothesis. But timing also merged natural philosophy with moral philosophy. Appropriately, the *Tertiary History* appeared the same year that Herbert Spencer made his triumphal tour of the United States. Simply substitute "fluvial erosion," in the one case, and "contraction," in the other, for Spencer's "struggle for existence" to discover that Dutton and Fischer approximated the famous Spencerian epitome of evolution as a progression from incoherent homogeneity to increasingly coherent heterogeneity. From the vague sweep of the Aquarius Plateau, Dutton's narrative had advanced, stage by stage, to a grand climax, an intricate integration of interdependent pieces, at Point Sublime. So the Canyon's evolution underwrote the belief that similar principles of progress informed all aspects of the universe. That earth history could progress foreshadowed—destined—an epoch of social progress. That such an exotic spectacle could be reduced to precepts common to prevailing scholarship validated the robustness of those principles. The Canyon gave as well as got.

Dutton's career did not end on the rim. As Point Sublime was the climax but not the conclusion to the *Tertiary History*, so the *Tertiary History* was an apex but not a end to Dutton's oeuvre.

Even before he departed the Colorado Plateau—in fact as part of his reconnaissance of the High Plateaus—he had supplied some of the scientific muscle to bolster Powell's famous *Arid Lands* report (1878). His volcanic researches continued in Nicaragua and Hawaii. His inquiry into the Charleston earthquake of 1886 brought international acclaim. When Powell successfully lobbied in 1888 for an Irrigation Survey within the Geological Survey—an institution that would direct much of western settlement if Powell had his way—he appointed Dutton chief engineer. The assignment was to last only two years. In 1890 a new chief of ordnance appeared who was less sympathetic toward Dutton's annual furlough to the civilians. In 1890, too, Congress began a serious attack on Powell's more geopolitical ambitions, and the Irrigation Survey folded. During congressional hearings Dutton admitted that the topographic maps on which Powell placed such hope, and on which he had pinned the future of the survey, were not suitable for reclamation engineering. The maps, Dutton insisted, were a good investment; they were not, however, essential or suitable for irrigation. Powell never forgave him.

But there were changes within the Geological Survey as well. When he first took to the field, Dutton had high hopes. "I cherish the belief that the Survey in the course of a few years will accomplish much for geology," he wrote Geikie in 1880. "The spirit which has been infused into it is most gratifying. . . . Mr. King is more than justifying all the high expectations which attended his appointment & his skill & ability to organize & administer have proved to be of the highest order. He succeeds in everything. . . ." It was Clarence King who placed Dutton in charge of the Division of the Colorado after the consolidation of the surveys, and King who supported his work at the Grand Canyon.[36]

By 1885, however, at the end of his years on the Colorado Plateau and after nearly four years of the Powell administration, Dutton had other thoughts for Geikie. "Our Survey is now at its zenith & I prophesy its decline. The 'organization' is rapidly 'perfecting,' i.e., more clerks, more rules, more red tape, less freedom of movement, less discretion on the part of the geologists & less outturn of scientific product. This is inevitable. It is the law of nature & can no more be stopped than the growth & decadence of the human body." But it was not a future calculated to inspire a man like Dutton.[37]

When he left the Geological Survey in 1890, he found himself in "virtual banishment" at the arsenal in San Antonio, Texas. He pursued some scientific work, but not single-mindedly and then with difficulty after illness broke his famously robust health. Still, Dutton so impressed George Breckenridge, a San Antonio banker, that the two went on a world cruise. There was a manuscript on China too, though it was never published. In 1899 Dutton and Breckenridge decided to tour Mexico, and for this Dutton invited his Canyon comrades William Holmes and G. K. Gilbert. "Shall be delighted to see you once more," Dutton wrote his favorite artist, "and recall old times when we were young and beautiful and when the roses bloomed—or rather when the coyotes howled and the cactus spines got into our shins." They visited ruins and volcanoes and spent the long hours on the train playing cribbage, far from coyotes and cacti. Holmes sketched, Gilbert jotted stray observations into his omnipresent notebooks, and Dutton puffed on his cigars.[38]

Later a new chief of ordnance rehabilitated Dutton's Army career and returned him as his personal assistant to Washington, D.C. There Dutton delivered his final scientific paper, on radioactivity and volcanoes, and there in 1912 he died. Perhaps apocryphally, but surely appropriately, his last words recalled his "old friends on the Geological Survey." His years on the plateaus were those he remembered most vividly, and for them history has best preserved his memory. When he arrived, the Canyon was one of many natural marvels clamoring for celebrity. When he left, it stood alone.[39]

In the end, the *Tertiary History*—and the Grand Canyon—were about seeing. Graphic art was as indispensable as Dutton's graphic prose. Its illustrations, especially its *Atlas*, are primary reasons why the *Tertiary History* has endured.

Begin with the photography. The Wheeler Survey had priority here. Timothy O'Sullivan made the first photographs of the Canyon, from the river, and after he departed, William Bell extended the view to include the rim of the western Canyon. Both, however, sank into the general morass of that troubled survey. By then Powell had introduced two other photographers, E. O. Beaman to the river, and J. K. Hillers to the rim. Their photo portfolios, done under impossibly laborious conditions, made the Grand Canyon one of the first western spetacles to receive a thorough photographic inquiry, the Wheeler and Powell survey pictures coming at nearly the same time as the photographs of Yellowstone taken by W. H. Jackson for the Hayden Survey.

Reputations were made here. For his work with the King and Wheeler surveys, O'Sullivan achieved deserved fame. For Hillers the Canyon portfolio launched him on a celebrated career that made him chief photographer for both the Bureau of American Ethnology and the U.S. Geological Survey and earned him international renown for developing techniques to render photographic transparencies on glass. In the *Tertiary History* the heliotype reproduction of Hillers's photos is poor, but the photos were included because photography was too important a visual medium to ignore and because like Dutton's habit of continually relocating himself on the landscape, they sharpen by contrast the illustrations of Thomas Moran and William Holmes.

Probably, however, their real significance was subtextual. Hillers's photographs were taken back to studios and studies where they provided, for the others, a visual archive. They complemented field sketches; they furnished a frequently consulted reference. From them Moran refreshed and reconstructed his memory. Almost certainly the best of Hillers's work was co-opted into Dutton's prose, Thomas Moran's colors, and William Holmes's indestructible lines.

The ensemble's artist qua artist was Thomas Moran. He came to the *Tertiary History* with a glowing tradition of Second Age artist-explorers to sustain him and with plenty of Canyon art already behind him.

An English emigrant from a family of painters and etchers, Moran was born in 1837, a year after Emerson's *Nature* and Cole's *The Oxbow*. He evolved as an artist by fusing the two and by investing in the natural scenes of the American West something of the landscape aesthetics of J. M. W. Turner, whom Moran admired, and the Düsseldorf school, whose American practitioners often rivaled him. Moran had Turner's eye for color, Albert Bierstadt's exuberance for the monumental, Frederick Church's passion for wild landscapes—and a nationalist's delight in the scenery of the country in which he grew up. "That there is a nationalism in art needs no proof," Moran asserted. An artist "should paint his own land."[40]

So Thomas Moran did. In 1871 he had joined the Hayden Survey to the Yellowstone. From that summer's experience came a portfolio of dazzling watercolors of geysers and bubbling hot springs and the magnificent panorama, *Grand Canyon of the Yellowstone*, an immediate sensation. Congress purchased the work for ten thousand dollars, hung it in the Capitol, and proceeded under its radiant majesty to authorize Yellowstone as the first of America's national parks. Not one to pass by publicity, Powell brought Moran to the Grand Canyon in 1873, and from the North Rim, Moran painted a companion piece, *Chasm of the Colorado*, also bought by Congress and hung next to its Yellowstone cognate. Later both traveled to the Centennial Exhibition in Philadelphia where they boasted the scenic splendor of the American empire. Powell further convinced Moran to illustrate his *Exploration of the Colorado River*, a collusion of purple prose and chromatic landscape, though Moran had to mute his vision into engravings. Alone among Canyon artists, Moran had to convey both rim and river. When Dutton began his research on the *Tertiary History*, he naturally looked to Moran, and in 1880 Moran returned to the Canyon with Dutton. It would not be his last trip.

Though in his early years he often lived by his engravings, his instincts were those of the painter for whom Art transcends Nature. "I place no value upon literal transcripts from Nature. My general scope is not realistic; all my tendencies are toward idealization." Though "of course" all art must come "through Nature," Moran believed "that a place, as a place, has no value in itself for the artist only so far as it furnished the material from which to construct a picture." In particular, "topography in art is valueless."[41]

Rather, art expressed emotion; representational art was intrinsically inferior to the "impression produced by nature" on the painter. Moran freely, promiscuously rearranged landscape features so that their positions would be true to their "pictorial," not their topographic nature. Citing Turner, Moran declaimed that "Art is not Nature; an aggregation of ten thousand facts may add nothing to a picture, but be rather the destruction of it." Literal truth counted for nothing; representation was "never a work of art, is never a picture." The artist was free to rearrange features as he saw fit. His only ambition must be to express a region's "character"; his only standard, his success at "sacrificing the literal truth of the parts to the higher truth of the whole." That Morgan did on a grand scale. The *Chasm of the Colorado* was landscape as opera.[42]

For a graphic artist, the Canyon presented special problems, technical as well as aesthetic. Dutton recognized two: the lack of perspective and the false perspective. The rim offered no simple pictorial focus. No peak, waterfall, or single gorge concentrates the eye, while a blank horizon inscribes a vast plane. In the *Grand Canyon of the Yellowstone* Moran could include the falls and gorge of the Yellowstone River within a contained vantage point. The Grand Canyon of the Colorado, from the rim, allowed no such perspective. The false perspective, a "defect which usually mars all canyon scenery," was particularly pronounced at Powell Plateau, where Moran sited his *Chasm*. It involved "the flattening of objects through want of gradations in tones and shades, and the obscurity of form and detail produced by the great distances and hazey atmosphere."[43]

But Moran's philosophy of landscape art allowed him, demanded of him, that he invent his own perspective. He constructed artificial platforms for introduced viewers and contrived foregrounds that forced the eye toward the picture's center. He orchestrated individual terrain features, repositioned them, exaggerated them, according to the overall "impression" he sought. He distinguished separate objects by their radiant colors, unmarred by sun or shade. He unified whole panoramas by an interstitial medium of cloud and haze. The obscurity of form and detail that Dutton lamented Moran turned to positive effect. "This Grand Cañon," Moran explained, "offers a new and comparatively untrodden field for pictorial interpretation, and only awaits the men of original thoughts and ideas to prove to their countrymen that we possess a land of beauty and grandeur with which no other can compare."[44]

Most fundamentally Moran devised ways to transfigure canyons into a range of mountains. By falsely lowering the foregound, he introduced a focus; by flooding the upper canvas with cloud and peaks, he erased the vast panorama of sky that filled the natural horizon. Improbably the two perspectives, rim and river, so geographically and aesthetically at odds, here combine. Instead of viewing the Grand Canyon from the top, looking down, the viewer of a Moran Canyon looks up. The river becomes a focal gorge; the inner Canyon vaguely resembles a Yosemite Valley viewed from afar. On the North Rim he had stalled and needed the prod of Powell's enthusiasm to kick-start his own. In a sense he also transferred Powell's river-dominated perspective to the rim, a move that agreed as well with conventions of landscape art and that merged with his successful illustrations for Powell's *Exploration*. The rim becomes a kind of valley that peers into a gorge behind which lies a braided tangle of other gorges.

Moran's was a transcendentalist landscape. Emerson's insistence that words were signs of natural facts, and natural facts only signs of spiritual facts, found perfect expression in a Moran Canyon. Paint replaces words. The meticulously drawn foreground, so detailed a viewer can identify lichen species on limestone boulders, substitutes for the realm of natural facts. The cloud-filled background of soaring summits and light becomes the world of spiritual fact, no longer lashed to the laws or limitations of topographic or geologic reality but rearranged to convey the larger truths and sublimity of Nature and unified by ubiquitous spirit clouds. The first nature of things becomes a second nature of spirit. So too the eye moves from Canyon gloom to Canyon glory, from Powell's Great Unknown at the center to an illuminated panorama of sun-splashed peaks that constitute the rim and then moves up and beyond with an arc of rainbow.

Everything in fact is exaggerated, in part to fit the Canyon into conventions of landscape art and in part to celebrate nature on a grand and unexpected scale. It was his "Big Picture," Moran confessed, big in ambition as well as size (seven by twelve feet). It swept aside all previous Canyon images. It shrinks Egloffstein's *Big Cañon* into a cameo, overwhelmed by a larger geographic and aesthetic perspective. Like nearly all paintings of the Canyon, it shows at once too much and too little. Moran could not capture all of the Canyon, though he tried heroically; still less could he do it by projecting the rim view as though it were seen simultaneously from the river in a kind of Romantic cubism. Yet for all its distortions, the fantasy of its vantage point, its geography of misty marvels, no one would mistake a Moran Canyon for anything but the Grand Canyon. And for all its bombast, the *Chasm of the Colorado* marks as much the effective onset of Canyon art as Powell's *Exploration* does Canyon literature.

The *Grand Canyon of the Yellowstone* touched a more instinctive chord. Mountains, not canyons, still dominated popular aesthetics. The first of the Great Survey leaders, Clarence King, made his reputation by climbing Mount Whitney, by discovering a glacier (the first in America) on the slopes of Mount Shasta, and by writing *Moutaineering in the Sierra Nevada*. Forested Yellowstone, ringed with mountains, could be set aside as a "pleasuring ground" for the people of the United States. The Grand Canyon was more problematic. As Dutton recognized, it required special cultivation. It remained preeminently a scientific spectacle, perhaps a nationalist emblem, not a source of popular entertainment, easy recognition, or public endorsement. Appreciation of Canyon scenery did not grow organically either out of folk contact or from existing traditions. It was created—had its meaning invented almost in defiance of convention—by an extraordinary elite. That act of will is reflected in the heroic contrivance of Moran's *Chasm*.

Yet he returned; the *Chasm of the Colorado* was only a prologue. Though his career began at Yellowstone, it ended at the Grand Canyon. Moran revisited the Canyon in 1880 with Dutton, courtesy of the Geological Survey; in 1892 with William H. Jackson, the great photographer of the West; and in 1901 with a coterie of artists from New York. In the latter two cases he came as the guest of the Santa Fe Railroad. By 1904 Moran was undertaking almost annual visits to the Canyon rim. A senior member of the National Academy of Design and a charter member of the Society of Men Who Paint the West, honored as the dean of American landscape painters and increasingly popularized by chromolithographs of his Canyon canvases published by the Santa Fe in an effort to publicize its Arizona route as a tourist mecca, Moran in his later years became obsessed with the Canyon. The Canyon was color—that was its maddening aesthetic challenge—but it was nature too, and it was American, uniquely so. The Canyon's rim was American art's greatest gallery and its greatest pulpit.

Moran expressed this best when he returned to the South Rim in 1901. He had always insisted that the "business of the great painter should be the representation of great scenes in nature." The grand spectacles of nature lay in America: from here too should come the world's grandest art. The one American artist to earn John Ruskin's praise, Moran now led the fight against foreign, usually French, influences—against impressionism and later cubism, against the celebration of new subjects other than landscape, against the spirit of expatriation. Such art was "false to nature" and such artists, by ignoring their proper heritage, were falsifying their future. More and more Moran's podium was the Canyon rim, a scene without any European equivalent.[45]

When the National Gallery of Art staged an exhibition on national parks in 1917, four of the forty-five paintings were Moran's, and largely on the strength of his example, seventeen of the collection were of the Grand Canyon. For his catalytic work at Yellowstone, the National Park Service proclaimed him the "father of the park system." Two years later, assisted by the exhibition, the Grand Canyon finally achieved national park status itself. Surely Moran's paintings had contributed. What Moran had fixed in paint was now fixed in law. The scene was finally preserved in statute more enduring than varnish and gilt. The director of the gallery, William Holmes himself, was no less lavish in his praise. Moran, he declared, is "the greatest landscape painter the world has ever known."[46]

Yet success had its price. By substituting an idealized landscape for the actual one, Moran had subordinated the topographic Canyon to reigning cultural ideas, aesthetic conventions, and painterly mannerisms. It may be that some of Moran's use of mist reflects the impact of Oriental art, much as Dutton (with his allusion to Oriental pagodas and Fujiyama) shows the influence of Japan in particular. But more likely Moran was simply indulging in Turnerian conventions and in the idealization of nature that, particularly in landscape art, survived the onslaught of Darwinism, realism, and naturalism, much as its techniques survived impressionism. That is what made his imagery recognizable and what made his Canyon "art." But it also bound the Moran Canyon to the beliefs and norms of those times. However prolonged their tenure, they could not survive indefinitely. The "harmonious" whole that Moran sought—the social significance of his landscape as art—would be lost when those ideas faded. The Canyon as landscape feature might, through law, be preserved, but the Canyon as landscape art could not.

"Those who have long and carefully studied the Grand Cañon of the Colorado," Dutton wrote, "do not hesitate for a moment to pronounce it by the most sublime of all earthly spectacles." Thomas Moran had studied it longer and more carefully than any other artist. The idealization of Nature that he embodied persisted in both genteel and wilder forms—in Robert Underwood Johnson and John Muir, William Keith and Albert Bierstadt. Increasingly, however, it became itself conventional. In Moran's later Canyon paintings, perspective becomes formalized, the Romantic genteel, and the operatic decadent. So stylized did Moran's Canyon become that he took to signing his paintings with a thumbprint to frustrate forgeries. His repaintings had the quality of rite; his art, not the Canyon, had become their object. From his rim ramparts Moran fought a vain rearguard action against avant-garde modernism.[47]

What he lost, ironically, was the Canyon, the real Canyon of rock, strata, open sky, silty streams, and indestructible shapes. Art, it appears, was short; life, long. The topographic Canyon that Moran dismissed as irrelevant continued long after the landscape art that he practiced morphed into other genres or passed away. What Moran lacked was the capacity to see those stones in a way outside his idealized vision. In particular he lacked a science disciplined by topography. Yet unlike Yellowstone, where art would shape science, at the Grand Canyon science would instruct art. The meaning of the Canyon depended on its scientific, not its artistic, significance. An art disconnected from those geologic values would fade with artistic fads. Dutton's disciplined text is a literary fugue, with contrapuntal science and art; unchecked, Moran's canvases swell into an opera of almost Wagnerian excess.

If not the discipline of science, art needed, at a minimum, the particulars of place. The aging Moran lost both, if he had ever possessed the former. His Canyons became the scene of painterly excess, gilt-edged relics from another time, like the split-twig figurines recovered from Paleo hunter caves in the Redwall; historical curiosities like Casteñada's and Ives's misreadings of the Canyon's future. Without a believable transcendentalism, Moran's "harmonious whole" looked as quaint as Victorian bric-a-brac, as relevant as Emerson's *Nature* in an age of automobiles and quantum mechanics. The capacity of the Canyon to surprise was gone. Enduring Canyon art would be art that stayed close to the stone.

Paradoxically, some of the most durable of Canyon art came from the man who had praised Moran as the greatest of all landscape artists.

William Henry Holmes was an ideal foil to Thomas Moran. He stands to Moran as Dutton does to Powell. Among them the four men mark the ordinal points of the heroic age; they contain the compass of the Canyon's meaning. If Dutton fused aesthetics with geology, Holmes bonded science to art.

He was in many ways typical of those untypical travelers from high culture who set out for the High Plateaus in the 1870s. He was a master of the panorama; a craftsman with line, recalling the horizontal linearity that typified much of American painting at mid-century; and a self-taught naturalist, who specialized in the material artifacts of geology and archaeology. But most important, he was a splendid specimen of the artist as traveler, illustrator, and reporter so typical of the Second Age. Holmes's panoramic landscapes, fusing enthusiasm with exactitude, belong with Audubon's encyclopedia of wildlife, George Catlin's portfolio of Indians, and Frederick Catherwood's inventory of Mayan ruins. At the Grand Canyon a man who specialized in representational art met a landscape that needed only full-scale representation.

Formally trained in art, Holmes was recruited as an illustrator for the Hayden Survey and sent west from 1872 to 1877. His keen eye soon made him a competent geologist and, from his experiences on the Colorado Plateau, a fine archaeologist, attracted particularly to the hard shape of landforms and artifacts. Later he worked for the Geological Survey, then transferred into the Bureau of American Ethnology. From there he spent three years as curator of anthropology at the Field Museum in Chicago before returning to the Smithsonian Institution, where he remained for twenty-three years and continued his passion for exploration by directing the Armour Expedition to the Yucatán. When Powell died in 1902, Holmes succeeded him as director of the Bureau of

American Ethnology. His *Handbook of Aboriginal American Antiquities* (1919) immediately established itself as the standard reference. A remarkable career in all, yet it was art that glued the various shards together, art, his first love, as William Goetzmann notes, "to which he always in some fashion returned." Appropriately his administrative tenure ended in 1920, when at age seventy-four, he became director of the National Gallery of Art. He remained for twelve years.[48]

Rehired by the Geological Survey, Holmes went to the Grand Canyon in 1880 to assist Dutton. Like his other professional work, his drawings were functional. In the *Atlas* to the *Tertiary History*, sandwiched between geologic maps, the panoramas give texture where the maps, lacking a suitable topographic contour base, show only the symbolic color of geologic eras and the gross structure of faults and uplift. The pictures give visual texture as well to Dutton's prose. What makes the *Tertiary History* more than a collection of sketches is what also makes the *Handbook of Aboriginal American Antiquities* more than the riprap of pothunters and the impressions of dilettantes in search of the picturesque: it communicates ideas as well as images. The same principles of natural history that inform Dutton's text shape Holmes's mighty panoramas as well.

A Moran landscape is a study in grandiloquence; every Moran painting has every Canyon element in it. Holmes, however, evolves the great out of the tiny. He gathers individual scenes as though they were rock samples, saved for later assembly into a composite stratigraphic column or, in the case of the *Tertiary History*, a composite history. The cliff, the gorge, the butte—all are separately featured, then combined into a succession of syntheses at Zion Canyon, Toroweap Overlook, and Point Sublime. Consider each in turn.

For Zion Holmes drew *The Temples and Towers of the Virgen*. Reinforcing Dutton's architectural analogies, Zion Canyon looms out of the desert like a cityscape, reminiscent of Frederick Church's panoramas of Greek antiquities and the Holy Land. The rock strata and land sculpture gather lines into a focus with almost mathematical perspective. It is as though the land explained itself, as if it needed only to be discovered like a fossil ammonite and recorded. Probably the panorama's most remarkable feature is the immense scale and emptiness of its sky, which consumes more than half the scene. One effect of course is to prevent a vertical exaggeration of the buttes, to shape panoramas much wider than they are high. But another, perhaps more significant consequence is that the picture illustrates one of the themes of Dutton's text, the concept of a Great Denudation, a period of erosion that stripped off the greater proportion of the rocks that had once covered the region and of which the isolated buttes and receding cliffs are but a relic. The principal scientific significance in the scene is precisely those missing strata.

Consider, next, *The Grand Cañon at the Foot of the Toroweap*, a study in fluvial downcutting, dominated by the excavations of the western Canyon. Even here, however, there are countervailing horizontal planes with which to balance the vertiginous gorge. One is the horizon; the other, the red shelf of the Esplanade, a great erosional terrace between the rim and the gorge. The geologic text is that the Canyon eroded in three stages: first the Great Denudation, which stripped away the overlaying strata; then a lesser downcutting to (and horizontal recession along) the Esplanade; and finally a renewed burst of downcutting to the inner gorge. The proportioning of the panorama records these facts precisely. The quarter or so of the panorama committed to sky retains the lessons of the Great Denudation. The Esplanade then balances the gorge. The river appears only as a patch, as though stone curtains had parted to reveal it. Matching it is a pond on the Esplanade, a reminder that water has been the sculptor of both. Still, the gorge is the most active feature, and it explodes at the viewer. Quite possibly, *The Grand Cañon at the Foot of the Toroweap* is the most successful of all Canyon art, surely the finest synthesis of rim and river.

Holmes's most ambitious pieces, however, are the three panoramas—east, south, and west—from Point Sublime, which portray the eastern Canyon and collectively illustrate the climax to Dutton's text. Here all the processes and forms of land sculpturing and all the geologic themes of the Canyon converge. Here Dutton declared was the Grand Ensemble. And here Holmes demonstrated his mastery of Canyon art. He broke the point's 270-degree sweep into three parts. Only one, the view south, includes the river, though again only as a symbolic emblem. The vast sculpting of the Canyon through the Kaibab Plateau was not the result of a river-cut gorge but an immense process of excavation by retreating cliffs, a modern exemplar of what must have occurred during the Great Denudation. Every feature is included, each in its proper place, each stratum distinct and identifiable.

The most instructive feature, however, is the foreground of the *Panorama from Point Sublime* (looking east). Two figures reside. One sketches, obviously an artist, while the other, instructing over his shoulder, is surely a geologist. Holmes and Dutton—or equally the two personas of William Henry Holmes. Viewing the panorama from the Aquarius Plateau, Dutton once declared that the geologist must find himself a poet. At Point Sublime the reverse has occurred; the artist has found himself a geologist. What made the Grand Canyon a significant landscape for Western civilization was its scientific lessons. It came too late and was too much sui generis to reform western art. Even as Moran and Holmes painted, landscape art had crossed the summit and was descending down the lee side of Western aesthetics. But in 1880 it spoke with the clarity of a Holmes line and the vitality of Moran's colors—and with the cultural authority of geologic science. Dutton the poet met Holmes the geologist.

Yet the Holmes panorama was far more than simple photographic realism inflated to an enormous scale. It had artistry and necessary distortions. No one can see line and structure in the Canyon with the clarity with which Holmes drew them. Canyon haze is real, and though Dutton warned that it could deceive, it is as fundamental to the scene as Canyon colors, with which Holmes

Surely this latter exchange was not unilateral. In eulogizing Powell, Gilbert declared that Powell's greatest contributions were those he never published but passed out freely as ideas to his colleagues. Clarence Dutton said much the same: among himself, Gilbert, and Powell there was such a full and frank circulation of ideas that no one knew who had originated what concept. Yet the self-effacing Gilbert, the real successor to Newberry in the plateau province, should not be forgotten. He lacked the pulpit oratory of Powell that would make the *Exploration* a perennial classic or the suppleness of mind and grace of prose that did the same for Dutton's *Tertiary History of the Grand Cañon District*. But the science of erosion in the Colorado Plateau was spectacularly his.

Bailey Willis, who watched both men closely on the national survey, spoke of Gilbert as "Powell's better half. Perhaps no one else ever thought of them in that way, but in constant relations with the two I learned to know how much Gilbert, the true scientist, contributed to the geological thinking of Powell, the man of action. I do not think that they themselves were conscious of the degree to which the latter absorbed and gave out as his own ideas that the former had silently passed through." Where Powell preferred a dramatic revelation, Gilbert proceeded by systematic contrasts between known and unknown, exploring analogies that linked new with old, that bonded a novel science like geology to traditional physics. Gilbert, for example, ignored Powell's intricate taxonomy of structures and streams because they were not "founded on principles of causation, and cannot therefore be assumed to be final." Instead he searched for those informing principles, finding them by analogy to mechanics rather than, as Powell had, by analogy to paleontology and stratigraphy.[22]

So too, while Powell brought the Canyon into exploration lore, Gilbert transported it into natural science. The American school of geology boosted by William Morris Davis celebrated fluvialism, mountain building, and geomorphology, all dramatically revealed in the plateau province and published by that fabled triumvirate

Powell, Dutton, and Gilbert. Yet Powell's bravura had behind it Gilbert's scientific muscle, and Dutton's word paintings of Canyon land sculpture decorated the nearly mathematical perspective of Gilbertian geomorphology. Gilbert went on to a celebrated career: a pioneer of experimental geology and the philosophy of method, the discoverer of two mountain-building processes and enunciator of the modern theory of the moon's origin, the third American to receive the coveted Wollaston Medal from the London Geological Society, a member of the National Academy of Sciences, and the president of numerous scientific societies, including the Geological Society of America, the only man twice so honored. His *Lake Bonneville* was awarded pride of place in the U.S. Geological Survey's monograph series, much as his career burned inextinguishably in the institutional memory of the survey. For its centennial the survey established a G. K. Gilbert fellowship to honor its outstanding practitioners.

Gilbert left to Powell the grand gesture and the purple-prosed popularizing of the Canyon. Within Powell's public career, he buried his own. No memorial to him rises along the rim. Yet the science he did so much to validate was what, in the critical years, did so much to validate the Canyon. Geology remembered. Over evening campfires in 1965 the geologists of the USGS Colorado River Expedition, the last survey before Glen Canyon Dam closed the free flow of the Colorado through the Grand Canyon, debated the question of who was America's greatest practitioner of what had surely become America's greatest science. They chose Grove Karl Gilbert. The setting as much as the selection was exactly right.[23]

A GREAT INNOVATION:
GRAND ENSEMBLE

The Second Great Age of Discovery unveiled—more than that, endowed with meaning—many landscapes. But the Canyon may also dispenses, or Canyon shadows, which are equally absent. Even perspective in the Point Sublime panoramas does not rely on a gathering of linear movement into a single focus, so much as it presents a foreground of curves that tend toward a planar horizon. In fact, the scene inverts traditional perspective in which an open foreground rises to a focal object. Instead, horizon takes the place of foreground, and a descending feature of Canyon topography, like a butte or gorge, substitutes for the focal figure. The eye flows naturally into the depths. Holmes neatly conveys what Moran had to contort. Every portion of the Canyon is seemingly exposed with equal exactness and transparency. One has the illusion of peering into, not merely at, the panorama, as if the picture actually exfoliated toward the viewer, opening in all directions to expose more of the scene than would actually be possible to see. Much as Dutton's word panoramas enlarge the unaided mind, so Holmes's panoramas instruct the unaided eye.

The contrast with Moran is enlightening. As befits their shared arts education, their rough compositions are often comparable. Holmes blocked out *The Temples and Towers of the Virgen*, for example, much the same way Moran did the *Chasm*. But Holmes savored the horizontal, willing to let the eye sweep across the horizon, while Moran demanded a vertical thrust, from gorge to cloud, an ascent from Canyon gloom to Canyon glory. Where Moran drew meticulous foregrounds that extend to progressively misty horizons, Holmes sketched vague foregrounds that lead to greater detail in the distance. A Moran horizon is filled with clouds and reaches to the top of the canvas; the upper half of a Holmes horizon is often empty sky. Where Moran exploits color to distinguish objects and relies on mist to organize them, Holmes uses line. Moran overwhelms; Holmes instructs. Behind Moran lay a transcendentalist philosophy; behind Holmes, commonsense realism. Whether at the rim of the Grand Canyon or at the ruins of Oaxaca, whether dealing with a vanished culture or a relic mountain range, Holmes was attracted to its material stuff—its artifacts, antiquities, rock strata, peaks. The topographic landscape that Moran denigrated Holmes celebrated. At the Canyon illustration, informed by science, became art.

Each too suffered the vice of his virtue; each exaggerated. Moran's was an exaggeration of things added, of features inserted, of colors heightened, of painterly flourish. Holmes exaggerated by removing. He achieved a false clarity by substracting unnecessary attributes, stripping away features not essential to a geologic description, like a physicist denying all attributes to an object except its mass and motion. Missing are color, shadow, cloud, haze, all of which are as fundamental to the seen Canyon as its gorges and strata. The outcome is a landscape whose emotive power derives from the scientific ideas behind it. Where a Moran landscape denies any presence but his own, the Holmes panorama boasts a deceptive emptiness that has allowed later generations to see in the scene what they wish.

William Holmes did not return to the Canyon to brood over it as Thomas Moran did or to relive past triumphs in the way Powell did. Instead, like Dutton, he finished his statement with the *Tertiary History*. Nor did Holmes feel the need to urge American scenes on to those who would produce an American art. Again unlike Moran, he worked naturally in a long tradition of American illustrators and exploring artists who emphasized reportorial fact rather than the psychological impression; who preferred line over color; who promoted a commonsense realism (through often a Romantic realism) over painterly imagination. Enchanted by ever-subtle hues and dissolving mists, mesmerized by Turnerian aesthetics, Moran could paint and repaint the same Canyon scene—was compelled to paint it over and over—and he saw his reputation rise and fall with the ebb and flow of painterly conventions. Praised by Ruskin, he was ignored by Apollinaire. Holmes drew once. There was no ambiguity about either source or significance.

William Henry Holmes could be stubborn and showed plenty of ego in his scientific work. His dogmatism while director of the Bureau of American Ethnology retarded for decades the study of early humans in the New World. But as an illustrator he consistently subordinated his talent to the subject at hand, to whatever landscape or field of inquiry he applied his art. As an artist he remained, like so much of his published work in government documents, relatively invisible to the public, shaping popular culture through his influence on high culture. Fame and power he found in the institutions of the Washington establishment; popular acclaim followed from his design and curatorial labors—the western exhibits at the Philadelphia Centennial and Columbian Exposition, the ethnographic collections at the Smithsonian, the art of the National Gallery.

And, one should add, with his enduring interpretation of the Grand Canyon. His panoramas lifted the *Tertiary History* far beyond the usual character of government monographs. They made its *Atlas* one of the magnificent books of western American art. More than Moran's *Chasm*, but like his *Grand Canyon of the Yellowstone*, they made plausible the assertion that the Canyon deserved protected status. When the National Park Service wanted to rally sentiment behind the park system and to incorporate the Grand Canyon within that realm, it was William Holmes, then director, who staged a major exhibition of western paintings at the National Gallery of Art. To help make the Canyon a park was by then easy. The real triumph had come four decades earlier, when he had made it Grand.

LEAVE IT AS IT IS: .
ONE OF THE GREAT SIGHTS

In less than twenty-five years American civilization had gone to the brink of the Canyon rim, ridden the rapids of its informing river, and reclassified the place from an "unprofitable locale" to the "sublimest thing on earth." What the Ives Expedition began, the U.S. Geological Survey completed. With Thomas Moran and William Henry Holmes, Timothy O'Sullivan and Jack Hillers, the Canyon entered American art. With John Wesley Powell and

Clarence Dutton, it inspired classics of western American literature. Together with John Strong Newberry and Grove Karl Gilbert they made the Canyon a centerpiece of American geology, and its larger setting, the arid lands, the focus for public land reform. Through its revelations of geologic time, the Canyon entered a larger intellectual discourse regarding the order of the universe and humanity's place within it.

Geologists were at the core, not only because the Canyon was a singularly geologic spectacle but because geologic time, like the world sea, touched the shorelines of all the great questions of the culture. They navigated that sea with the conceptual instruments of historical discourse. With laws of evolutionary progress, Newberry had joined geology to biological and theological thought. Powell demonstrated how, by similar means, the broader questions of the earth coincided with social and philosophical schemes. In practical terms he endeavored to adapt American social, political, and economic institutions to the environmental conditions of the West. Gilbert's achievement was to pioneer in the effort to unify geology by analogy to mechanics and mathematics. It was Dutton's role to fuse geology to the large questions of chemistry, geophysics, and landscape aesthetics. By assuming that evolution affected every geological phenomenon, he could relate the development of landforms, the petrological sequence of volcanic extrusions, and the history of the earth. His practical contribution was to adapt aesthetic theory, especially that common to architecture and painting, to an appreciation of the new scenery. After a hundred years the larger interpretation of the plateau province is still the one that Powell, Gilbert, Moran, Holmes, and Dutton collectively gave to it.

Yet the Canyon's assimilation into American society remained skewed. Revelation, appreciation, comprehension—all had derived from the cosmopolitan culture of a mobile elite, not from long residence or out of folk traditions. Settlers had shunned the place, as Casteñada and Ives had predicted they would, as fur trappers and frontier guides had labored to see that they did.

Even those most indomitable of intermountain pioneers, the Mormons, had done little more than run summer sheep onto the Kaibab. No one lived within the gorge.

Almost alone an educated elite had seen merit in the Canyon's bizarre land sculpture, recognized that the river intersected important intellectual questions, and sought out the rim in defiance of popular taste, Gilded Age mores, and laissez-faire politics. The High Plateaus were an overlook for high culture; the Colorado's canyons, a traverse through the cultural preoccupations of the era's intelligentsia. Yet the cultural Canyon remained incomplete. The heroic age had cut the gorge, as it were; the widening of its cliffs fell to a second generation of intellectuals and a miscellany of frontier folk, from miners to tourists, who slowly gathered into the widening gyre of the Canyon's call.

Utilization was not far behind appreciation. Its principal intellectual proponent, Robert Brewster Stanton, extended the Romantic imagination to engineering with the proposal (which became an obsession) to bring a railroad through the inner gorge. Stanton came to the project with nearly two decades of practical experience in the West and several construction triumphs to his credit, a reputation as a brilliant young engineer, and an imagination inflamed by Powell's narrative about what Stanton ever after referred to as "the River."

Though Stanton later downplayed the epic scale of the project—insisting that he was merely putting numbers on land features—the scheme had become for him, as his earlier expedition had for Ives, a dream, a vision of linking America's greatest landscape feature with its mightiest technology. In fact Stanton's 1889–90 trips down the Colorado gorges were a logical successor to Ives's investigation of the Colorado's navigability for steamboats. They established Stanton as a pioneer among river runners and marked the return of the engineer as explorer. The historical researches that he began in 1906, though never published in full, made Stanton, along with Frederick Dellenbaugh, the foremost early historian of the Colorado River.

Yet little practical came from it. The tragic death of Frank Brown, his sponsor, that marred Stanton's first expedition, the collapse of his railroad project, the popular triumph of the Powell and Dellenbaugh chronicles—all put Stanton's Canyon reputation, and that of Canyon engineering, into a recession from which it has never fully recovered. Not until 1923 was a real engineering survey of the Canyon conducted, and then for reservoir sites. Not until the 1960s was another engineering scheme on this scale proposed, only to face a more furious public skepticism than even Stanton had endured. Not its economic but its intellectual resources continued to shape the interpretation of the Canyon and the politics of its development.

That meant geology.

The mantle fell first to Charles Doolittle Walcott. Walcott had studied for a while under Louis Agassiz at Harvard University, then worked for James Hall at the New York State Museum, soon distinguishing himself as a paleontologist and stratigrapher. When the Geological Survey was formed in 1879, Clarence King quickly hired him. He promptly joined Dutton for stratigraphic work on the High Plateaus, and two years later he went into the Grand Canyon itself. Powell led the assault in person, carving a horse trail down into the Nankoweap Basin. Walcott recalled how "encamped in snow, often concealed for days in the driving frozen mist and whirling snow, the party gradually overcame the apparently insurmountable obstacles in its way. . . ." The result was a "perfectly frightful trail," Dutton informed Geikie.[49]

The excitement over, Powell departed, and Walcott overwintered, working out with painstaking care the stratigraphy of the Grand Canyon and Chuar groups. It was entirely in keeping with Powell's temperament that with great gusto and in defiance of winter storms, he should blaze a trail into a remote region and then leave the real scientific work to another. He had done it with Gilbert; he did it with Dutton. And it is entirely indicative of Charles Walcott that he would follow Powell's path and with meticulous care make its possibilities known. Whether he realized it or not, in taking this promising protégé to the place at which he had made his own reputation, Powell was setting Walcott on an administrative career that would far surpass his own.

While he showed talent as a scientist, Walcott demonstrated genius as a politician of science and an administrator of scientific organizations. Within a year after he had emerged from the Nankoweap Trail, Walcott was promoted to the post of chief paleontologist for the Geological Survey and almost immediately thereafter he succeeded a weary Gilbert as chief geologist. He began his Grand Canyon investigations shortly after Powell took charge of the survey; when he concluded them in 1895, he had replaced Powell as survey director and was entering a fabulously successful career as the chief administrator of half a dozen bureaus and the instigator of half a dozen more. But his scientific reputation, upon which those appointments first depended, stemmed from five papers on Canyon geology that he published between 1880 and 1895.

Walcott rebuilt the USGS after Powell had plunged it to political depths with the kind of reckless abandon he had shown in constructing the Nankoweap Trail. Later he applied the same patient hand to the development of other institutions: the Bureau of Mines, the Carnegie Institution of Washington with its Geophysical Laboratory, the National Research Council, the National Advisory Committee on Aeronautics, the Smithsonian Institution and National Museum of Natural History, and the National Academy of Sciences, of which he was president. For a while in 1907 Walcott actually administered three organizations simultaneously: the Geological Survey, the Reclamation Service, and the Smithsonian Institution. As quiet as Powell was flamboyant, Walcott translated ideas into institutions. That the U.S. Geological Survey became the prototype of the Progressive Era technocratic bureau, that as "the Mother of Bureaus" it spawned new offspring almost annually, was largely a tribute to Charles Doolittle Walcott.

What he got from the Canyon, he returned. His behind-the-scenes politicking was instrumental in promoting the forest reserve program, under the provisions of which the Grand Canyon was first set aside as protected land, and he was active in the drive to establish the National Park Service, under whose rule the Canyon has been administered since 1919. Through his investigations in the basins of the Nankoweap, the Kwagunt, and Chuar, Walcott worked out the stratigraphy of the eastern Canyon, thus complementing the stratigraphic profile of the western Canyon published by Newberry and Gilbert; recommended theories of structural and fluvial history for the evolution of the Canyon, modifying and challenging the simple model Powell had proposed; and correlated Canyon strata to the historical geology of North America, a much-needed modernization of Newberry's pioneering studies. Eventually he carried that stratigraphy, and the evolutionary perspective it archived, far beyond the Colorado Plateau.

Most famously Walcott mined the Burgess shale of the Canadian Rockies for fossils that, better than anywhere else, mapped out the explosion of life that had characterized the Cambrian era. A century later, after another round of scientific revolutions in biology and geology, Walcott's evolutionary vision could seem archaic. But when the earth's age was believed to be less than one hundred million years, when the texture of fossil-preserved evolution remained thin, those excavations had come as a revelation. The scientific reputation that Walcott inaugurated at the Canyon, he confirmed in the Rockies.

Nothing endures forever, ideas no less than things. An evolutionist like Charles Walcott, a man who commenced his career in the gorges of the Grand Canyon, knew that all too well. He had seen the evidence both in the rocks he had cored for fossils and in the more impressive testimony of erosion that had stripped whole strata away, ripping out great chapters from the text of time. The cairns along the Nankoweap Trail resembled so many geodetic markers by which to triangulate into unknown basins of earth time, and for Walcott they continued that task long after the talus of new discoveries had buried his old track. Behind the Burgess shale stood the Hermit, Bright Angel, and Hakatai shales of the Nankoweap and Chuar basins; behind his vision of evolutionary history stood the whole stratigraphic column of the Canyon like an immense stele. Not his conception of evolution but the evidentiary fossils he gathered would endure; not his ideas but the institutions he collected, packed, and stored as he did his trilobites. For Charles Walcott that was likely enough.

Time also had its shape. The stratigraphy of the Canyon was one dimension; the sculpturing of those strata another. Explaining the geomorphology of Grand fell largely to William Morris Davis and his student François Matthes.

The first systematizer of physiography (geomorphology, as it later became known), Davis dominated the science for half a century. He publicized as well as consolidated the Powell Survey's insights, cultivated his reputation on theirs, made the place and the people fundamental to his endless proselytizing on behalf of the American school of earth science. He wrote biographical memoirs of both Powell and Gilbert for the National Academy of Sciences; Gilbert's was the largest in the series. And he spent nearly two decades propagandizing about the Canyon country as a paradigm of fluvial erosion.

He summed his insights in the concept of a geographical cycle. This was a model that synthesized geologic structure, erosional processes, and boundless time into regular patterns of land sculpture and, especially, of landscape evolution. Every climate, every geomorphic province had its distinctive variants, but each played out a universal trend. Landscapes were closed systems that eroded: they began as uplifted, high-energy systems and then decayed through the entropy of erosion into level, low-energy systems. Landscapes proceeded through cycles in the same thermodynamic sense that heat engines did. The process was irreversible, though it was possible to restart the cycle with renewed uplift. Thus landscapes were a kind of entropy clock, and sculpted landforms, a variety of earth fossil. Recognize the pattern, and you know a landscape's stage of evolution; you know its age.

This was an extraordinary premise. The geologic vision that stratigraphy had built up, piling stratum upon stratum in chronological ascension, the geographical cycle metaphorically tore down, methodically stripping away layer upon layer. Instead of stratigraphic columns, Davis proposed a series of systematic declinations by which, for every imaginable climate, uplifted landscapes wore away until they culminated in a nearly level erosional baseline he termed a peneplain. Erosion thus produced a parallel chronology to deposition. Landscapes became geomorphic fossils that tracked the tread of geologic time. It was possible to date the earth even when its preserved records were being removed, not a trivial achievement, given that most of geologic time was lost to erosion's erasure. Davis proposed means to measure that void.

For a geology of denudation rather than of deposition, there were few spectacles to rival the Grand Canyon. In the early twentieth century William Morris Davis went there more than once to see for himself the fluvial mechanics that Gilbert had discovered, to inspect the Canyon terraces that Dutton had recommended as marking epochs of erosion, and to ponder the meaning of the Great Denudation taking place along the distant cliffs and of the Great Unconformity, which mapped an ancient peneplain deep in the gorge. All the critical parts were here, and so was the medium for their synthesis. From the rim Davis marveled at the supremacy of geologic time over all things, even the Grand Canyon. "The most emphatic lesson that the canyon teaches is that it is not a very old feature of the earth's surface, but a very modern one; that it does not mark the accomplishment of a great task of earth sculpture, but only the beginning of such a task; and that in spite of its great dimension, it is properly described as a young valley." In brief, Davis played Dryden to Dutton's Shake-speare, pruning and systematizing, reducing the captain's aesthetic flights of geopoetry to the heroic couplets of an inspired pedagogue.[50]

Wherever the Davisian model traveled, it did so with the authority of the Colorado Plateau and the Grand Canyon behind it. As he had made the Powell Survey fundamental to the historiography of the American school, so Davis made the Canyon indispensable as the symbol of its lessons. He first wrote of the Canyon in 1892, relying on the published studies of the Powell group. But between 1900 and 1904 he led parties of American geologists to the rim four times, and in 1912, under his inspiration, the American Transcontinental Excursion organized by the American Geographical Society established the Canyon as a centerpiece in its travels.

Meanwhile Davis wrote and spoke avidly about the significance of the Canyon—"my crack piece," he called his stock lecture, one he tirelessly propagated throughout the world. He helped make the Grand Canyon as familiar to Europeans as the Alps were to Americans.[51]

But even before Davis began his famous European campaign on behalf of the precepts of the American school, Europeans were themselves coming to the rim. Karl Baedeker included a map of the Canyon and instructions on how to reach it by stagecoach in his 1899 edition of *The United States*. Buffalo Bill Cody escorted British nobles to the North Rim in a vain effort to have them purchase the land as a private hunting preserve. Baedeker's approach to the Canyon as commodity proved more successful, and among the many spectators arriving at the rims were geologists. Some came as members of international congresses; others, as private pilgrims; most, as skeptics regarding the grandiloquent reports of their American colleagues.

For Archibald Geikie the intriguing precepts of American

fluvialism appeared to be singularly dependent on the observations freighted back from the Colorado Plateau, and he finally went west to see for himself. He was not disappointed. "It is unquestionably true that had the birthplace of geology lain on the west side of the Rocky Mountains," he wrote to critics of fluvialism, "this controversy would never have arisen." Dutton had said much the same, though, with respect to the impact the Canyon might have made on Western art. It had not influenced European art as much as Fujiyama had Japanese art, but it did so influence Western science. Geikie, who had reviewed Dutton's *Tertiary History* for *Nature*, brought just that message back to Europe. As his point of departure he compared the "gorges of the Old World and the New."[52]

The Canyon became to geology what the Louvre was to art or St. Peter's Square to architecture. In 1891 it was thus wholly appropriate that Powell and Gilbert should direct the International Congress of Geologists to the rim and that in 1904, a part of the St. Louis fair, the World's Geological Congress should arrange a special excursion as well. For perhaps fifty years afterward, however, it was not necessary to bring the Muhammads of the earth science to the Canyon; the lessons of the Canyon were brought to them in abundance and without further contention. It had become an effective symbol of American geology: its exploring traditions, its conceptual lessons, its relationship to American nationalism. But it had also become a symbol of the earth, available to all.

Science dominated Canyon culture, and geology ruled Canyon science. When C. Hart Merriam, then director of the Biological Survey, came to the region in 1899, he was more interested in the stratification of life zones he saw in the San Francisco Peaks than in the stratification of evolutionary ages in the Canyon. For this the Canyon may perhaps be grateful. Merriam's life zone concept was almost pure Humboldt, practically a plagiarism of outmoded

ideas Humboldt had developed for the slopes of Mount Chimborazo in Ecuador.

From anthropology, however, the Canyon may have given as
much as it got. Its meager human ruins were dwarfed by the magnificent cliff palaces at Mesa Verde, Chaco, and Canyon de Chelly;
its inner Canyon residents, the Havasupai, proved consistently
less interesting than the well-ceremonialed Hopi; the outlying
Paiute and Hualapai claimed the fringe of anthropology as they
did the margins of the Great Basin.

Yet the Canyon influenced the careers of at least two men who
did much to shape American anthropology, in both its ideas and
its institutions. Powell became the first director of the Bureau of
American Ethnology in the Smithsonian, and William Henry
Holmes succeeded him. The BAE later sent ethnographers back
to the scenes of the founders, while the Havasupai, as they had
time and again since Spanish times, attracted others. Meanwhile
its discovered ruins, however diminutive by regional standards,
did provide the political pretext for President Theodore Roosevelt to invoke the Antiquities Act and set the area aside for special protection within the public domain.

So also Canyon art remained subordinated to Canyon science.
The Canyon never became a distinct genre, the way the Sierras or
the Hudson River did; it contributed nothing by way of new techniques or a new oeuvre. The Canyon had to compete with more
traditional Alpine landscapes, and even Thomas Moran remained
popularly acclaimed as an "artist of the mountains." It had to
compete too with that other genre of western painting, the West
as action. Charles Russell, Frederic Remington, and their imitators—none went to the Canyon to paint. They needed human figures, not sculpted buttes, and human drama, not the inexorable
patience of geologic time. They demanded events, not scenery.

By the time Moran, assisted by free passes from the Santa Fe
Railroad, returned and made the rim into a pulpit, landscape was

fast fading from the forefront of art, an avant-garde was poised to replace the artist-explorer, and even Remington was turning to impressionism. More and more the Canyon became the symbol of past glories, not an emblem of new ideas. On its rim Moran found a great constant with which to preserve American traditions that he thought representative. It seemed that artists might paint the Canyon as they would the old masters in the Louvre or the classic scenes of picturesque Italy, as a form of instruction by imitation. The Canyon received rather than inspired.

Perhaps there was no need for anything further. In 1902 the torch effectively passed. Frederick Dellenbaugh, the seventeen-year-old artist on Powell's second voyage, published a comprehensive history, *The Romance of the Colorado River*. For its frontispiece it had a watercolor sketch from Thomas Moran, who a year before had made the visit to the Canyon rim that led to his American art essay; for its epilogue, the book included a biography of John Wesley Powell, who died shortly before publication. The *Romance* became a kind of panegyric to Powell, and Powell before his death urged Dellenbaugh to complete the saga with the full narrative of the 1871–72 voyage, a task Dellenbaugh finished a few years later. Together the books consolidated the Powell epic, transformed a popular saga into scholarship, and brought the Canyon into the canon of American history.

But if the *Romance* summarized the region's heroic past, the *Grand Canyon of Arizona*—a compendium of photographs and word pictures about the Canyon promulgated that same year by the Santa Fe Railroad—pointed to its future. Filled with original essays by Powell, Moran, Stanton, and R. D. Salisbury of the Yale Geology Department, the book also contained poetic bromides from writers like Harriet Monroe, overwrought effusions from professional lecturers like John L. Stoddard, and trite apostrophes from recycled hacks like Joaquin Miller and Charles Dudley Warner, all of it intertwined indiscriminately like the cross-bedding

CANYON
AND COSMOS

No place, not even a wild place, is a place until it has had that human attention that at its highest reach we call poetry.
—WALLACE STEGNER

Even after 100 years, however, the explanation of this landscape still defies us.
—CHARLES HUNT

Before the nineteenth century had ended, the Grand Canyon had found its poet. It also had its troubadours, its court painters, its cultural viziers. The achievements of that exploring elite, whose reputations had grown symbiotically with the Canyon's, had shattered its intellectual and aesthetic isolation, had smelted its unearthly novelty into prevailing genres, had hammered its common stone into the statuary of a national icon. The Canyon was not merely assimilated by American culture; it was smothered, polished, celebrated. A fearsome landscape had become a precious object.

What ideas had valorized, politics moved to preserve. In 1893 President Harrison included the eastern Canyon within a forest reserve. In 1906 President Roosevelt proclaimed it a game reserve and two years later a national monument, thanks to its scattered Indian ruins and its significance to geologic science. In 1919, after extensive lobbying, Grand Canyon became a national park under the jurisdiction of the recently (1916) established National Park Service. What began as a symbol significant to a cultural elite became a pleasuring ground for the public. And more: the Canyon was transfigured into a sacred site. Like Hindu pilgrims in a *yatra* of Shaivite shrines, Americans (and foreign visitors in search of America) toured the national parks, of which the Grand Canyon was the most distinctive, the one without comparison anywhere else. The Canyon put America First.

Interest was sufficient for a spur track from the main Atchison, Topeka, and Santa Fe railway line to replace the stagecoach in 1901, and the luxurious El Tovar Hotel, a legacy of tents and rustic cabins. The rails brought the Canyon into the realm of industrial tourism. Ease of geographic access soon demanded an equal ease of intellectual access. Powell had pronounced the Canyon the most sublime of earthly phenomena but one that demanded patience and toil; Dutton had insisted that the scene could be appreciated only through strenuous cultivation, the hard labor of thinking. Neither suited the Santa Fe Railroad, the National Park Service, or the touring public. The visitor replaced the explorer, the Kodak snapshot the grand canvas, the inscribed overlook the monographs, atlases, and personal narratives of its bold creators. Visitation shifted from the lofty North Rim to the more proximate South. The Grand Canyon was fast becoming a commercial commodity and a cultural cliché. And there were fewer intellectuals of stature to say otherwise.

Even as the public crowded Canyon overlooks, intellectuals were walking away. The new high culture of modernism had little use for the High Plateaus. Modernism busied itself with other projects, above all itself. It preferred to search its own depths, not those of the river-excavated Kaibab and Uinkaret plateaus. Scenes and values that had previously joined elite to folk were worn away, a Great Denudation within American culture. Modernism cut through their once-common ground until intellectuals and the public were as distant and incommensurable as the two rims. A commercial popular culture rushed in to fill the void.

MODERNISM MOVES ON: THE POPULIST CANYON

Still, a few of that cultural elite came to the Canyon, and they filled the yet empty places with books, paintings, scientific essays, even exploring sorties. But in this silver age the emphasis was on refinement of data and technique. The larger vision had been established; the remaining chore was to inventory, document, fill in, and, above all, to disseminate. High culture had to compete with purveyors of the Canyon as experience, not simply as idea; with the Canyon as a promotional medium, not the expression of scientific information. The genius of the age was to bring the viewer to the Canyon, not the Canyon to the inquirer in the form of print or painting or principle. In literature the trend was almost wholly toward tourist books or sketches from the perspective of the tourist. Canyon oracles were those specimens of local color, like John Hance who affected the pose of frontier sage or William Bass with his homespun doggerel. They were all figures who could entertain as well as guide, who could, with a little professional promotion, become objects of interest in themselves.

So the cultural chasm between elite and mass widened, partly because high culture was going elsewhere and partly because popular culture became ever more estranged from modernism. The Canyon's silver age produced the splendidly intricate topographic maps of François Matthes, the sparkling watercolors of Gunnar Widforss, the stratigraphic inquiries consummated by Edwin McKee, and the painstaking engineering survey of the

Colorado River by the U.S. Geological Survey. But the popular interpretation of the Grand Canyon passed to the promotional department of the Santa Fe Railroad, to the photographs and
motion pictures of the Kolb brothers, to naturalists in the employ
of the National Park Service, and especially around the turn of the
century to assorted characters in residence like Bass and Hance
who catered to the tourist trade. Buffalo Bill tried to flog off the
North Rim as a hunting preserve to British nobility; Buffalo Jones
became a national celebrity for roping mountain lions out of
Kaibab pines; Uncle Jim Owens, government hunter, became a
character study for literary hacks like Zane Grey; stuntmen landed
biplanes on the Tonto Shelf; Tom Mix rode up Canyon trails for
Hollywood's silver screen. Cultural artifacts scattered like pebbles
under the tracks of the Model Ts that swarmed to the rim. The
Canyon was less a national oracle than a promotional backdrop.

Yet there was more at work than raw American commercialism.
The Second Great Age of Discovery had inspired the heroic age
of Canyon exploration and the golden age of its interpretation. By
the time Teddy Roosevelt stood on the South Rim, however, the
Second Age had fled to the poles, and the perspective-framing
Enlightenment was fast becoming moribund. By the time Grand
Canyon acquired national park status, the Second Age had died
on the Antarctic ice sheets, imperialism had fallen into exhaustion
in the trenches of the Great War, and Western art and science
were sucked into the maelstrom of full-blown revolution. The
Canyon was caught in that cultural wind shear. The gusts that had
carried an age to the Grand Canyon now blew elsewhere. Even as
the tourist Canyon became ever more popular, as visitation
swelled and commercial interest boomed, the intellectual Canyon
tumbled down the cliffs of high culture like boulders pushed over
the rim by bored sightseers.

What had previously converged on the Canyon now split. In
painting and the plastic arts, impressionism, cubism, surrealism,

dadaism, and their proliferating progeny introduced new conceptions of perspective, broke down representational aesthetics, insisted that truth did not reside in the object but in the viewing artist. In natural science, Newtonian physics splintered against the new worlds of nature—the microcosm of atom and gene and the macrocosm of cosmology. Quantum physics and Einsteinian relativity challenged the epistemology of Newtonian science and the orthodoxy of omniscience that the Enlightenment had constructed out of its presumptions. The sheer multiplicity of human experience, the discovery of fundamental principles of indeterminacy, and the inescapable reality of relativized perspectives—all shattered the grand design of historicism. The observer prevailed over the observed. Modernists privileged irony over purpose. For philosophy William James satirized Herbert Spencer's evolutionary synthesis in an unforgettable parody: "Evolution is a change from nowish untalkaboutable all-alikeness by continuous stick-togetherations and somethingelseifications." Make it new, Ezra Pound insisted. Modernism did, with a vengeance.[1]

The old, even the geologically old, was no longer novel, could no longer serve as a universal repository of events and ideas. Modernism prepared to raze the past as Le Corbusier proposed for Paris in order to construct his Radiant City. In literature, in philosophy, in mathematics, science, and the plastic arts, avant-gardes appeared that had little use for the techniques with which the Grand Canyon had been revealed and valorized. Intellectuals were more likely to follow Joseph Conrad into a heart of imperial darkness or Sigmund Freud into the depths of the unconscious and the labyrinth of dreams than to gaze once more with John Wesley Powell into the Great Unknown of the Inner Gorge. The formative event in American art was not the exhibition of paintings that Stephen Mather and William Henry Holmes organized at the National Gallery in 1917, much less the promotional exhibits sponsored by the Santa Fe Railroad, but the exhibition of The Eight and especially the 1913 Armory Show that brought for the first time that panoply of modernist art to the United

States. The revolutionary sciences were those that scrambled after the new physics, downgrading Isaac Newton from the rank of philosopher to engineer, and that pursued the new genetics, consigning Charles Darwin from the Sage of Down to butterfly collector. In the earth sciences the controversy that gripped geology was directed not at the 1923 Birdseye Expedition through the Colorado canyons but at the international debate three years later on the theory of continental drift.

Even with the Sante Fe and the National Park Service as patrons, even with the National Gallery willing to host exhibitions, modernists were more inclined to choose Taos or Carmel than Grand Canyon. The siren song of Mabel Luhan Dodge proved more compelling than Powell's commands; the attractions of a Taos populated with pueblo Indians more stimulating than the empty immensity of Toroweap; a colony of fellow-traveling artists more comforting than a corps of far-ranging naturalists. In practice Taos artists were more modernizers than modernists, more willing to adapt new techniques than to surrender America's commonsense realism. But their shift in style necessarily meant a shift in subject as well. The Canyon became peripheral, more a sink for sketches than a source of inspiration. Regional artists preferred the mesas and ravines of northern New Mexico, which were not only closer at hand but closer in composition to Cézanne's archetypal Mont Victoire; they preferred sunburned natives in picturesque villages to cosmopolitan scientists confronting the great questions posed by a monumental nature. Emblematically the defining Southwest novel of the era, Willa Cather's *Death Comes for the Archbishop* (1927), ends with the erection of a cathedral, not the evolution of a canyon.

The intellectual elite no longer heard the call of the Canyon because they no longer spoke to it, no longer listened for its reply. High culture left the high rims for other ideas and other places, though its legacy and many of its agents remained at the Canyon, lingering like the last refracted rays of an autumnal sunset.

* * *

Among those who did come was composer Ferde Grofé who produced the Canyon's most enduring musical composition, *Grand Canyon Suite*.

Grofé had encountered the Canyon during the course of travels in Arizona as a pianist in vaudeville houses, hotels, and dance halls. His *Suite*, begun in 1921 and completed twelve years later, typically modernized musical effects without adopting a full-blown modernist philosophy. It told the same story through sound that Dutton had with words, the evolution of a day. *Grand Canyon Suite* built logically on Grofé's earlier *Mississippi Suite*.

An "obsessed" Grofé demanded a full palette of "orchestral colors," for he not only saw but "heard" color. With its mimicry of mule and storm and sunset, the symphony created a kind of musical representationalism of the sort that had fallen out of favor with musical culture much as representational painting had with the avant-garde of the plastic arts. The suite was to music what Thomas Hart Benton's muscular landscapes and Carl Sandburg's verse were to the painting and poetry of the day, an American accommodation, an adaptation of new techniques to traditional subjects. Self-consciously Grofé sought an "American idiom" that would fall "easily on the average ear." At his best Grofé was a Gershwin for American nature.[2]

But perhaps the most telling of its contrapuntal passages was historical. By the time the *Suite* was fully performed, modernism was rewriting the software of American culture like a computer virus. An intellectual migration, fleeing fascism in Europe, reinforced that trend. Equally, however popular the Canyon's depiction in concert halls, the actual Canyon had its tourism gutted by the Great Depression and subsequent wartime rationing. Visitation stalled. The Canyon lost not only its economic patrons but its political clientele as well. Grofé's work stands virtually alone, a monadnock rising from a base-leveled cultural countryside like the Mesozoic Red Butte and, like it too, a relic from an earlier era, in this case the 1920s when most of the work was written.

The Canyon remained a supremely visual spectacle, and as long as there was patronage, painters erected their easels on the rim. But modernism posed important challenges during the 1920s, as did the Great Depression of the 1930s, and there remained the imposing presence of Thomas Moran.

Moran remained the patriarch of Canyon artists, subsidized by a Santa Fe Railroad that also reproduced his paintings as chromolithographs. From the *Chasm of the Colorado* in 1873–74 to *Grand Canyon* in 1920, his art had spanned forty-seven years. No one had pondered the Canyon longer. More and more, however, his gilt-edged, heavily varnished canvases seemed like Victorian relics from a time when art read nature for its lessons, when the larger the spectacle, the grander its significance. His idiom was set. He repeated himself as a traveling bard might retell Homer or a concert pianist replay a favorite Beethoven sonata. Yet although the aging Moran continued to harangue from his Canyon lectern, increasingly big looked like bombast. His panoramas were as empty of modernist irony as they were filled with Emersonian mist.

Others sought more appropriate stances and less grandiloquent gestures and, loosely orbiting around the Taos and Santa Fe schools, developed more suitable techniques. Louis Akin, William Leigh, Oscar Berninghaus, Gustave Baumann, and Ferdinand Burgdorff all incorporated elements of impressionism or modernist mannerisms though in ways that did not lose the ultimate presence of the Canyon itself. In the end the Canyon carried their art, not their art the Canyon. Akin lamented that there was a limited market for Canyon pictures. Revolutionary modernism looked elsewhere. Modernist art explored the foundations of painting the way modernist mathematics did the symbolic logic of numbers. The era's most celebrated meditation on time was Salvador Dali's *Persistence of Memory*; surrealism, not stratigraphy, shaped its contours. Intellectually the rift between Canyon and art widened. Geographically the Canyon was suspended between two regional colonies, the Taos-Santa Fe artists and the Southern California impressionists. It remained peripheral to both.[3]

There were two exceptions, two artists—curiously amid the vogue for American regionalism—both émigré Swedes, both born in 1879. Both painted broadly representational landscapes. There the similarities between Carl Oscar Borg and Gunnar Widforss end. For Borg the Canyon (and its surrounding plateau province) were the backdrop to a spiritual quest, one that never ceased. For Widforss the Canyon became home.

Borg had a hardscrabble childhood, salvaged by personal mysticism and a sympathetic pastor who recognized the youngster's talent for drawing. A series of misadventures took him to France and England, where he languished in poverty until he began painting sets at the Drury Lane Theatre. In 1901 he sailed to America, which he entered illegally while sequestered in a propeller shaft. Two years later he arrived in Los Angeles, found work and friends, made a reputation and contacts. Through Charles Lummis he learned about the Southwest's landscapes and native cultures, and through Eva Lummis he was introduced to patrons, most notably Phoebe Apperson Hearst, who subsequently sponsored his career and travels. In particular she arranged for him to paint the Hopi and Navajo Indians under the auspices of the University of California and Bureau of American Ethnology.

His 1916 sojourn to the Southwest was an epiphany. He immediately empathized with the natives; place and people matched perfectly his own temperament. His career boomed, further supported by work for United Artists studio as an art director and bolstered by national enthusiasm for southwestern scenes. Like most of the Taos and Santa Fe artists, he was interested primarily in the native peoples, secondarily in landscape by itself.

Landscapes served most often as backdrop, a way of placing the people. What he had done for theaters and studios, he repeated in his paintings. The land was a stage for the human presence.

Despite praise from Moran himself, who reportedly considered Borg "preeminently the highest grade of any artist in America today," Borg's Canyon paintings are curiously weak, among his most feeble. A few succeed where, as with *The Great River, Grand Canyon*, the viewer is situated at mid-level and the Colorado provides a strong, sinuous focus. But in comparison with Borg's Canyon de Chelly landscapes, his Grand Canyon seems uninspired. Perhaps the scale was too immense, the contrast between the Canyon and the human presence too great. The open sky that serves the transcendentalist Borg as mist did Moran is lost amid the Canyon's closed strata. In instances where he inserts human figures, the proportion often seems odd or the commentary almost comical, as when in *Hush of Evening* Borg has a party of Navajo horsemen peering improbably into the gorge. Without those figures, however, the canvases seem weirdly vacant, neither charged with spirit nor filled with human aspiration, but simply empty, like stage backdrops shorn of their performance.[4]

The Depression coincided with personal disappointments and dampened Borg's enthusiasms. In 1932 he wrote that he could no longer look "with longing romantic eyes at the great American desert." Art had been a "religion" for him; now the ritual rather than the spirit remained. The painting continued, though wanderlust and drink increasingly filled his days. His travels returned him to Sweden, and in 1938 he married a Swede and took up residence in Gothenburg. But he was no longer Swedish and returned to California to discover that he was not American either. He died dining alone in a Santa Barbara restaurant.[5]

The contrast with Gunnar Widforss is curiously complete. Trained as a decorative painter (with a certificate from the Royal Technical Institute in Stockholm), Widforss abandoned the business to become an artist and indulged in years of travel throughout Europe and the United States. He soon specialized particularly in landscapes and watercolors. In 1912 he began exhibiting his works, successfully. He resumed his rhythm of travel and painting, even through World War I, shifting from war-torn central Europe to its nordic perimeter.

In 1921 he traversed the United States on his way to the Orient. At Yosemite he met Steven Mather, director of the National Park Service, who persuaded him that the national parks would provide a suitable subject, and Mather adequate patronage. Widforss began to tour and paint the major parks, including Grand Canyon. By 1924 he had enough works—seventy-two in all—to sustain a one-man exhibition at the National Gallery of Art. Acclaim followed. So did other exhibitions and commissions; more travel took him to Mesa Verde and then to Taos and Santa Fe.

But the Canyon most gripped him. There he set up permanent residence, becoming a U.S. citizen in 1929. There too he produced in a series of watercolors some of the most vivid and scenically honest of all Grand Canyon art. For nearly twenty years Widforss focused his art on the Canyon, claiming in effect the mantles of Moran and Holmes. At his best no one has synthesized Canyon form and Canyon color so successfully. No less an authority than William Holmes himself declared, during a Widforss exhibition at the National Gallery, that "these are the finest things of their kind that have come out of the West . . . [by] possibly the greatest watercolorist in America today."[6]

Strong words, backed by an oeuvre of Canyon art unmatched for half a century. Widforss's field of vision is more restricted than in the macroscopic panoramas of either Holmes or Moran, but it encompasses all the essential Canyon features, and it maintains a sense of definition from foreground to horizon. In Widforss's finest works, the foreground crowds to one side, the slope of the rim matches the slash of the river, the backdrop fills with mesa or butte. There is depth without an appeal to defiles, a sense of recognition without the drama of revelation, a realism that values the observed object as much as the observing artist. With his meticulous draftsmanship Canyon shape never dissolves into mist and Canyon color reinforces that sense of definition rather than, as in the cases of Moran and the later quasi impressionists, smears it. Had he been born half a century earlier, Widforss might have become a rival to Winslow Homer; or had he directed his brush to the modern landscape of machine America, to Charles Sheeler; or had he used the Southwest scenery to delve into a psychological landscape, of Georgia O'Keeffe. Instead Widforss was too committed to representational art to contribute to modernism, and too late to join the formative era of Canyon painting.

It is reported that one of the Taos artists said of Widforss, "If he just wouldn't copy nature so closely he'd be the greatest living painter in America," and that when Widforss was told of the comment, he swept his hand toward the Canyon and asked, "Could imagination improve on that?" That was not the posture of a modernist. Besides, Canyon art—the best of it—had communicated idea as well as image, and ideas are conspicuously lacking in Widforss. Neither geologic time nor transcendentalist nature figures forth. Perhaps Widforss was constrained by his public image as "the painter of the National Parks," the promotional uses to which his painting were put, the need to connect to a touring public not enthusiastic about abstract art. Perhaps the Canyon, where he died and lies buried, was greater than his art of naive realism.[7]

Widforss painted nature less as landscape than as still life. Revealingly the human figure is absent from a Widforss watercolor. There are no awestruck travelers like those Moran and Egloffstein included, respectively, in the *Chasm of the Colorado* and *Big Cañon at Diamond River*, no emissaries of high culture inserted as Holmes did at Point Sublime. So too it is hard to place Gunnar Widforss. In the panorama of Canyon history, he is at once undeniable and invisible. Like one of the buttes he loved to paint, segregated from both rims, Gunnar Widforss stands by himself, oddly isolated from the great eras of Canyon culture. Yet unlike Carl Borg, he had found a home, and unlike even the Taos artists, excepting perhaps O'Keeffe, he is indelibly identified with the scenes of that chosen place.

* * *

There were others content, eager to detail with scientific and engineering exactitude what the heroic age had poetically envisioned. Together they moved rim and river beyond the realm of science into engineering. For each the Canyon confirmed a career and established a reputation. As Widforss had become the "painter of the national parks," so François Matthes became their cartographer. The political journey that Powell had launched from Green River and that ended with the Geological Survey, the survey continued when it dispatched Claude Birdseye to map the river following the 1922 Colorado River Compact, which apportioned the waters of the Colorado among the states within its watershed and liberated those waters for reclamation projects.

An immigrant from the Netherlands, Matthes approached the rim with an excellent technical education, supplemented by engineering studies at the Massachusetts Institute of Technology. In 1896 he joined the cartographic division of the U.S. Geological Survey, serving his apprenticeship in such rugged locales as the Bighorn Mountains of Wyoming and the Bradshaws of Arizona. Impressed, Director Walcott assigned him to the Grand Canyon, a year after the Santa Fe railhead reached the South Rim. There Matthes began to map out the Canyon's most celebrated features and so helped triangulate from its exploring past into its tourist future.

The challenge was formidable, and like Walcott, Matthes was compelled to blaze trails to the North Rim (first along Bass Canyon, then Bright Angel) as well as develop new techniques for analysis. With only an alidade and plane table as instruments, the mapping of the Bright Angel and Vishnu quadrangles became a technical triumph, a tour de force of draftsmanship that demanded a different scale of contoured line and developed concepts that were to be applied to other regions. In 1904 and 1905, moreover, Matthes studied geomorphology under William Morris Davis at Harvard, and when the Bright Angel quadrangle was published, it included on its back side a geomorphic analysis written by Matthes.

The pioneering Matthes then moved on to other parks. His maps helped do for the creation of Glacier National Park what Moran's watercolors had done for Yellowstone, and decades of study helped confirm the Sierra Nevada as a testimony to glacial erosion as the Colorado Plateau was for fluvial. Compared with the Grand Canyon, Yosemite Valley seemed geographically quaint, though its exfoliating granites and glacial-polish walls made the Canyon's angular features seem cartographically benevolent. The Bright Angel quadrangle, in particular, endured as an aesthetic and technical standard, unsurpassed until the advent of laser-based theodolites and aerial photography allowed for a revision.

The remainder of the project devolved on to Richard Evans, a Matthes protégé. Over the period 1920–23 Evans mapped most of the eastern Canyon and complemented Dutton's Oriental place-names and Matthes's Nordic ones with allusions drawn from Arthurian legendry. Lancelot Point and Excalibur joined Vishnu Temple and Wotan's Throne. By the time the survey ceased, the most complex of western landscapes had become the foremost of its mapped terrains, and the Canyon had launched still more national careers.

The Geological Survey matched rim with river. The cartographic inventory that Matthes and his associates had made for the excavated plateaus, the survey's Grand Canyon Expedition of 1923 did for the gorge of the Colorado River. Under the direction of Claude Birdseye, then its chief topographic engineer, the survey recapitulated the journey of its old charismatic chief, John Wesley Powell, but with a rigor unknown to Powell's intrepid adventurers. E. C. La Rue surveyed potential damsites. Lewis Freeman reported the adventure. Emery Kolb served as chief boatman. At its conclusion one of the boats (the *Grand*) was shipped to the Smithsonian Institution for "permanent exhibition." Such was the self-consciousness of the Canyon's silver age.

The work demanded precision, which meant it proceeded with a caution that bordered on tedium. Since the compact had made Lee's Ferry the divide between the upper and the lower basin states, the expedition launched from there and made it Mile 0, a base line for the language of topographic engineering. Then they overwrote Powell's fulsome prose with a new Canyon graphic. Previously unnamed features—rapids, bends, sandbars—were to be named by their distance from the Lee's Ferry baseline. Six Mile Wash, 104 Mile Rapids, Mile 181, a most exotic landscape, a scene that left professional poets babbling platitudes, had become among the most precisely delineated places on the planet. A gauging station at the confluence of the Colorado and Bright Angel Creek completed the mathematization of the Canyon. Not only the river's shape but its dynamics came under constant, quantitative scrutiny. Numbers replaced figures of speech. Reservoir sites (eight in all, with thirteen alternates) complemented scenic overlooks. Contour maps complemented the tradition of the panoramas with which Holmes had recorded Canyon topography.

Among them, Matthes and Evans, Dutton and Powell, and the Birdseye Expedition effectively numbered as well as named the Canyon. They made the Canyon one of the most instantly recognizable sites on earth. But despite the real hazards of travel, the virtuoso technical skills displayed, and often the intellectual achievement of these projects, they were, in a sense, a colossal infilling of exploratory trenches dug by the heroic age. They marked in blanks; they fussed over details; they cleaned up untidy corners of topography. They resolved many of the minor questions of Canyon science and answered none of the fundamentals. If anything, the detailing cluttered the founding clarity of the Canyon's importance. By the 1920s no one could say, with much confidence, just how the Canyon had formed. In fact, no one could say without irony just what the place of this supremely geological phenomenon was within geologic science.

* * *

Geology mattered.

Of all the emissaries of high culture that had elevated the Canyon into significance, none had been more important. Geology as an intellectual enterprise had made the Canyon, for an American intelligentsia and its institutions, something more than a freak of nature. Geology had posed and answered vital questions of what it meant to be human and, at places like Niagara Falls, Yellowstone, and Grand Canyon, what it meant to be an American. Geology had sponsored Canyon art, Canyon word paintings, Canyon science, Canyon politics. For its geological significance, the Supreme Court had legitimized the reservation of the Canyon under the provisions of the Antiquities Act. And the Canyon had reciprocated. It had given American earth science a most cherished symbol. Reviewing the *Tertiary History*, the British journal *Nature* had even then considered the Canyon "the grandest and most unique feature in the geology of the United States, and in which indeed there is no parallel elsewhere in the world."[8]

By the late 1920s geology and especially the American school had reached a cultural equilibrium. The long revolution had ended, replaced by professional norms and bureaucratic mores. As Dutton had prophesied, editors deleted *sublime* as they would *traprock,* excised aesthetic meditations as though they were paranormal séances, and dismantled grand ensembles into working hypotheses and annotated bibliographies. No longer cascading from newfound mountains, the stream of geologic discovery slid into a lake of governmental and academic institutionalization, depositing its data like silt into library deltas. But the full impact was not obvious at the time.

A climax came in 1928, when two giants from its formative era published their final studies: Thomas Chamberlin his *Two Solar Families*, which expanded midwestern and western geology into an evolutionary cosmology, and G. K. Gilbert his *Studies of the Basin-Range Structure*, posthumously completing the cycle of works of one of the Canyon's greatest scientific explorers. That same year Norman L. Bowen published *The Evolution of the Igneous*

Rocks, a summa of another American tradition, petrology. Bowen proposed a geochemical progression by which an undifferentiated pool of magma could successively evolve into an abundance of mineral species. There was more: radiometric dating techniques were announced that promised an absolute time scale that could resolve the age of the earth; Richard Byrd launched his expedition to Antarctica, with its flight over the South Pole, that would complete the last geographic ambition of the Second Great Age of Discovery; and Herbert Hoover, a mining engineer, had become president. From minerals to planets the American school had achieved a spectacular synthesis of historical geology centered on the concept of evolution. It was a tradition often leveraged from a fulcrum at the Grand Canyon.

It was appropriately in 1928, then, that American geologists published the proceedings of a symposium in which they rejected the concept of continental drift. Over the past thirty years modernism's storms had blown through physics, biology, painting, philosophy, astronomy, and literature. A year earlier Werner Heisenberg had announced his principle of indeterminacy; a year later P. A. M. Dirac had fused the two extremes of the new physics into relativistic quantum mechanics. The theory of continental drift, as proposed by Alfred Wegener, promised to do the same for the earth sciences. Yet American geologists, especially, resisted. They had their own heroic history, their own landscape confirmations of great ideas; they preferred to follow the Great Surveys over the Great Basin and the Sierra Nevada, to Yellowstone and Yosemite and of course Grand Canyon, rather than trudge behind Wegener over the Greenland ice sheet. Continental drift was not only untrue; it was also unnecessary.

Yet their imagined climax was, as it so often proves to be, a prideful pause before the fall. By the 1930s the American school of earth science was in serious trouble, and within another decade it was moribund, as quaint before modernist science as the American regionalism of Grant Wood, much less the still-reproduced lithographs of Thomas Moran, was to dadaism, cubism, and surrealism. American geology had run out of frontiers. Geologic re-connaissance went the way of free land, fenced by intellectual equivalents to the Taylor Grazing Act. Its informing question, the age of the earth, was close to solution. Where they once revealed ancient geologic empires, geologists now subdivided strata with the intensity that Padua scholastics had glossed Aristotle.

More and more often American geologists engaged in a kind of ritualistic re-creation of past glories, resurveying the classic study areas of their heroic age, debating endlessly the theses and con-cepts of the great masters, recounting over and over the sagas of western exploration. The library replaced the field as a source of data. Senior scientists argued questions like the origin of granite or the stratigraphy of the deep ocean as though they were disput-ing free will or the existence of angels, unconcerned that no em-pirical test or experiment could drive toward a conclusion. They revisited the puzzle of rim and river as mathematicians would Fer-mat's Last Theorem. The Canyon became more museum than laboratory. It endured primarily as a symbol, no longer a dynamic source of vital information.

Ideas and energy that would have launched an international ca-reer a half century before languished in dry dock. Despite the long tenure of Edwin McKee—first as chief naturalist of the park (1929–40) and then as de facto chief scientist of the Canyon region—his classic stratigraphy of the Paleozoic Canyon went onto library shelves rather than into the backpacks of a new gen-eration of exploring geologists. A historical geologist like McKee would have appreciated the importance of timing: the Canyon could no longer make a career. The great monographs and per-sonal narratives of the heroic age were the ammonites and pelecy-pods of a lithified past—horizon fossils of an age that no longer flourished. Instead McKee's magisterial studies of the Kaibab and Redwall limestones, of the Supai and Toroweap formations, and of the Coconino sandstone largely banked the coals of Canyon sci-ence. Even geologists still read the rocks with the texts of Powell,

Dutton, Walcott, and Davis before them. The revolution in earth science came later, and it looked elsewhere.

The dominant audience was tourism. Perhaps the most interesting of those who catered to it were the Kolb brothers, Emery and Ellsworth. Arriving at the Canyon in 1902 to "follow the work of scenic photography," they eventually traversed the Colorado River from Green River, Wyoming, to the Sea of Cortés. The bulk of the journey came in late 1911, the stretch from Needles south in 1912 and 1913. They lagged ten years behind the railroad to the rim and two years behind the first strictly tourist trip down the river (that by Julius Stone), but they systematically photographed their adventure, using both still and motion pictures, and wrote a widely distributed account, *Through the Grand Canyon from Wyoming to Mexico* (1913).[9]

The voyage was adventure, to be sure, but it was enterprise too, done so that it could be photographed. The Kolbs didn't reveal the Canyon; they used the notoriety of the Canyon to promote themselves and their work. Ellsworth confessed ingenuously that "the success of our expedition depended on our success as photographers. We could not hope to add anything of importance to the scientific and topographic knowledge of the canyons already existing; and merely to come out alive at the other end did not make a strong appeal to our vanity. We were there as scenic photographers in love with their work. . . ." A scenic photographer needed a scene; that the Canyon provided. In truth the idea of scenic photography as a career came to the Kolbs after they had arrived at the South Rim, and they began their collective career by photographing the mule trail parties that ventured down the Bright Angel Trail.[10]

Here was Everyman as explorer, describing for a nation of Everymans how they did it and telling the story through popular mediums—a motion picture and a picture book, the first really of the modern era. More than anyone else, even more than the Santa Fe Railroad, which after all brought in professional writers and painters, the Kolbs transformed the genres of high culture into the medium of popular culture. The whole package of voyage and book had been staged so as to present the story, and the Canyon filmed to satisfy the eyes of the average tourist. That they faced real dangers and that the practice of photographing from the gorge required muscle, pluck, and wit spared them from being shills of the pseudoevent. They were originals, though popular culture over the decades commercialized them into a cliché.

The timing of their trip as much as its subject determined the success of the Kolb enterprise. It was an era in which alarm at the closing of the frontier and years of sloganeering by social Darwinists had led to a vigorous search for personal adventure, by elite and folk equally. The Kolbs completed their descent through the Canyon the same year that Teddy Roosevelt delivered his invocation to the "life of strenuous endeavor," and Ellsworth's book came with an introduction by Owen Wister, a Roosevelt crony, whose novel *The Virginian* had appeared the same year the Kolbs arrived at the Canyon and whose theme was the cowboy as western folk hero.

But unlike Wister, or his friend Frederic Remington, or their mutual friend Roosevelt, the Kolbs—and their colleagues and imitators—offered adventure without the trappings of high culture. Their motion picture was followed by others, as Hollywood made the West into the western, with Tom Mix, to name one star among many, riding up canyon trails and swimming Colorado gorges. Their photographs of the tourist Canyon were, as Robert Euler has remarked, the first of an avalanche, the art form of Everyman. "In sheer numbers, there probably have been more pictures taken than words written about Grand Canyon, but not much more...."[11]

The changed perspective followed a change in audience. The interpreters of the Canyon were no longer intellectuals, or the Canyon's patrons even the affluent late-nineteenth-century travelers of railroad and resort, but Everyman and his Model T. By 1926 auto travel exceeded rail. Within a few years paved roads reached to all the major overlooks, a footbridge spanned the Colorado, and a park naturalist regularly lectured eager visitors. The average stay could be measured in minutes, hours at most, enough to authenticate the visit with a souvenir and to circle the overlooks as Muslim pilgrims did the Kaaba. The Kolbs retired to their studio on the Bright Angel Trailhead, as much a tourist feature as Powell's memorial or Mather Point. There they replayed their motion picture and for decades ended as they began, by selling photo supplies to visitors and photos of mule trains to tourist tenderfeet. They had become themselves part of the scene.

All this is not to say that the coming of mass culture and its intimate ally, mass tourism, to the Grand Canyon was unimportant. Upon it was predicated the public conservation of the Canyon, and its preservation in a form that would retard the crudest forms of commercialism that had, for example, blemished Niagara Falls. Nor is it to say that those who catered to tourism saw the Canyon only over the rise of a cash register. Nor, again, does this imply that the art of Gunnar Widforss was trivial, or that Edwin McKee's studies of Paleozoic stratigraphy were merely self-indulgent, or that François Matthes and Richard Evans and Claude Birdseye were dilettantes. Their contributions were as important to the Canyon's cultural history as that history had become to the American experience.

But they were minor events in intellectual history, almost provincial in comparison with the ferment in relativistic cosmology, quantum theory, the modern synthesis of evolution and genetics, the breakthroughs in formal logic, or the stunning revolution in modern art and literature. The Canyon's cliffs were no mirror for modernism, as they had been a palette for Romantic art and a slate for natural science. No Nobel laureate began a career on rim or river. No major artist shattered old genres or announced an avant-garde manifesto among its sunset-blasted buttes. No book foamed up from its rapids to demand a place in the modernist canon. Yet just such triumphs had happened in the preceding half century.

Instead the Canyon was becoming a museum piece, a fixture like statuary on the lawn of the national manor. Purveyors of the populist Canyon promoted their wares by and large without the aid of cultural elites. Tourists came to see what they were told to see; they saw (or heard or read what they were supposed to see) without seeking to turn personal vision into cultural insight. They rushed to the El Tovar Hotel, Verkamp's, the Kolb Studios, or the Hopi House for souvenirs and entertainment as much as to the Bright Angel Trailhead or Hopi Point. They visited the Canyon as they did other sites of national pilgrimage. They saw and touched an iconic Canyon. They impressed their perspective with their sheer numbers.

The Canyon was becoming culturally moribund and, for that reason, politically vulnerable. Dutton had imagined a time when the Canyon itself succumbed to the continued ravages of the Great Denudation, and William Morris Davis had exploited that image to impress on his listeners the immensity and power of geologic time. Geologically that event, if it ever proceeded to completion, was millions of years away. Its intellectual equivalent, however, was almost at hand. The cultural Canyon had reached grade.

The Canyon remained a supreme spectacle, though of what precisely was less certain. "I have heard rumors of visitors who were disappointed," wrote J. B. Priestley in the best Canyon essay of the era. "The same people will be disappointed at the Day of Judgment." A British man of letters, Priestley was a visitor twice over, and he sensed both the strangeness of the place and its significance. "If I were an American," he concluded, "I should make my remembrance of it the final test of men, art, and policies. I

CANYON GLOOM TO CANYON GLORY

Thomas Moran, *Chasm of the Colorado*. Moran succeeded in translating Alpine art into a Canyon setting. No one more actively promoted the place as a setting for landscape art. His Canyons span forty years.

SILVER AGE: ART

Gunnar Widforss, *Powell Plateau, Grand Canyon*. Widforss at his finest, and an interesting artistic backsiting on Moran's *Chasm*, which, geographically, views this scene in reverse.

THE COMMERCIAL CANYON

ABOVE: The opening of the Sante Fe rail link between Williams and the South Rim, the beginning of wholesale tourism and the construction of modern facilities to service it, 17 September 1901.

OPPOSITE, TOP: Buffalo Bill shilling in 1892 on behalf of speculators trying to flog the North Rim off as a hunting preserve to British nobility. While rich in deer and cougars, the place was simply too remote. Here the group admires the South Rim.

OPPOSITE, BOTTOM: The Kolb brothers' studio, perched on the rim like a box camera, ready to photograph mule trains.

Preserving One of the Great Sights

Above: Theodore Roosevelt on mule, John Hance mounted behind him, and Ida Tarbell two farther back.

Opposite, bottom: Steven Mather, director of the National Park Service, at the dedication of the Powell Memorial, an event where history, myth, government, and scenic values all converged. The photograph is by Francis Farquahar, who later assembled a masterful first bibliography of the Grand Canyon and Colorado River.

THE GRAND ENSEMBLE AT THE CAPITAL

After he was assigned to the Geological Survey's national office, Gilbert and some colleagues began to stage commemorative lunches, which they called the Great Basin Mess. These evolved into elaborate affairs. Much of the Washington scientific establishment, including those whose careers were tied to the Canyon, attended. The photograph above shows Gilbert (seated, third from left); Powell (seated, front); William Holmes (standing behind Powell); Charles Walcott (seated, far right); and WJ McGee (seated, left), a Powell protégé and one of the architects of a philosophy of national conservation.

SILVER AGE: SCIENCE

OPPOSITE, TOP: Edwin McKee as a young naturalist lecturing on the South Rim, near Mather's memorial plaque.

OPPOSITE, BOTTOM: Mapping the river—the U.S. Geological Survey's Grand Canyon Expedition of 1923 under Claude Birdseye.

ABOVE: Mapping the rims—a survey team under François Matthes.

RIGHT: Dr. David White and Edwin McKee examine fossils on a canyon trail.

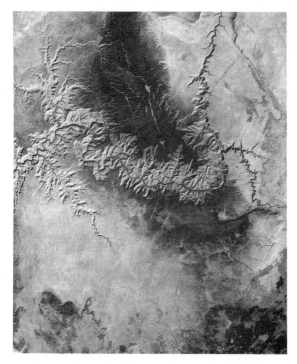

THE COSMIC CANYON

LEFT: Landat views the Grand Canyon, reducing its immense complexity to the status of a mudcrack.

BELOW: Comparative status of the Grand Canyon and the Valle Marineris on Mars.

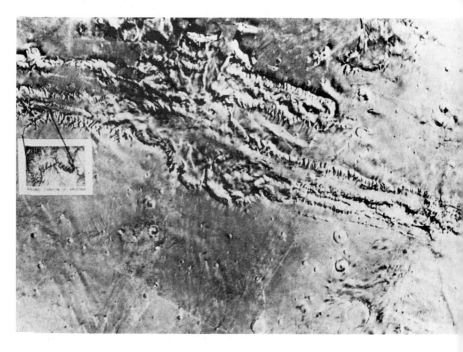

re sketches of all the participants. While Powell remained at
e core, Dutton earned a lengthy portrait (Stegner had written
s doctoral thesis on Dutton).

The book was an immense success, an instant classic that tran-
ended inherited categories of literary biography, history, and
estern literature. It immediately overwhelmed two feeble studies
om the 1940s, Edwin Corle's improbably named *Listen, Bright
gel* (1946) and Roderick Peattie's anthology *The Inverted
ountains* (1948). It even found a children's cognate of sorts in
arguerite Henry's Newberry Award–winning *Brighty of the
and Canyon* (1953). Brighty did for the Grand Canyon what
nokey Bear did for forest fire. The baby boomers who grew up
th it learned that, like the burro Brighty, the Grand Canyon
ould remain "wild and free."

So while Brighty roamed as a free spirit, Stegner's book carried
e load. Twenty years later Sally Gregory Fairfax, summarizing
o decades of vigorous environmental reform, declared for an
mpressive consensus" that "if you are going to read one book in
s area, it should be Wallace Stegner's *Beyond the Hundredth
eridian. . . .*" If the Canyon had made Powell's reputation, his
ok about Powell's Canyon made Stegner's. More than anyone
e Wallace Stegner became the West's man of letters and a sage
r a new era of environmentalism. The heroic age had its poet. If
was through Dutton's eyes that tourists saw the Canyon's sun-
s, it was with Stegner's voice that they read his words.[15]

e lesson arrived just in time. Two postwar development
nemes, both promoted in 1956, proposed fundamentally to re-
ucture both rim and river. The river's redefinition began in
48 with the completion of the Upper Colorado River Basin
ompact, which liberated the Bureau of Reclamation to plan for
e wholesale reconstruction that in time made the Colorado one
the most engineered waterways in the world. Following an im-
rtant controversy, the process culminated in the Upper Colo-

Canyon broke apart. What cultural elites sought t
not hold, and populist experiments like the Shiva '
tion ended in near parody. The real "lost world"
Great Age of Discovery.[14]

DOWN THE RIVER AND BACK FROM THE BRINK: THE ENVIRONMENTALIST CANYON

Yet the Canyon remained. Tourism might sag, intel
asm falter, and the Canyon's very familiarity bre
tempt, then a complacency about what it signified
remained, its meaning ready for rehabilitation. Just
rado rapids renewed when side canyons debouch
into its channel, so new interests poured into the
larger cultural watersheds and revived the vigor
The Grand Canyon entered—helped define—the
of postwar environmentalism.

The first of the rejuvenating rapids was a literary
heroic age.

When Wallace Stegner published *Beyond the
ridian: John Wesley Powell and the Second Opening*
1954, his evocation had a bardic quality, a sweepi
times past. Stegner claimed he was writing the "bic
reer," whatever that was. In fact, the result was a n
cation of the whole Powell Survey and the landscap
had made a reputation. The book's "biography" w
place, the Canyon Country, as it was of Powell;
a "career" was, as much as anything, a wonderful
the Canyon in particular had been explored, bee
celebrated, and become assimilated into American

rado River Storage Project Act of 1956. The rim's redefinition sprang from the National Park Service, which argued successfully for a decade-long, system-wide rehabilitation of facilities and infrastructure that it called Mission 66. If the river's reconstruction recalled the traditional economics of power and water, the rim's pointed to the recreational demands of a consumer society. Both schemes inspired an environmentalist reaction.

The political drama began slightly earlier, coincident with Stegner's *Beyond the Hundredth Meridian*. The Bureau of Reclamation had originally proposed to develop, as part of the Upper Colorado Basin Project, a dam at Echo Park that would inundate part of Dinosaur National Monument. The precedent for flooding a piece of the national park system horrified conservationists who had never quite recovered from the flooding of Yosemite's Hetch Hetchy Valley. Fighting the dam at Echo Park marked the political metamorphosis of an aging conservation agenda into a new-era environmentalism. The transformation was one of style as much as theme.

Almost all the activist apparatus applied to later controversies emerged at Echo Park. There was a picture book, *This Is Dinosaur* (1955), an anthology promoted and published by Alfred Knopf and edited by Wallace Stegner. Though it appears quaint when compared with the slick-page writing and high-voltage politics packed by its successors, the volume established a new genre. Not surprisingly the story of Powell and his Colorado adventure figured prominently. Not only was a principle at stake—the inviolability of the national parks—so was a part of American history. There was a film about Dinosaur too, another precedent. And there were hard, fascinating lessons in mobilizing public opinion to oppose large-scale development projects on the public lands. Like the old forty-niner who seemed to materialize at every western mining strike and instruct the community on how to proceed, the successful veterans of the Echo Park fight wandered widely among the public lands and controversies and provided leadership for a generation of environmental activists. In particular, dams became favorite targets for bringing public protest to critical mass.

Through those fights, through the arguments and ideas that underlay that movement, an intellectual culture began returning to Grand Canyon. Unwittingly the Bureau of Reclamation helped point the way. In return for abandoning the Echo Park site, it constructed a high dam at Glen Canyon, upstream from Lee's Ferry, and as part of its construction wave, like a slow flood down the river, it proposed hydropower dams at Marble Canyon and Bridge Canyon that would encase the flanks of the eastern Grand Canyon in reservoirs. Incredibly, the scheme even argued for a tunnel to carry waters from the Marble Canyon reservoir beneath the Kaibab Plateau and empty into Kanab Canyon, where another dam would impound it. Some 90 percent of the flow through the classic Grand Canyon would cease. Although the dams avoided the park itself and were allowed under the provisions of the park's organic act, they clearly compromised the natural integrity of the Canyon. And they thrust the Canyon center stage into American environmentalism.

Neither was the rim spared. The National Park Service itself saw to that. The Santa Fe Railroad had kept Canyon visitation on a parity with national rates during the Depression while the Roosevelt administration, through the Civilian Conservation Corps, had upgraded much of the park's facilities. Both crashed during the war. When visitation revived, tourists were trading rail for roads. The National Park Service—not only at Grand Canyon but throughout its holdings—found that its infrastructure was inadequate. In his column for *Harper's*, Bernard De Voto proposed the country abolish the parks if it wasn't willing to maintain them. The public rallied behind the parks, and the Park Service responded with a grand scheme to accommodate the automotive tourist.

The outcome was a decade-long construction intended to conclude on the fiftieth anniversary of the service's organic act. Mission 66 brought Levittown, through the interstate highway system, to the national parks, reconciled outdoor recreation with a consumer society, and ensured public access to a motoring public eager to fill the new infrastructure. Yet while it built visitor centers, it did little to explain the meaning of the parks beyond bureaucratic celebration of the Park Service. Mission 66 revived the wholesale construction projects of the CCC and coincided, historically and culturally, with the creation of Disneyland; critics charged that neither was an appropriate model for a national park. If the Bureau of Reclamation could see rivers only as damsites and kilowatts, the Park Service seemed driven by visitation rates and paved overlooks, the nature reserve as theme park.

Both schemes questioned what a park meant and especially what this particular park meant. The Echo Park controversy partially answered the first query, but Grand Canyon National Park would not itself be flooded. The dams would not attack a sacrosanct principle or submerge a visual heritage. (The Colorado River had in fact been dammed by volcanic flows during the Pleistocene and had flooded the Canyon more than once; the soils farmed by the Havasupai were the deposits of one such episode.) The traditional conception of the Canyon as a scenic and scientific spectacle was an insufficient reply. The replumbed Colorado would not be visible from the rim, and Mission 66 would bring ever-larger numbers of tourists to not see those effects. If the projects were offensive or inappropriate, the reasons had to be found elsewhere.

Yet even as physical access improved, intellectual access declined. More cars brought more visitors to more overlooks, but it was not evident that they saw more deeply into the scene. If the Canyon was to endure as a culturally powerful presence, the public needed to find a meaning beyond souvenirs, hydropower, and scenic pullouts. A simple revival of Powell, Dutton, Holmes, and Moran was of limited use; they spoke the language of another age. The Canyon needed to express values deeper than pop culture and more contemporary than a recycled Romanticism.

*   *   *

The critical act of interpretation came when Joseph Wood Krutch published *Grand Canyon: Today and All Its Yesterdays* (1957). It was not a great book, not in the sense that the *Exploration of the Colorado River* and the *Tertiary History* had been, though the book had plenty of quotable passages. It was often sentimental and its science old-fashioned, premodernist in its simple evolutionism and its attachment to concepts like the Great Chain of Being. Its major audience had to wait until a few years afterward, when the book was converted into a successful television documentary. But with exquisite timing Krutch had written the prolegomenon to the conception of the Grand Canyon as wilderness.

Here was a bona fide man of letters, an éminence grise of high culture. Krutch, who had begun his career as a critic of books, plays, and society, was a man very much attuned to the spirit of the 1920s highbrow violently smitten by the village virus. In 1929 he consolidated a sophisticated case for intellectual despair with *The Modern Temper*, until the stock market crash pushed his book off a literary ledge and gave him genuine cause for grief. Even as sales fell, however, his reputation rose. Krutch settled into Columbia University and a role as a prominent drama critic. Gradually his strident, affected modernism mellowed, then vanished. After publishing a biography of Henry David Thoreau in 1948, Krutch made a Thoreauvian gesture and retired to open air and fresh thoughts in the Southwest. Now an apostate from modernism, Krutch recanted *The Modern Temper* with *The Measure of Man* (1954), a humanist paean; he began to write natural history books, in the spirit of Gilbert White and the reclusive Thoreau. Then he visited the Grand Canyon.

There the former spokesman for a world in which there was nothing to believe found a great constant, an eternal verity, and in writing of the Canyon, Krutch affirmed what had become for him a fundamental truth: "The wilderness and the idea of wilderness is

one of the permanent abodes of the human spirit." He successfully repositioned the Canyon within the moral geography of postwar America in which the wild and the synthetic, like two poles of
a bar magnet, defined the lines of force for understanding environmental issues. At the Canyon Krutch discovered a perfect expression in the contrast between the relict life of the Havasupai
Indians living in their side canyon Eden and the grotesque commercialism of Las Vegas, sprouting like a plastic mushroom in the
desert. Both were to compete for the waters of the Colorado; both
were to compete for the right to give meaning to the Canyon the
river had carved. One spoke with stone-inscribed truths; the
other, to a throwaway consumerism.[16]

The Canyon was known, but its significance had been relegated
to library shelves and its celebration to *Arizona Highways*; its
scenery was recognizable, and its visual effects seemed less stunning to a generation that had acquired television. Shrewdly
Krutch transcended utilitarian politics with an appeal to the wild
itself. The Grand Canyon was not hostile or even tangential to the
American Way of Life. Rather, it expressed the raw promise of
that new world and would continue to do so if Americans would
only leave it alone. "If we do not preserve it," Krutch concluded,
"then we shall have diminished by just that much the unique
privilege of being an American."[17]

Between them Stegner and Krutch redefined the Canyon's
meaning. They created a new poetry for the place and, unlike
those of the heroic age, did so on a basis other than science.
Though they wrote of scientists and alluded to scientific ideas,
they positioned the Canyon within a broad humanism; hagiogra-
phy and wilderness are not scientific concepts. It was well they did
so because modern science was engaged in its own developmental
schemes, the "endless frontier" proposed by Vannevar Bush and
funded by a host of military and civilian agencies, including the
freshly minted National Science Foundation. The old cultural alliance of the Second Age, like the Grand Alliance of the Second

World War, had disintegrated, leaving behind the intellectual iron curtain of C. P. Snow's "two cultures." Big Science now visited the Canyon as a tourist, not as a researcher.

Since the 1920s the earth sciences had been too often reduced to scholarly ritual and petroleum prospecting. Now that was changing. The same year that Krutch published his prose poem, on the centennial of the Ives Expedition, the International Geophysical Year (IGY) announced a Third Great Age of Discovery by launching Sputnik into earth orbit, lowering the bathyscape *Trieste* into the depths of the Marianas Trench, and dispatching a swarm of aircraft and tracked vehicles across the icy wastes of Antarctica. Geology at last roused from its long hibernation.

The Third Age took as its greater geographic domain the solar system. Its premier expression was the geophysical inventory of a planet, typically by remote sensing, a technique field-tested during IGY on planet Earth. The Earth-Moon system served the Third Age as the interior seas of Europe had the First Age and the natural history excursion and grand tour had the Second. Its defining gesture was a trek across the solar system, best epitomized by the two Voyager spacecraft. Its intellectual syndrome orbited eccentrically around modernism. The new explorations finally brought the revolution in earth science so long postponed during the twentieth century.

The Third Age resuscitated the American school. Its understanding of planet Earth culminated in the theory of plate tectonics. Comparative planetology, not the comparative frontiers of Western civilization, underwrote its prime insights. The Third Age did not even need human explorers, only robotic probes, and it was searching not for exotic peoples or lost civilizations but for evidence of life itself. Its moral drama was ambiguous. Contact with the terrains of the Third Age, often through prosthetic instruments, wiped away the moral crisis of prior exploring ventures but at the cost, it seemed, of moral drama and social significance.

If there was nothing to find, there was little reason to look. If there was little by way of new peoples and biotas to compromise exploration with empire, neither was there a compelling reason to proceed.

Of particular interest to the Grand Canyon was the character of geologic time. The new geophysical chronometers were not entropy clocks or life cycles. Like paleomagnetic reversals, or circadian rhythms, or the steady-state time of general systems theory, they were based on open rather than closed systems. The concept of information suggested that in such systems structures could maintain themselves, not necessarily decay. Meanwhile the development of modern genetics helped found evolution on chance rather than on design and helped destroy the value of the life cycle as a principle of metahistory. The world lines of quarks and tachyons replaced the depositional and diastrophic chronologies of epic earth history. Time was relativized; time's arrow, given a feedback loop. Colliding plates, unlike a contracting earth, suggested no necessary direction to geologic history. Impact craters, not canyons, recorded the early history of the solar system. Smashing moonlets explained the stratigraphy of the moon and Mercury. The Geological Survey's Branch of Astrogeology in Flagstaff scrambled down Meteor Crater rather than the Inner Gorge.

Its contact with new lands had meant the American school could claim a share of the national creation story: America as the frontier fusion of Old World civilization with New World wilderness. The vision of empty landscapes had encouraged an appeal for natural processes as geologic agents, working with infinite patience over aeons of time and a preference for long, exfoliating narratives. But the modern landscape was often rapidly resynthesized by human engineering, and it was necessary to understand and predict the almost instantaneous changes that might result. A sixty-million-year Tertiary history seemed arcane next to regional development schemes whose planning horizon extended over a decade. William Morris Davis's geographical cycle was powerless before the Upper Colorado River Storage Project. Geologic time compressed to a surface as nearly flat as LANDSAT imagery of the Canyon.

For the new earth sciences there was remarkably little of importance at the Grand Canyon. Their surveys migrated to the boundaries of plates, to the San Andreas fault, the East Pacific rise, the Hawaiian hot spot, the Mid-Atlantic Ridge; their ideas, to the macrofeatures of other Earthlike planets: the shield volcanoes and rift valleys of Mars, the highlands of Venus, the methane atmosphere of Titan, the seared dead surface of Mercury. They celebrated those macro features of the Earth that were comparable. The East African rift zone, the shield volcanoes of the Pacific, the channeled scablands of eastern Washington, the Sudbury crater in Ontario—here was the comparative geology that bound the Earth to the solar system. Vulcan's Throne from which Dutton and Holmes had peered into the western Canyon had to compete with volcanoes on Io and geysers on frigid Triton. Stratigraphers of plate tectonics looked to the Franciscan mélange in California's Coast Range rather than to the Redwall limestone. Where the dark schists of the Inner Gorge pointed to a Great Unknown, still older stromatolites from the West Australian craton spoke to the origin of life. In an era focused on gravity anomalies, paleomagnetism, heat flows, and continent-sized chunks of lithosphere that rammed into one another, the geomorphology that had once synthesized the American school—had traced the frontier between humanity and geology and between art and science—seemed merely decorative, like carved cornices in a steel skyscraper.

The Canyon no longer framed earth science as it had a century before. The Great Unconformity as testimony to the unbounded patience of geologic time faced the Chicxulub Crater, formed when an extraterrestrial body slammed into the Yucatán and precipitated the extinction of 90 percent of the planet's species, and made its far-scattered iridium a universal stratigraphic index. The slow recession of Canyon cliffs, testimony to the dynamics of the Great Denudation, had to match the immense storms of Jupiter's

Great Red Spot and Neptune's Great Dark Spot; the banded limestone, shale, and sandstone of Canyon buttes, the rings of Saturn and Uranus; the revelation of earth time with the cosmographic image of the Earth as a celestial body, like a sapphire set in black velvet.

On the centennial of John Wesley Powell's voyage in the *Emma Dean*, Neil Armstrong and Buzz Aldrin landed *Apollo 11* on the Sea of Tranquillity, and scientific eyes looked up, not down. In a memorial symposium on Powell, whose proceedings the Geological Survey published, Charles Hunt could ponder the evolution of the Colorado River system, noting that the fundamental questions of Canyon geology, including how it originated, remained unanswered. Luna Leopold, chief hydraulic engineer of the survey, replaced the evolutionary model of the Colorado with the proposal that it existed in a state of quasi equilibrium, transporting debris and water but no longer downcutting, and likened its rapids to thermodynamic engines. Mechanical metaphors seemed only appropriate when one was confronted with the geomorphology of wholesale engineering, when the floodgates of Glen Canyon had choked off spring floods, when the rhythm of the river beat to power demands created by regional air conditioners. The geologic puzzle endured as a historical curiosity, like unexplained artifacts at an Anasazi ruin.

That symposium built on one chaired by Edwin McKee in 1964. This session had attacked directly the question of an originating mechanism for the Canyon and retired in ordered ambiguity. Between those inconclusive symposia, meanwhile, a revitalized earth science had rapidly consolidated the formative concepts of plate tectonics. Even as the Powell symposium pondered the insoluble, a representative of the Museum of Northern Arizona—the institutional sponsor of the McKee symposium and a prominent promoter of Canyon science—discovered a fossil of *Lystrosaurus* that helped confirm the macromovement of continents. Ironically the find came not from the Colorado Plateau but from the mountains of Antarctica. The discovery by Edwin

Colbert was immediately hailed as major, confirmatory evidence to that already plucked from the deep ocean floor, traced along transcurrent faults, and mapped as volcanic arcs and overthrust zones where plates had subducted or overridden one another. The acceptance of plate theory further shifted attention to the boundaries of those lithospheric slabs, none of which framed the Grand Canyon. The Canyon resembled more a pothole on a plate's travels than the journey's end. The gorge ceased to be a scientific oracle.

The escalating Third Age challenged the Canyon's authority as a planetary spectacle. It revealed oceanic trenches like the Marianas, many times deeper; the sandswept Valle Marineris on Mars, many times wider and as long as the continental United States; ice-smothered basins in Antarctica, integral to the breakup of Gondwana. As an intellectual spectacle the geological aesthetics of Dutton had to confront the "geo-poetry" of Harry Hess, whose paper on mantle convection crystallized the revival of continental drift as a concept. The new imagery of the Canyon from orbiting spacecraft simplified its complexity and flattened its panorama of time; the Grand Canyon looked like a mud crack in the solar system. The organic ensemble that had made the Canyon so important a symbol to the American school now seemed as irrelevant as the Spencerian formula with which Clarence Dutton had described it, or the transcendentalism that animated Moran's paintings, or the sense of scientific revelation evident in the detail of Holmes's panoramas. The Canyon seemed to testify to a science as antiquated as trilobites.

The Third Great Age of Discovery would not revalorize the Grand Canyon.

It didn't need to. By an immense cultural metamorphosis the Canyon was being rediscovered. Tourists drove to the rim in renewed numbers and, more significantly, journeyed to and rode down the river at exponential rates. Even as Glen Canyon Dam throttled the Colorado's flow, the mainstream of American thought compensated and poured ideas through its gorges. Once again Americans were looking to nature for inspiration. It was not long before they looked to the Canyon.

By 1962 the two poles of postwar environmentalism each had a literary model: for the synthetic landscape, Rachel Carson's *Silent Spring*, which dramatized the horrors of "chemical fallout"; and for wilderness, Eliot Porter's *"In Wildness Is the Preservation of the World"*, a blend of photography and prose. Even the National Park Service, still mesmerized by Mission 66, was ready for reform. Wallace Stegner meanwhile wrote an influential essay arguing for wild landscapes as part of "the geography of hope." Secretary of Interior Stewart Udall appointed a special committee to recommend better policies of wildlife management, particularly at Yellowstone. Chaired by A. Starker Leopold, a professor of wildlife biology at the University of California-Berkeley, a son of Aldo Leopold, the great philosopher of wilderness, and a brother of Luna Leopold, soon to begin the final hydraulic survey of the once-wild Colorado, the Leopold Committee quickly expanded its charge into a review of how the Park Service administered natural areas. In 1963 the committee's report recommended that parks should represent "vignettes of Primitive America." The next year Congress passed the Wilderness Act, which gave statutory standing to the concept of the wild and committed lands to its realization.[18]

Competition over the park's meaning, and controversy over its political future, heated up. The Bureau of Reclamation's Upper Colorado River Storage Project scheme was so enormous it demanded the two Canyon dams solely to sell hydropower to help underwrite its costs. This time there were two scenarios possible, symbolized by two books. If *This Is Dinosaur* memorialized a success story, its Sierra Club successor, *The Place No One Knew: Glen Canyon on the Colorado* (1963) documented a failure, the place the compromised Echo Park Dam had gone to. The choice seemed agonizingly clear. Grand Canyon could recapitulate either Echo

Park or Glen Canyon. That waters were already backing up behind Glen Canyon Dam—water that would otherwise flow through the sanctum of the Inner Gorge—gave urgency to the threat. The Grand Canyon dam controversy, as Roderick Nash observed, became "one of the classic confrontations in the history of American conservation."[19]

Glen Canyon had been flooded because its sandstone gorges had insufficient connections to American culture. Echo Park had been spared because a cultural elite had quickly found, or where necessary created, such connections. Meaning already resided in the Canyon, but the significance of the Canyon as scenic spectacle and as paean to earth time was insufficient by itself as counterarguments. The dams need not be seen from the principal overlooks; the contemplation of geologic time was lost on a throwaway culture that was committed to instant gratification and for which fifteen minutes of Warholian fame summed a celebrity lifetime. Public media were more interested in astronauts hiking down the Bright Angel Trail, promising to plant humanity's footprints on the moon, than on abstract arguments for the erasure of the human presence, hardly a telegenic subject.

The Canyon needed a cultural counterforce of equal magnitude and found it in wilderness. Like an old building gutted and rebuilt with a new interior, the cultural Canyon presented its classic facade while being internally rewired with the politics of ecology and reconstructed with more modern furnishings from the wilderness movement. Attention refocused on the river, as tourism did. Coincident with the Wilderness Act, the Sierra Club published a Grand Canyon book in the style of the Glen Canyon and Echo Park predecessors, François Leydet's *Time and the River Flowing: Grand Canyon*, and produced some films. While Leydet and company popularized the Canyon by boat, Colin Fletcher did it by backpack. Fletcher made his trip in 1963, published in 1967, and echoed the themes of Leydet et al.: the river and the awesomeness of earth time. But it was not really the Canyon as exhibitor of earth history that attracted them or drew a large audience. It was the Colorado as emblem of a wild and free-flowing river and the Canyon as timeless symbol of untrammeled nature, of rhythms longer than human experience and deeper than human knowledge.

The Canyon shone as park, as wilderness, as symbol of environmentalism's resolve. The court battles that followed the initial preservation of the Canyon had centered on the Antiquities Act and on the value of the Canyon for history and science; the new political fights were to focus on the meaning of wilderness. As Congress scheduled hearings in the summer of 1966 on the Pacific Southwest Water Plan, which was to oversee development on the lower Colorado, the Sierra Club sponsored a series of full-page ads in the *New York Times* and *Washington Post* in protest. The first argued that "there is only one simple, incredible issue here: this time it's the Grand Canyon they want to flood. *The Grand Canyon.*" A July ad mocked the Bureau of Reclamation's arguments that reservoirs would open the Canyon to public appreciation and shamed a constituency committed to conservation. "SHOULD WE ALSO FLOOD THE SISTINE CHAPEL SO TOURISTS CAN GET NEARER THE CEILING?" That put the matter to the public. David Brower, head of the Sierra Club and a veteran of Echo Park, put the matter to environmentalists. "If we can't save the Grand Canyon," he asked, "what the hell can we save?"[20]

The campaign succeeded, although the controversy did not cease until 1968, when Congress approved the Central Arizona Project without the offending dams, and also legislated a National Wild and Scenic Rivers System to expand the dominion of America's white-water wilderness of which the Canyon had become the paradigm. Simultaneously, now that Mission 66 had concluded, the National Park Service reformed its own house with a reconsidered set of guidelines for the management of the units under its care. The parks had a new meaning.

So did the Grand Canyon. What the dam episode symbolizes, and in some degree helped formulate, and what should not be obscured by the activist environmentalism, the politicization of "ecology," and all the consciousness-raising that went on are that the Canyon had reconnected with educated elites. Ideas came from intellectuals who had read not only Dutton and Powell but John Muir and Henry Thoreau and especially Aldo Leopold and who saw wilderness as a great cultural resource, intimately bound up with the American creation myth and American exceptionalism and with the human stewardship of nature everywhere. For all its popular, sometimes mindless permutations, the cult of wilderness had real ideas behind it, and thanks to the dam controversy, the Canyon became a repository for them. Wilderness advocates had needed a symbol the public would recognize; the Canyon needed a significance grander than scenery.

Like a broken bone, the fracture between the Canyon and intellectual culture knit together, stronger than ever. The Grand Canyon became, for postwar environmentalism, both talisman and oracle. It would again inspire as well as inform. Between a white-water Grand and a dam-chocked Glen, intellectual energy sparked, like an electrical arc leaping between oppositely charged diodes. Edward Abbey set his novel of ecotage, *The Monkey Wrench Gang* (1974), exactly within that force field.

In this revival the works of the heroic age were commonly quoted, those from the Canyon's silver age hardly at all. With the exception of a few choice passages from J. B. Priestley, from the era between Dutton and Stegner there is barely a whisper. It hardly mattered.

The renaissance rippled widely outward. Science returned; art reappeared; literature renewed; the Canyon was rediscovered, revisited, redefined. The Geological Survey restudied the river preparatory to its symposium on the occasions of the Powell centennial. The Museum of Northern Arizona and the Grand Canyon Natural History Association published an anthology summarizing the state of Canyon geologic studies in 1974. Particularly significant was a scientific transfer from geology to ecology as the dam-restructured river prompted a biological survey of the gorge. Separately the Geological Survey and the National Geographic Society remapped the Canyon. The National Endowment for the Arts began an artists-in-residence program in 1972, coinciding with a popular revival of western American subjects and representationalism as a genre; an Arts for the Parks program, under the aegis of the National Parks Association, superseded it. Still, landscape photography in the Eliot Porter and David Muench mode remained the principal form of Canyon art, finding ready patrons in the environmental periodicals or calendars, *Arizona Highways* magazine, and innumerable popular books. In 1983 a consortium of cultural institutions launched an annual Grand Canyon Chamber Music Festival. Within the long current of Canyon history, this brief era was a kind of Lava Falls, books foaming out of presses like white water against rock, as ideas met politics.

The river in fact became the Canyon's central metaphor. Because the park had been threatened by dams, the Canyon became equated with the Colorado River. The fate of one would be that of the other. The perspective of the river determined almost wholly the interpretation of the Canyon. Before the dam controversy, few tourists had traversed the gorge. Commercial boat trips, interrupted briefly by the impounding of Lake Powell, began to increase exponentially as controlled releases restored flow. Before 1963, when Glen Canyon Dam closed, fewer than 100 people had boated through Grand Canyon. By 1967 some 2,000 tourists were on the river, and by 1972, 16,400; the National Park Service found it necessary to regulate access with permits. The survival of Grand Canyon as a wilderness, it was argued, depended on the continuity of the river, which followed from the mechanics of boat travel. The Canyon's Colorado thus began at Lee's Ferry and ended in Lake Mead. Nothing should interrupt its free flow.

Virtually every work of significance described the integrity of the Canyon in terms of the unity of the river. For this too Echo

Park had established a precedent, as celebrity boat trips helped advertise the area. For Grand Canyon, Leydet dismissed the view from the rim as that of "an outsider looking in." Only by journeying "can you fully appreciate the work of the two great architects of the Grand Canyon, time and the flowing river," an observation that would surely have astonished Holmes and Moran, no less than Dutton and Powell, both of whom ascribed the splendor of the Canyon to the height and complexity of the Kaibab Plateau and found the relationship of rim to river the fundamental question of Canyon geology. "You sense it from an airplane," wrote Roderick Nash, author of *Wilderness and the American Mind*, a history of the idea of wilderness first published in 1967, but "you know it running the river." To the views of the writer and historian were added those of the artist. "You cannot grasp the scope of the Grand Canyon from the rim, however you try," explained Philip Hyde, photographer. "It is at the meeting of the river and the rock that those little things happen that make the landscape have meaning and sympathetic scale." It was an orientation that the Powell centennial did nothing to dispel.[21]

When the Park Service underwrote scientific work on the Canyon, as it attempted to do in the early 1970s, the emphasis was on the river. Even as recreational vehicles brought increasing throngs to the Canyon rim, a surge like those the Model T and railroad had swept up in earlier times, the Canyon had come to mean the river; the river, wilderness; and wilderness, ecology. In the nineteenth and twentieth centuries, geology and the institutions of geology had dominated conservation; now that mantle descended on biology. The river, curiously, had to be "alive," and the Canyon "living." The emphasis on the river was natural enough, not lessened by the arguments advanced on behalf of proponents of the dams that the water would not be visible from the eastern Grand Canyon viewpoints. It was natural to appeal to the river in order to define the Canyon as both a physical unit and a concept. But the equation with life was something new. To the uninitiated, political ecology might seem as curious a conceit with which to inform the Grand Canyon as Dutton's appeal to Spencerian evolution a century before.

Yet the propagandists and the intellectuals and even the public who argued that the Colorado River was Grand Canyon were on to something. As the Third Great Age of Discovery sent back its images and inventories of other planets, the uniqueness of planet Earth became more apparent. There it spun, with its stunning blues and whites, alone in the void, the Earth as precious object. Those shining colors came from water, which the Earth, perhaps solely, possessed in abundance and then, no less miraculously, within a temperature range near water's triple point. Water clouds, water oceans, water ice caps, and, of course, rivers—all were unique to Earth.

As a natural spectacle the Grand Canyon would be hard pressed to compete with the image of mass-fractured Miranda, gas storms on Jupiter that flared for centuries, filigree rings around white Saturn; a commercial boat trip through Colorado rapids was hardly on the order of a voyage across interplanetary space. But the history revealed by the Canyon was Earth history, not merely a history of geologic time, and it was a history unlikely to be found elsewhere in the solar system. The physical history of the Earth was distinctive in being by and large a geology of water: a history of erosion by water, deposition by water, sculpture by water. The Grand Canyon with its dramatic juxtaposition of rim and river served not only as a national but a planetary monument to that fact.

In this new cosmos the Canyon claims standing not because of its size or antiquity but, as Dutton had insisted, by virtue of its ever-evolving ensemble and the ideas continually made available by which to interpret it. How these might now converge is not obvious, but then it was never certain that Dutton and his colleagues were going to succeed in synthesizing landscape art, geology, expansionist politics, Romantic history, social Darwinism, aesthetic philosophy, travel literature, and the raw landforms of the West a century ago. The Canyon is unique, idiographic, dynamic; so are its interpretations.

But the grand convergence has endured, equally as a place and as a perspective. The importance of the Canyon will likely outlive the parochial American idea of wilderness, designation as a world heritage site, and mass tourism. A place that can hold a score of Yosemite Valleys and in which Niagara Falls would vanish behind a butte, that could absorb the shock of American expansionism and democratic politics, that could transcend a century of intellectual inquiry, from Charles Darwin to Jacques Derrida has not exhausted its capacity to refract whatever light nature or humanity casts toward it, provided a suitable overlook exists from which to view it.

That of course is Dutton's Point, which will be visited time and again, and made and remade. The Canyon has something yet to say, even if each visitor hears only the echo of his or her own voice.

Afterword:

A Review from Point Sublime

Each man sees himself in the Grand Canyon.
                                    —Carl Sandburg

In September 1996 the North Rim Longshots held a reunion. The climactic event for the fire crew was an expedition to Point Sublime. We crawled over washed-out fire roads in whatever vehicles we could scrape together, recapitulating the numberless times we had raced to Sublime for a final look or a leisurely lunch. I sat on the outcrop at the point, lunch in hand, old comrades to my sides, and looked out. Suddenly time vanished. There was nothing before us to suggest that anything—anything *at all*—had happened in the last twenty-five years. There was no means by which to date the putative passage of time. There were no decaying trees, no new sprouts, no since-sculpted buttes; there was, at high noon, not even the measured tread of shadows. The scene was compelling testimony to the power of the Canyon not to reveal time so much as to obliterate it through sheer immensity. Twenty-five years blanked off like a deleted file. We sank into reverie.

That is not an experience possible with the present study. Its history is, for me, only too obvious, and the marks of editorial time both too apparent and too cautious. No one could confuse this edition with its callow first draft.

The present study began as a graduate term paper and in 1974 metamorphosed into a report in lieu of a thesis for a Master of Arts degree in American civilization at the University of Texas at Austin. Anyone familiar with the works of William H. Goetzmann and John E. Sunder will recognize their presence in its prose, a professorial mix of shock and patience that seems to me peculiarly suited to the study of a place like Grand Canyon. The extended essay was never intended to be published, nor deserved to be. Now that it has found a suitable form, I am pleased to dedicate it to those who first allowed me to push my homemade craft into the stream.

It was at the recommendation of Robert C. Euler, however, that I began to prepare the manuscript for publication by the Grand Canyon Natural History Association. That such a distinguished scholar of the Canyon should show interest was extremely flattering, for at the time I was a seasonal employee, the foreman of the North Rim fire crew; I am grateful for his faith in the project. Consequently I undertook extensive revisions. The text was almost completely recast, new insights introduced, some passages borrowed from my dissertation (a biography of Grove Karl Gilbert), and a good bit of old prose and shaky editorializing expunged. By then I had some tangible support from an unexpected quarter and, with it, a clearer sense of an organizing principle.

In 1981 I received the Antarctic Fellowship from the National Endowment for the Humanities and, after leaving the North Rim for the last time, spent an austral summer on the Ice. The two projects share a common conceit, the idea (first proposed by William Goetzmann) of organizing history according to ages of discovery. To Goeztmann's argument for a second great age, I added a third, and to *Dutton's Point*, as an inquiry into an earth emblem of the second age, I projected *The Ice*, a meditation on an earth emblem of the third age, Antarctica. This strategy was not obvious to NEH. In the end we survived. I thank the agency also for its support and patience.

A transfer to Arizona State University's main campus, after a decade at ASU West, introduced me to graduate assistants, and to our mutual surprise, I assigned Tonia Horton to help with clerical matters and data collection and then to review the old manuscript critically, which she did with zeal and insight. She has my thanks. So has my daughter, Lydia, who assisted on an expedition to the Grand Canyon research library. At Grand Canyon, Sarah Stebbins and Colleen Hyde helped me navigate through research collections. Hal Rothman has earned my gratitude for shocking me out of my Canyon coma long enough to revisit a favorite place. Cliff Nelson allowed me to reconnect with an old friend, even if I did it clumsily as a taxpayer. Thanks to Gerry McCauley for finding the manuscript a good home, and to Wendy Wolf for making it welcome and for forcing me to see the Canyon for the first time all over again.

Not least, thanks go to Sonja, my wife. Our lives together began on the North Rim. The Canyon continues to hang on our walls, salt our speech, and fill our lengthening lives, and remind us that we have never really left Dutton's Point.

APPENDIX

The Grand Canyon: A Graphical Profile

How the Canyon Became Grand is an extended interpretive essay that assumes rather than argues a variety of theses. While the following figures will not prove those arguments, they offer visual and, in places, quantitative support. They help place select Canyon processes within Canyon history and Canyon history within a larger landscape of historical scholarship.

Discovery

Figure A-1 plots out the major events of Canyon history by using the Colorado River as a time line. European history begins in 1540 with Cárdenas, located here at Mile 0, Lee's Ferry. The time line ends at Pearce's Ferry, 178 miles and 450 years later.

Figure A-2 graphs European exploring expeditions by fifty-year periods. There is a good bit of arbitrariness in counting, but there is every reason to believe the general contour is accurate. The First Age quickly reaches equilibrium. In effect, trade replaces exploration, while the dynamic of discovery continues because new nations send out exploring parties to try to outflank the established powers. The Second Age shows clearly; the heroic age of Canyon exploration occupies nearly the dead center of the era. The Third Age is still ambiguous. One scenario holds that the numbers will continue to decline to something like those of the First Age. Another, shown here, suggests that there is a revival under way, though far from the scale of the Second Age. Not fully counted for the Third Age are deep-ocean exploring sorties, many still classified from their Cold War origins. What will distinguish the Third Age is its peculiar ahuman (and abiotic) domain and its cultural alliance with modernism, broadly conceived. Sources: J. N. L. Baker, *A History of Geographical Discovery and Exploration* (New York: Cooper Square Publishers, 1967); J. H. Parry, *The Discovery of the Sea* (Berkeley: University of California Press, 1981); and Alex Roland, ed., *A Spacefaring People: Perspectives on Early Spaceflight*. NASA SP-4405 (Washington, D.C.: Government Printing Office, 1985).

GEOLOGIC TIME

Figure A-3 plots over the past four hundred years the commonly accepted ages of the earth. The significance of the Canyon as a demonstration of geologic time is immediately apparent. The valorization of the Canyon occurred amid this debate over earth history. Adapted from Preston Cloud, *Oasis in Space* (New York: Norton, 1988).

THE TOURIST CANYON

Figure A-4 records the annual visitation to the Grand Canyon, as measured against visitation rates to the national park system overall. The vulnerability of the Canyon during the late 1950s is clear, not only in terms of elite culture but in sheer numbers of tourists.

Figure A-5 isolates the Colorado River as a tourist experience. Made possible by the closing of Glen Canyon Dam, river running explodes exponentially at precisely the time that the dam controversy occurs. Those dams would have made the "natural" trip through the Canyon impossible. The rafting trip, in fact, helped redefine the dimensions of the Canyon overall. Source: Grand Canyon National Park.

THE CULTURAL CANYON

Figure A-6 shows the output of Canyon-related publications. General population growth provides a standard against which to measure the vigor of Canyon scholarship. The collapse from 1930 to the mid-1960s is striking and helps explain why the Canyon could be considered during that time as a site for high dam construction. Data from Earle Spamer, *Bibliography of the Grand Canyon and the Lower Colorado River* (Grand Canyon Association, 1990 edition).

A GRAND GEOLOGY

Figure A-7 traces the publication of Canyon-related scientific literature. Although geology consistently dominates, the post–Glen Canyon Dam research made biology an important challenger for interest and funding. Data from Spamer, *Bibliography of the Grand Canyon and the Lower Colorado River* (1990).

Geology's depressed publication output from 1920 to the 1960s resulted from changes within the science as well as from its relationship to the Canyon. Figure A-8 plots the age of citations within the literature of American geology. As the science became moribund, it shifted more and more away from the field and into the library. Not until the Third Age does the tempo of the science quicken. Source: Henry Menard, *Science: Growth and Change* (Cambridge: Harvard University Press, 1974).

THE PAINTED CANYON

Figure A-9 traces the growth of Canyon paintings, as "published" in some form or another: within books, exhibition catalogs, gallery collections, etc. Undoubtedly the list is incomplete, particularly in more recent years, but almost certainly the general contour is correct. Several items are clear. First, the early works had an impact out of proportion to their numbers. Second, after the heroic age, art followed rather than led the valorization of the Canyon. Third, until recently, one artist has tended to dominate the Canyon scene, in both numbers and influence. Astonishingly, Thomas Moran's influence extended for over forty years. Sources various.

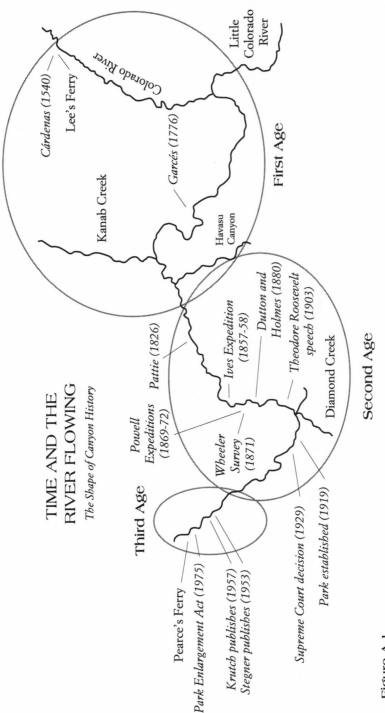

TIME AND THE
RIVER FLOWING
The Shape of Canyon History

First Age

Colorado River

Cárdenas (1540)

Lee's Ferry

Little
Colorado
River

Kanab Creek

Garcés (1776)

Havasu
Canyon

Second Age

Pattie (1826)

Ives Expedition
(1857-58)

Dutton and
Holmes (1880)

Theodore Roosevelt
speech (1903)

Diamond Creek

Third Age

Powell
Expeditions
(1869-72)

Wheeler
Survey
(1871)

Park established (1919)

Supreme Court decision (1929)

Stegner publishes (1953)

Krutch publishes (1957)

Park Enlargement Act (1975)

Pearce's Ferry

Figure A-1.

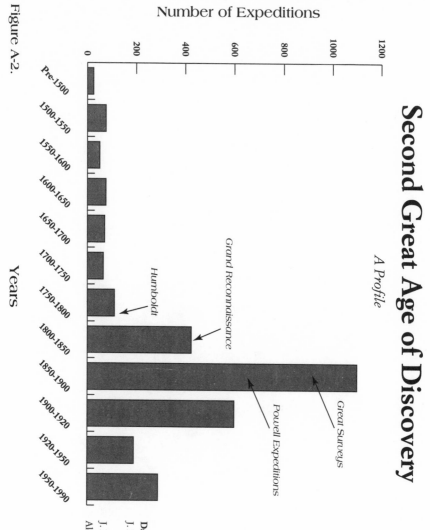

Figure A-2.

Second Great Age of Discovery

A Profile

Number of Expeditions

Years

Pre-1500
1500-1550
1550-1600
1600-1650
1650-1700
1700-1750
1750-1800
1800-1850
1850-1900
1900-1920
1920-1950
1950-1990

Humboldt

Grand Reconnaissance

Powell Expeditions

Great Surveys

Data Sources:
J. N. L. Baker, *A History of Geographical
    Discovery and Exploration*
J. H. Parry, *The Discovery of the Sea*
Alex Roland, ed., *A Spacefaring People*

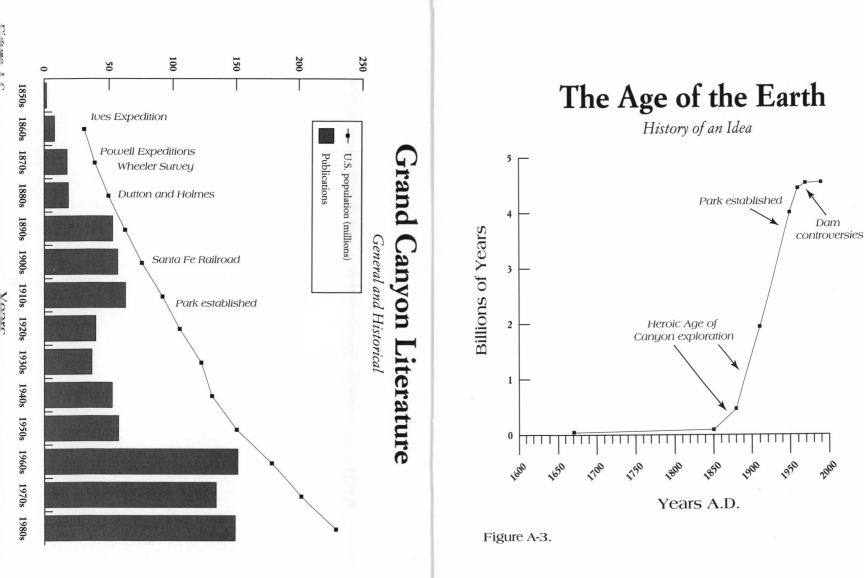

Grand Canyon Literature

General and Historical

- ■ | U.S. population (millions)
- ■ Publications

Ives Expedition

Powell Expeditions
Wheeler Survey

Dutton and Holmes

Santa Fe Railroad

Park established

1850s 1860s 1870s 1880s 1890s 1900s 1910s 1920s 1930s 1940s 1950s 1960s 1970s 1980s

0 50 100 150 200 250

The Age of the Earth

History of an Idea

Park established

Dam
controversies

Heroic Age of
Canyon exploration

Billions of Years

5
4
3
2
1
0

1600 1650 1700 1750 1800 1850 1900 1950 2000

Years A.D.

Figure A-3.

Grand Canyon

Contact and Visitation

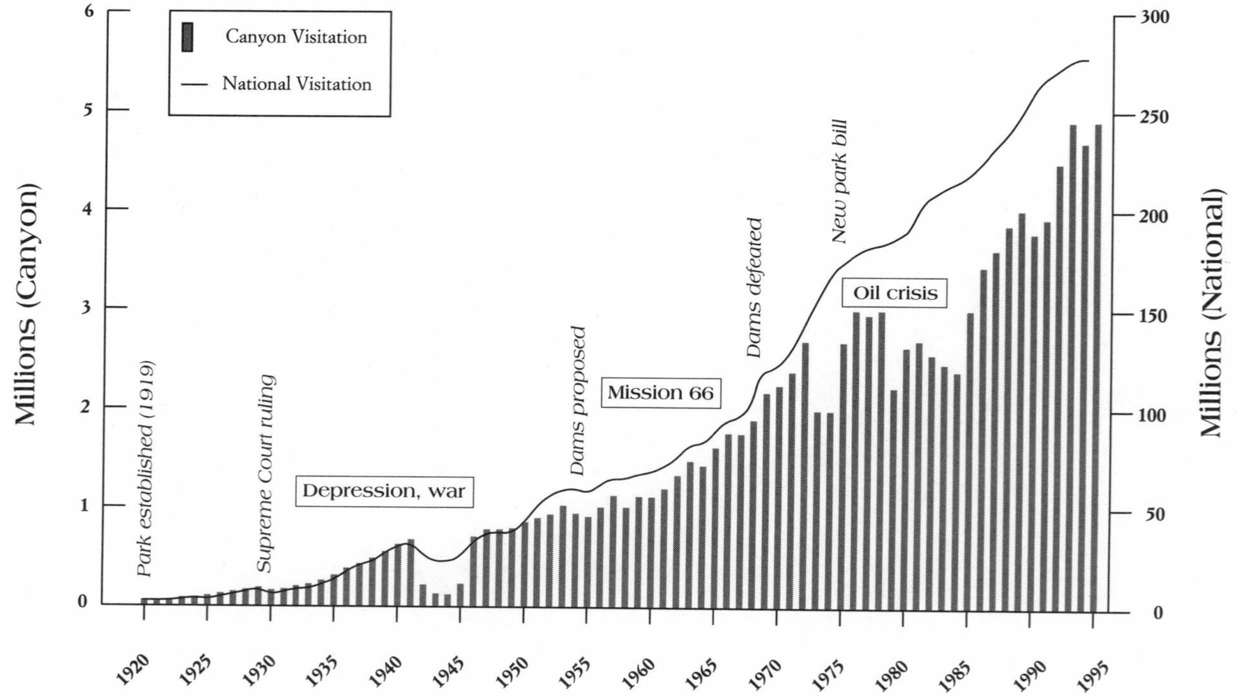
Canyon Visitation
National Visitation
Millions (Canyon)
Millions (National)
0
1
2
3
4
5
6
0
50
100
150
200
250
300
1920
1925
1930
1935
1940
1945
1950
1955
1960
1965
1970
1975
1980
1985
1990
1995
Park established (1919)
Supreme Court ruling
Depression, war
Dams proposed
Mission 66
Dams defeated
New park bill
Oil crisis

Figure A-4.

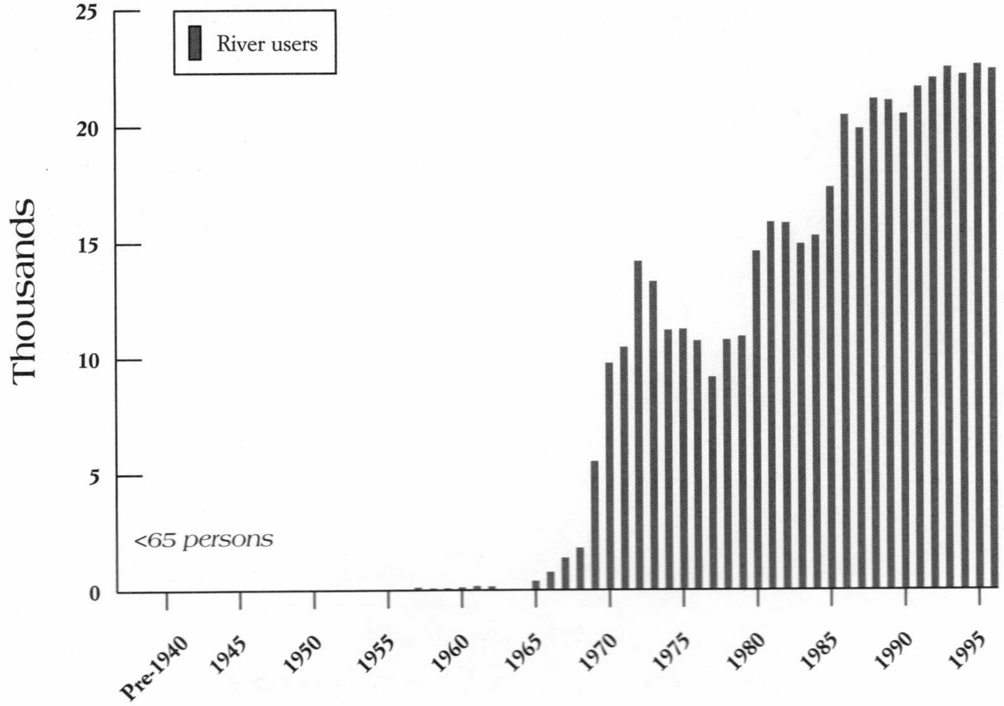
River users
Thousands
0
5
10
15
20
25
<65 persons
Pre-1940
1945
1950
1955
1960
1965
1970
1975
1980
1985
1990
1995

Figure A-5.

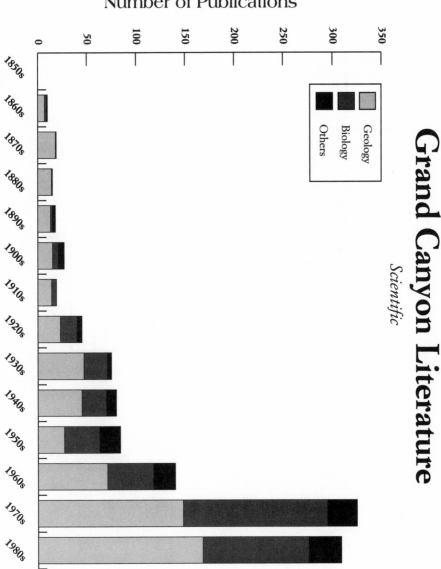

Figure A-7.

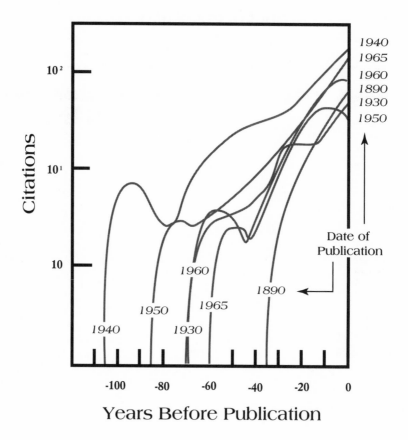

Figure A-8.

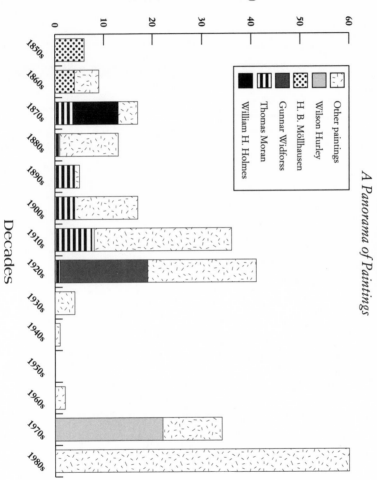

Figure A-9.

NOTES

TWO NEW WORLDS

1. Quoted from "Castañeda's History of the Expedition," p. 11, in Bruce Babbitt, ed., *Grand Canyon: An Anthology* (Flagstaff: Northland Press, 1978).
2. Ibid., p. 12.
3. See William Goetzmann, *New Lands, New Men: The United States and the Second Great Age of Discovery* (New York: Viking, 1986).
4. Elliott Coues, *On the Trail of a Spanish Pioneer*, vol. II (Francis P. Harper, 1900), pp. 347–50.
5. James Ohio Pattie, *Personal Narrative of James O. Pattie of Kentucky*, ed. Timothy Flint and Reuben Thwaites (Arthur H. Clark, 1905), p. 97.
6. Lieutenant Joseph C. Ives, *Report upon the Colorado River of the West*, Senate Ex. Doc., 36th Congress, 1st Session (Washington, D.C.: Government Printing Office, 1861), p. 21.
7. Humboldt, quoted in Douglas Botting, *Humboldt and the Cosmos* (New York: Harper and Row, 1973), p. 76.
8. See Edward S. Wallace, *The Great Reconnaissance: Soldiers, Artists, and Scientists on the Frontier, 1848–1861* (Boston: Little, Brown, 1955) and William Goetzmann, *Army Exploration in the American West, 1803–1863* (New Haven: Yale, 1959) and *Exploration and Empire* (New York: Knopf, 1966). Quote from Goetzmann, *Army Exploration*, p. 5.

RIM AND RIVER

1. Roosevelt quoted, Babbitt, *Grand Canyon*, pp. 187–88.
2. Ives, *Report*, p. 81.
3. Alonso Johnson quoted in Goetzmann, *Army Exploration*, p. 379.
4. See, for example, Ives, *Report*, p. 109.
5. Ibid., p. 110.
6. Humboldt quoted in Ben W. Huseman, *Wild River, Timeless Canyons: Balduin Möllhausen's Watercolors of the Colorado* (Fort Worth: Amon Carter Museum, 1995), p. 30.
7. Ibid., p. 68.
8. Ibid., p. 221.
9. Goetzmann makes this point twice, first in *Army Exploration in the American West, 1803–1861* (New Haven, CT: Yale University Press, 1959), p. 389, and again in *Exploration and Empire* (New York: Knopf, 1966), p. 330.
10. John S. Newberry, in Captain John Macomb, *Exploring Expedition from Santa Fe, New Mexico, to the Junction of the Grand and Green Rivers of the Great Colorado of the West* (Washington, D.C.: Government Printing Office, 1876), p. 54.
11. Dr. J. S. Newberry, "Geological Report," in Ives, *Report*, Part III, p. 45.
12. John S. Newberry, "Report of Progress in 1870," *Geological Survey of Ohio* (Columbus, Ohio: Columbus Printing Co., 1870), p. 14.
13. See Otis "Dock" R. Marston, "Who Named the Grand Canyon?," *Pacific Historian*, Vol. 12, no. 3 (Summer 1968), pp. 4–8; Samuel Bowles, *Our New West* (Hartford, Conn.: Hartford Publishing Co., 1869), p. 500; Powell quoted in William Culp Darrah, *Powell of the Colorado* (Princeton: Princeton University Press, 1962), p. 93.
14. John Wesley Powell, the *Exploration of the Colorado River of the West* (Cambridge: Harvard University Press, 1962, reprint), p. 83; Alexander von Humboldt, *Personal Narrative of a Journey to the Equinoctial Regions of the New Continent*, trans. Jason Wilson (New York: Penguin Books, 1995), p. 203.
15. J. W. Powell, *The Exploration of the Colorado River and Its Canyons*, (New York: Dover Publications, 1961; reprint of *Canyon of the Colorado* [Flood & Vincent, 1895], p. 275.
16. Powell, *Exploration* (Harvard edition), p. 93.
17. Powell, *Exploration* (Dover edition), pp. 390, 397.
18. Wallace Stegner makes the point nicely when he observes that no place, even a wild place, is a place until it has a poet. Certainly this was true for the Canyon and aptly describes Powell's contribution. Stegner, *Where the*

Bluebird Sings to the Lemonade Springs (New York: Penguin Books, 1992), p. 295.

19. Captain George M. Wheeler, "Geographical Report," *U.S. Geographical Survey West of the 100th Meridian* (Washington, D.C.: Government Printing Office, 1889), p. 170.

20. G. K. Gilbert to J. W. Powell, 09-24-75, "Letters Received," Powell Survey, Record Group 57, National Archives.

21. Captain G. M. Wheeler, *Report Upon United States Geographical Surveys West of the One Hundredth Meridian*, vol. I, Geographical Report (Washington, D.C.: Government Printing Office, 1889) p. 170.

22. Bailey Willis, *A Yanqui in Patagonia* (Palo Alto, Calif.: Stanford University Press, 1947), p. 33.

23. Personal telephone interview with Edwin McKee.

24. John Muir, "Wild Parks and Forest Reservations of the West," *Atlantic Monthly* (January 1898), p. 28.

25. Clarence E. Dutton, *Tertiary History of the Grand Cañon District*, U.S. Geological Survey Monograph 2 (Washington, D.C.: Government Printing Office, 1882), p. 141.

26. Wallace Stegner, *Beyond the Hundredth Meridian* (Boston: Houghton Mifflin, 1954), pp. 173–74.

27. The primary sources of biographical material on Dutton are: Wallace E. Stegner, "Clarence Edward Dutton: Geologist and Man of Letters," Ph.D. thesis (University of Iowa, 1935), later published as *Clarence Edward Dutton: An Appraisal* (Salt Lake City: University of Utah, 1936); George F. Becker, "Major C. E. Dutton [obituary]," *American Journal of Science*, 4th ser., vol. 33, no. 196 (1912), pp. 387–88; J. S. Diller, "Major Clarence Edward Dutton," *Bulletin of the Seismological Society of America*, vol. 1, no. 4 (1911), pp. 137–42, and "Memoir of Clarence Edward Dutton," *Geological Society of America Bulletin*, vol. 24 (1913), pp. 10–18; and an autobiographical sketch, dated December 20, 1886, contained in the Marcus Benjamin Papers, Record Unit 7085, Smithsonian Institution Archives, which is the major source of Dutton quotes in the referenced passage.

28. See autobiographical sketch in Marcus Benjamin Papers, loc. cit.

29. Clarence Dutton to J. W. Powell, September 17, 1876, "Letters Received," Powell Survey, Record Group 57, National Archives.

30. Clarence E. Dutton, "Mount Taylor and the Zuñi Plateau," U.S. Geological Survey, *Annual Report*, vol. 6 (Washington, D.C.: Government Printing Office, 1885), p. 113.

31. Clarence E. Dutton, *Report on the Geology of the High Plateaus, Utah* (Washington, D.C.: Government Printing Office, 1880), p. 284.

32. Dutton, *Tertiary History*, p. 141.
33. Ibid., p. xvi.
34. Ibid., pp. 142–43.
35. Samuel Emmons to G. F. Becker, June 16, 1882, "General Correspondence," George F. Becker Papers, Library of Congress.
36. Dutton quoted in Mary Rabbitt, *Minerals, Lands, and Geology for the Common Defense and General Welfare, vol. 2, 1879–1904* (Washington, D.C.: U.S. Geological Survey, 1980), p. 42.
37. Ibid., p. 104.
38. Dutton to W. H. Holmes, 1899, "Random Records . . . ," vol. 8, pp. 91–94, William H. Holmes Papers, National Portrait Gallery.
39. Dutton quoted by Diller, "Major Clarence Edward Dutton," p. 18.
40. Thomas Moran, "New World," in Charles Lummis, *Mesa, Cañon, and Pueblo* (New York: Century Co., 1925), p. 504. The exact date for Cole's *The Oxbow* is unclear. The best guess is that Cole worked on the painting between 1836 and 1838, with the latter date marking its completion.
41. Moran, quoted in G. W. Sheldon, *American Painters* (New York: D. Appleton and Co., 1879), p. 125.
42. Moran, ibid., p. 124.
43. Dutton, *Tertiary History*, p. 164.
44. Moran, "New World," p. 505
45. Moran quoted in Thurman Wilkens, *Thomas Moran: Artist of the Mountains* (Norman: University of Oklahoma Press, 1966), p. 4.
46. Quoted in Wilken, *Thomas Moran*, p. 238.
47. Dutton, *Tertiary History*, p. 142.
48. William H. Goetzmann, *William H. Holmes: Panoramic Art* (Fort Worth: Amon Carter Museum, 1977).
49. C. L. Walcott, "Pre-Carboniferous Strata in the Grand Canyon of the Colorado, Arizona," *American Journal of Science*, 3d ser., vol. 26 (1883), p. 437; Dutton letter to Geikie, quoted in Rabbitt, *Minerals, Lands*, p. 71. I have benefited from an unpublished paper, "C. D. Walcott and the Grand Canyon," that Ellis L. Yochelson, its author, generously shared with me.
50. William Morris Davis, "The Lessons of the Colorado Canyon," *American Geographical Society Bulletin*, vol. 41 (1909), p. 346.
51. Davis, "crack piece," quoted in Richard Chorley et al., *The History of the Study of Landforms; or, The Development of Geomorphology*, vol. 2, *The Life and Work of William Morris Davis* (London: Methuen, 1974), p. 727.
52. Geikie quoted in Gordon Davies, *Earth in Decay* (New York: Neal Watson, 1969), p. 352.
53. Roosevelt quoted in Paul Schullery, ed., *The Grand Canyon: Early*

Impressions (Boulder: Colorado Associated University Press, 1981), pp. 101–02.

CANYON AND COSMOS

1. James quoted in Richard Hofstadter, *Social Darwinism in American Thought* (Boston: Beacon Press, 1944), p. 129.
2. See Ferde Grofé, "Story of Grand Canyon Suite," *Arizona Highways*, vol. 14 (December 1938), pp. 6–9.
3. Bruce E. Babbitt, *Color and Light: The Southwest Canvases of Louis Akin* (Flagstaff: Northland Press, 1973), p. 23.
4. Katherine Plake Hough et al., *Carl Oscar Borg: A Niche in Time* (Palm Springs, Calif.: Palm Springs Desert Museum, 1990), p. 57.
5. Helen Laird, "Carl Oscar Borg," ibid., p. 43.
6. Bill Belknap and Frances Spencer Belknap, *Gunnar Widforss: Painter of the Grand Canyon* (Flagstaff: Northland Press, 1969), p. 25.
7. Ibid., pp. 74–75.
8. Archibald Geikie, "*The Tertiary History of the Grand Cañon District*," *Nature* (February 15, 1883), p. 357.
9. Ellsworth Kolb, *Through the Grand Canyon from Wyoming to Mexico* (New York: Macmillan, 1914), p. 3.
10. Ibid., p. 4.
11. Robert C. Euler, "Foreword," in Babbitt, *Grand Canyon,* p. ix.
12. J. B. Priestley, "Midnight on the Desert," ibid., pp. 103–04
13. For the expedition's story, see "Harold E. Anthony, "The Facts About Shiva," pp. 709–22, 766, and George B. Andrews, "Scaling Wotan's Throne," pp. 723–24, 766, *Natural History*, vol. XL, no. 5 (December 1937).
14. Priestley, "Midnight on the Desert," p. 104.
15. Samuel Trask Dana and Sally K. Fairfax, *Forest and Range Policy: Its Development in the United States*, 2d ed. (New York: McGraw-Hill Book Co., 1980), p. 426.
16. Joseph Wood Krutch, *Grand Canyon: Today and All Its Yesterdays* (New York: William Morrow and Co., 1957), p. 275.
17. Ibid., p. 276.
18. Stegner's quote from p. 197, as reproduced in Wallace Stegner, "The Meaning of Wilderness in American Civilization," pp. 192–97, in Roderick Nash, *The American Environment: Readings in the History of Conservation* (Menlo Park, Calif.: Addison-Wesley Publishing Co., 1968); A. S. Leopold et al., "Wildlife Management in the National Parks," *Compilation of the Adminis-*

trative Policies for the National Parks and National Monuments of Scientific Significance, rev. ed. (Washington, D.C.: Government Printing Office, 1970), p. 101.

19. Roderick Nash, "The Perils and Possibilities of a Park," in Roderick Nash, ed., *Grand Canyon of the Living Colorado* (New York: Sierra Club-Ballantine Books, 1970), p. 102.

20. Roderick Nash, *Wilderness and the American Mind*, 3d ed. (New Haven: Yale University Press, 1982), p. 230.

21. François Leydet, *Time and the River Flowing: Grand Canyon* (San Francisco: Sierra Club, 1964), p. 84; Nash, "Perils and Possibilities," p. 107; Hyde quoted in Robert Weinstein and Roger Olmstead, "Image Makers of the Colorado Canyons," *American West*, vol. IV, no. 2 (May 1967), p. 38.

SOURCES
AND FURTHER READINGS

The existence of Earle Spamer's magisterial bibliography of the Grand Canyon, regularly updated, makes it pointless for me to offer some perfunctory summary of sources. Besides, that kind of archival research was not my purpose in writing this book. The notes provide full citations for all the quotations lodged within the text. For any other literature connecting to the Canyon, consult Earle E. Spamer, compiler, *Bibliography of the Grand Canyon and the Lower Colorado River from 1540*, Monograph Number 8, Grand Canyon Natural History Association (1990).

Instead I would like to elaborate on those materials that helped me contextualize the Grand Canyon story and that might not turn up in conventional, place-specific bibliographies. Many are biographical studies of significant Canyon figures. Often these works were my point of departure into other realms of scholarship, and it should go without saying that I could have included hundreds of other studies. But these are the books with which I began and to which I continually returned.

EXPLORATION. Begin with William H. Goetzmann's classic trilogy: *Army Exploration in the American West, 1803–1863* (1959), which reaches a climax with the Ives Expedition; *Exploration and Empire: The Explorer and the Scientist in the Winning of the American West* (1966), which places Canyon discovery within the context of western American exploration; and *New Lands, New Men: The United States and the Second Great Age of Discovery* (1986), which situates American exploration within a global setting. Very useful too is William Goetzmann and Glyndwr Williams, *The Atlas of North American Exploration* (1992), which distills five hundred years of European discovery into a delightful suite of maps. Pair it with Carl I. Wheat, *Mapping the Trans-Mississippi West, 1540–1861*, 5 vols. (1957–63).

A useful summary of global surveys, despite its British bias, is J. N. L. Baker, *A History of Geographical Discovery and Exploration*, rev. ed. (1967). To complement it with a more visually graphic style, see Eric Newby, *The Rand McNally World Atlas of Exploration* (1975) and especially Glyn Williams and Felipe Fernandez Armesto, eds., *The Times Atlas of World Exploration* (1991). For understanding the character of the First Age, see the many marvelous works of J. H. Parry, but especially *The Establishment of the European Hegemony, 1415–1715* (1961), *The Discovery of the Sea* (1974), and *The Age of the Reconnaissance* (1963). For the ocean-based transition to the Second Age, see J. C. Beaglehole, *The Exploration of the Pacific*, 3d ed. (1966) and Jacques Brosse, *Great Voyages of Discovery: Circumnavigators and Scientists, 1764–1843* (1983). Goetzmann's *New Lands, New Men* (above) is the defining study of the Second Age. To appreciate New Spain's contributions, see Iris Engstrand, *Spanish Scientists in the New World: The Eighteenth-Century Expeditions* (1981). To understand Humboldt's status, see Helmut de Terra, *Humboldt: The Life and Times of Alexander von Humboldt, 1769–1959* (1955). And for John Wesley Powell's, see, in addition to Wallace Stegner's "biography of a career," *Beyond the Hundredth Meridian* (1953), William Culp Darrah, *Powell of the Colorado* (1950). For an introduction to the Third Age, see Stephen Pyne, *The Ice* (1986), and "Space: the Third Great Age of Discovery" in Martin Collins and Sylvia Fries, eds., *Space: Discovery and Exploration* (1994). Contemporary reviews of IGY are available in Sydney Chapman, *IGY: Year of Discovery* (1960) and J. Tuzo Wilson, *IGY: The Year of the New Moons* (1961).

EARTH SCIENCE. The historical literature on geology is large. William Sarjeant, *Geologists and the History of Geology: An International Bibliography from the Origins to 1978. Supplement, 1979–84* (1987), and the U.S. Geological Survey's *Bibliography of North American Geology* remain indispensable references.

Intellectual and institutional histories continue to thrive. Still useful is

Frank Dawson Adams, *The Birth and Development of the Geological Sciences* (1954). For physical geography, see Preston James, *All Possible Worlds: A History of Geographical Ideas* (1972). Of special significance to Canyon interpretation, however, are the three volumes by Richard Chorley et al., *The History of the Study of Landforms; or, The Development of Geomorphology* (1964–82). Volume 2 is an intellectual biography of William Morris Davis.

For American geology, George Merrill, *The First Hundred Years of American Geology* (1924) remains unsurpassed for breadth and detail. For an effort to tell the larger story through the career of one geologist, see Stephen Pyne, *Grove Karl Gilbert* (1980). On the U.S. Geological Survey, see Thomas Manning, *Government in Science: The U.S. Geological Survey* (1967) and Mary E. Rabbitt's multivolumed series, *Minerals, Lands and Geology for the Common Defense and General Welfare,* (1979–), and in distilled form, *The United States Geological Survey, 1879–1989* (1989). Overwritten but helpful as a complement to Goetzmann's *Exploration and Empire* is Richard Bartlett, *Great Surveys of the American West* (1962). For a comparison of themes and styles with the Third Age, see Don E. Wilhelm, *To a Rocky Moon: A Geologist's History of Lunar Exploration* (1993) and Henry Menard, *The Ocean of Truth: A Personal History of Global Tectonics* (1986).

Many critical Canyon scientists still lack bona fide biographies. In their absence, consider the following sketches: Ellis L. Yochelson, "Charles D. Walcott," *Geotimes* (March 1979), pp. 26–29, for a wonderful profile of an oft-overlooked individual; J. F. Kemp, "Memorial of J. S. Newberry," *Geological Society of America Bulletin*, vol. 4 (1893), pp. 393–406; Clifford M. Nelson, "William Henry Holmes: Beginning a Career in Art and Science," *Columbia Historical Society* 50 (1980), pp. 252–78; and Fritiof Fryxell, ed., *François Matthes and the Marks of Time* (1962). Ellis Yochelson has written a biography of Walcott's career in the Geological Survey, *Charles Doolittle Walcott, Paleontologist*, to be published by Kent State University Press.

The controversy over the age of the earth was so fundamental in defining geology that it is difficult to tease it out of general histories. A good introduction to the early eras is Charles Gillespie's classic *Genesis and Geology* (1951), while Martin J. S. Rudwick, *The Meaning of Fossils: Episodes in the History of Paleontology* (1985) helps move the story along. Perhaps the best source is the evolution of Arthur Holmes's *The Age of the Earth* (many editions). A survey of the debate as it existed at the time Dutton et al. were interpreting the Canyon is Joe Birchfield, *Lord Kelvin and the Age of the Earth* (1975).

The related controversy over Darwin shows few signs of abating; there is no point here in elaborating on that scholarly industry. As good a contextual summary as any is Ernst Mayr, *The Growth of Biological Thought* (1982).

ARTS. Western art, landscapes, and national traditions are the subject of innumerable studies. Three books that I have found notably useful are Barbara Novak, *Nature and Culture. American Landscape and Painting, 1825–1875* (1980), for its explication of trends that culminated in the heroic age of Canyon painting; Simon Schama, *Landscape and Memory* (1995), for showing how art contributes to a valorization of landscapes; and William H. Goetzmann and William N. Goetzmann, *The West of the Imagination* (1986), for elaborating the art criticism contained in the senior author's earlier *Exploration and Empire*. Several books illuminate the northern New Mexico school; consider, for example, Arrell Gibson, *The Santa Fe and Taos Colonies: Age of the Muses 1900–1942* (1983).

The Mesa Southwest Museum sponsored an exhibition on Canyon art in 1987, published as Tray C. Mead, ed., *Capturing the Canyon: Artists in the Grand Canyon* (1987). But most Canyon art remains within the context of biographical studies or retrospective exhibitions by individual artists. Published collections include: Bruce Babbitt, *Color and Light: The Southwest Canvases of Louis Akin* (1973); Helen Laird, *Carl Oscar Borg and the Magic Region* (1986); Katherine Plake Hough et al., *Carl Oscar Borg: A Niche in Time* (1990); Peter Hassrick and Ellen J. Landis, *Wilson Hurley: A Retrospective Exhibition* (1985); Bill Kelknap and Frances Spencer Belknap, *Gunnar Widforss: Painter of the Grand Canyon* (1969); and Donald J. Hagerty, *Beyond the Visible Landscape: The Art of Ed Mell* (1996). Uneven but enlightening is James D. Horan, *Timothy O'Sullivan: America's Forgotten Photographer* (1966).

Perhaps appropriately Thomas Moran has inspired a virtual cottage industry of studies and plentiful exhibitions. A good biography is Thurman Wilkins, *Thomas Moran: Artist of the Mountains* (1966). Recent commentaries include Nancy K. Anderson, *Thomas Moran* (1997).

ENVIRONMENTAL HISTORY AND CANYON HISTORY. For the reinterpretation of the Canyon as wilderness, there is no better beginning than Roderick Nash, *Wilderness and the American Mind*, 3d ed. (1983). The

Echo Park controversy that led to the Canyon dam controversy is the subject of several studies, especially Elmo Richardson, *Dams, Parks, and Politics: Resource Development and Preservation in the Truman-Eisenhower Era* (1973) and Mark Harvey, *A Symbol of Wilderness: Echo Park and the American Conservation Movement* (1994). A fascinating scientific critique from the same era is L. B. Leopold and T. Maddock, *The Flood Control Controversy* (1954). To see how the controversy merged with the general history of the park, see J. Donald Hughes's mysteriously named *In the House of Stone and Light* (1978). The political history is continued in Barbara J. Morehouse, *A Place Called Grand Canyon: Contested Geographies* (1996).

In recent years biographies have appeared for several major Canyon interpreters. Powell continues to fascinate (see Exploration). John D. Margolis, *Joseph Wood Krutch: A Writer's Life* (1980) places Krutch's Canyon book within his larger career, as Jackson Benson, *Wallace Stegner: His Life and Work* (1996) does for Stegner's Powell study.

INDEX

Army Corps of Topographical
Engineers (U.S.), 34–36
early, of Colorado River, 17
Egloffstein, 44
inventory of the Canyon, 128–29
Ives Expedition, 40
Matthes's contribution, 127–28
Renaissance-era, 4, 5, 9
Cataract Canyon, 39
Catesby, Mark, 33
Cather, Willa, 120
Catlin, George, 33
Central Arizona Project, 153
Chamberlin, Thomas, 130
Chasm of the Colorado, 89, 91, 92
Chicxulub Crater, 148
Church, Frederick, 30, 33
circumnavigation, 12, 14, 15
Civilian Conservation Corps (CCC),
142
Civil War, 35, 55
cliff recession, theory of, 82
Coconino Plateau, 25
Cody, Buffalo Bill, 109
Colbert, Edwin, 149–50
Colorado Exploring Expedition,
38
Colorado Plateau, 47–48
Dutton surveys, 75–84
Colorado River, 153
as Canyon's central metaphor,
155–57
erosion, xi
Escalante-Domínguez Expedition,
17
maps, 6
quasi equilibrium model, 149
Spanish view, 21
as time line, 163, 167
Colorado River Expedition, 68
commercialism, 117–18
photography, 133–35

Condamine, Charles-Marie de la, 14,
16
conservation, 135
continental drift, 131, 150
Cook, Captain James, 14–15
Corle, Edwin, 140
Coronado, Francisco Vásquez de, 5, 9
Cosmos Club, 73
Council of Trent, 8
cultural history of canyon,
heroic age, xv, 169
cultural landscape, xii

dam system proposed, 142–43
Dana, James Dwight, 49
Darwin, Charles, 32
Darwinism, 38
antiquity of the earth, 51
debates, 56
neo-Darwinian synthesis, 138
Newberry reconciling theology
with, 49–50
Davis, William Morris, 67, 107–9, 127
Death Comes for the Archbishop
(1927), 120
Dellenbaugh, Frederick, 112
development schemes, postwar,
140–43
De Voto, Bernard, 142
Diamond Creek, 40–41
Dinosaur National Monument, 141
Dirac, P. A. M., 131
discovery of canyon
ancient peoples, 3–4
nineteenth century, 2–3
sixteenth century, 2
Spanish conquistadors, 4–10
Domínguez, Francisco, 17
Doré, Gustave, 45
Düsseldorf school, 33
influencing Moran, 88

Late Nights on Air

BOOKS BY ELIZABETH HAY

FICTION

Crossing the Snow Line (stories, 1989)
Small Change (stories, 1997)
A Student of Weather (2000)
Garbo Laughs (2003)

NON-FICTION

The Only Snow in Havana (1992)
Captivity Tales: Canadians in New York (1993)

LATE

NIGHTS

ON

AIR

ELIZABETH
HAY

McClelland & Stewart

LIBRARY AND ARCHIVES CANADA CATALOGUING IN PUBLICATION

Hay, Elizabeth, 1951-

Late nights on air / Elizabeth Hay.

ISBN 978-0-7710-3811-2

I. Title.

PS8565.A875L38 2007   C813'.54   C2007-902009-7

We acknowledge the financial support of the Government of Canada through the Book Publishing Industry Development Program and that of the Government of Ontario through the Ontario Media Development Corporation's Ontario Book Initiative. We further acknowledge the support of the Canada Council for the Arts and the Ontario Arts Council for our publishing program.

Typeset in Fournier by M&S, Toronto
Printed and bound in Canada

ANCIENT FOREST
FRIENDLY

This book was produced using ancient-forest friendly papers.

McClelland & Stewart Ltd.
75 Sherbourne Street
Toronto, Ontario
M5A 2P9
www.mcclelland.com

4 5   11 10 09 08 07

In memory of David Turney

1952 – 1988

Late Nights on Air

HARRY WAS IN HIS LITTLE HOUSE on the edge of Back Bay when at half past twelve her voice came over the radio for the first time. A voice unusual in its sound and unusual in itself, since there were no other female announcers on air. He listened to the slow, clear, almost unnatural confidence, the low-pitched sexiness, the elusive accent as she read the local news. More than curious, already in love, he walked into the station the next day at precisely the same time.

It was the beginning of June, the start of the long, golden summer of 1975 when northern light held that little radio station in the large palm of its hand. Eleanor Dew was behind the receptionist's desk and behind clever Eleanor was the studio. She looked up, surprised. Harry rarely darkened the station door except at night when he came in to do the late shift and got away with saying and playing whatever he liked. He paused beside her desk and with a broad wink asked about the new person on air.

"Hired off the street," she told him. "The parting shot of our erstwhile manager."

"Well, well, well," said Harry.

Despite the red glow of the on-air light, he then pushed through the studio door, only to be met by one of the great mysteries of life. We look so very different from the way we sound. It's a shock, similar to hearing your own voice for the first time, when you're forced to wonder how the rest of you comes across if you sound nothing like the way you think you sound. You feel dislodged from the old shoe of yourself.

Harry had pictured somebody short and compact with sun-bleached hair, fine blue eyes, great legs, a woman in her thirties. But Dido Paris was tall, big-boned, olive-skinned, younger. Glasses. Thick, dark, springy hair held back off a wide face. Faintest shadow on her upper lip. An unreasonably beautiful woman. She didn't look up, too intent on the newscast typed in capital letters on green paper, three-part greens, the paper-and-carbon combination the newsmen typed on.

He turned to check who was in the control room. Eddy at the controls and one of the newsmen standing at Eddy's shoulder. An audience, in other words.

Harry took out his lighter, flicked it, and put the flame to the top corner of the green. And still she didn't look up.

An upper lip as downy as he imagined her legs might be. And yes, when she stood up later and came around the table, her legs were visible below a loose blue skirt, and the mystery of her voice was solved. She was European. European in her straightforwardness, her appearance, her way of speaking, which was almost too calm, except when the page was alight. Then her voice caught fire. She stopped turning her long pencil end on end, pacing herself. Stopped speaking altogether. Her eyes went in two directions – one leg on shore, the other in the canoe, but the canoe was pulling away from shore and *shit* – she picked up her glass, poured water on the flames, and read with jolting speed, repressed panic, to the very last word at the bottom of the page.

The news clip came on, she switched off her microphone and looked up wildly at the man with the boyish gleam in his eye. But he wasn't boyish, he was balding, bespectacled, square-jawed. She noticed his cauliflower ear.

"You're Harry Boyd," she said.

And she, too, had imagined another face – a big, bushy head to go with the relaxed, late-night growl that she heard only as she fell asleep. The man who'd once been a big name in radio, she'd been told. He was shorter than she'd expected and his hands trembled.

Half an hour later, perched on Dido's desk, bumming a cigarette, Harry asked her how she'd come by her intriguing accent. She studied him, not quite willing to forgive his outrageous behaviour, until he asked if she was Greek. Then out bubbled her easy and seductive laugh.

No chance. She'd grown up in the Netherlands near the German border, the daughter of a Latin teacher who'd listened to the BBC and written questions to "London Calling" about expressions he didn't understand. Her father had a reel-to-reel tape recorder and taped programs off the radio. She learned English at school, she told Harry, but her pronunciation was terrible and so she'd asked her father to make some tapes for her, and then she practised her English listening to Margaret Leighton reading Noel Coward and to Noel Coward himself, acquiring in that way her peculiar European-English accent, which she hated. "I figured marriage to a Canadian would solve my problem, but it hasn't."

"Two minutes," said Harry, "and you're already breaking my heart."

"It didn't last," she said.

"Then we have something in common, you and I."

He slipped her glasses off her face and breathed on the lenses and polished them with his handkerchief, then slid them back over her nose, saying, "And Dorothy Parker said men never make passes at girls with glasses."

"Parker?"

"Dorothy. A writerly wit who famously claimed to be 'too fucking busy and vice versa.'"

Dido was only semi-amused. To Eleanor the next day she called Harry "the loser," a put-down softened by her accent; it came out "lose-air." She said he'd taken a drag off her lit cigarette, then set it back on the ashtray. "So cheap," she said with a shake of her head and a faint, unimpressed smile.

"But not without charm," countered Eleanor. "Charm, sex, insecurity: that's what Harry has to offer."

Dido was more interested now.

"He's too old for you, Dido."

But his age was the last thing Dido minded.

Harry was forty-two. Winds of ill repute had blown him back up on these shores – a man with a nearly forgotten reputation for brilliance, one of those lucky luckless people who finds his element early on and then makes the mistake of leaving it – radio for a television talk show, where he'd bombed. In short order, he was fired, his personal life fell apart, rumours rose up and settled down. A year ago an old boss stumbled across him sleeping in a hotel lobby in Toronto and pulled a few strings to get him a night shift in the Northern Service, the very place where he'd started out fifteen years ago. At square one again, but with a difference. Now he was an *old* fish in a small pond.

And yet it suited him – the place, the hours, the relative obscurity.

Stories about him circulated: how he had numerous ex-wives, and a tremendous tolerance for liquor, and some dark deed in his past – some disgrace. Professional, certainly. Sexual? No one was quite sure. His cauliflower ear suggested a life touched by violence. His trembling hands sent granules of instant coffee scattering in all directions. "Harry's been here," they would say in the morning, surveying the little table that held mugs, spoons, the electric kettle, the big jar of Maxwell House.

In that first conversation Harry asked Dido about her husband, tell me all about him, and she jested that she'd married almost the first person who asked her, a fellow student at McGill, but when he brought her from Montreal through the gates of his rich Halifax neighbourhood, she saw his father in the driveway. "And we just looked at each other," she said, turning the oversized man's watch on her wrist in what Harry would come to understand was a yearning, nervous habit. "We just looked." Harry saw them, a man and woman unable to take their eyes off each other, and the picture cut into his heart.

After a moment Dido shrugged, but her face still ran with longing and regret. The situation became impossible, she admitted. She escaped the triangle by coming north.

"And your father-in-law let you go?"

She gestured towards the entrance of the station. "I half expect him to come through that door."

———

The radio station occupied a quiet corner a block away from main street. It had been an electrical supplies store once, Top Electric, and was that size. A one-storey shoebox in a town that had sprung up in the 1930s on the gold-rich shores of Great Slave Lake, an inland sea one-third the size of troubled Ireland.

Entering, the first person you saw was Eleanor Dew, who managed to be pretty even though no part of her was pretty. She had rather bulging eyes and a chin that blended into her throat, yet she gave off an idea of Blondness, a sort of radiance that came from having her feet on the ground and her head in heaven. At thirty-six she was almost the oldest person in the station and a poet at heart, reading Milton between phone calls – the community announcements coming in, the complaints and song requests, the mixture of personal and business calls for the six announcer-operators or the two newsmen or the station manager, who had run off with a waitress a week ago.

Her desk stood next to a plate-glass window that overlooked the dusty street leading up to the Gold Range, also known as the Strange Range, and to Franklin Avenue, the main street with two stoplights. Turn left on Franklin Avenue and you passed on one side MacLeod's Hardware and the Hudson's Bay Store and on the other side the Capitol Theatre with its third-run movies and fifth-rate popcorn machine. Continue on in the same direction through the newest part of New Town, and then angle left, and eventually you came around to

Cominco, one of the two operating gold mines that gave the town its initial reason for being. If, instead, you turned right on Franklin Avenue you passed the Yellowknife Inn on one side and the post office on the other, you passed the public library and the clothing store known as Eve of the Arctic. Proceed in a down-sloping northerly direction and you reached the oldest part of Old Town, an array of little houses and shacks and log cabins and privies, of Quonset huts and trailers and motley businesses, all of which seemed perfectly at ease on this rocky peninsula under the enormous sky. Well, they weren't competing with it. Yellowknife had only one high-rise and it wasn't on main street, it was a lonely apartment building in the southeastern part of town.

A rudimentary place of ten thousand people named after an indigenous tribe that used knives made of copper, and in many ways it was a white blot on the native landscape. But it was as far north as most southerners had ever come. It was north of the sixtieth parallel and shared in the romance of the North, emanating not mystery but uniqueness and not right away. It had no breathtaking scenery. No mountains, no glaciers, in the winter not even that much snow. But after a while it grew on them, on some of them at least, on the ones who would never forget, who would think back on their lives and say, My time there was the most vivid time in my life.

Only two stoplights, perhaps, but such a traffic in voices. That summer a small but steady parade of poets came through town, unconnected to the parade of experts addressing Judge Berger at his inquiry into what would be, if it went ahead, the largest single development project ever undertaken in the Western world, a gas pipeline running across the top of the Arctic and down the eight-hundred-mile-length of the Mackenzie River. Politics overshadowed poetry, as it always does. The poets came one at a time throughout the summer, a modest incursion and the first of its kind, organized by a local poetry lover and financed by the national council for the arts. The pipeline experts came in droves, it seemed, gathering at the gleaming white Explorer Hotel that dominated the road on the way to the airport. It was a time when Yellowknife was on the map, when the North was on everyone's minds, when the latest scheme to extract its riches had gained so much ground that this summer of 1975 took on the mythical quality of a cloudless summer before the outbreak of war, or before the onset of the kind of restlessness, social, spiritual, that remakes the world.

Harry went to a few of the literary readings at the public library. He went with Eleanor, who wrote poetry for her own pleasure, until he lost patience with what he called the empty wordplay. How can a poem last, he cried, if it doesn't touch your heart? You might remember the poet, he declared, but you won't remember the poem. To underscore his point he typed out verses from a poem he admired and taped them to the wall in the one and only announce booth, where their message about death and its haunting aftermath was like a skull sitting on the console. The poem was by Alden Nowlan, who came from Harry's part of southern New Brunswick, and it described the foolish time in the poet's life when he worked alone at night in a radio station and couldn't believe anyone was listening, for "it seemed I was talking / only to myself in a room no bigger / than an ordinary bathroom." Then one day he had to cover a fatal collision between a car and a train, and Nowlan the broadcaster turned into Nowlan the appalled listener. "Inside the wreckage" of the car, three young men were dead, but the car radio was still playing and "nobody could get at it" to turn it off. Across the top margin Harry scrawled, *Do you ever wonder where your voice goes?*

The more personal question he avoided asking himself. How had he ended up back here, where he'd started, in the little rabbit warren of rooms known as CFYK? Sitting in the announce booth, feeling his own life collide with itself.

Eleanor was the station's gatekeeper. From her desk she controlled access to a single hallway that led like a short main street directly through the guts of the station to an exit that tumbled you back out into the northern summer – to a garbage bin full to overflowing with tape so edited, so beknuckled and thickened with white splicing tape as to be deemed unsalvageable, finally, by the head technician in his basement lair. Crusty Andrew McNab presided over the station's nether region of workbenches, labelled shelves, crowded corners, and his own tidy desk. For seventeen years he'd practised frugality and extravagant disdain, *fathead* being his favourite term for anyone conceited enough to go on air.

Andrew's wasn't the only lair. The newsroom, just large enough for two newsmen and two desks and one editing machine, was another. Its firmly closed door lay directly in the line of fire between Eleanor's desk and the front door of the station through which the town's characters liked to come. Mrs. Dargabble, for instance, with her lofty, loquacious, regular plea for classical music. I don't expect opera, but a little Mozart from time to time? Eleanor couldn't have

agreed more. She wrote down the request, then tossed it sadly
into the wastebasket as soon as the poor woman turned her
back, since there was no hope, she knew. No hope for Mozart
in Yellowknife.

Until Harry Boyd passed by one day recently and
rumbled at the hefty, flapping, fragile woman, "Do you like
Lucia Popp?"

"She sings the Queen of the Night," said the startled Mrs.
Dargabble.

"Tonight I'll play her for you. Turn on your radio at midnight."

"You *mar*vellous man. You under*stand*."

By now Harry was haunting the station at all hours and
it was obvious to everyone why. He wanted to be around
Dido Paris.

"How will I recognize him?" Harry had asked her, his
voice a-growl with mock irony and serious intent. "This
fancy man of yours. Your father-in-law."

She had a long, slow smile. "You're a romantic, Harry."

"I'm not ashamed of it."

He saw her face give way once again to such tender
sadness that his lonely insides twisted and tightened. But then
he took heart. "You like older men."

Dido leaned back and laughed at him. "Harry, you're so
transparent."

He wasn't ashamed of that either. He recognized in Dido a
deep streak of melancholy that he happened to share, and he
was fascinated, not least by a childhood he guessed was partly
to blame. Holland after the war. Not Holland, she corrected.
The Netherlands. She told him her mother sewed warm winter

pants for her from old army uniforms and she had to wear pyjamas underneath, otherwise the khaki chafed her thighs and made them bleed. At the look on his face, she smiled and touched his arm. It wasn't so bad, she said. In a way, I didn't mind. And you won't believe how much I miss what I ate then, chocolate sprinkles on bread, we put the butter on top of the sprinkles to keep them in place, and speculaas – you know? the Dutch windmill cookie? – between two slices of buttered bread. I bicycled to school and took that for my lunch. Her voice had a buoyant, velvety sound. Sensual, but not so sensual it lost energy or authority. Had her father been her teacher? he wanted to know. Not officially, she said, and she grew pensive again. Her father had died quite recently, in March, still listening to the BBC. At the time of his death she'd been here, substitute teaching Math and French at the local high school, a job that merely met her need to be as far away as possible from her romantic entanglements. After her father's death she felt impelled to rethink her life. In a first step, she came to the station offering to volunteer. "And the rest is history," said Harry.

He couldn't imagine this beautiful woman, whose manner he could only describe as regal, lasting very long in a town like Yellowknife. And when he asked about her intentions, she said she had no idea whether she'd even stay in Canada. "Canada" she pronounced with a certain contempt. Canadians were spoiled, she said. Look at the size and weight of their over-crammed garbage cans, the number and newness of their cars, the houses standing unoccupied, the closets bursting with clothes, the daily showers. She didn't go on, but she could have. Her ex-husband's family had used water as if there were no tomorrow, but with her sense of economy and quality – in the Netherlands even a tea towel was made to last for decades – with her sense of history, tragedy, and time, she knew better than these dishwashing guzzlers, these showering fools, these lawn-lovers and land-wasters. Yellowknife, however, was different. Here, she felt that she'd stepped backwards into small-town life, especially in the unplanned old part of town where there was outdoor plumbing and the streets were unpaved and had names like Ragged Ass Road. Such a curious mixture, the city was, of brand-new and raw-old, of government buildings and beer parlours and bush planes and little shack-like houses close to the water, which seemed to lie in all directions, as did the vast wilderness. The place was full of opportunities, she said, especially if you were white and even if you were a woman.

Harry drew a map of Yellowknife for Dido, marking the location of his house on Latham Island at the far end of Old Town, not with an X but with a • like a beauty mark. And was it deliberate or unconscious, she wondered, that his rendition of the island (separated from the mainland by the narrowest of narrows) made it look like a penis with personality? An erect penis with a noticeable rightward curve. His house was near the base of the left-hand side of this curvaceous, prancing, happy, circumcised cock.

In watching him rapidly sketch the map, Dido Paris learned a few things and guessed a few others. Since Harry knew the coastline like the back of his hand, he must be a sailor, he must be happiest on water. His sketch was fast and deft and to the point. It showed no interest in the town itself, except insofar as Franklin Avenue ran down to the tip of the island-erection that bestrode the waters of Great Slave Lake. In manly capital letters he had written GIANT on the west shore of Back Bay and CON near Yellowknife Bay to indicate the two gold mines. But his focus was on the water and on inviting her, she assumed, to take an entertaining plunge.

THE DAY AFTER HARRY BRAVED the station in order to see Dido, a cloud of weather so warm had descended that Eleanor Dew went for a long walk before bed. She lived in the new part of town, in a basic but comfortable trailer home not far from Frame Lake. Occasionally that night she felt a cool breeze come off the water. Otherwise, warmth descended from the sky, then a little soft rain. The next morning the air outside was like one of those so-called white children – hair so blond it's white – a heavy mist obscuring the trailer next door. She was reminded of her grandfather, who had washed his fine head of white hair once a week with Old Dutch Cleanser.

This was the day Gwen Symon came into the station for the first time, and nobody noticed. It was the third day of June, a Tuesday.

Eleanor was caught up in playful banter with Ralph Cody, the freelance book reviewer. "You've drunk nineteen cups of coffee already. Do you plan to stay awake for a month?"

Ralph was a small man, about sixty, in a tweed jacket with patched elbows. His appetite for talk was barely whetted by the ten minutes allowed him on air. His teeth were darkly stained with coffee and tobacco. His nicotined hands were the smallest, daintiest hands Eleanor had ever seen on a man.

The two of them were discussing discomfort, how much better everyone used to be at enduring it, but especially the voyageurs during the fur trade and all the storied travellers in the Arctic.

Gwen stood there. They weren't aware of her. Or pretended they weren't. After a moment she said, "Some of those travellers weren't comfortable unless they were *un*comfortable."

Then they looked over and saw a pair of shocking blue eyes coming straight at them out of a young woman's white face. She had a large bruise on her throat – the size of a dollar bill torn in half, the purple ten-dollar bill. Dead-white skin (as white, thought Eleanor, as someone's feet, in shoes all year round, might be). A very bad haircut. And those blue eyes.

"Where did *you* come from?" asked Ralph.

"I just arrived," she said, and pointed out the window to the soft-shaped, ten-year-old Volvo parked in the street. Attached to it was a very small trailer.

She said, "I was wondering. Who could I talk to about a job?"

They established that she was twenty-four, she'd driven from Georgian Bay in Ontario, more than three thousand miles, camping in her trailer along the way, and if she could find work she would stay for a while. In Toronto she'd been told that anyone as inexperienced in radio as she was should try the hinterlands first.

Ralph's lips twitched in amusement; he could just picture some bureaucrat with a grand vocabulary. "So you came all this way to be on air."

"Not on air," came the hasty answer. "In the background. And I came all this way for other reasons too. I've always wanted to see the North."

It turned out she was intent on becoming a script assistant for radio drama.

"I don't mean to be harsh," said Ralph, "but have you been listening to the radio up here? Have you heard any radio dramas? Have you even heard a skit?"

"I think you need them," she said quietly.

Ah, thought Eleanor. She had trapped a mouse in her trailer a few days ago and this girl was just as subtle in her camouflage: a buff-grey shirt with a pale brown collar, and darker brown pants. No adornment except for the impressive bruise on her throat. An embarrassment, that, or something worse. But her sense of purpose was unmistakable, it cut through the static of her pale, brown personality. Someone else to watch. The girl's face was flushed now, the underarms of her shirt visibly wet. And Eleanor was reminded of her aunt who had to towel herself dry after she spoke on the telephone, the effort took so much out of her. Yet this same aunt had travelled cities the world over, and she'd done it alone.

This place could be the making of you, Eleanor thought, smiling at Gwen. But then everyone thought the North would be the making of them, as she knew perfectly well. That's exactly what led to so many disasters.

Eleanor told young Gwen that she wasn't sure who she should talk to, since their station manager had absconded. Ralph cracked that where he came from it was the weather that was transient: all you had to do was wait five minutes if you didn't like it; here, all you had to do was wait five minutes if you didn't like the people.

Eleanor laughed and went on to say that head office had been talking to Harry Boyd and she guessed they would ask him to step into the breach.

"What if I watched in the meantime," said Gwen. "I could learn a lot by watching."

"Have you got a place to stay?"

Gwen indicated her little Boler trailer parked outside, and Eleanor offered her own backyard as a parking place until she found an apartment.

"You're brave to have driven all this way."

Gwen considered for a moment whether this made her brave. In truth, she was always afraid, always worried. She shook her head. "Like I said, I've wanted to come north for as long as I can remember."

"Three thousand miles!"

"Yes," still unimpressed by herself, "but I never went over fifty."

Eleanor gave Gwen Symon a tour of the station, and for the next couple of days Gwen sat in master control with silent Eddy the red-headed tech and watched him operate the big console. She listened to the announcers, became familiar with their habits. There was the morning man, so prodigiously at ease on radio that it was like sleeping for him. The rest of his life was work – his troubled marriage, his full-time drinking – this was where he came to rest. There was the silver-haired treaty Indian, trim and immaculate and quiet, who did the news in Dogrib. There was the restless, fast-talking Metis sportscaster, who also hosted the late afternoon request show, since in the Northern Service announcers did more than one job and operated the equipment for themselves, besides. There was the utterly reliable newsreader and host of Radio Noon, who was training Dido to take his place, since he would be leaving soon for a job in the south. And there was Dido, who struggled with pronunciation, but had the most beautiful speaking voice Gwen had ever heard.

As it turned out, Harry was indeed made acting manager. *Acting*, as head office took pains to point out, until a permanent manager was hired. Somebody had to cover temporarily, and Harry, despite his lamentable history, was the most experienced person at hand.

Gwen went to see him in his new office, the first room down the hall past Eleanor's desk. She arrived just as he swivelled in his chair and picked up his phone, giving her his back but not because he meant to. She hovered at the open door, having nerved herself to enter, and now was unwilling to go away. She knew his voice. She'd heard him on her car radio as she drove the final leg to Yellowknife, drawn on by the endless light into a sunset that blended into sunrise, and accompanied for a while by this irreverent, handsome-sounding man who said things like, "The time may not be out of joint, but this joint is out of time." Now here he was in the flesh and her sense of letdown was part of a larger disappointment, since the North looked nothing like what she'd expected either. It wasn't a dramatic scene of rugged simplicity, rather, mile after mile of stunted trees covered with dust from the gravel road.

From the door she had a good view of the back of his balding head and his fat left ear. He hung up the phone, and she stepped all the way into his office, saying, "You don't look *anything* like how you sound."

Harry turned. He took off his glasses with one hand and studied her. "That," he said gravely, "is the tragedy of radio."

Gwen felt disarmed. Her face lit up, and Harry's relaxed into a smile. The old seducer, mutual honesty, had walked in the door and joined them.

"You remind me of *Johnny Q*," she said, voicing her sudden thought.

Her favourite comic strip growing up. On her stomach, the Saturday paper spread wide and still warm from having been under her bum all through lunch (staking her claim before her brother did), she drank in the intoxicating smell of newsprint – a potent, throat-catching, alcoholic smell – and devoured *On Stage*, the ongoing story of the actress Mary Perkins, who married the reporter Pete Fletcher, because he was handsome and reliable, even though she was deeply attracted to roguish Johnny Q of the cauliflower ear. Johnny Q came and went, other adventures intervened, but you always knew when he was back because his cauliflower ear appeared at the edge of the strip. Often his voice came first, a teasing sexy comment directed at a stewardess who was bringing him yet another drink. Then the back of his head appeared with the cauliflower ear jutting to one side. There was no greater pleasure in her childhood than knowing Johnny Q would be around for several weeks at least.

Harry Boyd wasn't handsome, but he was appealing in his own idiosyncratic way. Polka-dot silk shirt, dress pants, tennis sneakers. His face broad, underslept, middle-aged. Less a twinkle in his eye than an interested, half-irritated gleam. Like a pilot from the Second World War. Amused and thirsty.

"Sit down and make yourself homely."

She sat across from him in his little office, and he asked her why she wanted a job in northern radio. Her answer surprised and gripped him. When she was a girl, she said, she heard a radio program about John Hornby, the Englishman who starved to death along with his young cousin Edgar Christian, and a third companion, Harold Adlard, when they over-wintered in the Barrens in 1927. She'd never forgotten it.

"'Death in the Barren Ground.'" He leaned back in his chair. "Alan King took the role of Hornby, Douglas Rain was Edgar Christian. I think Bud Knapp did the narration. An incredible story," he said, glad to be remembering it again. "George Whalley wrote the script."

"And the biography too," she said. "*The Legend of John Hornby*. I've read it three times."

Her eagerness made Harry smile. "Whalley's daughter lives here, you know. Just down the road from me on Latham Island. She told me her father's really a Coleridge scholar. His obsession with Hornby is something he pursued on the side. His 'love child' she called it. I made her promise to bring him round and introduce him if he ever comes to Yellowknife."

Gwen said, "I've wanted to make radio dramas ever since I heard that broadcast."

Harry cradled his glasses in his left hand. "I hate to break it to you, but we're a one-thousand-watt radio station. We don't do drama."

"Is that in the regulations?"

A simple question that scored a point without intending to.

Harry said, "You've got Hornby's eyes. Has anybody told you that?" He pushed back and swung his feet up on his desk, a sign that he was interested, that she was worth his while. Harry had a weakness for shy, young travellers who'd fallen in love with the North, having been one himself. "So what was it about Hornby's story that hooked you?"

Gwen didn't hesitate. She told him it was Hornby's feeling for the Barrens. She understood the pull of that sort of desolate, rugged landscape; it's what made her travel a year ago to Newfoundland. The Barrens were far more remote, she knew, and even more dangerously exposed in the treeless interior of the Arctic. She wanted to see them too. And Hornby himself fascinated her, she said. He went to such extremes, getting by on so little, pushing himself to the brink. And then there was the way he died. He was to blame for what happened, but young Edgar never blamed him. That's what she found so moving.

Harry was nodding. "It's one of those unforgettable northern tales that break your heart."

"But," she leapt in, "it was a tragedy that avoided a greater tragedy, since they never turned against each other."

His cigarette stopped halfway to his mouth.

"I just mean," and she stuttered a little and pulled at the jagged ends of her short brown hair, "I just mean sometimes people misunderstand each other after a while, and then they turn against each other. They don't want to," she said softly, "but they can't help it."

Harry felt suddenly alert. "That sounds like personal experience talking."

He saw her move back in her chair and suspected he was right. "So how did you get to be so wise?"

It seemed she might not answer his question, but she did. "I read," she smiled, and he chuckled. Small-town honesty. He could recognize it a mile away. Small-town honesty, and big-city drive.

The girl reminded him of somebody he hadn't thought about for a long time. Somebody he'd met all too briefly at a reception years ago. A thin, young graduate student with short hair and a big shoulder bag into which she slipped food off the tables. She was making assiduous progress from the cheese to the butter tarts, wrapping the food in paper napkins, when he offered her a sausage roll for her collection, and her face crinkled with delight. How marvellous and rare, meeting a woman who liked to be teased. She made room for the sausage roll in her bag and he noticed the book tucked inside; the very book he was reading: Dashiell Hammett's *The Thin Man*. Then she gave him a warm smile and continued to the end of the table and then out the side door. He should have gone after her, but he let her go. He let her slip through his fingers.

Gwen Symon had the same kind of smile. She was telling him that Yellowknife wasn't what she'd expected, but the light was remarkable and she was looking forward to the darkness and cold of winter. And she could see that it was a place where anyone could make a fresh start.

"Why would *you* need a fresh start?" he asked. "You look almost prepubescent."

Her sky-blue eyes stabbed him. She didn't know the word, to her own surprise, and almost asked what it meant. Pre-what? Typewriters were clacking away on the other side of the wall and she was aware that his eyes had shifted to the bruise on her throat. "Why not?" she said at last.

A surprisingly self-possessed response. *Why not?* Harry straightened his shoulders, swung his feet back on the floor. A fresh start was exactly what he needed too.

"We have an opening, it so happens. Actually, two openings. I need someone to replace me on the night shift and soon I'll need a host for Radio Noon." He began to shuffle papers on his desk. "You're in luck. But whether we can *afford* to hire somebody else who needs to be trained is another matter. I know this will surprise the hell out of the CBC, but I'm a cheap bastard." Without looking at her, he spread his arms and lifted his shoulders. "I can't help it."

"Mr. Boyd," she said. "Mr. Boyd!" Leaning forward to get his attention.

"Harry's the name."

"I'm *cheaper*." Her eyes were bright, sharp, amused.

"You are?" His own eyes widened to take in this suddenly competitive girl. "*How* cheap?"

She was wearing sandals. Never in her life had she paid full price for sandals.

She raised her foot. "End of summer sale."

He pointed to his own feet. "Salvation Army."

That's where Gwen got her brassieres.

Harry said, "In Mexico I bargained so hard the street vendors turned their backs on me and walked away. I'm so cheap that when I go out with my buddies I forget to take my wallet."

"I've never sunk that low," she said.

"Honey, you don't know what my life has been like."

It wasn't hard, what she did next. Turning the conversation. Most men love to talk about themselves to women, even to a woman like her. "What has your life been like?" she asked, and he told her about what he called the violet hours of drinking that followed on the heels of his television disgrace, when he found himself eating corn flakes with a shoehorn since he didn't own a spoon. "I was no good on television," he said, expecting her to contradict him. But she didn't.

"My father was a drinker," she said.

"Then you know every sordid detail. You're not frightened."

"Not of that."

Harry waved her into the studio, the door of which was only a few feet from Eleanor's desk. He handed her the news story lying on the table, told her where to sit, lowered the microphone to her small, thin face. Then he went back out and down the hall to master control and asked Eddy to slap up a tape.

The studio in which Gwen sat at a big baize-covered table had an upright piano in the corner, and she wondered if musicians came in to play on air. The studio was connected by a picture window to master control, which was connected in the same way to the announce booth and the editing booth beyond that. She could see the length of the little station and into the hallway too. And thus she was inducted into the visibility and invisibility of radio, the intimacy and the isolation. Harry turned on his mike and spoke to her through the glass: Introduce yourself, then read the news story.

It was a story about a single car crash near Fort Rae, a settlement seventy miles west of Yellowknife. The car had skidded on loose gravel and had gone out of control on a lonely curve of bumpy road, the so-called highway she'd driven on to get to Yellowknife. The man had been killed, the woman escaped with minor cuts. Five dogs were in the car at the time of the accident, one of them still hadn't been recovered.

Harry listened. He pulled a notepad out of his back pocket and jotted down: *Interesting. Monotonous. Worth a chance.*

"What do you think, Eddy?" he said.

"Not great," said Eddy.

"Not yet."

There was something about her voice. It sounded parched and boyish and defenceless, a little like Douglas Rain's voice – the eerie, naked, innocent quality he brought to Edgar Christian, the seventeen-year-old cousin who accompanied Hornby into the Barrens and stayed loyal until his last breath.

The next day Harry offered Gwen a summer contract as an announcer-operator, thinking of it as a trial run, and she accepted.

<hr />

Gwen asked herself later why she agreed to the job. Why would someone who wanted to be in the background agree to be in the foreground? It was the only job going, she told herself. Then why was she so ecstatic about the prospect of being on air?

She went for a walk down to Old Town and without her being aware of it the interviewing voice started up inside her head, asking, "As a child, did you realize how famous you were going to be?" And in a modest voice she answered, "Not as a child. Not then. Believe me, I've combed through my childhood looking for signs and there weren't any." An answer so honest and self-deprecating and gently humorous it provoked even more admiration from her imagined interviewer and she became aware that it was happening again, her mental tape recorder was on. She was being questioned about her long and famous life and she was talking easily, confidently, amusingly, without a trace of self-consciousness.

Gwen took over reading the news from the smooth-voiced favourite of the two newsmen, Roland Clark, who would be leaving in a week for Vancouver. Dido was given Radio Noon. The night shift would fall to a casual who regularly filled in on holidays, at least for now. Harry wanted to keep his options open until he saw how the women worked out.

Shake it up, he thought, when he leaned into the newsroom to announce the change, making his fresh start on Gwen's shoulders. How could she know that she'd hitched her wagon to a murky star, to a man who'd been written off by the real powers in the station as one more example of head office's ineptitude? But she discovered soon enough. The enmity of newsmen is no small thing.

IT WOULD BE ONE OF THOSE RARE summers when the light is crystalline, the sky deep blue, the air continuously warm. Yellowknife was like a summer residence, a northern resort. It was Summer itself. Children were in the playgrounds all night long.

Harry's little white house on Latham Island overlooked Back Bay, an extension of Yellowknife Bay, itself an arm of Great Slave Lake. One evening he enticed Dido to spend time with him by offering to take her sailing on the bay. Later the same week they went out in his canoe, paddling across Back Bay to the tiny abandoned cemetery on the opposite shore. Dido asked to get out and wander about, and it was there, in that spot, that she first smelled invisible apples.

"'Transparent fruit,'" nodded Eleanor a few days later when Dido thought it wise to bring her along as a chaperone. The pleasant odour, pervasive but without a source, made Eleanor think of other phrases that captured the North as it lit up the human imagination. "Garden of Desire." "Country of the Mind." She was sitting in the middle of the canoe as if she were a factor for the Hudson's Bay Company. "My father would have loved this," she murmured as they paddled her around, a woman who seemed older than she was, closer to fifty than forty, but she'd always seemed older than she was, always an Eleanor, never an Ellie.

That evening Dido stayed alone in the cemetery, while Harry and Eleanor explored the shore. She was kneeling in the long grass, trying to make out the name on a weathered wooden cross and thinking of her father in his tweed cap and trench coat, an anglophile until the last. She'd learned about his sudden death three weeks after it happened, in a letter from her mother, an act of casualness that still dumbfounds her. Now, in the sloping, overgrown shadiness of a faraway cemetery, something extraordinary happens. She hears him call her name. *Dido.* And she looks around, exactly as she did when she first caught the sweet smell of apples in the air. *Dido.*

Her heart opens wide and she trembles. The voice is real. Not old or quavery, but clear, unmistakable, as confident in her as ever. A steady, loving voice. Not wanting to break the spell, she stays kneeling for several minutes and says nothing to the others.

That night she sleeps a long, deep, uninterrupted sleep, and in the morning she dresses for work knowing she's equal to whatever lies ahead. At 5:30 p.m., when she reads the news, her accent is gone and each word seems to pronounce itself.

It was like putting my foot on firm ground, she marvelled a few days later when she confessed what had happened.

Gwen gave her a look of honest envy, keen and wistful. She had always wanted the same kind of miraculous release. To be caught up in something so remarkable that she was taken completely out of herself.

Slender-hipped Dido. Who didn't fall in love with her that summer? Who didn't notice her habit of holding her mug backwards, embracing it with both hands and lacing her fingers through the handle? Or recall that she drank her coffee black? Or remember her boast that she had a Thermos of coffee at her bedside in order to indulge herself first thing in the morning before getting up?

Harry thought her voice sounded like a tarnished silver spoon. He listened for it coming down the hall, catching her unusual scent first. Patchouli, she told him. A heavy, dark-brown fragrance from the other side of the world.

Dido was slender despite having wide shoulders and thick wrists and big hands. Reliably kind despite being reliably hurtful. A long, pleasant evening might be the prelude to a single, crushing remark: "Harry, you grunt like an old man when you lift that canoe." Yet she was zealous in her compliments and capable of the most reckless intimacy.

That she would marry a man younger than herself, for instance, yet be more intrigued by his father even before she met him, her sense of attraction building from the son's initial description and abetted by his answers to her many questions, until she had a clear picture of the driven, moody, hugely successful businessman so good with his hands he'd built his own forty-foot sailboat and named it *Nansen*.

Then she did meet him and he was brown as a nut from sailing – in a black polo shirt, white cotton pants, bare feet. Immensely good-looking in his deep tan. Holding by the hand a diapered, towheaded grandson. Standing in the driveway as she drove up for the first time.

They walked to the beach together, they swam. He carried a bathing cap of sea water to wash off her sandy feet, put sun-warmed stones into her cold hands, took her sailing. Married, he was, to a woman who was afraid of water, whereas she of the soft, unshaven legs loved the sea.

In her father-in-law's home there were no rooms where they could hide, an open-concept, gravity-defying house on the side of a hill. A mistake, he said to her. If you don't have a door to close, you don't have a door to open.

Then move, she said.

You make it sound simple.

You're not *old*, she said.

She was twenty-seven, he was fifty-eight.

It was she who moved, leaving his son one day and coming north. If her father-in-law loved her enough, he would find her. But a year had gone by.

Whenever Dido entered or left a room, eyes followed her. "You watch her just like a man," Eddy the tech said to Gwen one day. Red hair, small eyes, tall, lean, older, in a town where "older" meant thirty-two, Eddy was an unsettling presence. He looked right through Gwen as she flushed, the innocent up and down of her scrutiny under scrutiny. "Your eyes were on her body," he said, "just like a man's."

Uncomfortable, uncomfortable. And just a taste of what was to come.

A station break. All she had to do was sit at the control board in the announce booth, lower the round dial – it was called a pot – that controlled the feed from the network, flip the switch, and open her mike by turning another pot, then give the local and regional weather.

Harry was with her. "Watch the clock," he told her. "At twenty-nine seconds, get the network back up."

At thirty-one seconds, Harry reached over her shoulder with experienced hands and lowered one pot (her mike) and raised the other (the network). Toronto came back in mid-word, and Gwen was giving the final temperatures to a dead microphone.

She turned around and located his face.

"The first time is the worst," he said. "I've known announcers who opened their mouths and nothing came out."

She clenched her hands. Cold, clammy.

Harry said firmly, "You've got to keep one eye on the clock as you read."

Then he took her hands, his own being warm, and held them for a moment. At his comforting touch, life came into her again and she said, "That was awful!"

She'd been dropped in front of a microphone, like a child dropped out of a sack: no mother, no father, all alone on the highway of sound.

"'Thro' the jaws of Death,'" quoted Harry, "'Back from the mouth of Hell.'"

"The Bible?"

"'The Charge of the Light Brigade.'"

"Kipling," she said.

"*Tennyson.*"

And she buried her ignorant head in her hands.

After two weeks in Yellowknife, Gwen managed to find a furnished basement apartment on an unpaved side street that ran off Franklin Avenue. She was told she was lucky. In general, decent housing was hard to find and rents were atrocious. In her small, anonymous living room, however, she missed the domestic companionship of Eleanor and her roommate. We shared suppers and breakfasts and the stories of our lives, she thought.

Dust drifted in through her open window and gathered on the books piled on the floor beside her bed. She wrote her name on the mirror. A block away was the public library, where she'd gone to hear a visiting poet read. To the southeast, a five-minute walk away, was the radio station, where she wasn't doing very well at all. A place utterly contained, enclosed, yet voices carried beyond the horizon. She *was* the horizon to those listening.

One day Dido came upon her standing stock still in the record library, moaning to herself. "Don't think you're the only one," Dido assured her. "I cringe when I hear myself too."

But Gwen didn't believe her. Dido lived outside embarrassment — in the free and easy woods of herself.

Dido was never slapdash, never in a hurry. She brought to every task the same care that Gwen's father brought to the repair of a wristwatch or necklace or alarm clock. After eating a sandwich at her desk, Dido would brush her teeth in the washroom in the basement, taking twice as long as Gwen would have taken had she bothered, plying her toothbrush like an artisan working with ivory.

"You're so good on air, Dido." Gwen was standing with her arms wrapped around herself. "You make it sound simple."

Dido smiled. It *was* simple. What could she say? It came naturally. "It's a piece of cake for me. Do I say it correctly?"

"You say everything correctly."

Dido smiled again. She liked Gwen – the way her face lit up and she stopped whatever she was doing to talk for a while, to ask her opinion, to listen.

"Try to slow down," Dido advised her. "You go too fast. But you sound better than you think you do." She pushed Gwen's hair off her troubled forehead. "You don't believe me. But I always say what I think."

Dido's unconventional beauty went hand in hand with the light. Officially, the June sun set close to midnight and rose three hours later, but it never got dark. Dusk, yes. Between sunset and sunrise there was a soft sort of dusk and the street lights came on, but nobody needed them or noticed them. The constant light was like endless caffeine.

One afternoon, as Dido stood talking to Eleanor, Mrs. Dargabble came through the door, wearing a white-and-black scarf on her head. A wrap of sorts half fell off her shoulders and her red lipstick was in motion too, travelling like water through sand into the fine wrinkles above her lips and the deep fissures below. Mrs. Dargabble exclaimed to Eleanor, "I had to see Dido here in Yellowknife!" Then she greeted the woman in question by quoting Shakespeare, "'In such a night stood Dido with a willow in her hand.'"

From her receptionist's desk, Eleanor watched Dido deal with one admirer after another. It was like being close to a beehive, the steady hum of light and attraction, and the mystery at the core. People were drawn to the North and in the North they were drawn to Dido, so it seemed, and Dido managed herself very well. It was an art, appearing interested while saving the main part of yourself for something better.

Mrs. Dargabble was telling Dido that once upon a time she had been a hard-working seamstress with a lucrative business designing clothes. But then she met her husband – her first husband – a lovely man, from Boston like herself, who begged her to "jump." He urged her to be colourful and rambunctious and carefree, to shed her responsibilities and marry him instead. We came north together, she was saying, we set up a business raising dogs until – may he rest – he drowned ten years ago.

Gwen came out of the newsroom, and the old woman caught her hand as she walked by. "You're so soft," Mrs. Dargabble said to Gwen with traces, still, of her Boston accent: yo-ah for you're. "So soft. My husband told me to jump. You must *jump*."

"Jump?"

"You must *jump*."

Gwen made an agonized face and continued on into the studio.

Mrs. Dargabble had taken the chair that Eleanor always offered. It was on the side of her desk near the window and next to a small table of plants, avocadoes and oranges in pots, started by her from seed, and a handsome jade plant of uncertain age that Ralph Cody had given her after he saw her reading Ezra Pound's *Cathay*. She'd heard his voice once, the poet who slowly went mad on the air. A short clip of one of his fascist broadcasts for Radio Rome. Young Gwen couldn't have sounded more different. She was reading the news now, coming over the speakers in the hallway. Her voice irritating, whispery. Like someone standing behind you and playing with your hair.

Dido was listening too, without comment, but she felt like stepping into the studio and taking over. She became aware of Eddy, who was leaning his long, sinewy body against Eleanor's desk, ignoring everyone except herself. He fixed her with his small, intent eyes. He wanted to know if she'd ever been to Prosperous Lake. He was driving out there tonight.

"I'm sorry," Dido said, feeling and sounding invincible in her formality. "I have another engagement."

"What engagement?"

His expressive eyes – how small they were – didn't let up, and against her will she laughed a little.

"What engagement?"

"We're going to the movies."

"Who's 'we'?"

Dido licked her dry lips. She didn't like this man and didn't feel the need to answer. He smiled and shrugged and headed out the door.

After he left, Mrs. Dargabble said something so quietly Dido wasn't sure she'd heard properly.

"Perhaps I'm wrong," Mrs. Dargabble said. "But I don't think so."

"You don't think I should get mixed up with him." Dido looked thoughtfully out the big plate-glass window with its view of the street and saw Eddy heading up to Franklin Avenue. He carried himself with easy pride, like a professional soldier on leave. And she took away the image of a man pacing himself to outlast any number of wars.

IN THE LITTLE BOOTH OF LIGHT, speaking into the silver fruit hanging off the silver bough, Gwen struggled with the words on the greens. They twisted a little and moved away, capitalized, cagey. She tightened her grip on the page and stumbled. Alone, but heard for miles, she winced and stumbled again.

The news. Gwen Symon was reading the news. She heard herself make the mistake in her head and then she made it on air in a small voice flattened by panic. She remembered the fat actress with stage fright in *On Stage*, who lost weight by eating lettuce without any salad dressing and got over her fright by imagining that everyone in the audience was a rabbit.

Her voice came over the speakers in the hallway and then she herself came out into the hall – greens in hand and white-faced – as white-faced, thought Eleanor, as George VI after the crown was put on his stuttering head. Gwen carried the greens back to the newsroom and gave them to one of the two newsmen, who took them without looking at her – she who had ruined their long day's work in fifteen minutes by booting one story after another.

Eleanor, from her safe perch, heard it all. Harry stopped on his way past her desk and said with a grimace, "I could hear the sheets rustling." He recognized the softness of uncertainty, of nakedness, of no confidence at all. The loneliest voice he'd ever heard.

"You should help her," Eleanor said to him.

He jigged his head back and forth, as if considering it, and turned towards the door.

"You're helping Dido," Eleanor called after him, "who needs it less."

All right. He would teach Gwen how to read, as he'd taught his sister how to drive, how to navigate the lines of words, the lanes of vocabulary without embarrassment, accident. How to look ahead so that her voice flowed, rather than straight down at one stumpy phrase after another.

"I pretend I'm talking to one person," he told her the next afternoon in his office.

"I'm no good at that. I seize up. I run out of things to say."

She was watching his sensitive mouth. She would take away the memory of him smoking, and the spit-spit sound of getting the bits of tobacco off his tongue and lip. And of the three unfortunate things that were to happen to him that winter, one after the other, three months in a row.

The question she asked: How can you be a personality on the air when you have no personality?

That's good, came Harry's answer. Self-doubt is good. Most announcers are full of themselves, they're so in love with the sound of their own voices. You don't want a plummy sound. You don't want to be Henry Comor the second.

Gwen flared up. She loved Henry Comor, she told him. She had listened to "Hermit's Choice" every Saturday night when she was sixteen.

"Gwen, Gwen. Why weren't you out partying?"

Because nobody invited her. Curled up in the big arm-chair beside the varnished standing cabinet that contained the radio, she listened to Henry Comor interview well-known actors, writers, professors, journalists, politicians about what four books and four records they would take to a desert island, what in their solitude they would rely on for company. It was Robinson Crusoe-in-advance. Emotional seafaring on the airwaves.

She liked Comor's voice speaking *to* her, unhurried, and then to his guests. One of his guests, she remembered, was a professor of French who chose Stendhal's *Scarlet and Black* as one of his four books and talked about the very sad moment in his life when he discovered that Stendhal, who was short, fat, ugly, and too intelligent to be agreeable, died young, in his fifties, without having achieved his simple aim of being loved for himself. Then there was the Montreal poet Louis Dudek, who sounded like a farm boy and chose Joyce's *Ulysses*, since he wanted a book he could labour on. There was J. Frank Willis, the voice that reported the 1936 Moose River mine disaster with three-minute broadcasts every half hour for sixty-nine hours, day and night, without sleep. His breathing was heavy the night she heard him with Henry Comor, his voice like tires on a gravel road leading to a summer lake. He chose George Gershwin, saying that the night Gershwin died, artists gathered at the Hollywood Bowl and played his music for seven hours straight.

Henry Comor's voice changed, depending on his guest. Anyone with an English accent, and his own voice got more posh. But she didn't blame him, or any of them. She found it all too interesting. "It was wonderful company," she said to Harry.

Harry didn't seem to be paying attention. But he was.

"How did you come by that bruise?" He pointed to her throat, and her fingers went to the fading colour. "If you don't mind my asking."

Outside, a car door slammed. A town where you could hear every sound. She saw a piece of paper fly across the street and wondered how much snow would fall in the winter and how cold it would get and whether she would still have a job in radio by then.

What happened, she said finally, still staring out the window behind Harry, was a scary encounter on her way to Yellowknife. She was north of Edmonton, near the Alberta–Northwest Territories border, when she asked a nice-seeming farmer, thirty or so, not old, about a campground and he offered his lane as an overnight camping spot. In the middle of the night he came into her tiny trailer and she jerked awake, sitting up with a pounding heart. He put his finger to his lips and whispered that he liked long hair on a girl. Then he bent over and pushed his mouth hard against hers. She shoved him away and his voice turned mean. *What's the matter? You don't like men?* He must have used the side of his hand. Striking her across the windpipe so hard she choked. But then, amazingly, he left. She got herself dressed and peeled out of there, and when it began to get light she pulled over to the side of the road and dug out her nail scissors and cut off her long hair.

Gwen looked over at Harry's concerned, assessing face and said, "I know. I know what you're thinking." He was thinking – she thought – that she'd put herself in danger and was lucky to have escaped. That she was asking for trouble.

"What am I thinking, Gwen?"

"That I'll never get work in a hair salon."

He liked the joke. But that wasn't what had been in his mind. Gwen waited.

"I think you're intrepid," he said.

She ducked her head to hide her pleasure. Her face was warm. "Harry?" Looking at her hands.

"Gwen."

"That person you pretend you're talking to when you're on the air?" She looked up. "Who is it?"

Harry smiled. "My imaginary listener? He's a man in his sixties who comes home tired from work and he goes down to the basement to his workbench and builds model boats. And while he's doing that he listens with rapt attention to me."

"So it's not somebody you know?"

"Not somebody I've met," he said.

She nodded slowly, and Harry asked, "Who do you feel comfortable talking to?"

You, she thought. "Nobody," she said.

"My favourite person. Now give him a hat."

She thought for a moment. "A fedora."

"Fine. What else is he wearing?"

Into Gwen's mind came a middle-aged man puttering around a kitchen. He wore a wedding band, but he lived alone. A widower. He cooked for himself. His radio sat on the kitchen table. He had it on whenever he ate – it was always on. Before he went to bed he cleaned up, doing the dishes, setting up his coffee for the morning, sipping a final glass of Scotch. I could talk to someone like that, she thought.

＝

In the quiet house in Ontario where Gwen grew up, her father used to sit at the head of the table and crack Brazil nuts so painstakingly they came out whole, while her bruised and fractured walnuts whizzed through the air. Nearby was Owen Sound, which gave her the notion that you could be stuck in a certain sound for the whole of your natural life.

Her mother's throat music, for instance. Those purring sounds of affection meant to reassure Gwen's dad. And her soft throat clearing whenever company came and awkward silences fell. It was what "not being able to think of anything to say at the moment" sounds like.

Gwen had a radio in her room, installed the summer she got poison ivy. 1961. In that little town of woods and rocks, trails and leafiness, it had been her fond habit when small to pull leaves off the mock orange and stuff them as money into her dead grandpa's old tobacco pouch that closed with a zipper. Her homely, slight, small-bodied grandpa from Manchester, who had wanted to go to China as a missionary but ended up in Canada instead – a spiritual man, an odd duck. One day, out and about with the family dog, Gwen forgot to think – forgot to look out for the three glossy leaves, and besides, where she was they were everywhere. She pulled down her shorts to pee, and her bottom was tickled by the leaves she wasn't paying attention to. Then, in an excess of affection for the dog, she hugged him, this well-travelled connoisseur of every poison-ivy patch, and rubbed her face against his fur.

The itching began several hours later and had a visual equivalent. For dinner her mother served sausages, fat fingers with a grease-gagging flavour that brought tears to her eyes. Two halves of one misery. She shifted in her seat, her bottom crawling, but wasn't allowed to rise until the sausages were gone. (One day, in her late twenties, she would meet someone – her future mother-in-law – who would say, If I knew my kids didn't like something, I didn't serve it. Gwen would look at her with the wonder most mortals reserve for sight-ings of God.)

From ankles up to and across her bottom, then up to her face and into her eyes, she was soon ablaze and oozing with rash, blisters, torment. Her mother had her lie naked on the bedsheet, where she was too far gone for books or even the ink-induced spasm of excitement that came with the arrival of the *London Free Press* and the ongoing story of Mary Perkins.

A solution of cool water and baking soda, everywhere but on her private parts, which also raged, since her fingers had wandered there too. Her mother wrapped her hands in strips of flannel and Gwen ran her swathed hands across her chest, and the gentle relief of that light scratch, followed by the renewed, Job-like escalation of itching, made her understand the word *torture*.

Then one day came the radio. Installed beside her bed, turned on. She escaped on the highways of the air. The Archers, John Drainie (reading a story she would never forget about a woman strangled by her long scarf when it caught in the wheel of her convertible), Max Ferguson as Rawhide, the weather, the farm broadcast. Once, as part of the farm broadcast, there was a horse auction with all the sounds of buying and selling, while in the background a young girl sobbed. There were suffering people in the world besides herself, Gwen learned. There were people who were heartbroken.

Thinking back, it was a childhood of warts, wens, carbuncles, poison ivy, and trench mouth, this last affliction treated with gentian violet, her gums painted an astonishing violet-blue. Buttons were lost in the schoolyard. Shirts torn. All this was before television, though not technically. But her parents remained in the pre-television era, doing without one, eventually cancelling their subscription to the *London Free Press*. Living in silence, except for the radio.

The dusty pale pink of calamine lotion.

In her bedroom loose white curtains moved in the breeze. A sleeping-porch spacious with lack of anything but a white bed and bedside table and straight-backed chair and chest of drawers – and the movement of air through screened windows as gauzy curtains swelled inward. In another part of the house the telephone rang. But not here. Not in this outpost of quiet.

And over the radio one night came the story of John Hornby, and something happened that she had almost despaired of ever happening. From having been locked in (at the end of a chapter, the poison-ivy chapter), she entered somebody else's life and saw it from beginning to end. A man who starved to death. A man whose mistakes caused the death by starvation of his two young companions. A blue-eyed, soft-voiced, lucid madman, who courted hardship and seemed absolutely fearless. Gwen liked him enormously and fell under the spell of the desolate North.

"YOU CAN TELL SO MUCH about a person by hearing his voice," said Dido. She was in Eleanor's kitchen, drinking up her coffee. The radio was on in the background, an announcer introducing choral music.

"I wonder," replied Eleanor, who'd gone to church that morning, reviving a habit she'd given up years ago. "I wonder how much you can really tell." She remembered what her father had said about hearing Stalin on the radio in 1943: he had the warmest, sturdiest, most trustworthy voice he'd ever heard.

Dido's hands were wrapped around her coffee mug. Her hair was loose, her reading glasses in her pocket. "Gwen sounds like she's falling asleep on air. I can't listen to her."

"Give her time," said Eleanor.

She knew more about Gwen's past than Dido did, she knew Gwen had been having troubles with her family, she'd run away in a sense. But even if Gwen hadn't confided in her, she would have assumed something was wrong. There was her strange pallor, which made Eleanor think of Byron's ivory-pale skin, the result of overeating, then eating nothing, and since she'd watched Gwen starve herself at breakfast only to overindulge at dinner, she guessed the girl might be

self-denying and gluttonous, in turn. There was her consistently drab wardrobe, and not a trace of makeup or bit
of jewellery.

"She seems to want to erase herself," Eleanor said, "so it's
strange she's on the radio. It must be hard to have everybody
listening to you."

"Or does she want to draw attention to herself?" Dido,
impatient, swept her dark hair off her face. "She's always
talking to me about how bad she looks. I don't mean to say,"
altering her tone, "that she's aware of how she talks. I don't
think she knows herself very well, actually. Anyway," she said
abruptly, "let's get back to me."

Their eyes met – amused – and Eleanor forgot about
Gwen for the moment.

"When can I move in?" asked Dido.

"Tomorrow, if you like."

Lucky Dido. For almost a year she'd been sharing a
small bungalow with two other women who didn't know the
meaning of the words *quiet* or *clean*, and it was more like
camping out than living. Tomorrow she would move her
things into the small and tidy bedroom left vacant by
Eleanor's previous roommate, who'd decided suddenly she
couldn't face one more day in Yellowknife, let alone one
more winter. Dido would have the run of the mobile home,
the use of Eleanor's books, the pleasure of her civilized
company at a monthly rent that was lower by a third than
what she'd been paying. I'll stay here one more year, Dido
thought, and then I'll go somewhere entirely different.

One night in mid-June Dido and a former teaching colleague went to a party in Old Town that featured caribou burgers and kegs of beer. On a big deck overlooking a rocky slope with the bay in the distance, she discovered a crowd of strangers, men with huge bellies and heavy-handed hospitality and horrible opinions. She wondered if Texas was like this. She heard someone say, "If you're a white man, vote for a white man." She heard someone else say, "Any girl can type. We'll just drag a squaw in off the streets."

Dido saw the racism more clearly, seeing it with a new-comer's eyes. These were businessmen who believed the North belonged to them. They smelled money, she thought. They couldn't wait for the gas and oil to flow, and so they had no time for the inquiry into the proposed Mackenzie Valley pipeline. They hated the tax dollars it was soaking up and the delays it was causing. They resented the platform it was giving to natives, environmentalists, do-gooders of every stripe. They belittled the government-appointed judge who was running it. *Berger.* She heard the name being bandied about with contempt. But the pipeline was going ahead, she also heard them say, nothing would stop it. Government was behind it, big money was behind it, real northerners like them-selves, who put their shoulders to the wheel and prospered, they were behind it.

Overhead were ravens and lake gulls, all around were low hills made of the oldest rock in the world bathed by the most beautiful light on earth, and lovely miniature birches, and small flowers clinging and spreading. Dido had learned recently that this rock was the very rock she had failed to drive tent pegs into three thousand miles away in Ontario, on an ill-conceived camping trip with her ex-husband: it was all part of the great Canadian Shield, a connection that ran deep and underfoot, though on the surface it failed to bring even two quarrelsome people together.

After a while, she gravitated towards a less crowded corner of the deck and saw Eddy leaning on the railing, his loose hips, long legs. He was staring off into the distance. She glanced his way several times, but not once did he acknowledge her. She went to stand next to him. She rested her arms on the railing beside his, and he said to her, "These people are despicable."

"Then we agree about something."

He looked her in the face, his eyes full of anger. "Racists run the show up here," he said.

"I know."

His harshness appealed to her and surprised her. She began to ask him about himself, and he responded and not with small talk.

He'd grown up in California, the son of a house builder who died at the age of thirty-eight, leaving his mom with three kids and no money. Now his troubled boyhood had been stirred up again by the sudden death of his sister-in-law, who'd left behind a little girl, only five years old. He'd been five, too, when his father died.

"How did he die, your father?"

"He was up on a roof and they say he lost his balance."

His voice was quiet and clean, she thought, unlike Harry's fleshy growl. Eddy was leaning back now, against the railing, his fingers pushed into the front pockets of his jeans.

"Tracey asked me how you spell disappointment," he said.

His niece, she thought. "Disappointment," she repeated softly.

"I helped her sound it out and she got it all except for the second *p*."

Dido made her excuses to her friend, and she and Eddy left the party together. It was midnight. A car went by, having no need of headlights despite the hour. They walked south on Franklin Avenue, uphill, for they both lived in the new part of town. A drunk in a white shirt came weaving down the hill towards them. On his way by he reached out and grabbed Dido's arm and brought his dazed, liquored-up face to within a few inches of hers. Eddy stepped neatly between them and the man reeled off. "Incredible," muttered Eddy, "that he'd do that when I'm right here."

They walked on.

Dido was touched by his account of his niece. She could picture him sitting on the floor beside the little girl, helping her spell out her state of mind, and the girl would feel protected, cherished.

They reached the Yellowknife Inn and Dido said she would take a taxi the rest of the way home. Eddy offered to drive her. He had a truck, his place was just a couple of blocks away – he hadn't driven to the party, he'd ended up there, he didn't bother to explain how. No, she smiled, this was fine. He opened the taxi door for her, and once she was safely inside he asked her where she lived, then told the driver where to go, and in the back seat Dido felt a little amused but not displeased. Eddy was looking out for her.

The next morning she was in the bank. Another perfect summer's day, and she was congratulating herself on having come to a part of the world that was dry and light and spacious. I understand infinity now, she was saying to her father in her head. From my base point I've come a huge distance to a place consisting, in itself, of infinite distance.

She was at the side counter, signing a money order for her mother in Nijmegen, when a single red rose was set down beside her right hand. She stared at it, then turned, and there he was. Unsmiling, aggressively gallant, intent on being understood. Eddy touched his hand to his heart and held her gaze. And then he turned and walked out of the bank.

Dido followed him with her eyes, then looked down at the long-stemmed rose. And again, from nothing, or almost nothing, her attraction grew.

That night she lay beside Eleanor on Eleanor's double bed, listening to music on the radio, turning the big watch on her wrist and thinking aloud "about a day on the beach when I was as close to my father-in-law as I am to you, watching all these little birds race along the water's edge." They'd found a sheltered place in between the sand dunes, she said, and her father-in-law had told her about the first time he made something with his hands and discovered he was good at it, and it surprised him, not that he was good, but that anyone could be who was interested enough in what he was doing. "'Find something you're really interested in and everything else falls into place.' I was lying on my side, watching the light on his face, and I said, 'Okay, what about some*body*. If you find somebody

you're really interested in, does everything fall into place?'"
Her voice dropped a little, moved into another register. "I
remember the hour exactly, because he spotted this watch in the
sand and picked it up and slipped it on my wrist. Half past four
and he said, 'This is what I think about at night, if you ever
wondered,' and he bent down and began to kiss me through
my blouse, everywhere, not just my breasts, everywhere.

"Like this," and Dido demonstrated on Eleanor's sleeve.
Eleanor giggled.

He'd drawn her blouse into his mouth, sucking it up with
light puffs of air, a sort of reverse kiss, warm, amazing, the
most arousing thing she'd ever felt.

To Eleanor the demonstration felt like being vacuumed by
a little vacuum cleaner. "And then?"

"Then he stopped himself. 'I can't do this to my son.'"

The rose was in her room down the hall. Being given a
rose shouldn't make such a difference, and yet it did. "Father
and son," said Dido. "That's what mattered." She was remembering how every Friday her father had brought fresh flowers
home from the market to her delighted mother, whatever was
in season, gladiolas, dahlias, margaritas, lilies, tulips.

"You mattered," said Eleanor. She was trying to read the
changing expression on Dido's face.

"Not enough."

Their heads were inches apart. For another moment
Eleanor studied the faraway look on the face beside her. Then
she turned on her back and stared up at the ceiling. Dido's
words – candid, confiding, self-absorbed – had come so easily
that they infected Eleanor with the same ability to touch upon
things normally never spoken about. And so on this June night

filled with light, when so little sleep was required or attainable, she divulged the secret of her own failed marriage.

She was teaching English in those days and she'd fallen in love with a colleague, a married man whose wife was mentally ill. He was very good to his wife, very kind, but always sad. "He talked to me about her all the time, and now and again I went to visit them. He always called her sweetheart. Sweetheart, here's Eleanor. This went on for years, but then she got worse. Well, she became violent. She tore up his clothes, one day she threatened to kill him. In the end she was institutionalized and a year later he got a divorce. I thought he was right – not everybody did – but he had a life to live and so did I. After the divorce I persuaded him to marry me. On our wedding night we lay on the bed – like this – side by side, and he let me touch him but he didn't touch me back. On our honeymoon he removed his wedding ring. When we got home he wouldn't tell anyone we were married. And then he began crying, he couldn't stop crying."

"Are you saying you never made love?"

"We never did."

"How long were you together?"

"About six months in 1970."

"That's the year I came to Canada. I arrived in August and in October there was the War Measures Act. I couldn't believe it. I thought Canada stood for peace, and suddenly, tanks in the streets."

"It was a bad year," said Eleanor.

Dido raised herself on one elbow and looked down at her. She smoothed the long wisps of blond hair off Eleanor's forehead, then bent down and kissed her briefly on the mouth, an act of affectionate sympathy that moved Eleanor and took her aback. Then Dido said, "We both came north to escape love affairs. At least you left him."

"No. He left me. I would have stayed."

Dido flashed her a look of disbelief, and Eleanor said, "Sex isn't the most important thing to me."

Dido responded by once again turning the watch on her wrist. She seemed to Eleanor miles away. In another world.

"Tell me," Eleanor asked quietly, "where was your husband while you were on the beach with his father?"

Dido looked directly into her face. "Danny adored his mother. He pretty much forgot about me when he was with her."

Eleanor didn't think that could have been possible. But she said, "My husband doted on his mother too. What's his name? Your father-in-law."

"Daniel Moir."

"And you're still thinking he'll come to find you one day?"

"I don't know any more."

"But he knows you're here."

"He knows."

Eleanor woke up the next morning and discovered she wasn't alone. In the night Dido had slipped in beside her; she was curled up on her side, sound asleep. Eleanor lay still for a moment. Then she got out of bed and made coffee. From the kitchen she heard Dido stretch and yawn. She filled another mug and took the two mugs down the hall, aware of the sound of her feet on the carpet. Dido plumped up her pillows gratefully. Eleanor sat at the foot of the bed and watched her friend take her first sip.

Dido smiled at her. "I couldn't sleep."

"It's all right."

"I don't like sleeping alone," she admitted. "I fall asleep, but then I have bad dreams." She sipped her coffee and said slowly, "I woke up from a dream about Nijmegen and I had a real feeling of homesickness."

"I don't mind. It's like having a sister."

"I knew you wouldn't mind."

Dido intended a compliment and Eleanor took it as such, benign flattery. But it wasn't really like having a sister, she thought. It wasn't quite like anything she'd experienced before.

———

She remembers as a girl climbing into an apple tree with a cushion and a copy of Palgrave's *Golden Treasury of Poems*, and staying there till tea time. Her pretty mother had so wanted a pretty daughter, but Eleanor had her father's unfortunate chin and needed thick glasses before she was eight. She was fifteen when they moved to Canada, propelled by the legendary moment in her father's life when he stumbled into a news theatre on Piccadilly, escaping one of London's killer fogs, and saw *The Romance of Transportation* – a jazzy, funny, animated film about a northern country so clean and simple and fresh and refreshing that he asked himself what they were waiting for. It was 1954.

Her father had been an impetuous man, a poetry-loving physician as beguiled by bad verse as by good. McIntyre's deathless ode to the Ingersoll cheese never failed to cheer him up. *We have seen thee queen of cheese / Lying quietly at your ease, / Gently fanned by evening breeze, / Thy fair form no flies dare seize.* He'd read aloud to her. Walter de la Mare, Tennyson, Christina Rossetti, Shakespeare. The trouble with Othello, he told her, was that he had no sense of humour, poor wretch. Even Macbeth had a sense of humour.

Her father bought a house near the Ottawa River, then a canoe and an old Hillman, following in the strokes of his beloved explorers in one, retracing the steps of early settlers in the other, and instilling in his reluctant wife and eager daughter a sense of Canada as a northern country. That's what made it special. He had a library of books about the Far North and an old dream of seeing it with his own eyes. Eleanor knew all the names: Franklin, Ross, Peary, Cook, Rasmussen, Stefansson, Samuel Hearne, David Thompson, John Hornby.

On their local travels it was usually just the two of them, since the motion of the car made her mother sick. Eleanor was navigator, co-pilot, chronicler, copying into a notebook words and dates on plaques, such as, AUGUST 28, 1955. *In memory of the services, self-devotion and tragic death of Charles Lennox, Fourth Duke of Richmond, a gallant soldier and governor in chief of Canada, who died here, 28th August, 1819.*

Self-devotion? He was devoted to himself? That couldn't be good, she remembers saying, and her father told her she was quick to pick that up. But no, devotion of self to duty.

Spreading the picnic rug near the stone cairn, setting out the Thermos of tea and the bread and butter and hard-boiled eggs, he'd then told her the sad and remarkable story of the fourth Duke of Richmond, who went mad after he was bitten by a pet fox. Nothing happened to him for a little while, but there came a night when he couldn't swallow his mulled wine and a morning when the sight of water in his shaving basin sent him into a convulsion. At the time, he was travelling by bush trail from Perth back to Richmond, and he kept travelling, careful to avert his eyes from streams or any running water, hydrophobia being a classic symptom of what he was suffering from, namely rabies. His final hours were eked out on Chapman's farm, close to this very spot. Not in the cabin, which overlooked the unsettling waters of the Jock River, but in a dimly lit barn, where he lay on a pile of corn shucks suffering excruciating pain and delirium. At dusk, when the river was hidden from view, they moved him into the cabin and he died soon after, poor wretch.

Wretch was one of Ring Lardner's favourite words, her father informed her. Mr. Funk, the poet and dictionary publisher, had compiled a list of the ten most beautiful words in the English language, namely: mist, hush, luminous, murmuring, dawn, chimes, lullaby, melody, tranquil, and golden; and the American humorist had responded with a list of his own: gangrene, flit, scram, mange, wretch, smoot with a small "s," guzzle, McNaboe, blute, crene. A blute being a smoker who doesn't inhale, and a crene a man who inhales but doesn't smoke.

"Those aren't real words," she'd said, "blute and crene."

Her father sucked happily on his pipe.

"*Your* favourite word is knucklehead," she said.

"No. My favourite word is daughter."

"Don't be a blute," she said.

They were thick as thieves.

One December day, close to Christmas, her father invited
her to come with him into the country to see a patient, which
is how they found themselves driving down a lane at the end
of which stood something of a miracle. A tall maple tree in full
leaf. Closer, and the tree appeared to be hung with clumps of
sod. Closer still, and Eleanor asked what they were. They
were partridges, sixteen in number. Sun-seekers, her father
said, and he stopped the car. The Burnt Lands of Almonte
were behind them, an area of flat, scrubby heath, a natural
home for partridges, pheasants, quail. It was a mild December
with what the weatherman on the radio called snow-licking
temperatures. As they watched, the sun came out and the tree
shone with its unusual fruit. Like something out of antiquity,
her father said.

There was another time she remembered as vividly.
They'd gone one Sunday afternoon for a walk in Rockcliffe
Park above the Ottawa River, when suddenly the wind rose
and her father, putting his hand on her shoulder, told her to
listen. Do you hear the different sounds in different trees?
They stood entranced. The wind whispered through the pines
and roared through the elms, mournful then tumultuous,
reminding him of a line from the past, and he quoted it: *like a
lost wave seeking a forgotten shore.* His fine Dew memory often
retrieved quotations without identifying them. There would
be plenty of time for that. They had a lifetime of poetry to
look forward to.

But less than a year later, on the evening of October 22,
1957, her father closed a book halfway through. He'd been
reading to her as part of his campaign to improve his boyhood
French "at your expense," he'd say, since she was near the end

of high school by this time and her French was better than his. *La fille qui était laide.* A picture book about a girl so ugly no one in her village would have anything to do with her, and so she ran away to the forest, where, day after day, one page at a time, the fresh air brightened her eyes, the sun bronzed her skin, the wind lifted and ruffled her hair, and she became beautiful.

But her father closed the book. He wasn't feeling well. He needed to lie down.

"Sorry. Tomorrow."

He went upstairs to bed and at nine o'clock he died.

There was a day, a few weeks after the funeral, when she put her grief to one side and tried to do something for her mother. She took her for an outing, a change of scene. They went to the National Gallery in the east wing of the Victoria Museum at the end of Metcalfe Street and stood in front of Rembrandt at his less-than-best. The doughy face of Esther, her skin so obviously the product of a cold, northern climate – its range of splotchy colour – and the thin, awful hair. It could be a portrait of you, thought Eleanor, turning to look at the parent she'd been left with.

She had been her father's daughter, and she consoled herself by spending long hours at his L-shaped desk in a corner of his second-floor study, surrounded by volume after volume about the North. The faded spines of blue, green, red, and gold were like an ancient springtime that took her back to the earliest scenes of affection. She would always be living her life backwards, she realized, trying to regain something perfect that she'd lost.

Her mother, frantic about money, sold the library a year later to Gladys Pyke, owner of Ye Olde Book Shoppe on

Gilmour Street. They moved to the small town of Almonte, where everything was cheaper, including their rented bungalow on the highway. Among the books her mother packed up and sold were a Japanese marine book tied together with shoelaces that showed coastlines and islands and clouds and rain, and a book about Japanese artists who would go out into the weather and observe it, absorbing it in every level of their being, before coming back inside to paint. *La fille qui était laide* Eleanor never found. It must have come from the library, her mother said. It must have been returned. But no librarian then or since had ever heard of the tale.

Finally, Eleanor went north herself, and now in the summer of 1975, a variation of the story was about to unfold in front of her eyes.

ON THE SHORTEST NIGHT OF THE YEAR, a golden evening without end, Dido climbed the wooden steps to Pilot's Monument on top of the great Rock that formed the heart of old Yellowknife. In the Netherlands the light was long and gradual too, but more meadowy, more watery, or else hazier, depending on where you were. In her part of the Netherlands, the rolling and agricultural southeast, winds from the west brought a marvellous, sea-swept clarity, while from the east came all the dust of landlocked Europe. Here, it was subarctic desert, virtually unpopulated, and the light was uniformly clear.

On the road below, a small man in a black beret was bending over his tripod just as her father used to bend over his tape recorder. Her father's voice had become the wallpaper inside her skull, he'd made a home for himself there as improvised and unexpected as these little houses on the side of the Rock – houses with histories of instability, of changing from gambling den to barbershop to sheet metal shop to private home, and of being moved from one part of town to another since they had no foundations. All the little and large efforts of settlement intrigued her. Down the shore from the old cemetery on Back Bay there used to be market gardens. Some of the log buildings remained; it wasn't impossible, with green-houses, to produce melons and tomatoes in Yellowknife. We Dutch would have stopped at nothing, she thought, we would have turned this place into a northern garden. And that's what pained her most about her Canadian father-in-law, how easily he'd given up on her. She remembered one of her father's questions to "London Calling." "What did you mean by the phrase 'a month of Wednesdays'?" And the answer came over the air: "The expression is 'a month of Sundays,' but in the particular context 'a month of Wednesdays' made sense." Her father-in-law wasn't going to come after her, not in a month of Sundays, and not in a month of Wednesdays, either.

The man in the beret was Ralph Cody, she realized. She'd seen him around the station when he came in to do his book reviews. He folded his tripod and moved along Ingraham Drive, as it was fancifully called, since the narrow little roads on and around the Rock were more cow path than grand driveway. She'd read that the Ingraham of Ingraham Drive had been an early settler and hotel-builder who lost both feet and most of his fingers in a terrible boat accident on Great Bear Lake: fire then frostbite then amputation. All of these pioneer families were colourful, storied, and a diversion, Dido firmly believed, from the real story of the First Peoples, dis-placed and impoverished and now having their audience with Judge Berger, who wouldn't be radical enough in his recom-mendations. That went without saying.

Dido turned 360 degrees to take in the west, north, east, south of Back Bay, Giant Mine, Latham Island, Yellowknife Bay, Willow Flats, New Town, Peace River Flats. Then she made her way back down the flight of wooden steps to

Ingraham Drive and took a side road to another road that led past float plane bases and around to the government dock on Yellowknife Bay. Here there were small warehouses and from one of them came the sound of gentle hammering. She poked her head in the open door, surprised to see Eddy sitting at a workbench. He didn't look up and she could have stepped away unseen.

She went in.

He was working on a big old radio set, adapting it to his own purposes, he said when she asked. What purposes? His smile came suddenly, transforming his small eyes. Their depths came alive with an amused, seductive light that went right through her. He told her he knew about electronics from the U.S. army, he'd been in the communications corps. What purposes? she asked again, but again he didn't answer. So she confessed she'd grown up on war stories, or stories of liberation, to be accurate; her father adored both England and Canada.

Eddy had rented one corner of this warehouse, the rest of the space was occupied by rolled-up carpets. He didn't have the room in his apartment or the freedom at the station to spread out, and he indicated the array of tools and parts on the long table beside him.

"I wish I knew even half as much as you do," she said, conferring praise, singling him out as special. "Where are your people from?" she asked, and spoke his last name. *Fitzgerald.*

"Ireland originally," he told her. "We don't adore England."

She smiled too and turned the loose watch around her wrist, but she wasn't finished with her questions or he with his evasions. She asked him where he got the parts he needed. He ordered them, he said. And they arrived in the mail? Exactly.

"What are you doing, Eddy? What are you up to?"

"Do I have to be up to something?"

Their eyes met and it was clear that she hoped he *was* up to something, and he knew it and didn't mind.

For a few minutes she watched and said nothing. He was working with the tiniest of screws, using tweezers to pick them up. Eddy's fastidious hands and the rolled-up carpets behind him worked on her receptive mind, and she was brought back to her home in Nijmegen, to their practice of spreading heavy and valuable rugs over tables rather than across the floor. Strangely, she smelled apples again as a light breeze came in through open windows.

Eddy asked her what her plans were for the next few hours.

"Do you want the truth?"

"Always," he said.

"I think I'll stay up all night. I want to see all the changes in the light, the sequence from sunset to sunrise."

He offered to keep her company, if she liked. He'd make a pot of coffee at midnight, and he indicated the hot plate on the table. If she got tired he'd unroll one of those carpets and they could lie down together for a while. Dido laughed and shook her head. No, she said, she'd be fine alone. But her heart quickened and her body opened and ached.

"I'll have the coffee on," he called to her departing back. He couldn't see her face and the big, shining smile she couldn't keep from her lips.

Eddy was still at his workbench a little after midnight. She came in and stood close to him. Without looking up, he reached for her wrist and circled it with his hand.

She said, "I've come for my cup of coffee."

⸻

Eleanor no longer found Dido in bed very often now – neither in her bed nor her own.

The first time she noticed her absence she got up and wandered outside, unable to sleep, and looked for Dido's brown car. The shortest night of the year, and no sign of the woman or the car. She had to wonder at the loneliness she felt. Eleanor, Eleanor, you're almost forty, working in a lowly job, writing poetry you don't publish, essentially alone. What are you doing with yourself?

At the station the next day, Dido was as friendly to her as ever, but less talkative. Apparently, Dido wasn't a woman who felt the need to explain herself, and Eleanor was left to read on her own the signs of something new between her friend and Eddy.

That night, once again, Eleanor couldn't sleep. She'd made a mistake with the measurements when she'd ordered new window shades for her bedroom, and light poured in on all sides, giving her what she called Marilyn Monroe nights, they were so blond and sleepless. Finally, she went into her windowless bathroom, closed the door, rolled up a towel and shoved it into the crack between door and floor. Then she sat on the floor in the perfect darkness and suddenly tears were rolling down her face and she didn't understand why. I'm not unhappy, she thought. I'm really not unhappy. I've been much unhappier in the past.

About three in the morning she made tea and took her cup outside. She sat on the steps and fell to brooding about her ex-husband, his life with poor Barbara, his life with her, his unresolved life. Then her thoughts drew her back to child-hood, to her father, to their joy in each other, their mutual devotion. Moved by some impulse, Eleanor went back inside, crossed to the bookshelves in the living room, and pulled down the first book her hand landed upon. Where the book fell open, she began to read, and the first words were *"like imperfect sleep."*

"Like imperfect sleep, which instead of giving more strength to the head, doth but leave it the more exhausted, the result of mere operations of the imagination is but to weaken the soul. Instead of nourishment and energy she reaps only lassitude and disgust: whereas a genuine heavenly vision yields to her a harvest of ineffable spiritual riches, and an admirable renewal of bodily strength."

Eleanor read the passage a second time. Saint Teresa was justifying her visions, saying they came from God, not the devil, because they left her changed for the better: not feeling as one feels after imperfect sleep, but renewed and strong.

A lovely coincidence, thought Eleanor, but it doesn't lead anywhere.

Nevertheless, she kept reading. The book was *Varieties of Religious Experience* by William James, and she found herself especially affected by the chapters about sick souls, the divided self, conversion. She came upon the old, recurrent phrases in use for centuries, "inexpressible joy took hold of my heart," "a great change came over me," and thought, These people who find God assume a new flesh tone. Instead of being clothed and lumbered with self, they step naked into a new world. She thought she understood how it worked. Just as you can know by the wreckage of a moment that life will never be the same – your father dies one night when you're eighteen – so an awakened soul understands that from this moment on everything will be different, but rather than pain and sorrow, a reliable joy will be yours. If you take up the challenge.

Eleanor set down the book and closed her tired eyes. Such a big *if*.

Later, as she stood under a hot shower, she wondered if any of her feelings would ever be consummated, or if she was one of those people who is religious without ever having a vision, just as she'd been married without ever making love.

WHEN GWEN WAS FOUR YEARS OLD, she had a yellow summer dress with an ice cream pattern. To eat an ice cream cone in that dress, to watch her cone melt and disintegrate while the pretty cones on her dress remained frozen, perfect, gave her a sensation not unlike this one, of seeing typed words on the page turn into a great big mess in her mouth.

She tried to describe to Eleanor what it was like being on air – feet dangling, heart pierced with doubt, head all tangled. And Eleanor thought of Absalom in the Bible – Absalom fleeing an angry King David by riding his mule through the woods, dodging trees and ducking under boughs, until his mass of curly hair got so entangled in the low branches of an oak tree that he hung there, suspended; then along came Joab and thrust three darts through his heart.

Eleanor didn't burden Gwen with her recent Bible reading, she just listened and sympathized and understood that time was running out for Gwen. She knew the two newsmen, Bill Thwaite and George Tupper, had stormed into Harry's office, demanding he get rid of her as the newsreader.

Harry had fobbed them off, telling them to have patience, the girl had been reading the news for two weeks, what did they expect? But privately, he began to alter his plans.

A week later, he took Gwen to the Gold Range for a beer. The bar had its own atmosphere. Winter or summer it was the same seedy, over-lit, smoke-filled, hotdog-smelling tavern of small round tables covered with fitted dark-red terry cloth and glasses of beer. "You have to let yourself enter the story," Harry told Gwen with a new note of impatience in his voice. "Enter it and let your eyes move ahead to the end of the line and down to the next line, and your voice will pick up and follow. Read as if you're searching out the meaning of the words."

"But you have a great voice," she told him.

"I've never cared for it."

"It's great."

She noticed Jim Murphy, the morning man, at a table in the corner. He'd been there for hours by the looks of it. Jim had given her a couple of lessons in editing tape. Tight-lipped and rushed, but not unhelpful, he'd sat in front of the old Studer in the editing cubicle and threaded the dark, slippery, quarter-inch tape through the playback head and up onto the take-up reel, then pressed fast-forward until he reached the part of the interview he wanted to cut. He liked to jockey the reels back and forth by hand, rather like a man screwing lids on two jars at the same time, his ear attentive to the dragged-out whump and thump of words on tape. Having located the precise end of the word he wanted to keep, he marked the tape at that spot with a red grease pencil, then let the expendable sentences spool onto the floor until he came to the next word he wanted, backed up to the intake of breath, marked the spot, smoothed that portion of tape into the grooved cutting slot of the editing block, and sliced the tape with his razor blade. He did the same with the earlier spot he'd marked, then he made the two ends meet, butting them up against each other, before pressing an inch-long piece of white splicing tape over the join with his fingertip. Jim was fast, Gwen quite slow at first. But she found the handwork restful and took pleasure and pride in making cuts that no listener would be able to decipher, and in eliminating the stumbles and repetitions and bad grammar of voices on tape. It felt like kindness and a form of magic.

Gwen sent a tentative smile Jim's way and got back something less, a raised-eye acknowledgement followed by a hostile glance at Harry. For the first time, she felt worried not for herself, but for Harry. One of the newsmen, it was skinny Bill Thwaite, joined Jim and then the dirty looks directed Harry's way became double-barrelled.

"Harry?"

He stopped drumming the table with his fingers and smiled at her, an honest shambles of a man who couldn't bring himself to tell her what he had to tell her.

"Is it hard being the manager? I mean, going from the night shift, when nobody bothered you, to all the hassles of running the station."

"Acting manager. I have no illusions. I've got the job while they figure out their long-term plans for television and the new station they've got in mind. But I'm going to use my time to do a few things."

She watched him tap another cigarette out of his pack, grateful for his faith in her so far, dubious about how much longer it could possibly last. "Such as," she prodded.

"I'm going to defend radio from TV."

His mood became more expansive, and she relaxed a little, believing he wouldn't bother to tell her these things if he'd written her off. Radio was like poetry, he told her. At its best it could be, while television was like a blockbuster novel: one made you think and feel, the other dulled your mind. "A radio program isn't a 'show,'" he went on. "It's not showbiz, it's not an assault. It's about one person learning something interesting and telling it to somebody else. You're speaking to one person, remember that. And don't say who you are every fifteen minutes, or give time checks to the second. Is there a listener alive who really cares if it's going to be 5:28 ten seconds from now? Just say it's five-thirty. We're not in Toronto, for Christ's sake."

She looked over at Jim and Bill, who were ordering more beer. "Jim never makes a mistake," she said, her voice envious, wistful. "He's so sure of himself."

"That's his problem."

A remark that made her eyes glisten with interest, for she'd had exactly the same thought. Jim was too smooth. He was so smooth you tuned him out.

Leaning forward, "What's his problem?"

"He doesn't think it's hard. To be any good you have to believe it's hard. It's called creative tension." Harry looked at her pale, intense face and read her mind. "And you won't be any good until you're dedicated to something outside yourself."

Gwen considered this. "Is Dido dedicated to something outside herself?"

"Dido's ambitious." His voice was bleak. "She won't stick around radio very long."

"You haven't answered my question," she said.

Harry smiled. He was impressed by these young women, who seemed to know what they wanted, and it wasn't marriage and children. They seemed smarter and more aware of themselves than men. On the other hand, they lacked what he would call proper arrogance – the arrogance necessary to succeed at something over the long haul, despite your insecurities. Not that he was one to talk, of course.

"You're competitive," he allowed.

"I don't think I am," she answered slowly. "Except maybe in an ingrown way."

Harry laughed and drained his glass. He felt his pockets, patted himself front and back.

"I suppose you've forgotten your wallet," she cracked.

"Hang on." He located it in his back pocket, slapped it on the table, then narrowed his eyes. "But I bet my mother is cheaper than your mother."

"That's impossible."

"My mother was so cheap," he said with energy, "that when she made raspberry jam it was mostly rhubarb. And she never turned on the oven unless she had several things to bake. 'Not for twenty minutes, for *one* thing.'"

"Mine too," cried Gwen, "mine too. She had to have something in every corner of the oven or the heat was going to waste. We used to make a game of hunting for the chips in her chocolate chip cookies. 'Mom? How can you call these chocolate chip cookies?'"

Harry snickered. "They don't call them chocolate *chips* cookies for a reason, Gwen."

They became aware of the bar again – of Jim Murphy and Bill Thwaite on one dark horizon, while from a nearby table came the low and thunderous rumble of a female voice talking about all these well-meaning left-wing lawyers from southern universities coming up here and telling the natives what to think and what to say to Berger. She personally thought, she did, that everybody should cut the dramatization and stop talking about the past. What matters is now and tomorrow.

"Who's that?" whispered Gwen as the voice blared on about all the bullshit being shovelled around, since who in his right mind would give up clean water from a tap and a centrally heated house and food at the Bay to go back on the land? Why not talk about all the good things we've brought them, all the benefits that make life a lot easier?

"She's been around for years. A settlement manager for a while. A teacher before that. She's a pain in the neck, but she's no fool."

Years ago he'd paid a visit to her classroom in Nahanni Butte, where the children, using plasticine, had made uncannily accurate models of every kind of animal and every make of Ski-Doo. To her credit, she even had them writing haiku.

Harry paid the waiter for their beers, then studied Gwen for a moment. She was chewing her nails, staring at the floor.

He said, "I used to be scared too."

She looked up.

"But then I learned that making a mistake is just something you go on from."

Gwen's eyes didn't leave his face.

"I don't mean I felt secure," he said. "Feeling secure makes you lazy. You have to have an edge. The good ones are always nervous."

But you weren't good on television, she thought, you were terrible. She'd realized rather suddenly one day that it must have been him, must have been Harry, that night years ago when she was watching television. On her small screen he'd been a blurry figure, who seemed out of focus he was so out of place; she saw him stumble and thought oh no, he's going to fall, and she switched channels.

How it perplexed and disturbed her, this question of good nervousness versus bad nervousness.

They headed back to the station. This part of town was no different, really, to the place Harry had known in 1960, when he started out. In those days there were only three thousand people, instead of ten thousand, and there were no subdivisions in New Town, no high-rise, no Explorer Hotel. He'd arrived at the end of summer, a refugee from graduate school, and for a few months he'd worked at Cominco, one of the two gold mines in Yellowknife. Then he began to do some freelance radio pieces, and before he knew it he'd been offered a permanent job. Now, all these years later, he couldn't approach the station without feeling nostalgic and depressed, both, about life in general and himself in particular. At the corner he noticed a dog limping towards them, and knelt down. A small husky, who allowed him to lift and examine her sore paw. A shard of glass from a broken beer bottle had lodged between two badly scuffed pads: he removed it.

"If only you could fix my problems so easily," Gwen observed dryly, looking down at the top of his balding head and at his big hands, gardener's hands, she thought.

He let out a short laugh and stood up. Gwen wasn't bad company. He wondered if the dog might be the one missing from the car that skidded off the gravel near Fort Rae; he'd hold on to her and call the police. The dog followed them across the street and into the radio station.

On Eleanor's desk lay the pile of community announcements broadcast three times a day in five-minute time slots, a listing of events and of personal messages.

Would Henry Wandering Spirit please contact the R.C.M.P. as soon as possible.

Helen Jumbo, you have a C.O.D. parcel in the Ft. Simpson post office.

The pediatrician will be at the nurses' station in Ft. Smith on Thursday afternoon from one to four o'clock.

To Albert Drygeese: The plane won't be coming in today because of the fog. It will come tomorrow at three in the afternoon. Dad.

The Gene Bertoncini Jazz Trio performs in Yellowknife in the auditorium of Mildred Hall Elementary School this Sunday at 8 p.m.

To the Chocolates in Fort Rae: Debbie Lynn had a baby boy, six pounds, eight ounces. Both doing well.

They glanced at these and other announcements typed on the half sheets of yellow carbon paper. Nobody was looking for a lost dog.

Harry went searching for a water bowl for his new buddy, while Gwen reread the announcement about Saturday night's Raven Mad Daze All Night Golf Tournament on the town's nine-hole golf course, infamous for being made of sand and for having a special ground rule to cover the ravens that swooped down and stole your ball. Seize the moment, Gwen thought to herself. Time to jump. She went down to the technical shop in the basement to ask about signing out the Nagra tape recorder, and that's when she heard what Harry had been meaning to tell her.

In the basement Andrew McNab gave her a careful lesson in operating the Nagra, a beautiful Swiss machine, he said of the heavy reel-to-reel tape recorder encased in black leather. "You might as well," he allowed when she explained that she wanted to tape part of the midnight golf tournament. "You'll be getting used to late-night hours."

It turned out Harry had consigned her to the night shift, the radio wasteland of 6 p.m. to 1 a.m., but he hadn't quite got around to telling her.

The dog lay at his feet on the floor of his office when Gwen positioned herself in the open door. "Harry, there's something you haven't told me."

He looked at her over his glasses. She had seen this look before on her father's face when she'd come in tenth in a foot race, having previously done rather well in the hop, skip, and jump. Then he removed his glasses and asked her to sit down.

"I'm thinking of calling her Ella," he said, "if the police don't call me back to say someone's got a prior claim."

They both gazed at the dog, who didn't take her eyes off Harry.

"Old Eller," he quipped.

Having made Gwen smile, he said, "Don't take the night shift personally. It's where every apprentice starts and where some of us choose to end up." He was working the arms of his glasses, tapping them together. "Let me put it this way, you'll be able to work out your kinks a lot more easily." And he told her how much he'd enjoyed the solitude and freedom of being the only one in the station, hour after hour. He'd found his feet in radio again, regained some of his old confidence. After seven o'clock the station was pretty quiet, he said. There was a certain amount of busywork, tapes to set up, the logging machine to maintain, sound carts to record, sometimes a news feed to send or receive, weather stats to be gathered by phoning the weather-men at the airport, and the live station breaks every hour. But there was plenty of time to listen to music; he'd needle-dropped his way through innumerable records, selecting songs for the hour from midnight to 1 a.m., when local radio took over from the national network. At 1 a.m. you signed off and shut down the station. He missed it, he said. It was a great place for trying things out, you could be as creative as you liked. Besides, he added, she'd be doing him a favour; the casual who had been filling in for a month had taken full-time work elsewhere.

Gwen listened and adjusted, and by the end of their conversation felt almost pleased. Until the next day, that is, when she learned that Dido, who among other things had been doing Radio Noon, would become the permanent newsreader as well.

Later that day, Gwen took the gradual slope downhill to Old Town. To have water on both sides, to know which way was north, to be walking towards it – this was comfort by any measure.

It came to her suddenly that what she missed most was frankness. So much of the time you weren't allowed to say certain things. You weren't allowed to say you were lousy. Nobody wanted to hear it. You weren't allowed to say you were jealous. As she walked along, the voice started up inside her head, asking her about the biggest obstacle she had ever faced. Probably my own jealousy, she confessed to the shadowy, sympathetic, ever-impressed voice. In my early years in radio, I was very bad. I know, it's hard to believe, but something about radio made me even more self-conscious. In Yellowknife I worked with Dido Paris and she was such a natural. The name means nothing to you? Well, she was wonderful on air. I wasn't like that at all.

"You're deep in thought," said Ralph Cody.

She had slowed down and was saying these things to herself, so busy being a famous old woman looking back on her past that she wasn't aware of anything else.

Ralph had his camera bag over his shoulder and was heading to the causeway that joined Old Town to Latham Island, so Gwen went along, glad of the company, and learned that in the 1930s, before they built the causeway, a woman named Bertha used to row people across the narrows for a nickel a head, and that a family named Cinnamon had moved up from Vermilion and become prominent in Yellowknife, "creating a veritable rainbow of names," crowed Ralph. In those days, he said, you could meet a woman in the Wildcat Café and get married by a priest who doubled as a magician and have your wedding in the Squeeze Inn.

Ralph's fine grey hair blew about and his small, nicotined hands were deft with tripod and camera. To Gwen he seemed old and thin and irresistible, like her high school English teacher who taught her to love Shakespeare. Mr. Smiley had been a pilot in the war and had lost his sense of smell, a stroke of luck, he liked to say, since thereafter he was spared the smell of women's perfume. A cynic. Yet for all that, you knew he loved women, perhaps too much.

Gwen wanted Ralph to know the reason she was free in the middle of the day, and Ralph asked how she felt about it, being moved to the night shift. He himself was something of a nighthawk, he confessed, working on his educational contracts after dark, when he wasn't reading the books he reviewed for radio; daylight hours he saved for photography, though in the summer he could photograph around the clock. Gwen said she felt all right, but she wished she were better on air. Ralph told her she sounded fine.

Gwen considered this. "I wonder if you mean that." And her bleak challenge made him smile.

"A woman trolling for compliments," he said. "You sound fine. But if you *want* to be jealous," he added mischievously, "you're not as good as Dido."

He set up his tripod on a flat rock that extended into the water, then stepped back. "Take a look."

Gwen bent over and peered through the lens at weeds in water. To her eye the sinuous grasses were like long filaments of silver drowning in a watery sky. She came from a family of jewellers, after all. Her father and uncle, and a great-uncle too. The great-uncle had gone west from Ontario and opened up a jewellery store on the Prairies, and she liked to imagine him working with tiny, intricate objects under a vast Saskatchewan sky.

She said, "I don't want to be jealous, but I am." So jealous she'd even gone shopping for the kind of scoop-neck T-shirts Dido wore. She was wearing one now, as well as a short necklace of blue beads.

"I don't photograph people as a rule," Ralph said. "But I'd make an exception for Dido."

The hair on his head blew in the other direction and his scalp shone as he bent over his tripod. Thinning-haired Mr. Smiley used to lean against his desk and read Shakespeare's sonnets aloud, weaving in jokes about beautiful women losing their looks. We aren't here for long, he would say. And that turned out to be true, for he died very suddenly in his sixties.

"Dido's my first Dido," Ralph added after taking several shots. "Apart from the opera."

Gwen folded her arms. "Well, don't enlighten me. See if I care." And it relieved her feelings to speak with rough humour.

Ralph looked up and chuckled. So she wasn't a pushover, he thought, and he eyed her with more respect.

The opera he'd meant, he said, folding up his tripod, was *Les Troyens* by Berlioz – about the tragic passion of Dido and Aeneas, and the founding of Rome and the fall of Carthage.

"Dido was the Queen of Carthage and Berlioz learned her story at his father's knee. He was reading Virgil when you were reading Dick and Jane."

Ralph liked to talk, liked having a curious and attentive listener. He said the opera wasn't popular but it was very powerful, especially at the end when Dido kills herself, since in her dying moments she has a terrible awareness of what's to come — not only has Aeneas ruined her life by leaving her and sailing off to found Rome, but in founding Rome he's set in motion the last days of her beloved Carthage. "Do they teach you about Carthage these days?"

Gwen waved her hands to indicate vaguely, she knew vaguely.

"The Romans razed it to the ground. Then they sowed the surrounding fields with salt. That's the North, if the pipeline goes through." He was struck by his own analogy. "Not bad, Ralph. Write that down. Building the pipeline is like sowing the ground with salt."

They walked back to the road, and he told her that last year, during the opera season, he and Eleanor and Lorna Dargabble went into the station on Saturday afternoons and Eddy fed the broadcast from the Metropolitan Opera in New York into the lobby, since CFYK, in its wisdom, preempted the Saturday afternoon opera in favour of a country and western request show. "Bring on Merle Haggard," he intoned, revving himself up. "Get down with Johnny Cash. Let's hear it for Conway Twitty."

Gwen laughed, but she couldn't picture Eddy listening to opera, and she said so.

"Eddy's a surprising guy," Ralph said. "Eddy's the kind of guy who could be running guns for Angola or writing odes to his mistress."

"I don't think he likes women very much," she said, expressing a reservation she'd never articulated before. "On some level he *dislikes* them. Except for Dido, of course. He can't take his eyes off her. Any more than Harry can."

"*I* like women."

"I know you do." She smiled. "I've seen you flirting with Eleanor. I don't mean Eddy's interested in men," she went on, "I don't mean that at all. I just have the feeling he's got contempt for women."

"I would never underestimate a woman's intuition," said Ralph easily. But later, he would have reason to think back on young Gwen's assessment of Eddy.

＝

Gwen got bounced – out into the midnight woods. And there, night after night, through the month of July, she improved. No one was watching, few were listening, the light was entirely different. Alone in the announce booth, she turned off the overhead light and operated in the jewel-like glow of the little diodes and vu meters. She used headphones, since Andrew McNab wasn't around to chide her about announcers being addicted to the sound of their own voices, and thus she heard herself close by, not ricocheting around an empty room and careening out over empty wastes, but here, in the dark warm woods that resembled in a wonderful way the darkness backstage.

One night in the basement she found a little sound-effects door. Constructed of wood and about the size of an old-fashioned wall telephone, the wee door turned on a hinge and had a bell and a door knob of regular size. With Andrew's permission, she brought it upstairs into her snug little booth, where the control board was carved out as if to accommodate a well-filled belly. Sliding her wheeled chair into its embrace, she operated switches and pots, rolling to the left or right to work the turntables on either side, or to reach the standing rack equipped for reel-to-reel tapes and sound cartridges, the latter carrying station ID and music stings: press the square green button to start the cartridge and the yellow button to stop it. In the privacy of her late-night show (in her mind she called it "show" with apologies to Harry), which displaced the network from midnight till 1 a.m., she tried out the sound-effects door, shutting it hard on songs she didn't like and opening it wide on its squeaky hinges to welcome singers she enjoyed.

She gave herself a new name. Stella Round. And used it on air.

She experimented with sound. "Can you identify this bird?" she asked into the night, playing a persistent, rather eerie bird call she'd recorded through an open window in the early morning hours, not expecting an answer and not getting one either. She recorded Eleanor's impish, girlish, delighted laugh. She recorded a Venetian blind clicking in the wind and Bill Thwaite typing in the newsroom. Ella barking and a raven answering. Then she organized the sounds in a formal way, like music. A phrase, then a repeat of it, then a new sound, and a repeat, then back to the beginning, looping around her neck the long necklaces of dark-brown tape that she moved about and reinserted.

Jim Murphy, listening at home, phoned her at the station. "Let me air that what's-it, that sound thing again in the morning." Okay. But let her do some fine editing first.

At the old Studer, working with grease pencil, razor blade, splicing tape, and a few take-up reels, she made seamless joins between ambient noise and particular sounds, like a shoe-maker leaving behind a flawless shoe for the morning.

With time she'd grown more accustomed to the bracing experience of the microphone. It no longer felt like plunging into cold water – in and out – before towelling herself off. She could stay in much longer. A burka for the shy, the nighttime announce booth. A dark tent that covered her up as she crossed the wide desert of late-night radio.

IT WAS HARD TO SAY when the larger suspense began. At first, like almost everyone else, Harry had thought there wasn't much Judge Berger could do. His inquiry was window dressing and everyone knew it. But then Harry realized that the denigrators were missing the point. It wasn't Berger's job to decide whether or not a pipeline was to be built, but what conditions should be imposed if construction went ahead. Those conditions could be minor or they could be major. At stake was something immense, all the forms of life that lay in the path of a natural gas pipeline corridor that would rip open the Arctic, according to critics, like a razor slashing the face of the Mona Lisa.

Harry and Berger were the same age. In fact, although he hated to admit it, Thomas Berger was a year younger. Harry had met him and sized him up as casually formal, serious, unconceited, tireless, aware that he was facing the biggest challenge of his life and not about to blow it (the way Harry had), the sort of man who listened, the sort of man women couldn't get enough of. Harry came away impressed and nothing ever happened to make him less impressed. Berger was doing more to bring the issues of the day to the fore than anyone else he knew.

Now, voices that had never been on the radio had their chance to speak. Plain-spoken, same-spoken, tentative yet clear, young and old, in translation or speaking English, usually soft, sometimes strident, native people were convincing Judge Berger that the land gave them life, it was their flesh and blood, they were born and raised on it, they lived and survived by it, they loved and respected and belonged to it, as had their ancestors for thousands of years. Louis Caesar of Fort Good Hope, Lazarus Sittichinli of Aklavik, Fred Widow of Willow Lake, John Steen of Tuktoyaktuk, Jane Charlie of Fort McPherson. Up and down the Mackenzie River Valley the message was overwhelmingly the same. The past had never gone away, had no intention of going away.

The testimony wasn't unplanned (the native organizations were active in every settlement, urging everyone to speak out and speak with one voice), it wasn't left to chance, it was *almost* unrehearsed. Roy Fabian of Hay River told Judge Berger "there's very, very few white people that will be friends with native people. Any of these white people that are friends with native people, it's like a pearl in a pile of gravel."

Tom Berger was a pearl. He listened with grave, courteous, uncommon openness, being a careful speaker himself, and one who took his time. Reporters questioned him about his seemingly infinite patience, his ability to listen for hours to highly technical presentations on the one hand, and to meandering life stories on the other. He explained that from each speaker he tried to learn something new, and indicated that he felt at home with the way native people talked. If the Dene had nothing to say, they didn't say it, and the not saying could go on for a long time. "You often just sit there looking at the river."

Berger's distinctive voice became familiar to everyone in the North. Those who heard it would recognize it immediately, no matter how many years had gone by, his firm, thoughtful, soft-spoken voice soliciting expert testimony about the social, environmental, and economic impact of the pipeline, but also the opinions of anyone who would be affected by what would be the biggest project ever built in the history of free enterprise, if it went ahead. Every evening the opinions, arguments, voices were carried by all the stations in the Northern Service in the hour-long coverage prepared by the CBC's special team of six reporters working in English, Dogrib, Slavey, Hareskin, Loucheux, Chipewyan, and Inuktitut. "Let me put it this way," Berger would explain in his unhurried, tempered fashion, "we have never before in our country had an inquiry before large-scale frontier development was undertaken. So this inquiry is unique in the Canadian experience and really unique in the experience of any industrialized country in the West." And he invited everyone in "this vast Territory where we have people of four races speaking seven languages" to be a part of history in the making.

Although based in Yellowknife, where lawyers for the pipeline companies and the native organizations set out their formal positions, the inquiry would travel over the course of two years to settlements up and down the Mackenzie Valley, to communities on the Beaufort Sea and in the Yukon, and even to major cities in southern Canada, since at issue was the future of the northern wilderness, alternately considered a last frontier by developers and an indispensable homeland by the native people, but undeniably one of the last wonders of the earth.

With July came the smell of smoke in the air from distant forest fires. Trees and ground were tinder-dry after weeks of unbroken warmth and no rain.

Harry walked the thirty minutes home in the evening, his dog, Ella, bounding along beside him as she had in the morning when he'd gone to work. They followed Franklin Avenue to Old Town, then crossed the causeway to Latham Island, and the walk gave Harry time to ponder the struggle taking shape on his own small turf. A fancy new CBC station was in the works, to be built on the southern edge of town and to house the new regional television venture, with radio taking second place. In a few years TV would reach beyond Yellowknife to every remote settlement in the Arctic and produce a generation addicted to instant gratification – the final death knell, in Harry's opinion, for native language and culture. But did it have to be that way? He knew he was fighting a rearguard action, but so was Berger, and so were the settlements voting in favour of prohibition to turn back the tide of drunkenness and abuse. Harry couldn't stop the new station from being built, but he could champion radio as more flexible, more forward-thinking, far cheaper than television, and a natural home for northerners.

Most of the time, when he turned into his driveway, his neighbour Louise Corrie was sitting on her stoop next door, smoking her pipe. Louise in her bandana, her brown stockings and ankle socks, mukluks and low rubbers, old skirt and blue jacket. Black Louise, she was called, for her various illicit activities, making home brew for one, and certainly she had a steady stream of visitors, mostly men, at all hours of the day and night. But what she seemed to like best was to sit in the sunshine on the spot of lush green grass directly in front of the door of her shack. Harry would see her there and think "pigeons on the grass, alas," since gulls would land and pick about, drawn by the food she scraped out of her pot. This was where she'd sat on the morning a few weeks ago when she'd opened a can of paint and to Harry's wonderment and delight painted her brown cane completely white.

Harry went inside, made himself some supper, fed Ella, and then listened to Dido's voice on the sly. He'd made a tape of her reading the community announcements on Radio Noon, and though he tried to ration himself, still, every night her voice filled his house. It wasn't true that he never tired of it. He tired of it as one tires of even a beautiful song. But to reach that point took a lot of listening. There was a moment when she announced a call for local "thespians" to audition for the drama society, and she giggled, for all the world like a lamb kicking up its heels.

Late one night he phoned her. "I thought of dropping in to see you."

She was silent on the other end of the line.

"Silence," he said.

"No. It would be nice to see you. But tonight isn't a good night."

The next night, by chance, he happened to see her without being seen. Restless, he'd whistled for Ella and they'd gone out into the light-filled road around eight o'clock. Louise and her lopsided friend, Andrew, were sitting in front of her shack, Louise with her pipe, and Andrew lopsided, they said, from his habit of throwing himself in front of moving cars in the hope of collecting on the insurance, but never without a huge, goofy, good-natured grin for Harry, or anyone else, who greeted him.

Harry had nothing in mind except following the narrow road to the gently rising hill that overlooked Rainbow Valley at the end of the island – from the hill he'd be able to see the valley and the big lake beyond. As he walked along, he passed the snug, well-designed home that belonged to the daughter of George Whalley. Farther on, also on his left and in a clump of trees, was Father Fumoleau's little house, the political priest who'd spent years documenting the history of Treaties 8 and 11 to prove the natives had never extinguished their claim to the land. Harry stood just above the priest's house and looked down at the multicoloured little dwellings that gave the valley its name. Officially, it was Lot 500, fifty-six unsurveyed and unserviced acres set aside for the Indians, the people who'd lived on this land for hundreds, if not thousands, of years and now managed on the scraps tossed their way. Harry shifted his gaze to the vast, shining waters of Great Slave Lake.

It seemed to him that spiritual changes come like a gust of wind on a quiet day, blowing a door open or blowing it shut. He was thinking about Eleanor, who'd told him she was going to church again, and he knew she was reaching out for something and it touched him, but he felt more in tune with his mother, who had tried to pray for her sister's recovery from a stroke and suddenly realized there was no point; no one was listening. His mother had been a better mother than a minister's wife, a wonderful mother, really, despite her threats to feed him ground glass and arsenic if he didn't eat what was on his plate. Well, she should have lived here, he thought, where arsenic was all too plentiful from the milling of gold. For years rumours had circulated about native children eating snow and dying of arsenic poisoning. About children eating the plentiful red berries near Giant and Con mines and getting sick. About horses in the very early days drinking the spring runoff water lying about in puddles at Giant Mine and dying in the autumn, and of a similar fate befalling the cows that were brought north in the late 1940s by a Mr. and Mrs. Bevan.

Harry was about to turn around and head back to the fork in the road, following it to the less occupied side of the island, when he saw Eddy and Dido come out of a faded blue house down below. They crossed the road together and got into Eddy's white truck. The other day he'd watched Dido scratch her head with a pen. She'd run the end of the pen through her thick hair at the back of her head, repeatedly and from different angles, like the long handle of a comb, languidly, unconsciously. After she left her desk, he went over and picked up the pen and held it to his nose, pathetic man that he was, trying to smell her hair.

But now he turned and walked fast to get himself around the corner and out of sight. What were they doing there? he wondered. Dido and Eddy.

The curving road on this side of the island was lined with trees, the few houses were hidden, or not so hidden, and most of them occupied by white northerners, a somewhat anxious breed, he'd always thought, composed of transients, new-comers, long-timers, old-timers, pioneers – they were the rungs on an ascending ladder of possessive pride about one's stamina and attachment to the North. Who had Dido and Eddy been visiting? he wondered. And why?

That night he was lying on his bed thinking about the station – his station – and radio people he'd known. Quarrelsome as sparrows guarding their territory, but what issued from them was song, birdsong being proprietary and exclusive. What were people imagining as they listened to radio? How friendly everyone was. How well they must get along, how intimate they must be. Not knowing how they fought to get air time, resisted anything new, stewed in their own jealousy and ill will.

These were Harry's jaded thoughts. He knew he was too friendly with some of his staff, too cantankerous with the rest; it came from being an announcer himself, and from not having his heart in management – programming, yes, but not man-agement. For his own sake, and the station's, he should court the newsmen, bolster them, encourage them, make them feel valued. His radio was on, a low-level irritation at the moment with its yap yap yap of excessive information and mediocre music coming from Toronto. Ella lay on the floor beside him, awake, alert, always ready for a walk. He reached over and rubbed her ears and an idea came to him for a program of old songs, old tales, old remedies, old places. He heard the wind and the familiar thudding sounds of ravens on the roof, and stroked his dog's thick fur. His grandfather had been a furrier. Edgar Farnham, his mother's father, a man with wide-set eyes, floppy ears, floppy moustache, a man who liked to talk but only in a quiet room. As a small boy, Harry loved going into his shop in Winnipeg, loved all the fluff on the floor, the pigeon feathers in the windows, the girlie calendars on the walls, the winking men bent over their sewing machines. In the back office, he learned some bits of fur terminology: a thin pelt that crackles is called *a paper*, a thick pelt *a heavy*. He learned that you can clean fur by tumbling it with sawdust inside a drum; that mink is much cleaner and easier to work with than fox or coyote – shake a coyote pelt and you get clouds of dust. On his fifth birthday, his grandfather gave him a small swatch of mink and it became precious. Without it rubbing back and forth under his nose he couldn't fall asleep.

He was seven when they left Winnipeg. His father took over the Presbyterian parish in Woodstock, New Brunswick, and Harry drifted naturally into a friendship with a boy who made him think of his grandfather. The two things got mixed sentimentally in his mind: leaving his grandfather, then finding Mark Green, whose family had the only fur store in town.

Not surprising that the first he saw of his wife was her hair. Several long black hairs on the back of a chair. He'd picked them off distractedly, thinking they looked oriental, but they turned out to belong to the head of a dark and temperamental Scot.

After she left him, he opened a book one day and noticed a long pencil mark down the page. But it was one of Evelyn's long, dark hairs.

Later that night Harry had the idea of giving a party as a way of seeing more of Dido. He would invite everyone at work and then she would come too. He chose a Saturday in mid-July and spread the word around the station. However, news got bruited about the Strange Range that there was a party on Latham Island at the white house with the red canoe out front, and all sorts of people Harry had never seen before turned up.

Jim Murphy got particularly drunk and had to utter each word very carefully. He kept saying, "You're missing the whole point. Everything you do ought to be bilingual. Every program ought to be bilingual." And Eleanor listened, surprised he'd even have thought about it, and agreeing with him, though why he was telling her rather than Harry was a mystery.

She turned with relief to Ralph, who asked if the name Agnes Deans Cameron meant anything to her. It didn't mean a thing, so Ralph told her about the fascinating schoolmarm from Victoria who wrote a book about her travels to the Arctic in 1908. She visited Hudson's Bay trading posts along her route and read their logs, he said, and discovered in the process an account of the two starving Indian women who attacked and killed a pair of mail carriers on the Mackenzie River, partially devoured them, then made the leftovers into pemmican. Ralph said, "The Hudson's Bay factor asked the women what the flesh tasted like and they replied that 'one of the men was very good but the little red Scotchman tasted of tobacco.'" And he roared with laughter.

For his part, Harry watched Dido. He took heart when she needled Eddy about being a teetotaller. Eddy, without rising to the bait, filled her glass whenever she held it out: his wrists narrower than hers, more wiry. They were never more than a few feet apart — if Dido moved away, Eddy was soon at her side, and if Eddy moved away, it was the same.

But there came a moment when Eddy set the wine bottle on the coffee table, and the hard, neat sound of glass on wood marked a shift in the party. In his abrupt, inscrutable way, Eddy stood up to leave, and Harry had all his suspicions confirmed. Between Dido and Eddy things were more advanced than he'd wanted to believe, more advanced, more aggressive, more potent.

He growled, "Eddy," halting him in his progress to the door. "How did you end up in Yellowknife, anyway?"

Eddy stayed where he was standing. The music had stopped and the noise of the party had fallen off for a moment. "It's a long story, Harry."

"I'm not going anywhere."

With mild contempt, "Is that right?"

A pause, and then Eddy deigned to give a cold sober account of his movements. About a year ago, he said, leaning against the wall, he was driving around one day, aimless and bored, and he came to a fork in the road. He was in Montana at the time. The sign had two arrows, one pointed north, the other south. He could have gone either way. But the singer on the car radio was Neil Young, so he turned north, and then he decided he might as well follow the road until it ran out, which it finally did on the north shore of Great Slave Lake.

"Are you always so impulsive?" asked Dido, who by now had joined them.

"Try decisive," Eddy replied.

"So what was Neil Young singing?" she persisted with a faint smile.

Harry, through the pain in his heart, saw exactly what he was up against. Eddy had no sense of humour, and Dido, serious Dido, didn't care. European to the core, she'd fallen for the lean, sardonic, tight-lipped cowboy in jeans.

Eddy flipped through Harry's records – then dropped the needle directly onto the first note of "Helpless."

After that Dido stopped giving Eddy a hard time, she yielded her rights to tormenting him. And Harry, watching the play of feeling on her face, understood the power of a song to advance a man in a woman's heart. Songs, he thought, were the seven-league boots of romance.

Dido didn't leave with Eddy, though. She stayed, and the party went in another direction. Rapidly downhill. Harry would stand in the bathroom doorway an hour later, and in a state of marvelling despair watch while one person threw up in the bathroom sink, a second put his head in the toilet, and a third vomited into the bathtub. Not long after that, all of the afflicted had passed out on his living-room floor.

Rocking in his rocking chair, Harry presided over the aftermath of his own poor judgment, since he'd been the one to open the bottle of tequila. Gwen was sound asleep on the sofa. Two strangers were sleeping next to her on the floor. Eleanor had nodded off in a chair, waiting for Dido. And Dido sat on the floor in the lotus position, awake, alert, wired.

Then began the conversation that Harry would return to whenever he tried to understand Dido and what happened to her. Had he only said something different, had he issued the right sort of warning, had he offered her some other view of herself – who knows, he might have rescued her in time. It was three o'clock in the morning and the rising sun began to touch everything in the room, rosy light on ashtrays, bottles, glasses, bodies. Dido was asking him what he thought of Eddy, what he knew about him. At the time Harry was so busy following the passage of light across her skin, and so disinclined to ponder anything or anybody else, that he simply said he barely knew the man. Dido pressed him, she asked if he thought Eddy was good at what he did. Then he had to admit that he was, that Andrew McNab considered him the best radio technician he'd ever had. A look of pleasure lit up and relaxed her face. That look — of basking in what she'd wanted to hear, perhaps without even knowing she'd wanted to hear it — made Harry realize that Dido was talking herself into something, talking herself into being serious about Eddy. So he said acidly that Eddy was obviously a reformed boozer given the way he turned down anything stronger than Pepsi. She smiled. "Did you know he served in Vietnam?" He nodded. He did know.

Silence. Till Harry hoisted himself to his feet, asking what she wanted to listen to, and Dido said he'd done well in choosing the previous record, she'd be curious to see what he chose next.

Gwen sat up with a groan at that point and rubbed her eyes. Eleanor and the strangers on the floor slept on.

"This is the last record for tonight," Harry said, searching for the bagpipe music he favoured whenever he wanted to blast everybody out of his house.

"He won't tell us what it is," Dido said to Gwen. "He likes to hold his chest to his cards. Do I say it correctly? Harry?" He looked over at her. "Do I say it correctly?"

She was so beautiful. Even at this hour she looked elegant, perfect. She was wearing a yellow sweater and he felt old.

"I've got to go home." Gwen was on her feet, swaying.

"You're white as a sheet," Dido cried, and she followed Gwen to the door. "Wait. Your shoelace is undone."

Then Gwen sat on a chair while Dido, quite tenderly, as if Gwen were a child, tied her shoe.

OVER THE SUMMER AIR came footsteps in the snow. Gwen had learned from Jim Murphy the trick of kneading cornstarch in a plastic bag to duplicate the sound. Also, how to make ocean waves by sloshing the contents of a hot-water bottle back and forth. Generally, she was alone at the station as she aired her playful sound effects, but sometimes Eddy haunted the record library until she signed off at one in the morning. He had a key to the station, too, and a few times she had gone home, leaving him to lock up.

"The mistakes don't matter," he informed her one night after she stumbled over a station ID and apologized on air. "It's the recovery that counts."

If she had a nickel for every one of his smiles, she'd have ten cents. She nodded sheepishly, preferring Harry's way of phrasing the same point. *I learned that a mistake is just something you go on from.* Harry's advice gave her a route to follow, a path forward. Somehow Eddy managed to exchange one form of stress for another.

He leaned against the doorway, a pocket Faulkner under his arm, a pen in his hand. Frequently, he brought her records, slipping them in and out of their covers as he introduced her to

Lester Young, Dexter Gordon, John Fahey, Sarah Vaughan. With Eddy she always felt even younger than she was. Not *disliked*, revising what she'd said to Ralph, not held in contempt, that was too strong. Just examined in passing and discarded. Sometimes Eddy answered her questions, sometimes he didn't.

"Harry's in love with Dido too," she said bravely, curious to see his reaction.

"Harry's not good enough for her."

"Are you?"

He had a way of working the clip on his pen with his thumbnail, making a series of aggressive click click clicks. "Why don't you ask if she's good enough for me?"

Something in his manner reminded her of her brother, whom it was never wise to cross. Her brother didn't rest until he got his own way; then, having won, he'd sweeten. Countless, countless, countless times, she'd been sucked in by his forceful personality, his general indifference to her, his occasional delight in her, and then, how did it happen? It was harder to breathe, because she was breathing his air.

"So what's it like to have a third-rate boss?" Eddy asked her, still in the doorway.

"Second-rate," she bristled, then had to laugh since her defence was hardly a ringing endorsement.

"No. Third-rate." Not giving an inch to Harry or to humour.

Then he reached over and began to stroke the back of her neck. "Relax," he ordered, moving directly behind her and massaging with both hands. "*Relax*." His fingers dug into her neck, hurting her.

She let herself be experimented upon. Or so it felt to her.

"I've got a great record for you," he said.

"What."

"It's perfect for your show."

"Are you going to tell me. Or am I supposed to guess."

"Promise you'll play it."

The record turned out to be *Kind of Blue* by Miles Davis, cool melodic jazz forever ruined by the feel of Eddy's fingers pressing into her neck.

A few days later Gwen went to the town dump near the airport to record the extensive vocabulary of the local ravens, their rasping croaks and rattles and gargles and gulps, their metallic *toks* and *awks* and *ku-uk-kuks* and *quorks*. She discovered in the process how to avoid the wind noises that wrecked the clear sounds she was after. An old umbrella lay on a heap of shoes. She held it open in front of her microphone and it worked like a charm, defeating the wind without blocking the weird and wonderful squawks, or the strong wing-beats overhead.

Eddy appeared while she was there and she asked him what he was looking for, since he didn't seem to have anything he was getting rid of. He didn't bother to answer. She took another tack. "Do you mind?" she asked, and she turned on her tape recorder and picked up the sound of their footsteps as they crossed the crunchy ground. Then she directed her microphone towards his mouth. "What brings you to the dump?" she asked. He frowned, but told her he was looking for bicycle spokes. Then he went on. He told her you could furnish a house with what got thrown into this dump. He'd found window frames and unbroken panes of glass, perfectly good doors and shelves and kitchen cupboards. He'd found radios and television sets and cameras — an excellent camera that he'd fixed in an hour.

"People are getting stupider with each passing day," he said. "It used to be that every little town had its repairman who made a nice living mending anything that broke; now something breaks: pitch it." Waving his hand at the dump, "I wouldn't mind if every corporate executive was put in jail."

"You want to be different," said Gwen.

"I *am* different. You want my view of the future? I see a handful of people. A few survivors. The Dene will be okay. Indigenous cultures. They've still got the basic skills. But the rest of society? Down the toilet."

The ravens croaked and Gwen smiled. "Have I finally found somebody cheaper than my mother?"

She saw his face stiffen. He didn't like the word *cheap*. Neither did her mother.

Gwen took the tape back to the station and put together a short radio piece that began with the hoarse and garrulous ravens, proceeded to steely Eddy, and ended with her own impression of what the dump looked like: a shipwreck on dry land. The station had become her workshop, reminding her not just of the backroom in the family jewellery store, but of camping, since everything she needed here was also close at hand. On air, in the dusky light of the booth, she was walking through homes with her voice, along leaf-covered trails, under a canopy of trees, and nobody minded. Listeners in pyjamas took themselves down the path past the outdoor pump to the screened-in toilets, where long-legged insects spent the night on walls and ceiling, around the light fixture, batting at the screen door.

$$===$$

Everyone noticed the change in Gwen. The girl had laced up the soft shoe of her voice. Now she spoke rather more confidently and not so close to the microphone. Her voice didn't make the same sad dive at the end of every sentence.

One night, towards the end of July, Harry appeared in the doorway of the announce booth. "I've been listening to you. You're getting better."

She fastened him with skeptical eyes.

"There's a new warmth to your voice, Gwen."

"I've always preferred the coolth. But thank you, Harry."

Seeing him like this, suddenly, made her ache a little, the way her teeth ached after she flossed them.

He'd come to tell her that an old radio hand from Toronto would be arriving the following week to give a six-day training workshop. A good friend of his and a veteran announcer. Abe Lamont. Harry had leaned on him to give up a week's holiday for the good of northern broadcasting. It would mean long hours, he said, doing her regular shift at night and the workshops during the day. But it was a great chance. She was doing fine, but it could only help.

"Harry?"

He was watching the way she sat sideways at the control board, shoulders hunched up around her ears like a kid in school just before an exam. He hadn't thought about school for a long time and now it flooded back, all his early doubts and vulnerabilities that seemed of a piece with his feelings for Dido. "What?"

"You said to be good you have to be afraid. But I'm better because I'm *less* afraid." She sat a little straighter and her shoulders dropped an inch.

He took the empty chair. She was monitoring the network, doing the hourly station breaks, there was plenty of time to talk. "You make me want to go back and start all over again," he said heavily.

And to her surprise the skin around his eyes went a subtle pink, as it does when you speak well of someone dead. At her mother's funeral she'd noticed this – that deep feeling comes in reds and blues, and in movement across the face. The tone of Harry's skin changed, the area around his eyes reddened, the rest of his face went pale, bluer. His eyes were suddenly too gleaming.

"Did I tell you this is where I started out?" He looked around the booth. "The clock is different. Everything else is pretty much the same."

Then his eyes settled on her again. The suggestion of tears had subsided, and the colour.

"Harry," and her voice was earnest, curious, "have you ever thought about going back to Toronto and doing radio there?"

"They don't want me," he said.

"That can't be true."

"They don't want anything to do with me, Gwen. Believe me."

That night she played a heartbreaker by Emmy Lou Harris. It ended, and she said, "That was so beautiful, let's hear it again."

And Judge Berger called out of the blue to thank her.

He agreed to go on the air for a moment, and Gwen introduced him as The Great Listener. She asked him what he did with his free time, and he confessed he'd gone to see *Shampoo* at the Capitol Theatre, Warren Beatty exposing all the pitfalls of being a certain kind of male. "Really it was a very good movie," he said with a wonderfully amused laugh.

There were times that summer when she found herself talking to Berger on air. That is, she imagined him listening as sympathetically to her as he listened to the witnesses in small settlements who were speaking for the first time into a microphone.

THE TRAINING SESSIONS HARRY ARRANGED led to a sea change at the station, opening wounds, fanning grievances, inspiring ambitions, and creating the alliances that would pave the way for his eventual downfall. His old friend, bearded, big-bellied Abe Lamont, set himself up in the studio at the baize-covered table, and that first day Abe saw every member of staff who worked on air, one at a time, for half an hour. It was easier if you had no illusions and little experience. Jim Murphy, a broadcaster for fifteen years, emerged from his initial meeting looking sour and asking Dido what "fatuous" meant. Dido went in eagerly, but also came out chastened and annoyed. Abe had told her that her delivery was almost too perfect, he'd warned her against sounding antiseptic. *Antiseptic?* She drew herself up and his eyes glinted in response. Dido joined Jim in the office where the announcers had their desks, and he told her not to pay any mind, Abe Lamont was as over the hill as Harry. Where they got these people was a mystery.

The station had to keep running, of course, so everyone fit their sessions with Abe around their regular shifts. Gwen came in at noon. She read the script he provided, and when he played her voice back, her body contorted in embarrassment.

Abe would have none of that. It's a discipline, he told her, holding her gaze with bloodshot eyes, working his hand through his beard. No horror allowed. No self-revulsion. It has nothing to do with *you* per se, and everything to do with what you're trying to achieve. If you're going to be a professional, he told her, then you have to listen to yourself in a detached way and work to correct what's wrong. He asked her to read the page again with as much energy and passion as she could muster. "You'll never overdo it," he said. "It's not in your nature."

Different instructions for the men. I'm going to take an octave off your voice, he told them. Put your head between your knees. Open your mouth. Are you drooling yet? When you're drooling, come back up, and you'll sound like you've got a third ball. Now let's record the last syllable of time, he would tell them. Let's have a little sound and fury.

But the same basic assignment for everyone. Go out into the field, as he called the world, gather tape, edit it, write an introduction, present it to me. Nothing longer than ten minutes.

Gwen headed to the post office, intending to ask people what letters they were dreading to get, but on the way she saw Lorna Dargabble seated on the steps of her house, her shoulders shaking with laughter. Gwen went up the walk, tape recorder running, but the laughter turned out to be heartbroken sobbing, and she stopped her machine. Then she sat down beside the sorrowful woman, who took her hand and fingered and kneaded it as she might a seam — as she did a seam, the frayed state of her sofa being all too apparent when Gwen passed through the living room on her way to a cup of coffee.

"You know, my dear," declared Lorna sadly, "you'd be beautiful if you made a little effort. Come downstairs and I'll cut your hair."

It turned out that Mrs. Dargabble had a hair-styling shop in one half of her basement and no, she didn't mind if Gwen taped the snipping and the running commentary: "Dear girl, all your clothes are brown. What are you afraid of? With skin like yours you need blues, lavender, off-white. Show some spirit."

"You mean jump?" smiled Gwen, remembering the elderly woman's advice.

"I mean *leap*. And you can start by calling me Lorna."

Next to the space occupied by chair, sink, mirror, and shelves was a standing cabinet like the one Gwen grew up with. Inside it, a radio with its large golden speaker and a record player with a deep shelf for records. Lorna confessed that she came down here to listen to music and to be alone. "But you'd better turn that thing off," she said, and once again Gwen pressed pause. Then Lorna confided that she'd had dozens of records until he broke them in a drunken fury. Her husband. For a moment, she looked around herself in despair. Also in the basement were boxes upon boxes of financial records – a painstaking paper trail of every one of her expenses, she said, and every bit of the income she'd earned in this second marriage that was destroying her. She said, "He'll take everything he can."

"I'm thinking," Gwen said gently, meaningfully, "that perhaps you jumped into the wrong marriage." She was sitting on a padded stool in front of a mirror with a hair-dressing cape over her shoulders.

Lorna took up her long scissors. "*Touché*, my dear. Just remember there are worse things than loneliness and you won't make my mistake. But winter here does terrible things to people. You'll find out." The old woman's Boston accent came out in her vowels. "Winter leaves a lasting mark, my dear," and it sounded like lasting mack. "You discover you're not so strong, after all."

"I'm looking forward to winter."

"Not so strong and that's a fact."

Lorna's breathing was heavy and she stopped in mid-snip to say there was something else she'd learned, something worse – "But let's have some music." She went to put on one of her few surviving records, then returned to her thought. "It's a terrible thing. But even the nicest people get corrupted by the company they keep."

Gwen guessed that Lorna was talking about marriage in general and her husband in particular.

"I mean to say," she continued, "you put an onion next to butter and you get butter that tastes like onion."

"You're talking about your onion-husband," said Gwen.

"Yes." Laughing. "My onion-husband."

But now it was Brahms who made her cry.

Gwen listened too, less moved by the music than fascinated by its effect on her friend. In the mirror Lorna's old chin began to wobble and work like a little machine of emotion, quite independently and alarmingly, all its pistons firing. And then the tears flowed down her cheeks. She stopped to mop her eyes with a towel and to blow her nose. The sad heaviness of her face reminded Gwen of thick frosting badly applied and shored up with stiff scrapings from the bowl. She stood up and put her arms around her. Lorna hugged her back, and then recommenced cutting.

Half an hour later, Gwen looked at herself in the mirror and thought, *Is that really me?* Lorna had shaped her hair and lifted it somehow so that her small face looked wider, prettier.

Opening a closet, Lorna began to pull out clothes. "I used to be as skinny as you are. Try these on. I told you I used to make clothes."

To Gwen's surprise they were simple tailored garments of cotton and linen in white and cream and blue and chocolate brown. A shift, a few pairs of pants, tunics with pockets. She gazed into the mirror again – new clothes, new colours, new haircut – and couldn't take her eyes away.

An hour later, Gwen approached the doorway of the announcers' office, then hung back for a moment, suddenly self-conscious. She could see that Dido was absorbed in conversation with Harry and Jim, but Dido looked up and let out a whistle. The other two turned around, and Harry said, "Oh no!"

"Don't listen to him," said Dido.

"What have you done?" Harry raised his hands to his ears to indicate her hair, but he was play-acting, exaggerating.

Dido examined Gwen from the back as well as the front. "It's a vast improvement," she said with finality.

And it was. But something about Gwen would get on her nerves in the coming days. Dido had seen similar types in the classroom when she was substitute teaching, fresh-faced girls trying too hard to succeed, feigning surprise at their good marks, being disingenuous. Girls who were more ambitious than they ever let on or perhaps ever realized.

Gwen would feel Dido's coolness and be puzzled, not sure what she'd done wrong. Perhaps she'd just been herself. Anyone might tire of that, she thought. It would take time before she realized that she and Dido were locked in one of those personal misunderstandings that has no clear entrance and no exit either.

Later that same afternoon, their first day of training at an end, they all went to the Strange Range and occupied a table in the corner. Harry told Gwen that he'd known her hairdresser when she was still Lorna Palliser. "Doug Palliser used to volunteer at the station. A wonderful guy. He was running a rapids on the Back River when his canoe flipped over and he drowned. Lorna's been a lost soul ever since."

Abe Lamont of the golden pipes and caustic opinions held forth – first about his days producing Harry's television show, then about his return to radio announcing. His week here was a favour to Harry, he said, though he'd done training before, he wasn't a neophyte; he'd gone into other stations and coached the staff on how to write, perform, interview, edit: radio skills, in short. Then, having established his credentials, Abe left the subject of radio altogether. He said he'd seen *Last Tango in Paris*, finally, having missed it when it first opened. A great movie. They should see it if they ever got the chance.

"Great, if you like creepiness," challenged Dido, who hadn't seen the movie, and who would recoil from it when she did. She turned her big watch on her big wrist, unaware that it clunked against the table. Gwen sat to her right, listening.

"I didn't find it creepy," Gwen said quietly.

The others looked at her in surprise, but she didn't continue.

"Go on," said Harry.

For a second she hesitated, gathering her thoughts. "I didn't find it creepy," she said again, "just interesting and very sad. You understood why she shot him in the end. He wouldn't let go."

She'd found the movie profoundly disturbing but enchanting. She didn't know if she fully understood it. The movie was sad, but even sadder, she thought, would be to never experience that sort of all-engulfing love. She was almost twenty-five. She wondered if it would ever happen, if she would ever be passionately in love with someone who was passionately in love with her.

A pause, during which Harry caught Abe's eye and saw Gwen rise in his estimation. Then Harry stood up. He reminded Gwen that her regular shift started in forty minutes and he headed off. Jim Murphy muttered something about a wife on the warpath, and he left too.

The others watched the two men thread their way past tables and Dido reached over and poked Abe Lamont's arm with one finger. "So, how long have you known Harry?"

"We were in high school together."

She put her elbows on the table then, and smiled. "Then you can tell us what the man is really like."

Gwen leaned forward.

Abe Lamont's bulk overspread his chair, his beard doubled the size of his face and gave his hand something to burrow into while he weighed how to answer this gorgeous, prickly woman who wasn't unlike Harry's ex-wife. Evelyn Boyd had also been dark-haired and bossy and built.

"He's a wonderful cutter, a wonderful editor. Better at

that than being a TV personality. We did a history of jazz series together and I remember how elegantly he cut from 'yes' on page three to the top of page seven, bridging the cut by inserting 'but.' Of course, he operates best on three double Scotches and on three he's cold sober, but it makes him irritable."

"He's not irritable with *me*," said Dido.

"No," giving her an appreciative look, "he wouldn't be irritable with you."

A pause. "I find it hard to imagine," Dido said, "what his wives were like."

"There was just one wife. She was nice enough."

"Oh, Abe," her voice low and commanding, "you can do better than that."

Her words dislodged an uncomfortable smile – he had good teeth, she thought, for a man who couldn't be bothered with the rest of himself. Take care of your teeth, he'd advised them all earlier in the day: false teeth will end your career on air.

He said, "You're annoyed with me. Don't be."

"Am I annoyed?"

"By the end of the week you'll see the value of what I'm doing. Trust me."

"All I'm doing," she said with a small hard smile, "is trying to find out about Harry."

He took another swallow of beer, then wiped his mouth and the beard around it with the side of his hand. He was thinking she couldn't take criticism and that was too bad.

"Harry's a minister's son," he said. "A son of the manse. So he's a complicated man with lots of hang-ups. He's brilliant and he's proud and he's touchy. They said he needed a co-host on TV and he refused. He said co-hosts don't work, they talk to each other instead of to the viewer or the listener. He had a point. But they had other ideas, so they fired him."

"He detests television," said Dido.

"He doesn't understand it." Abe rocked his empty beer glass with his free hand. "He's sneering and condescending about it, about anything he can't stand."

In Abe's opinion, Harry was unreasonable about television. A smarter man – not smarter, Harry was smart – a *wiser* and less vulnerable man would have taken his TV failure less personally and not gone around painting all television with the same bitter brush.

Dido chose her words carefully. "Harry is what I would call an anachronism, actually."

"Anachronism?"

"You like big words." In no hurry to forgive him for *antiseptic*, to say nothing of *fatuous*. "You know what anachronism means, I'm sure."

They were at a standoff – until Gwen interceded, her voice oddly emotional. "*I* think Harry's *shy*."

Abe nodded and looked pleased. "You're right. I was shy too."

The word ignited a connection between them, an identification, a deep interest. Shy. For Gwen it was a tiny, precise, potent word like air, like loam, rock, sand, clay, marl, silt, mud, one of the basic building blocks of the world she lived in. An old word, wonderfully adapted to what it described. Being shy. Which meant shying away from oneself and from others, from life itself.

Abe claimed that his shyness arrived when he was seventeen and he remembered the exact moment. He was standing beside an orange car parked in the street, looking back at his house, when he felt a wave of shyness followed by a wave of depression. What flooded through him was exactly the opposite of whatever it was – the ecstatic joy – that swept through gloomy Proust when he tasted his madeleine biscuit and recaptured his past.

Gwen's eyes didn't leave his face. She wanted to know what kind of shyness he meant. Did he feel that everybody was looking at him?

"No. I was alone in the street. Just suddenly I felt mediocre and worthless." His rich radio voice made his words sound even more singular. "A guy without a future."

Gwen was trying to put her finger on the same shift in herself. In her case, shyness arrived at puberty and shut down her carefree childhood. After that, everything was hard: talking, being with people, being in the world. "According to my mother, I was loud and boisterous when I was little. I know it's hard to believe."

"I don't believe it," said Dido.

"I do," Abe said. "I was like that. Gregarious and reasonably confident. But then everything changed. For one thing, I avoided people and they took it the wrong way."

"There's a *right* way?" The word *shy* rankled with Dido too. What did it really mean? Everybody was shy from time to time. But the two of them – Gwen and big, boozy Abe Lamont – seemed to be of one cozy mind on the subject.

"Except for Harry," he said, ignoring the sarcasm. "We fell into walking to school together. He didn't talk and I didn't talk."

"And you both ended up in radio," Gwen said.

"Harry has a great face for radio," cracked Abe.

It was a good line. Gwen would use it from now on. *I have a great face for radio.*

"You get to be invisible," Abe went on. "You control the interview, you ask the questions, you say when it's over. The theatre world is packed with the same kind of people. Extroverted introverts."

Dido was biting her thumbnail. "That's different. On stage you lose yourself in a part, in radio you have to be yourself."

Abe leaned back. "It's still a performance, Dido. You can't just be yourself on the radio."

"I thought that's what everybody was trying for."

"No. You're trying to be *almost* yourself. You see the difference? You're giving a performance as your natural self."

"It's not you," said Gwen, thinking aloud, mulling it over.

"It's almost you," Abe said.

That night Gwen was speaking on the phone to the weather office at the airport, gathering weather stats, when Eddy stuck his head into the booth. His chiselled face and mouth looked extra-hard somehow. He wanted to know if she'd seen Dido.

"She was in the Gold Range when I left."

Without saying a word, he turned on his heel, and she assumed he'd left for the night.

Later on, Harry appeared. He pretended to barricade the door of the announce booth with a chair, as if seeking refuge from all the nutcases hounding him, and Gwen felt agreeably flattered. She said, "Abe told me he used to be shy, and so were you."

"That can't surprise *you*."

This sounded like a compliment. She too sought out corners, or spots behind doors, much as Harry had done just now.

"At bottom we're afraid of people, you and I," he said, collapsing into the only other chair. "Or maybe intimidated's a better word."

Not a compliment, then.

At that moment Eddy reappeared – he walked into master control, not having left the station, after all. Through the glass window they saw him take off his black leather jacket and drape it over the back of a chair.

"Eddy's the sort who could intimidate me," Harry said.

Eddy was intent on the equipment, taping something off the network. They had a view of his lean, muscled back. He was a man in control, running things, daring you to contradict him, quiet in a way that made you feel anything you said would sound foolish. Once, late at night, Gwen had witnessed him in master control take his wheeled chair and slam it into the wall – the impact more than the sound made her look up. Something had infuriated him. But when she asked him later what it was, he shrugged it off, said he'd just wanted to give her another sound effect – if you ever want the slam of a steel door, that's how to get it.

"The alpha male," said Harry. "What does he do here at this hour?"

"He's often here. I don't think he sleeps."

Eddy caught sight of them, and stared for a moment without any expression, then went back to what he was doing.

"Stoned," murmured Harry.

"I thought he'd gone. He was looking for Dido a while ago."

"The mystery couple," said Harry, and his voice was so low-spirited, so defeated that Gwen didn't know how to respond.

Then Harry shook himself and brightened a little. He told her he'd got authorization to hire a woman to present the news in Dogrib. Teresa Lafferty would replace silver-haired Sam, who'd joined the special team of reporters covering the pipeline inquiry full-time. Teresa had grown up in Fort Rae, he told Gwen, and gone south years ago, but she'd come back for her mother's funeral, then decided to stay on. An older woman, Harry said, but a real live wire. It was Sam who'd suggested her name, he'd known her family for years, and described her as smart, fluent in both languages, conscientious. "She starts tomorrow," Harry said, "so she'll get the benefit of Abe's training too."

Her full name was Teresa Dolorosa Lafferty, the Dolorosa for Mary's seven sorrows. But Teresa wasn't sorrowful. She had a sweet brown face with eyes almost hidden by laughter-induced wrinkles and sun-darkened pouches of skin. Teresa was fifty-three, and she would turn out to be a completely natural broadcaster, moving back and forth between English and Dogrib, and speaking softly and persuasively in a slightly nasal, low-pitched voice. She would start out by translating the news into Dogrib and reading it twice a day, but within weeks she was doing two hours of talk and music on Saturday afternoons, ad libbing without effort as she cued up records, and sounding irreverent, down to earth, completely human.

Gwen learned all about Teresa's past when Abe Lamont had several of them sit around the table in the studio and interview each other. Think about the best first question, he told them. Ask something that will make listeners *wait* to hear the answer.

Gwen looked at this vibrant, independent woman, and asked what she'd been like at twenty-one, and instantly Teresa was full of mirth. She'd spent her twenty-first birthday in a nunnery, she said, shaking her head, laughing. Inspired by the local priest, she and her older sister Audrey entered together, though her sister lasted longer. "As children we would say fifty rosaries each. Audrey insisted we hold our arms out like Jesus on the cross, and alternate. So we'd stand, arms outstretched, for as long as it took to say one hundred rosaries. First our hands would go numb, then our arms, then our shoulders. I had to throw myself into a state of holy detachment," she laughed, taking undivided pleasure in the telling.

Teresa rolled her smokes from Player's tobacco and smoked while she talked, the paper clinging to her lips like skin you're trying to pull off. Short dark hair without a trace of grey, light blue jeans, pressed white shirt. Gwen admired her astonishing levity, her ability to lift up into a seventh heaven of teasing and being teased, a woman who had a way of defanging anyone else's intemperate remarks. Teresa didn't take offence when Abe told her that her reading skills were questionable. "Questionable," she chortled. It wasn't a matter of thick skin, but of this lightness, thought Gwen. A balloon, genial and serene, floating in the air, and not pulled down by the small, nervous people around her.

Under Abe's eye, Gwen practised her interviewing skills, and got an outpouring of stories — about Teresa's days teaching in Old Crow in the Yukon, teaching on a native reserve in Saskatchewan, running a roadside restaurant, getting busted for trafficking marijuana, spending three months in jail. First, in a holding cell in Regina — a bunk with a filthy mattress and one thin blanket that she arranged so her face wouldn't touch the mattress, her body shaking with the cold and with shock. "Michelle, just a kid," she said, "came in at midnight for murder." By then, in order to escape the insults of the police, the humiliation, she had "retreated to the moon," practising a version of the same holy detachment that brought her through the marathons of hundreds of rosaries.

It was in jail, she said, where she became part of a native healing circle. "And that changed everything. That's when I gave up my life of blaming. You claim your mistakes," she said, "you claim your good qualities, and you don't get stuck. You move around the wheel of life from one level to the next, from the emotional level to the spiritual, making room as you move for something else to enter."

That night Gwen was in the announce booth when she heard her name being called. She opened the door and Teresa was standing in the hallway. She had something to give her — a rosary she'd found while unpacking boxes in her apartment. Gwen slipped it into her pocket and pulled it out the next afternoon in the Gold Range café. She and Eleanor and

Teresa had gone there together for coffee. It was about three in the afternoon. Outside, the perfect summer weather held, hour after hour. Gwen would remember back to this time and it seemed to her it rained only once; a place where you had no need of an umbrella.

Unaccountably, the rosary had broken inside her pocket, and Teresa hooted. "You're going to hell. You'll have to buy a *big* indulgence for that."

Gwen and Eleanor laughed. Then Gwen, a little alarmed despite herself, laid the rosary flat on the table. She tried to refasten the broken wires, but two of the beads were missing. "Hell twice over," said Teresa.

As Gwen and Eleanor watched, Teresa went around the rosary showing them how to count off ten Hail Marys and when she came to the missing beads, instead of "Hail Mary," she said, "Roast in hell, Roast in hell."

Eleanor, with arms leaning on the table, was smiling at the banter. She confessed she'd been reading the Bible lately. "It's been coming on me gradually," she said.

Gwen stared at her soft and tired eyes, and Eleanor went on. "I'm talking about belief. The belief that Christ is a source of perpetual grace."

With these words Gwen's antipathy to religion came back. It was like a moth's antipathy to cedar, it filled her whole being. "I wish Christ didn't have to come into it," she groaned. "Why does grace have to be personified in Christ?"

Eleanor stared down at her hands. "Because Christ is a *person*," she said. She knew it sounded simple-minded. But Christianity wasn't a system, it was person-to-Person.

Dido and Eddy had come in while they were talking, they were at a table near the front. Teresa spotted them and said, "Nobody works. I love it."

Between spoonfuls of ice cream, Teresa claimed she had no regrets about her years as a nun. There were concepts like Devotion and Respect that she didn't know how she would have learned about otherwise. All religions had something to offer. Even the Jehovah's Witnesses. When they knocked on her door, she invited them inside for a cup of coffee. "To be rude is just not part of my diet."

Teresa had been watching Dido and Eddy out of the corner of her eye. When they stood up to leave, she watched as Eddy put his hand on the back of Dido's neck and guided her through the door. "Those two are cooking up a train wreck," she said.

Eleanor and Gwen swung round and saw the pair through the restaurant window. Teresa asked how long they'd been together, and Eleanor told her it had started in June, so a month.

Teresa said, "I've seen other couples like that. He won't let her do things and she likes that. He'll get her to do other things, and she'll like that too."

═══

The same afternoon Ralph Cody dropped into the station. The tobacco-stained bibliophile traded books back and forth with Harry. Today Ralph was returning *The Big Sleep*, hard-boiled reading for a hard-boiled town, and bringing Harry an issue of *Blackwood's Magazine* of interest for its engrossing article about stammering Frank, the fifth son of Charles Dickens.

"Dickens had seven sons," recounted Ralph with energy, "every one a disappointment. They all had what the great man called 'a curse of limpness' upon them. It must be the worst luck in the world, don't you think? Having a father who's a literary genius."

Harry had reached into a bottom drawer of his desk and pulled out a bottle, and now he and Ralph sat back and enjoyed the fruit of Scotland, while Ralph continued the tale of stammering Frank. Dickens tried to cure the boy by making him read Shakespeare out loud, but young Frank grew up tongue-tied and deaf to boot; he got work eventually, with the Bengal police, a job that paved the way to sunstroke, deep depression, full-scale dissipation. Then strings were pulled, Ralph said, and he came out to Canada in 1874, taking a post in the newly formed North-West Mounted Police, where his superiors immediately rated him an officer of "no promise." Over the years he saw many things, including the decline of buffalo herds and consequent emaciation of the Indians, and some of their more desperate battles, and in the end, concluded Ralph, he acquitted himself rather well. "He said if he himself ever wrote a book, he'd call it *Thirty Years Without Beer*."

Harry laughed and stared into his glass. "'The curse of limpness.' That sounds like a manager I could name."

Then he remembered to tell Ralph something not un-related. On Saturday morning Abe Lamont would be playing *Death in the Barren Ground* for anybody on staff who was interested, a copy from radio archives in Toronto, and he'd be welcome to join them. It was the narrative drama of Hornby's last journey written by George Whalley. Harry knew that Ralph had copies of Whalley's biography of Hornby and of the diary written by Hornby's young cousin, Edgar Christian – a diary published in 1937 with a title Harry admired, *Unflinching* – and he was right to think Ralph would be eager to come.

Harry waved his big hand to take in the station. "I should have prepared everybody for Abe. Warned them not to expect flattery. I don't know how to manage egos. I alienate people."

"You've heard rumblings of discontent?"

He had. He'd even heard himself referred to as the crunchy granola dictator. Bill Thwaite, not bothering to keep his voice down. "It's too bad I can't be a bit more charming," Harry said.

Ralph snorted with laughter. "You're charming."

"Who have I charmed?"

"Who do you want to charm?"

Harry rubbed his eyes and readjusted his glasses, then shifted the conversation back to safer ground. "What's got you reading *Blackwood's Magazine*?"

Ralph smiled and went along. He said it had been a command performance when he was young, his family all read it from cover to cover and his father stored every back issue in the attic in Vancouver. His father was a great character, he added, the one who'd got him interested in languages by introducing him to the Cyrillic alphabet. They'd spent hours together poring over stamps, enchanted especially by anything Russian.

"My old dad was something of a mystic," he added. "Like the Celts, he believed we're made up of invisible currents. He used to say there are 'thin places' where we're closer to the unseen world."

"Name a thin place."

"The ocean. You stand next to the sea and you're in touch with all your longings and all your losses."

"Longings and losses," repeated Harry. "That does sort of sum it up."

Ralph took in Harry's rumpled face. "Dido came to see me the other day."

"Lucky you," said Harry.

"She wanted to borrow a book."

"A book," said Harry.

"*Rules for Radicals*. I sent her home with a year's worth of reading. Her arms were full, lumbered, aching with books."

"Saul Alinsky," Harry said slowly. "A smart man."

"They've started a study group."

"Who has?"

"Dido and Eddy. You know. 'Concerned whites who oppose the pipeline and want to support the native cause.' Solidarity. Brotherhood. Resistance. They asked me to join."

They hadn't asked Harry to join.

"She's a serious woman, Dido. I told her I wasn't the studying type."

"I like serious women," said Harry, and in his mind he saw Dido and Eddy come out of the little blue house in Rainbow Valley, and thought, So she's into politics. Then came the second thought, and it was bitter. Not politics – love.

"IN THE SPRING OF 1926, *John Hornby's party, three men and one canoe, left Fort Resolution and travelled to the site of Fort Reliance at the eastern end of Great Slave Lake. Here they were delayed for a time by heavy ice. Then by the classic route of Pike's Portage, they entered Artillery Lake. After that there was silence.*"

So began the hour-long radio drama *Death in the Barren Ground*. A handful of staff had come to listen. In the studio were Harry and Dido, Eleanor, Gwen, and Ralph. Eddy and Abe were in master control.

The narrator, marvellous Bud Knapp, related how two years later, in July of 1928, a party of geologists led by Harry Wilson was travelling by canoe from Great Slave Lake to Hudson Bay. They were aware that Hornby and his two companions had gone into the Barrens the previous summer, intending to overwinter there as Hornby had done once before, and that the three men hadn't reappeared, and there was some anxiety about them. Thirty-five miles below the junction of the Hanbury and Thelon rivers, Wilson discovered the derelict cabin and two bodies "apparently sewn in blankets" to the right of the cabin door, and inside a third body on a bunk. A note on top of the stove directed them to the papers and diary laid in the cold ashes inside, papers that would identify the three men as John Hornby, Harold Adlard, and Edgar Christian.

Knapp's voice then took them forward to the Mounted Police investigation and the conclusion of "death due to starvation not foul play," and then he took listeners back to the beginning, to the man at the centre of the story, the small, wiry Englishman, the son of a famous cricketer, who came to Canada in 1904 and fell under the spell of the Arctic, soon acquiring a reputation for incredible physical endurance, for surviving against the odds, for considering the Barren Ground "his destined element." At the age of forty-six, he had determined to make at least one more journey into a part of the world that only a few people had ever travelled through.

Here were Hornby's own solitary, musing words taken from his writings and spoken by actor Alan King. "I'm jealous, I suppose. Jealous of that country. Jealous of any man who goes in there without me." To Harry, the man sounded compelling, candid, clear-headed. "The trees end at Artillery Lake. The timber doesn't straggle off, it just ends in a distinct line that cuts diagonally across the lake. Beyond that, the Barrens . . . I've seen it go down to eighty below. There are no cabins, no trading posts, no human beings. But in the season, and if you're lucky, there's plenty of game . . . The caribou! Wonderful. I've seen tens of thousands of them in the open and at the shallow river crossings. At a narrow ford they may take hours to go by, trotting in a solid mass, their eyes glazed, the air shaking with their funny gruntings, their hooves grinding the ice to a fine powder. There's no sight like it."

And here were Edgar Christian's perceptive, accepting young thoughts about his much-admired cousin whom he called Jack. "He doesn't talk very much and when he does it's as though he were talking to himself." Edgar's voice, as spoken by Douglas Rain, was haunting, milky – *I am as safe as a house with Jack.* The boy was only seventeen.

Harold Adlard, the third member of the party, who'd joined up with them in Edmonton, out of eagerness to see the North, was twenty-seven.

The three men travelled slowly that summer of 1926. It wasn't until October that Edgar's diary began in earnest, by which time they were putting the final touches on their cabin on the Thelon River and contemplating a last push to get caribou. But the effort to get meat failed and winter set in. Hornby, quixotic, eccentric, confident he would survive because he always had, was guilty of defying "the immemorial custom of the North; he had not laid in his winter's meat in September." Their food ran low, then it ran out, and the three men turned into Hansel without Gretel, starving in a winter cage. Hornby had always planned to write a book and call it *The Land of Feast and Famine.* Now his notes for the never-finished volume took on the colour of tragedy. "My life has been finding out how to eat when there's nothing to eat, finding game when there isn't any, crawling on hands and knees to find food when you aren't strong enough to stand up and when your will to live has shrivelled away . . . In the Barrens starvation is an intensely active process. You are more likely to die of exhaustion than of starvation. As your strength goes you become more methodical and remorseless. A kind of creeping obsession entirely focused on the need your body has for food, and you set about finding it with the ingenuity of a deliberate, cold-blooded murderer."

Time and again, they hunted desperately and unsuccessfully, their days a succession of blizzards, frostbite, enforced idleness, injury, slow starvation, quiet valour. Triumphs of composure offset their bodily sufferings. Young Edgar was devoted to Hornby, Hornby was as selfless as he was reckless, the two were alike in their courage and resolve, which seemed inhuman, sublime. Hornby died first, on April 16. Harold Adlard died next, on May 4. Edgar Christian lasted another month, all by himself, until early June. By then there was still no northward migration of birds or animals, and for several days it had been blowing a snowstorm. His last diary entry was June 1. *9 a.m. Weaker than ever. The sunshine is bright now. Make preparations now. Left things late.* He would write to his father, then to his mother. *Dearest Mother. Feeling weak now. Can only write a little. Sorry I left it so late. Please don't blame dear Jack.*

Make preparations now was heartbreaking shorthand. Making the preparations for imminent death that Hornby had failed to make to preserve their lives.

Whalley's script put it beautifully, Harry thought. "For in the end most of what can be said about John Hornby is outweighed by the record of his unrelenting courage in the face of a disaster that he must have known his own irresponsibility had produced." An enigma during his life, Hornby was fortunate after death in having the best of biographers.

It seemed to Harry as he listened that everyone had fallen under the same spell, except Dido, whose blank face he couldn't read. Now she caught his eye and his heart sank. She didn't like this documentary he loved, this unfolding drama of fascination. He shifted his gaze to Gwen, who had heard the program when it was originally broadcast, as had he, and from her expression he could see that she recognized certain voices, remembered certain turns of phrase, and was caught up all over again in the overwhelming pull of the story.

But *why* had Hornby dallied so long, so inexplicably? Why had he let September slip by without laying in the winter's meat, thus leaving himself and the others short of food as early as November? Harry had his own explanation. To him, Hornby was a George Orwell type, even in appearance. The two men shared an enormous appetite for doing without. *Down and Out in Paris and London. Down and Out in the Arctic.*

The program ended and Harry broke the silence with a resonating afterthought: he'd like to see the spot where Hornby died. It would be worth the trip, he said, casually setting in motion the events of the following summer.

Dido, listening to Hornby's story, remembered her father. She was back in their house where he was grading papers as he listened to the radio, pausing in his correction of a mangled line from the *Aeneid* to drift over to England in his mind. Their house a house of maps and books and foreign sounds, of coffee every evening at eight, of fresh cut flowers, of salty licorice. Her father would have liked this documentary, it would have appealed to his melancholy mind. She wished he had done more with his life. But what her mother used to say was true.

He didn't have a fighting temperament. Nothing could arouse the battling instincts of that mild and gentle man. His voice wasn't unlike the actor's who played Hornby, she thought, the same ruminating style and pace of someone who seemed to stand outside life — a kind of baffled backwards sound, as if the future was already in the past.

She glanced through the window at Eddy in master control and knew what he was thinking: the program was well and good in its minor way. This wasn't the North that interested him, these old tales of the glories and disasters of English travellers. The present called out for justice, not for nostalgia over another extravagant failure on the part of blind and incompetent white men. Teresa Lafferty wasn't here. Why would she be? Dido looked around at all the pale, absorbed faces and felt like an atheist in church. These Canadians, she thought, these old-fashioned, colonized Canadians. She saw Gwen's fingers steal up to her eyes and Eleanor's gentle smile of too easy, too automatic appreciation lingering on her face. Abe Lamont's beard jutted out like a furry flag. And Harry, she knew without even looking, Harry was watching her, measuring her reactions, wanting something she wasn't about to give. Don't look at me like that, she'd told him once, you'll wear out your eyes. She glanced at him now and raised her eyebrows and his face had that hungry look of special pleading — fill my bowl, give me seconds — that made her lose patience. Earlier in the week she'd complained to him about Abe. Said that in calling her antiseptic, he was being racist. It was an anti-Dutch slur, she said, and no, she wasn't kidding.

In this moment (this parting of the ways) she made up her mind to be more uncompromising, less like her father. She remembered something Eddy had said about Berger. The man was too *reasonable*.

Afterwards, they remained in the studio and talked. Dido said Hornby must have been a masochist. "He was demented," she said, enunciating too clearly, this habit of over-enunciation that made Abe Lamont call her too perfect on air.

Gwen flared up. She hated words like *masochist* and *narcissist* and, and, and – she tried to think of another such label and couldn't. "Call someone a masochist," she spluttered, "and there's nothing left to say. It's the end of the story. You've written him off. Explained him to death."

Dido replied in a steady, even tone. "You haven't explained everything maybe, but almost everything."

"No! Those labels just give you a fancy reason to stop thinking about people."

"What would *you* call Hornby then?"

"Complicated." Gwen couldn't bear the criticism – she never could bear it when anyone she treasured got pilloried and dismissed. "What did Whalley say?" she cried. "'Brave, desolate, and haunted.'"

Dido pursed her lips. "Poor Edgar," she murmured. She was tired of Gwen's vehemence. All week, whenever she'd floated a new idea, Gwen had leapt in with a differing opinion, as if she had some privileged understanding of radio. They'd made a ten-minute documentary together about a Dene play on alcohol abuse, it was being performed on an outdoor stage, and they'd interviewed the actors and the director, who said, "Mostly we don't really tell them how the play is, but we want them to make the story to themselves of how the play is." Gwen had overruled Dido's intention of running music below the interviews, shaking her head dismissively, not even considering it.

Eddy weighed in now. Usually you could count on his silence. He said that Edgar, without Hornby, was nothing; he would have lived an ordinary life and been completely forgotten. He was talking to Dido, asking her which she would choose if she had the choice. "A long, steady, unexciting life or a brief spurt of intensity?"

Dido traced circles on the table with her fingertips. A small smile parted her lips. At last she admitted it. "Intensity."

Harry couldn't help himself. "And you accused me of being a romantic!"

But Dido and Eddy weren't paying attention, not to him.

Eleanor tried to say that surely the two weren't incompatible, intensity and a long life, but nobody was listening and she didn't go on. The words that kept ringing in her head were Hornby's *I've come to love the silence.* After the others had left, she said to Harry that Hornby's description of the Barrens as sudden, featureless, endless, as land ground down and scoured by glaciers, put her in mind of the holy men of the desert starving themselves in order to have visions. Hornby had been drawn to a place that almost nobody had ever seen, where everything was severe, but where suddenly the air shook with life, with the sounds of tens of thousands of caribou. Eleanor said visionaries and mystics are always drawn to emptiness and silence as the necessary preconditions for an upwelling of the spirit. No wonder George Whalley turned to the Bible when he tried to describe the power of this world at the end of the world. "Stones of fire" was one of his phrases. From Ezekiel.

She said, "If you go to the Barrens, Harry, I'd give anything to go with you."

On the afternoon of the same day, several of them went canoeing on Frame Lake, the protected inland lake on the western edges of New Town. It was a day soaked in sunshine and threaded by blue damselflies, in twos, mating. Darning needles, Harry called them. They lit on everybody, but especially on Gwen's shoulders and hair, stitching her with colour – blue, delicate, darting, iridescent – mending her mental aches and pains and errors and embarrassments. She was in the bow of Harry's canoe, Eleanor was paddling with Ralph. Ralph called out, *Gwen, they like you. You're a flower.* And she turned around with a wide smile.

Eleanor caught her breath. *La fille qui était laide.* Gwen looked beautiful.

What would happen next? wondered Eleanor. Love would happen next, as it always does, she thought, even to the old heroes. She'd been reading her beloved Edith Hamilton, refreshing her memory about the twelve labours of Hercules and thinking, as she turned the pages, about what a long, eventful, exhausting life he had, poor wretch, only to be reminded that yet to come were all the complications of love. First for Iole, then for Deianara, this latter ending in unendurable pain and death.

The canoes carried the canoeists and the canoeists carried the damselflies and everything seemed weightless. They were heading towards the first day of August, the street lights were noticeable again, and a few leaves were turning yellow, indicating in their minimal, elegant way an end to this long, warm summer and the beginning of a darker chapter.

Harry and Gwen went for a walk later on, all the way to the lip of Rainbow Valley, at the end of Latham Island. Gwen's voice was animated as she told him what she'd learned from Abe about lifting words off the page. He'd coached her to raise her eyes as she read, and it was hard to do, she wasn't relaxed enough, but a few times she'd succeeded in delivering the words as if speaking directly to the listener, and it was wonderful, she said, to feel unlocked from the tyranny of the page.

She'd had a good week and he was glad. Her professional progress was a small part of what he was after – a new flow of languages and information on air. He wanted one long street of sound that would be interesting to anyone, white or Dene, at any time of day. If radio could be more relevant than ever, he reasoned, then it stood a better chance against television. He was sure of it. He'd also been thinking that if head office was going to waste money on an elaborate new building, then it could be argued they should spend generously on crucial new programming. Already he was picturing Teresa Lafferty's hour of blended Dogrib and English; he wanted to hire another Dene woman, young Tessa Blondin, to do reports in Slavey; and he was tempted to curry more disfavour with the newsroom by carving five minutes off the regular local newscasts and adding them to the Dene allotment.

He and Gwen reached Rainbow Valley. They stood together looking down at the colourful curve of poverty, the small prefab houses painted in pastel blues and greens and pinks. Scruffy children played in the road, an old woman hauled a pail of water up her steps, smoke rose from several chimneys. The scene of settled displacement pulled from Gwen a wistful, pointed question. "Are you ever lonely?" she asked Harry. Tacitly confessing, she knew, that she herself was lonely and glad for his company.

Harry didn't hesitate. He said yes, he knew he'd always be lonely. "But I always have good friends wherever I am."

And Gwen knew exactly where she stood. She was meant to feel included in that company – one of many. She fell silent as they walked back to his house, disappointed somehow in Harry's answer. He made tea, moving a large box off his kitchen table to make room for teapot and cups. The box was addressed to Harry, she saw, and had a return address in New Brunswick. But he hadn't opened it.

"Why not?" she asked, dumbfounded that anyone could receive a package in the mail and resist its mystery.

He laughed and said that opening boxes made him sad. "I get lost in them, Gwen. All sorts of ghosts pour out."

IT WAS ABE LAMONT'S LAST NIGHT in town before flying back to Toronto. Harry had arranged to join him in the Gold Range, and he found him there, soused and voluble, bending Dido's ear about the old days when thousands of geese shot in the Mackenzie River Delta were piled high on barges and shipped south. Travelling the other way by barge came Pete, the Lebanese peddler from Alberta, selling oranges at every stop for a dollar apiece.

Dido was wearing a necklace of red coral beads, and in Harry's mind the colours took over, the creamy-grey breasts of the geese, the precious oranges, the reddish beads. Eddy wasn't with her and Harry took heart: perhaps she wasn't so attached to him, after all. He kept looking at her, but she was having none of his glances, none of his big, obvious, smitten heart. He felt old and raw with wanting her and not having her. A few weeks ago he'd invited her to a cabin on Prosperous Lake for a day of what he imagined might be seclusion, confessions, concerted wooing, but she had declined to go.

"Then have dinner with me in town. I'll cook for you."

"If you insist."

"Oh, I never insist."

That made her smile. "All right, then."

He'd made his signature dish, cauliflower soup so delicious (a touch of curry powder, and thick cream) that Dido had a second helping. "You're young," he'd said, looking at her but speaking of himself, "you're doing something really interesting, you think your future holds more of the same, but better. Then you discover that the highlight of your working life occurred at the beginning. And you can't go back."

Dido had laughed his comments away. "You want me to believe the best is now, things will never be better than this. Of course they'll be better. Of course I'll try television if I get a chance. Who wouldn't?"

"Let me see your palm." He'd stroked her palm with his fingertips. "Is television in Dido Paris's future? I see mansions, tropical trees. A lot of water."

"Swimming pools."

"A flood."

"You can't drown me just for wanting to go into television, Harry."

She'd spoken from a mocking distance that kept him very effectively at bay.

Now he watched, bemused, as she chummed up to the man she'd derided earlier in the week. She was plying Abe Lamont with questions about the legendary lost valley of orange trees in the Arctic. Abe the windbag, he thought indulgently, Abe the big tub of talent gone awry; no wonder the two of us get on so well: we could have set the world on fire, but neither of us is going to.

"Lamont! You're full of shit!"

Abe made a show of glowering back. "I feel sorry for you," he said to Dido (who seemed to like nothing better than the blood sport of male one-upmanship, the fondly savage insults). "I pity you having the great Harry Boyd as your boss. As I was saying," and he deepened his studio voice in order to mock himself and amuse her, "explorers found the tropical valley but couldn't relocate it. There's an old trapper, Gus Kraus, he lived on the Nahanni River for years, and in the summer he grew melons and in the winter he walked across his cabin floor in bare feet, that's how warm it was from the hot springs below. I expect the Nahanni gave rise to the legend."

"Or it could have been the place where Hornby died," she said. "The Thelon River."

"It could have been," agreed Abe.

He'd made peace with her the day before. She was the equal of any announcer on the national network, he'd told her in the end, and he'd offered to recommend her to a producer he knew in Toronto.

That same night, much later and on the spur of the drunken moment, Harry hammered on the door of Eleanor's trailer, hoping Dido would be there. He was lucky. She opened the door, a glow of white nightgown and loose hair.

"Save me from my insanity," he pleaded.

Inside, he fell into an armchair and she curled up on the sofa.

"Are you all right?" he asked her. "I worry about you, I want you to know that."

"I was asleep," she said.

His face looked hollowed out, she thought, as though he had false teeth and they weren't in. His glasses had slid down his nose.

She said, "You should worry about Eleanor. You probably woke her up."

"Shhhh." Finger to his lips. "Sorry." He took out his unfiltered cigarettes and offered her one. She shook her head, then changed her mind.

"I almost killed myself twice," he said, "I want you to know that."

She held the cigarette between her fingers. His accent was different when he was drunk. It went Irish, maudlin. His face reminded her of an open book that's fallen into a puddle.

"Why do you want me to know that, Harry?"

"The first time I saw you," he said, and he fumbled for words, "the first time I *heard* you, you made such an impression on me. I felt such a connection." He heard his voice, the pleading, but couldn't help himself. "Was it only me?"

She gazed at this man, who sat in a cloud of smoke. He made her feel tired and cruel. Vulnerable men didn't appeal to her, they never had.

Without answering his question, she got up and went into the kitchen, which was an extension of the living room. Harry stayed where he was. When she came back with a mug of coffee for him, he said, "I was watching you."

"That's new."

"Ah, Dido. Be kind to an old man."

She sat beside him and straightened the collar of his shirt as if he were an old man. "So what did you see when you were watching me?"

"A bird hunting for a worm. A woman looking this way and that for a coffee cup." He paused. "A beautiful woman."

But she had been called beautiful before.

"It's time for you to go," she said after he took a few sips and set down the mug.

"You're right."

He stood up and looked around him, patting his pockets, and that's when he saw Eddy's leather jacket hanging over a chair in the corner. Then he sagged.

"I'm too old for you, aren't I?"

"You're not too old, Harry. You're too needy."

═══

Eddy picked up his leather jacket in the morning, and in the afternoon he and Dido were on the hill near School Draw watching immense clouds roll in from the north. Below them lay Old Town, glittering in the low-flung light like an inviting bed of nails. Dido wanted to take cover, but Eddy put his arm around her and held her in place. Eddy, so relaxed, talked about being a kid when it seemed every time he and his brothers climbed Blueberry Hill the sky churned up a wild and violent storm. They played chicken with the elements, their fingers going after the blue, almost-black berries on the open hillside until the first close CRACK sent them skidding down to lower ground, laughing like fools. Beautiful berries, hanging full and ripe and surprisingly heavy on the underside of bushes as low as these ones. And he bent down and with his pocket knife hacked off the tip of an arctic willow and put the willow twig in Dido's hand.

That morning they'd driven to the Yellowknife River, and once they were well underway, miles from town, he said casually that the gas tank was empty and smiled at her alarm. Eddy always knew what he could get away with. That was the lesson of the drive, and of his lingering now on the exposed hilltop, his arm around her as the first strokes of lightning flashed across the sky and she trembled. "Loon at three o'clock," he said.

A moment later, when he looked into her face, she seemed a million miles away. He asked her what she was thinking, and she said the North Sea.

She said, "My mother. I think she's losing her memory."

"She's old."

"Sixty-one."

"Well, that's too young."

Dido turned to look at Eddy's hard, steady face. "Why didn't she phone me when my father died? I have this terrible feeling she forgot."

"To phone you?"

"Forgot she hadn't phoned me. Her letters are full of half-explained things she expects me to know about, but there's no way I could know about them."

"Don't worry about it," he said, his arm firmly around her, his response practical, definitive. "There's nothing you can do from here."

After the wind fell away, and just before the rain began, they came down off the hilltop and saw Gwen hurrying home. So they swept her up with them into Eddy's small truck and he drove her to her door.

Later, out of curiosity not unmixed with jealousy, Gwen

said to Dido, "Well, I can see what you'll bring to him. But what will he bring to you?"

Dido didn't answer, stung by the very question that was in the back of her own mind, and irked by Gwen's presumption. She thought fiercely, defensively, about Eddy's kindness to his motherless niece, how he phoned her every week and was sending her gifts of toy animals, a seal, an ookpik, a polar bear, a caribou, one at a time, until soon the little girl would have a complete northern menagerie. Ordinary people had no idea how attentive Eddy could be.

"She's so judgmental," Dido complained to Eleanor during a quiet moment at the station several days later.

"She's young."

"She's not much younger than I am." Dido was making herself a cup of instant coffee, and Harry walked in to do the same. "She'll be twenty-five tomorrow. You heard her say it the other day."

"I know all that. But compared to you she's inexperienced and unsure of herself. She's shy."

"Is she? Or is she perfectly sure of herself?"

Harry lifted his head. "There's something to that." Gwen could be surprisingly self-possessed, an odd mixture of crippling modesty and immodest determination. "She's improved a lot since she began."

Dido said, "I think she knows it. I think she knows exactly how good she is."

In the hallway Gwen had stopped a few feet from the door, brought up short. Her arms were full of record albums.

To hear herself spoken of disparagingly — it hadn't happened since she was a child at camp. At the age of ten she'd stormed into the tent with her objections: *I heard you. I heard what you said.* And all the other girls looked at her, embarrassed, but also sorry for her. And what had come after the anger? More anger, but in a different form. Anger with herself for having spoken out, and with the situation that goaded her into speaking. After the illicit blaze of indignation, there was the long, dark walk to the shore.

She heard Dido's damning, dismissive voice. "I think she's the type that gets called shy and isn't shy at all."

She heard Harry clear his throat, then say, "Well, most of us don't have your confidence and poise." Ingratiating himself with Dido, not coming to her defence at all.

One of the albums slipped out of her grasp and hit the floor with a bang. She swooped to pick it up — aware of the sudden, awful silence.

"Shit." Dido drew her head in from the open doorway. She'd glimpsed the back of Gwen beetling into the record library.

"Did she hear us?" whispered Eleanor.

She must have. She must have heard every word.

═══

In the record library Gwen's eyes smarted, a wounded bear with voices in her head, *she knows exactly how good she is . . .* The voices lifted her up off her chair and out of the station and into the low wide town. They transported her over rocky ground, but not high enough to avoid the rocks. So bang and drag and jostle and bump she went on her way through Old Town, which was barely older than she was. She passed the vagabond-like disarray that was Peace River Flats on the left and Willow Flats on the right, then made her way around the base of the Rock to the causeway to Latham Island. On the island she walked past Harry's house and came to the little dirt road on the left that led to the shore of Back Bay.

Agitated, she went down to the water.

And there she saw a vision of happiness. A young woman with her hair in a braid was throwing a stick for a big, handsome dog. He tore back and forth on the narrow shore, bounding and leaping with pleasure. *Stan*, the woman called. *Good dog*, she praised.

Not far away from the woman and her dog was Ralph Cody. Once again, he had his tripod set up at the water's edge, and when he saw her, he waved. Her grateful heart propelled her feet. She went over to him.

"They're always changing," he said of the watery weeds he was enamoured of. "The light, the current, the wind, the way they float and move. I've taken dozens of pictures and each one is subtly different."

The events of the following summer would make these pictures of Ralph's almost intolerably moving. But Gwen couldn't know that now. The two of them stood together on the strip of sandy shore under high clouds, white and grey, feathering across a blue sky.

Ralph manoeuvred to get another angle and she asked him what he was looking for and he considered for a moment. "Energy. I recognize energy when I see it. It's more than just the scene in front of the camera," he said, peering through the lens. "It's a kind of electric connection. Almost a union between your intuitive side and your rational side." He looked up from his Nikon. "I heard Abe Lamont talking about how to shape an interview and write for radio. It's not so different, is it? One thought in each sentence. Not too many adjectives. Simplicity. Intimacy. Directness. That's what I'm after too."

She nodded and heard Abe's commanding voice in her head: "It's not about you, it's about the script, the story; think of that." And thinking of that, what did she see? Dido. Something the matter between Dido and her, something she didn't understand. What Abe had dinned into her over the course of the week was the need for excellence, the need to take risks to get excellence. She'd felt excited, raised up, inspired. Maybe she'd even seemed sure of herself. Maybe that's what Dido was talking about. And Gwen felt lost in the enormous gap between how she felt inside and what others thought of her. Dido was wrong. Wrong about her. Unless, of course, she was right.

On the way back to the station, she made a detour to the Explorer Hotel. Teresa had mentioned that the formal hearings of the Berger Inquiry were instructive and more interesting than you might expect. She went whenever she could to sit in the audience and listen. Now Gwen made her way through the hotel lobby and down the hall to the big meeting room, and Teresa was there, in one of the chairs set out for the public. Gwen sat down next to her. A lawyer for one of the pipeline companies was talking, a large man in a perfect suit and tie.

"Arctic Gas," whispered Teresa with a grin. "Watch out." He was cross-examining an expert witness, an engineer employed by his own oil and gas consortium, to explain and defend what they were proposing – a pipeline that would be bigger in diameter than any existing gas pipeline in North America, that would be operated at a maximum pressure of 1,680 pounds per square inch, and designed to withstand this pressure, and reinforced, besides, with steel bands or "crack arrestors," meaning it couldn't ever crack, rupture, burst. "Ha, ha," said Teresa, loud enough to turn a few heads.

Judge Berger sat alone at a small table at the front. He listened and made notes by hand. In keeping with the official nature of these formal sessions, he wore a navy blue pinstripe suit. Gwen was more familiar with his relaxed appearance in newspaper photographs taken at community hearings. Here, she gathered from Teresa, the expert witnesses sat at a table on his right. The reporters who covered the inquiry full-time sat on his left at an extended table that was spread, as were all the tables, with a white cloth. The lawyers – for Berger's commission of inquiry, for the pipeline companies, for the native organizations, for environmental groups – sat at other tables, their backs to the audience. When the hearing stopped for a coffee break, Teresa said she supposed she should get herself to work. Gwen left with her, and a moment later they were outside in the afternoon light walking back to the station. "Malarkey," Teresa said, and laughed. No purpose was served, she said, by all the malarkey that happens when people aren't honest.

"In white culture, people are so busy lying through their teeth. So busy thinking about getting ahead and making money, so busy thinking about how they come across, that they can't be themselves in a natural way. It builds up such a complicated and depressing web."

Teresa wasn't laughing any more. To Gwen she looked tired, uncharacteristically worn out.

Teresa went on, "If someone is sitting across from you and says, 'I want your land.' And you say no, I happen to like it here and I've been here forever, then they should respect what you've said, and that's an end to it. They shouldn't try to get around you. They shouldn't read something else into what you've said. They should *respect* you."

In the coming months, Gwen would often attend the inquiry. She noticed other townspeople who came repeatedly, a grey-haired woman who was always knitting, a wide-faced mother who breastfed her baby. They heard the native organizations push their moral high ground, and the pipeline companies don the cloak of thoughtful realism, and church and environmental groups attack the amorality of multi-national oil. Of equal interest to Gwen was the science. All the types of snow, all the complications of the soil, all the varieties of wildlife she'd never given much thought to. Everyone addressed Berger when they spoke, and he guided them forward, passionate about every aspect of the issue, you could tell, but sober, balanced, Leonard Bernstein as parson, a force field of quiet attention. If something wasn't clear he asked a question, and every single person listened.

After they realized they'd been overheard, Eleanor and Dido and Harry stood frozen in place for a moment until Dido began to laugh — embarrassed, shocked, working up a kind of carelessness to ease her guilt. Harry went over in his mind what he'd said — what the other two had said — not so bad, really, no great harm done, he hoped. But he'd better find Gwen. He went to the record library. A pile of records on a chair, but no Gwen, as he told them when he came back.

Eleanor wished that she'd nipped the whole thing in the bud. And yet she knew these regrettable conversations happened, were even necessary entertainment of a kind. Friends, good friends too, take the measure of each other behind the other's back, pronouncing with injudicious yet satisfying finality. They do it to make themselves feel better, only to end up feeling slightly ashamed. They do it as a form of emotional release. They do it, in some way, not to bury the relationship but to keep it alive.

But there were consequences. No one who hears ill of herself quite trusts the friend again.

What were they to do? Harry said he'd talk to Gwen the next time he saw her, he'd joke her out of it. But Eleanor said some gesture of friendship was needed, and Dido was the one who suggested they celebrate Gwen's birthday. It seemed to the others a generous thought, and Eleanor offered her place for the party.

"A *surprise* party," Dido specified. "Otherwise, she'll find an excuse not to come."

Eleanor was dubious, but she agreed to be the one to invite Gwen home for a drink without divulging what lay in store.

Later that afternoon, when she saw her come into the station with Teresa, she called to her and Gwen came over to her desk. Eleanor searched her face and said quietly, "You've been gone quite a while."

The sympathy in Eleanor's voice picked at the thread of her self-pity, and tugged, and Gwen felt herself unravel childishly. She bit her lip.

"You overheard us talking," said Eleanor.

Gwen looked down, her face a study in embarrassment, and a phrase came to Eleanor's mind: proud flesh. In an old medical book of her father's, its yellowed pages smelling of sweet dustiness, like an old church, she'd read among other things about burns and scalds, about suppuration, pain, excessive granulations or "proud flesh," and, unless skilfully treated, ugly scars.

"People say all sorts of things, Gwen. It doesn't mean much. It doesn't mean they aren't fond of the person, very fond."

Gwen still couldn't meet her eyes, and Eleanor reached across her desk and touched her hand. "Listen. Your birthday's tomorrow. Let's have a drink together."

Gwen looked at her then, a look of gratitude. She nodded and smiled. Then, fingering some of the papers on the desk, she said, "Dido," and stopped.

"Dido isn't as confident as she looks. And you can seem very sure of yourself sometimes."

Gwen stared back at her amazed. "I don't *feel* sure of myself."

"I know."

GWEN TURNED A QUARTER OF A CENTURY on her day off, Friday, August 1. Nothing from her brother, not a phone call, not a card. She thought of him in the jewellery store he'd taken over after their father died, her father a jeweller who never looked up, her brother a businessman who never stopped glancing around for another sale. Being on the radio, she'd discovered, was easier than dealing with certain people. There was a restfulness, an intimacy, a wonderful privacy when you didn't have to speak to someone face to face. She'd fallen into the habit of reading out a bedtime poem "for all you lie-awakes" before she signed off at night. Then afterwards she liked to take her time going home, roaming around on summer nights that at their darkest were still light enough to pick berries by. But things were changing now – it was becoming cooler, duskier.

Friday evening, she arrived for her birthday drink with Eleanor at seven o'clock, and Dido was there. Dido, making an effort, she could see that. A measured effort, a measured welcome, and as they worked at making conversation, and nothing was easy, Gwen understood that she was going to have to live with this – her negative effect on someone who used to like her, someone she still admired.

Between glasses of wine, and during an awkward pause, Gwen took herself to the bathroom. She followed the beige-carpeted hallway, pausing to look in through the door of the small spare bedroom, Dido's room, and it looked barely inhabited, its narrow bed more a shelf for books and papers than a place for sleeping. So she was spending her nights with Eddy. The second door was the bathroom, but a third door – the open door to Eleanor's bedroom – offered another view, another way of stalling, of avoiding Dido. Idly, she gazed in at the unmade double bed, the armchair, the window shades, when something caught her eye. A few feet away, a bottle of patchouli on top of the dresser. An unattractive scent, she'd always thought. She noticed a pair of Dido's slingback shoes on the floor.

As Gwen retraced her steps to the bathroom, a penny dropped in her mind.

At eight o'clock the bell rang, the door burst open, and in came Harry and Ralph and Teresa with overzealous cries of *Happy Birthday*.

Gwen felt tears spring to her eyes, and she smiled. She embraced everybody. "Thank you," she said, and her voice was husky. But, in truth, she hated surprise parties. She couldn't help feeling that it was cruel to string a person along, to say nothing all day in order to give her a hard, brotherly punch of affection at night.

For an hour or two she did her best. She mingled, listened, asked questions. She ate cake. After a while, she hid for a time inside a book she found on Eleanor's shelf, Rasmussen's *Observations on the Intellectual Culture of the Caribou Eskimos*. While Harry doctored himself with Scotch and Ralph satisfied his sweet tooth, Gwen was out in the arctic wastes and fifty years back in the past when the Inuit were still living much as they had for hundreds upon hundreds of years. *Small flocks of caribou were extremely shy and could not be hunted on the creaking snow in good weather, but only in a snowstorm, when it was sometimes possible to stalk quite close up to them.*

Rasmussen had entered the Barren Grounds in the spring of 1922, having heard as he travelled "many harrowing tales of the privation that had prevailed that winter." Everywhere Eskimos were starving. He followed the Kazan River looking for inland tribes, "the people of the whirlpools" and "the people of the willow thicket." The months of March and April were always the most dangerous time. Winter food caches had been used up, the May caribou migration hadn't begun.

"Hornby wasn't the only one who starved to death," Gwen thought, and she looked up to see Ralph watching her indulgently. "A serious reader," he said. "A woman after my own heart." He, too, liked to retreat behind a book or a magazine at parties, especially now that he had no wife to accuse him of being unforgivably and boyishly rude.

Gwen smiled and relaxed. She put the book down and returned to a party that seemed more complicated in its social tensions than the straightforward business of starving to death. A party she found touching and baffling and tiring and hard to navigate.

Dido was dancing by herself in bare feet. Teresa kicked off her shoes and joined her. Gwen watched from her armchair, fascinated by both women, afraid she'd be expected to dance too, charmed by their lack of inhibition, and envious.

Would she ever be like that? Dido was much the bigger of the two, yet her hips were almost as narrow as Teresa's. They were dancing to the Beatles – Dido reached over and jacked up the volume, she slipped her loose watch off her wrist and set it on the stereo – flirtatious, girlish, free, encouraged by applause from Ralph and Harry, who seemed as disinclined to dance as Gwen, and over the din Eleanor heard the doorbell.

It was Eddy on the doorstep. An entrance that changed everything. A visit in the manner of a visitation from an un-invited guest, although Eddy had been invited. He apologized for arriving late, he acknowledged Gwen with a squeeze of her shoulder. But the playful mood vanished, the women stopped dancing, and the music changed. Eddy had a new recording he wanted them to hear. Soon Joe Turner was singing slow, funky blues backed up by wailing trumpets. "I Know You Love Me Baby."

Eddy and Dido were dancing, and Gwen could see exactly what Eddy brought to Dido. Dido moved differently with Eddy. She was slower, unhurried. Her breasts looked heavier, riper, her hips wider, lower, fuller. She shone with a different glow, a dark, erotic radiance.

By now Teresa was sitting cross-legged on the carpet beside Gwen's armchair, rolling a smoke, her hands trembling. Looking down at her, Gwen could see the traces of grey that she'd never noticed before in the dark hair on top of Teresa's head. She could see the side of her face, and was struck by what seemed to be a sad and knowing smile. The other day Teresa had told her that although she'd followed her sister into the nunnery, she'd never followed her into a bad

marriage. That was the great sadness of her life, she said. Her
sister's terrible marriage.

It was late. Harry lay semi-sprawled on the floor. He gave up
trying to make his point, having forgotten what it was. Gwen
was curled up in an armchair, reading again. Eleanor's eyes
rested on the birthday girl and a memory came back of a boy
she knew growing up, Ronny Ferguson, a strange boy: other
kids would be playing outside and he would be inside reading
Marvel comics; even at his birthday party he kept on reading.
His mother let him, that was the marvellous thing.

Gwen closed the book and asked what time it was. She
asked the room at large. Everyone, except herself, was at this
point sitting on the floor.

Dido, across the room with her back against the wall and
Eddy beside her, waited a moment before she replied. "What
time do you want it to be?"

Dido had slipped her shoes back on, low heels, black. Her
bare arms were the colour of peeled almonds. Her watch was
conspicuous again on her wrist.

Gwen wanted it to be very late. She wanted to go home.
"I want it to be the time it is."

"But what time do you *want* it to be?"

Gwen felt herself being toyed with, baited by Dido's
amused, provocative, subtly hostile tone, and her own voice
came out hard and strained. "I. want. it. to. be. the. time. it. *is*."

Eleanor leaned her head back against the wall. It seemed
to her that something was going on here that was closer than

friendship, just as the scratchy label of a sweater is closer than the sweater.

The smile widened on Dido's lips. She shifted and looked at her watch. Then she looked at Gwen. "Why are you sitting on a chair? All the rest of us are on the floor."

"I'm comfortable on the chair." But she didn't feel comfortable. And didn't look it either, she knew that.

"You don't look comfortable," said Dido with that slightly mocking smile.

"I'm as comfortable as I ever am."

"But you're apart from us, sitting up there. You've set yourself apart."

"I know. I know I'm sitting on a chair and everyone else is on the floor."

"Do you *feel* apart from the rest of us?"

"Maybe a little. Is that a crime?"

Dido was watching Gwen, but nobody else was. "It's not a crime. I just wonder what's going on. And why you're so angry."

Somebody had to break the silence, but nobody did.

Then Harry spoke, his voice low, conversational, a little slurred. "What's the book, Gwen?"

She looked down at the book in her hands.

"Show me."

She stood up then and handed him the book. And that's how she got off the chair-island on which she'd been stranded. She knelt on the floor beside Harry. From here she could see partway down the hall and picture the rest – the underused small bedroom, the fully used big bedroom. She could scarcely credit it. Yet it nudged her again. The eerie feeling that she knew something she could use against Dido.

Only in a snowstorm, she thought, a flurry of stuff in the air, was it possible to outwit the caribou. Outwitting people, however, that was easy. They were at the door. Eleanor embraced her and soothed her heart by saying, "Let's have lunch tomorrow. I'll ring your bell at noon." But brazen Dido took her face between her hands and kissed her on the mouth. "Happy birthday, birthday girl."

Dido's lips felt thin and oversoft, innocent yet all wrong. Harmless, but not harmless at all.

$$\equiv$$

It was 1 a.m., and Dido and Eleanor were listening to Billie Holiday sing good morning to her heartache as they emptied ashtrays, stacked dishes, began to wash up after the party.

Dido dried a plate. She reached for another, and as she did so, she remembered something, and the towel went still.

"I had a terrible dream last night."

Eleanor stopped too, and turned to look at Dido, who stood transfixed. She was back in the dream.

"I was in a big city and it was very dark, pitch dark. It felt like Eastern Europe somewhere. Pitch *black*, I mean. A taxi pulled up and I got into it, and we began to drive down this old, narrow street. There were two men in the front seat in black suits. They were staring straight ahead. I couldn't see their faces. I had no idea who they were, I didn't know where we were going either, I didn't know where I was." Dido rubbed her forehead with one hand. "There was nothing in here," she said slowly. "I had no memory. I had no mind. I didn't know anything. It was as black in here as it was outside." She looked at Eleanor. "It was terrifying."

She's describing a hearse, thought Eleanor. She's describing her own journey into death.

She took the tea towel out of Dido's hand. "You're tired, honey. It's late."

Dido turned to stare at the clock on the kitchen wall. "Eddy said, 'Loon at three o'clock' the other day. I didn't know whether to turn my head right or left. I couldn't remember where three was on the clock."

Eleanor put her arm around Dido and drew her away from the clock. "I get confused by things too and I'm not trying to juggle two languages and two countries the way you are."

<hr>

Gwen had driven Harry home. On the way they didn't talk and were comfortable not talking. They came down Franklin Avenue, named for the man who ate his boots, the explorer who managed to lose the lives of all one hundred and twenty-nine of his men in one of those foolhardy attempts to find the Northwest Passage. Proof to Harry that if your disaster was on a large enough scale, your incompetence would be forgiven.

In passing the Capitol Theatre, Gwen saw *The Godfather Part II* on the marquee, and she said, "Eddy has cruel lips."

"Women go for that," replied Harry with a dry laugh.

She knew he meant the movie male aggressiveness that was undeniably exciting. "Dido has cruel lips too," she said.

Harry pretended not to hear this quiet remark. It was August 2 now, and the darkness was like a partially open drawer.

"There's Mrs. Dargabble," said Harry.

Lorna Dargabble was on the other side of the street, out for a walk at one in the morning, hands in her pockets, oversized *chapeau* on her head. A lonely figure, slow, heavy, troubled. The last time Gwen had knocked on her door, no one had answered, but she'd heard a radio, faintly; Lorna always had the radio on – it was her lifeline, she said. In the hallway Gwen had called out her name, and up came Lorna from the basement, full of apologies for not having her teeth in and dressed in much the same style as the half-renovated kitchen: she wore the most elegant shoes, green suede with straps at the back, a long green velvet skirt, and a lumber jacket. The kitchen had insulation but no drywall, a new stove not yet installed, and a true boarding house smell of none-too-clean.

"I don't see her at the station any more," said Harry.

"Oh, she still comes in. She's been talking about moving back to Boston. She says Yellowknife is no place for an old woman."

Harry nodded. Or an old man, for that matter.

When Gwen pulled into Harry's driveway, she turned off the motor and sat back, unwilling to end a night she'd held steadfastly at bay. There was something she wanted to ask.

"Harry?" She ran her necklace of blue beads back and forth across her lower lip.

The gesture reminded Harry of his ex-wife, who used to draw forward a strand of her long hair and curl it around and around her finger.

What she wanted to ask was why Dido had kissed her on the mouth like that. What was she trying to prove? And why were her personal things in Eleanor's bedroom when she was obviously sleeping with Eddy? She wanted to say, What's going on with Dido, this woman you're so in love with?

But an easier statement slipped out. "I'd like to live down here," she said.

Then she said something else. "I don't really like living alone. I liked it better when I lived with Eleanor. I mean, lived with her, sort of."

"Too bad she doesn't have more room."

She looked at him. "There's enough room. Dido's bedroom doesn't seem to get much use, even when she's there."

For a second his eyes drilled her. Then he looked ahead with a bleak little smile.

It had slipped out innocently enough, cloaked in honesty, even delicacy. She had observed something. How could she not take credit?

Iago. Iago had bobbed up inside her.

"It's late, Gwen." He reached for the door handle. "Thanks for the ride."

But she was Iago and Othello in one: insinuating and sorry. "I'm sorry. Forget what I just said. I don't know what I'm talking about." She was looking over at him. "I shouldn't have said that. I don't mean to be nasty."

Harry remained silent.

"Or maybe I do," she said.

Harry heard the misery in her voice. Now she was staring at her hands in her lap. It was cool enough that he was surprised she wasn't shivering in her light jacket.

Later, he would ponder on what she'd implied. *Dido's bedroom doesn't seem to get much use.* A shock — if it was true. But his world wasn't destroyed by the thought of Dido in Eleanor's bed. It's not the thought of a woman with another woman that makes a man unhappy, it's the thought of a woman with another man. Anyway, he didn't buy it — although he'd give anything to see Eddy's face if it were true. No, the remark said more about Gwen than it did about anyone else. She'd leapt to a conclusion for reasons of her own, and then she'd had the decency to regret it.

GWEN FOUND HERSELF THINKING about the vulnerable rivers and birds and plants and animals and old ways of life – all of it unprotected, much of it wary. At the Berger Inquiry she'd heard that snow geese in late August gathered in the thousands on the arctic coast, feeding for several weeks on berries and sedges before flying eight hundred miles non-stop to northern Alberta, then on to the wheat fields farther south. On these August staging grounds, said the biologists, the birds were easily frightened by planes overhead and activity on the ground – the noise of a compressor station at a distance of a mile and a half, or a small aircraft at the same distance, was enough to flush them into the air. Similarly, the white whales of the Beaufort Sea were wary of man, yet increasingly exposed. To give birth they came into the warmer, shallow waters of Mackenzie Bay, now the site, and increasingly so, of offshore drilling for oil and gas.

Then there were the caribou. In March they left their winter range among the trees and slowly travelled north across the tundra, arriving at their calving grounds near the arctic coast in late May. In early June, after the calves were born, the cows joined together in small, timid clusters, then larger bands, then greater herds that culminated in the post-calving aggregation, the gathering en masse in July that forms the sight over which everyone marvels, a spectacle equal to the long lost flights of passenger pigeons, or the once glorious massing of buffalo. But disturb them while calving, fly a helicopter low in the fog, and you cause the females to be separated from their young, with drastic results. At the same time these creatures were enormously resilient, able to withstand extreme cold and hunger, epic distances and plagues of maddening flies.

She learned the word *albedo*. An oil spill, in turning the ice black, ruins its albedo or reflective capacity, causing it to absorb light rather than reflect it, and to melt, thereby changing the environment in unforeseeable ways. Albedo like albino, went her connecting mind, like bezel – a ruby-eyed albino. Jewellery terms came back to her, and her father's slender explanations, his reticence. He would sit at his jeweller's bench, using a brush to sweep up piles of silver dust, or lemel, which he kept and melted up for reuse. He had little boxes of gold dust too. Every so often the big jewellery makers would take everything up, he told her once, all the floorboards, all the shelves, and burn them for the gold. He would bring his magnifying loupe to his eye, then raise the jewel to the loupe, checking for imperfections. It's all illusion, he'd murmured once as he fine-sandpapered a brooch: you make something smooth with a series of scratches. Cabochon was another old word used in the trade; it referred to any stone that was flat on one side and round on the other. In little drawers her father had cabochons of amber and turquoise, in other little drawers loose pearls, garnets, amethysts. Anneal. She loved to watch the process happen, the metal relax and change colour, soften and become supple under the steady heat of the gas flame. Her father would have said that Dido had a jeweller's hands and wrists and shoulders, square and strong and capable. It wasn't hard to imagine Dido doing what she herself had never managed to do, polish silver and gold on the rouge wheel without ever blackening her long, competent fingers.

In the coming months, Gwen formed an image of the North as an open page in a book of wonders illustrated and illuminated with rare animals and subtle plants. The North was the tropics made simple and cool. A rather more knowable place, since it held on to all traces of passage, to every weathered bone and fire-cracked rock. One scientist talked about the length of time it took anything to decay in the arctic air, on the one hand, and to grow, on the other, since food supplies were limited, summer was short, reproduction rates were meagre. In some parts of the North an arctic char didn't produce ripe eggs until it was twelve years old, and even after that it spawned only every second or third year. A world, where if you were a child and the world was a plate, then the plate would be huge and have lots of space between a few select foods. She had been that very sort of child, wanting everything kept separate, and not a lot of different things at once, or much of any one thing at all.

The inquiry was making so much visible and noteworthy. Something quickened inside her when she heard native testimony on the radio about living on the land, about existing in makeshift shelters as you went storm-tossed and sun-warmed through life. Many native people still spent May and June in their spring camps trapping muskrats, and summers at their fish camps in the Delta catching and drying fish or harvesting white whales, and parts of the winters inland, hunting and trapping. Berger was going to their doorsteps, settlement to settlement, thirty-five in all. He was visiting summer camps and fishing grounds, like the itinerant preachers of old, in his corduroy jacket with the leather patches on the elbows, wearing his large school-boy glasses on his pleasantly wide face. And people, of course, were coming to him. Countless witnesses were speaking into the microphone in a gathering, an aggregation if you like, of informants and information. A remarkable time of hope for anyone opposed to the pipeline, for anyone in favour of the present learning from the past.

Around Yellowknife, the miniature birches and poplars changed colour in August. For about two weeks they were a ravishing yellow-gold. It was quite astonishing, but so fast: every single leaf was on every single tree and every single leaf was yellow. Farther south, colour gathered on some leaves as others fell, and you only ever got a piece of the whole, but here you had all of the glory all at once, and then it was gone. In September, it snowed enough to cover the ground, and the roads turned icy. They wouldn't see water on the streets again until April.

Towards the end of September, a large package arrived at the station addressed to Gwen Symon. A round-shouldered bundle of heavy brown paper, bigger than a big sleeping bag, she thought. No return address. She'd thought immediately of a peace offering from her brother in Ontario – they hadn't spoken in months and months – but the postmark said YELLOWKNIFE.

Opening it, while Eleanor looked on, Gwen recalled Harry's comment about ghosts pouring out of boxes. He was right. It was a fur coat, a ghost of sorts.

She lifted it out of its wrappings, her expression open-mouthed and astounded, and Eleanor said, "We're going to remember this for the rest of our lives. You'll remember the look of the coat and I'll remember the look on your face."

Gwen held the coat by its shoulders and shook out its folds. She examined the dark, brownish-grey fur that seemed to shed light. It felt as soft as talcum powder. She checked the label, "Wright Furs," then looked for tags and found none, looked for signs of wear on the brown silk lining and found not wear, but the softness of having been worn. She slipped it on, bringing it close around her neck, and stepped up to the studio window to see her reflection.

"You look wonderful," said Eleanor.

Gwen put her hands in the pockets and pulled out a small card. *From a secret admirer.* Now her insides were as transformed as her outsides: she felt flattered and stunned. The first snowfall had worked a similar change on the town itself. It dazzled interiors by transforming the external world.

The beauty of fur. The coat was light in weight but immediately warm and luxurious. And Gwen did look wonderful. Even she could see that.

Teresa was able to identify the fur. Her father ran a trapline, and so she knew sheared beaver when she saw it. The coat had been perfectly cared for, she said, it was as good as new.

Dido had appeared too, drawn by all the fuss. She fingered the coat enviously. "It's beautiful, Gwen."

"Try it on."

Dido tried it on. She had to hunch her shoulders and when she stretched out her arms, inches of bare wrist protruded. "Whoever sent it knows your size," she said. "Maybe somebody's watching you. Did you think of that?"

Gwen took the coat back from her, and slowly, carefully folded it. She hadn't thought of that, and what had been latent, a slight feeling of alarm and suspicion, now overtook her joy. She stroked the fur. What a shame if she couldn't wear it.

"Come on," protested Teresa. "Who cares where it came from."

Then quite suddenly Gwen knew. In her childhood a big basket of precious blueberries from Manitoulin Island had been sent to a family down the street, the Johnsons, a gift from their island relatives. But the berries never arrived – they were delivered by mistake to another family with the same name – a story pieced together only after the relatives wondered aloud at never having been thanked. "There must be another Gwen Symon," she said.

But then why was the package addressed to her at her place of work? No, she realized, she was the one it was intended for.

In the end, Gwen would take Teresa's view. She wore the coat. She called it Dolly. Come on Dolly, let's go for a walk. And she would take long rambles, warm as toast and reasonably worry-free. She never ceased to puzzle over who might have given it to her, but no one stepped forward, and the riddle remained unsolved for more than a year.

A few days later, in the parking lot next to the liquor store, Harry pulled up behind Dido's parked car. She sat alone behind the wheel, so still that he wondered why, and then the light dawned. No doubt she was listening to the radio, and he turned his on to see what might have captured her attention.

It was Eliza Doolittle's spirited invective against Henry Higgins, but what Harry couldn't know was that Dido was reliving the skip on her childhood recording, a skip ingrained in her memory as much as the music itself. She heard it coming, then heard it happen, even as the song on the radio sailed smoothly on. It brought her whole childhood back. Her father would lift the needle and place it, delicately, a fraction of a centimetre ahead. As precisely as Eddy had located "Helpless." "My Fair Lady" had been a recording for daytime. At night, her father frequently put on "Harold in Italy," and she would fall asleep to those glorious, haunting strains, learning to love the viola because of Berlioz, because, in truth, of her father. Sitting here now, suspended with music that flooded her with the past, she wondered what her father, who'd been drawn to strong women, not to strong men, would have thought of Eddy. Eddy was so private, intense, possessive; he wanted to have a child with her, he wanted a son; and yet there were things he kept entirely to himself, and there were times when she didn't seem to matter to him at all. The radio news came on and she turned it up. Gravesites were being prepared for the winter, not at the old cemetery on Back Bay where she'd heard her father's voice, but at the new one

near the airport, twenty-five graves that would be covered
with wooden cribbing to protect them until needed, after
which the ground would freeze so hard it would be impossible
to turn it over with a spade. The innocence of these arrange-
ments struck her. Nobody expects anything bad to happen,
she thought, anything out of the ordinary. She, on the other
hand, had been having one violent dream after another and
they coloured her days with vague apprehension.

Harry's tuneful whistle greeted her when she got out of
the car. He was leaning against his van, whistling "I've Grown
Accustomed to Her Face," and she had to smile. She recognized the compliment, understood the connection; he'd been
listening to the radio too.

Harry was delighted to see her, delighted to catch her in
an unguarded moment. He was thinking that the age difference between them wasn't as vast as that between Higgins and
Eliza. He in his forties, Dido in her twenties. But Dido must
have read his mind because she said, "Harry, I'm not Eliza
Doolittle, you know."

He watched her head into the liquor store and admired her
more than ever for seeing through his foolish self.

———

Radio mattered more as the days grew shorter. Gwen, broadcasting at midnight, had more calls and more complaints about
the music she played. There were times when she put her disgruntled listeners on the air and defended herself, using the
little sound-effects door to good effect. "Thank you and good

night!" Or, "You think that's opera? Let me introduce you to opera. Here we are at Joan Sutherland's door." She rang the doorbell and invited Joan to sing an aria from *Norma*.

At the end of her summer contract, Harry had called her into his office and extended it for a year. For Gwen, that was more than enough. She felt a new surge of confidence that helped to balance other worries, like her ongoing estrangement from Dido. Their paths rarely crossed any more, and when they did, nothing transpired except the briefest of greetings. She had more contact, really, with Lorna Dargabble, who often phoned during her late night show, almost pitifully grateful for some of the music she played.

Sometimes when she closed down the station at one in the morning and stepped outside, she would see the elderly woman coming back from one of her solitary walks. In the summer, Lorna said, she ventured as far as Frame Lake, and walked along the shore, or went down to Old Town and circled the Rock. In the colder months, however, she stayed in the downtown area that was scented by the warm, stale, greasy puffs of air that issued from Jason's Chicken.

On this occasion, as Gwen accompanied Mrs. Dargabble home, they saw Eddy and a young Dene man ahead of them, the latter identifiable by his long black braid and a posture even more erect than Eddy's.

Lorna said, "I don't trust those two. I don't know what they're up to, but they're up to something."

Gwen looked at her, surprised to catch a hint of prejudice. "Do they have to be up to something? I mean, here we are, you and I. Would you say we're up to something?"

Lorna chuckled and put her arm through Gwen's. But soon she let out a heavy sigh. "My days of being up to anything are over," she said.

Gwen asked what was weighing on her mind, and Lorna told her that she'd almost decided to see a lawyer about getting a divorce.

"But that's good," encouraged Gwen.

"No," Lorna said. "Nothing's good."

Gwen's breakfast was everyone else's lunch; she got into the habit of joining Teresa in the Gold Range café around noon. One day, when Eleanor was with them, Teresa split her egg roll down the centre, poured the sweet sauce inside, and said, amused and mischievous, "Love is like a Chinese menu. It's not a question of meeting the one and only. There's infinite choice. All you have to do is pick."

"Listen to you," said Eleanor, who shared Teresa's side of the booth. Teresa leaned into her, capsized by mirth.

The café was busy and warm, dank with steam and grease and cigarette smoke. A framed photograph, "Lunchtime Atop a Skyscraper, 1932," on the wall: workers with lunch pails in their laps, balanced on a high beam above New York City. Teresa's relaxed work ethic meant for longer than usual lunch breaks and later than usual hours to make up for it. That suited Gwen, who didn't begin her shift until 6 p.m.

This was the day when Teresa let drop quite casually that she used to volunteer at the gay crisis line in Vancouver. "A

thirty-five-year-old woman called up," she said, "and I suggested we have coffee together. I told her don't worry. I'm an
ancient Chinese washerwoman. I won't come on to you."
Teresa recognized the look on Gwen's face, the slight shock,
and added with a small smile, "I try not to hide anything
about myself."

A pause. Eleanor said, "That's what I love about you."

For Gwen, Teresa's revelation brought her birthday party
into focus. She remembered Teresa's trembling hands after
Eddy claimed Dido for himself, and realized she'd been right
about something, after all, just wrong about the someone.

Eddy came in, and with him came not Dido this time, but
his Dene friend. The two men passed the three women and
nodded. Eleanor greeted them by name. "Eddy. Paul." They
took a booth at the very back of the restaurant. Eleanor said,
"Paul came to our northern support group to explain the
native land claim."

Teresa's face had darkened. Suddenly she looked every
inch her age.

"I wonder if *you'd* come one night," Eleanor said to her.
"We'd love to hear your views."

There was something wonderfully innocent and generous
about Eleanor Dew, thought Gwen on her side of the booth as
she watched her kind, lived-in face become animated with the
issues of the day. Eleanor filled Teresa in on the northern
support group formed by Dido and Eddy, a workshop of like-
minded whites who wanted to discuss the native land claim,
understand it better, support it publicly, offset the usual white
ignorance and mistrust of native rights. The North of Sixty
Support Group, they were calling themselves, and it wasn't

meant for journalists, she said with an apologetic smile for Gwen, just ordinary people in town. "Well, Dido's the exception. There's just a handful of us. We meet once a week in my trailer. There's a teacher. An architect. There's the United Church minister. One woman's a nurse. There's a painter. There's me. We're tasting the pleasures of radical thinking," she said with a gently ironic smile, "going to the root of what Eddy likes to call present reality. But it's good. Paul spoke to us a few weeks ago," indicating him with a movement of her finger, "I found it interesting, helpful."

Teresa said, "I know Paul Julien." She pushed her plate to one side. "He's a cousin of mine." The food she hadn't eaten would go into the garbage cans behind the restaurant and be squawked over by the flapping, theatrical ravens.

"We deserve a land claim settlement," Teresa said. "We deserve to have control of this country. But Paul's what I'd call a man on the prowl. He's bad news."

Late one night, Gwen, wearing Dolly, stood in the middle of the street, head craned back, marvelling, listening. She'd finished her shift and put on her borrowed finery, the mysterious loan, as she chose to think of it, that had fallen into her lap from the amazing sky. A sky that on this night towards the end of October was filled with a moving white fog, which began to shimmer and ripple downwards in long, shaggy icicles, then sideways in draperies of pale green and violet — a huge, heavenly version of the gas flame of a jeweller's torch shooting out to the side and shifting in colour from white to blue to green to orange. If she'd been outside the city, somewhere in the arctic wastes, she might have heard the northern lights swish and whisper as everyone said they did, Dene, Inuit, trappers, prospectors, everyone except the dreary scientists.

Earlier the same night, there had been earthly fireworks of a milder sort on Latham Island. Judge Berger was holding a community hearing in the hall a hundred yards or so from Harry's house. These community hearings, as distinct from the formal hearings in the Explorer Hotel, were casual and open-ended, continuing until everyone who wanted to speak had spoken. It was Berger's contention that every person who lived in this part of the world had a right to say what he or she felt about a pipeline.

Harry sat at the end of a row of chairs, listening to a smart, young Yellowknife doctor utter a series of warnings about the next southern invasion of the North. Look at Alaska, the doctor was saying, where the Alyeska pipeline was built *after* a land claims settlement with the native people, and even so, the effect has been catastrophic on rates of suicide, divorce, alcoholism, mental illness, violent crime: a horror story, and we haven't heard the final chapter. Here, said the doctor, the natives don't *have* a land claims settlement. So what's going to happen? For three winters a few of them will be hired as part of a big pipeline force and they'll receive high wages. Then what? They'll drift south looking for the same wages, they'll drift into unemployment and welfare in Vancouver or Winnipeg or Toronto, and the North will have lost its best young men just when the Dene are trying to establish their right to self-determination. Young native women will be enticed and sexually exploited by transient white labourers with lots of money and easy access to alcohol and no thought for the consequences of their actions. "Who is going to pay for all this?" he wanted to know. "The pipeline company? The oil company? The people of Canada? These people may pay the dollars; we already know who is going to pay the price in human misery."

The little hall was bright with lights and cameras. The possibility for spontaneous, unscripted drama made these informal hearings of special interest to journalists. Nothing went unnoticed.

Harry saw Eddy and Dido at the back, their coats over their arms. Lorna Dargabble sat in loose disarray at the end of a middle row. Berger, in jacket and tie, was at the front, seated at a small square table, a pedestal mike directly in front of him. On his left were the transcribers, getting down every word that was spoken. At another table were representatives from both pipeline companies, who were there to answer questions. Behind the judge, and tacked to the wall, was a huge map showing the proposed routes for the pipeline, there being two proposals, as Berger took pains to explain in his opening remarks. The one that was 2,200 miles long had been put forward by an international consortium (Arctic Gas). It was to bring gas from Prudhoe Bay, along the north slope of Alaska across the Yukon to the Mackenzie Valley, then pick up Canadian gas from the Mackenzie River Delta, and in a single pipeline bring it to markets in the south, Canadian and American. The other was an all-Canadian proposal (Foothills Pipe Lines) to bring Canadian gas from the Mackenzie Delta south to Canadian markets only. This one was eight hundred miles long. Arctic Gas claimed their bigger venture would be more economical in the long run, and gas would cost less than it would if the Foothills project went through. "Well, that's the argument between them," said Berger, setting himself apart from the companies even as he explained their intentions to the audience of about seventy people. No matter which pipeline project went ahead, he said, there would be thousands of men needed to build it and it would take years to build. And if a gas pipeline was built, an oil pipeline would surely follow. It was logical, then, for his inquiry to address not just the impact of a gas pipeline, but all the development that would come thereafter. Listening to him speak, Harry appreciated just how much Tom Berger had managed to turn his inquiry into an exercise in democracy, informing, questioning, teaching, listening. "I hope you'll feel free to speak up and tell me what's on your mind," Berger would say to the local people at these informal hearings, "just as if there were only yourselves and myself here tonight."

After the doctor finished speaking, a pilot for one of the small charter companies in Yellowknife went to the microphone, a man skeptical about the value of the inquiry, who referred to "the proposed, and it would seem from all accounts, inevitable pipeline." He said he'd welcome the boost to the economy, the extra business, but he felt depressed about what was bound to happen to the relaxed and easygoing town he loved.

After the pilot, Eddy got up to speak.

Teresa Lafferty had come in by then, and was standing at the back, curious to hear what these townspeople had to say. She wouldn't speak herself until Berger brought his inquiry to her hometown of Fort Rae the following summer. She wanted her relatives, her grandmother especially, to hear her voice added to theirs; she wanted them to be together on that historic day. Then she would say that what the pipeline companies were asking for was enormous and what the people were asking for wasn't much at all. It wasn't asking a lot to have the land claim settled first. If the pipeline should burst, what would happen to their traditional hunting grounds, to the animals and all the food they depended on? My people don't have any money at all, she would tell the judge, and I don't think they care to make money. The only ones who stand to benefit from a pipeline are the big oil companies and southern Canada and the United States. I'm afraid of the pipeline, she would tell him. I'm afraid for the elders, for all my relatives, for their traditional way of life, and for the land itself.

Tonight Teresa looked around at the mostly white faces and wondered where these people came from – where you came from being the question put to everyone in the North (everyone except the Indians, she thought). From outside, but from where outside?

Harry was motioning to her, asking if she wanted to sit down, and she took the chair beside him. Then Harry was holding his glasses, closing and opening the frames as he listened to Eddy.

"A Dene friend of mine," Eddy was saying, "told me he'd been to Vietnam too, and I thought he was joking. But we drove out to Fort Rae, and I wonder if you know this, Judge, that seventy miles from here there's a place they call Vietnam. Crappy houses, broken windows, dust and dirt and misery. Fort Rae isn't much, but part of it's so bad they call it Vietnam.

A real skid row. So what I want to say tonight is that I think you have good intentions, but good intentions aren't enough. Some friends and I started a northern support group to add our voices, in a very small way, to the call for social justice for the native people. We called ourselves the North of Sixty Support Group. Then a couple of weeks ago a few rednecks, I can't think of any other word for them, stole our name, registered themselves legally, and set about printing ads in favour of the pipeline. What can you do against people like that?" Eddy addressed his question to the audience at large. Then said to Berger, "You're an employee of the Government of Canada. You're part of the system. I've been living here for over a year, I've got a white boss, most of the folks I work with are white. That radio station I work at — it should be Dene-run. This inquiry should be Dene-run too. They're the majority, they should be in charge. But it's never going to happen, not by having nice, polite meetings."

Teresa shifted her embroidered parka in her lap. She thought, In a year he'll be gone, back to where he came from. All the white people went home eventually.

"Look," he gestured with both hands, his jaw working with suppressed anger, "you've already had some Dene witnesses say they'll lay down their lives to stop the pipeline and the whites all squawked about it. *They're threatening violence.* But I'm saying there's already violence. The conditions in the settlements. That's a form of violence. Why aren't the whites up in arms about that? Why aren't they up in arms about the underhanded disrespect and backroom wheeling and dealing that does violence to goodwill and good intentions? So I want to go on record as opposing the pipeline and supporting the Dene taking control by whatever means necessary."

There was a smattering of applause. One of the native reporters raised his fist and grinned with glee, one rabble-rouser congratulating another. Dido saw Harry Boyd tug on his ear, left-handed, good-hearted, ineffectual Harry. But Eddy was right. The world was divided into the majority who wanted to believe everything was okay and the radical few who knew it wasn't and were galvanized by that fact. Eddy had energy and so did she. She had an immigrant's energy and impatience and sense of purpose, and so did Eddy. Privately, they were both coming to believe you had to do something drastic to stop corporations from violating the land. Something to convince them the North wouldn't be a safe place to put their money.

Lorna Dargabble was on her way to the microphone. Harry glanced back at Dido. She was standing in front of Eddy, leaning against him. His hands were on her shoulders. The two of them shone with a powerful, self-righteous glow, it seemed to Harry, who considered self-righteousness a sin in itself, not that the thought made him feel any better. Lorna Dargabble was wishing everybody would stop romanticizing the past. She was an old woman, she was saying, and she'd seen what men do to women late at night and it didn't matter if they were white or native, or if it was ten years ago or today. There's a lot of ugliness in the North and a lot of abuse. We need kindness, she was saying, jobs and kindness. But she was losing her train of thought, and Harry noticed Eddy whispering in Dido's ear and Dido smiling and nodding. They seemed to be amused by the old woman. Not only self-righteous, he thought, but cruel. Then he was called back to Lorna, her voice suddenly clear as a bell. "I heard on the radio this man telling you the pipeline companies will rape the land. Well, this man ought to know. I mean to say, he's been up on rape charges more than once. There's a lot of talk about the terrible degradation the pipeline will bring. Oh, yes. And I'm worried too. But don't believe everything you hear, that's all I'm saying."

Lorna's short testimony was greeted by a shuffling of feet, a certain embarrassment. Berger, unfailingly polite, thanked her. At every one of these hearings the atmosphere was serious, unhurried; people wanted to express themselves. Frequently, someone would say, as a young woman was saying now, "I didn't intend to speak tonight, I just intended to listen. However, after listening to the last person, I felt I had to speak. I think it's time we believed in the native people. This is their land." A Dene fellow went to the microphone after that. "Like myself," he said, "I'm a young man. I'm only twenty-three years old and I'm thinking about my kids." Harry would see this man again on a cold winter's day under circumstances so different he wouldn't recognize him at first. "Today I was parking my truck downtown. Yes, I parked my truck because I was going to be gone about half an hour, but I was gone forty-five minutes. When I got back to my truck I got a ticket and it was going to cost me three dollars. I was thinking, well, this is Dene land. They should at least ask us before they do their regulations. At least they should ask the chiefs. They should say, what do you think?" There was a murmur of sympathy from the audience, some nodded their heads. "Before the white people came to Yellowknife, kids used to be learning lessons from their parents. Our kids don't listen now and even the dogs, we don't have any good dogs now. All the white people came and brought their small dogs around, they're all mixed up now. Everything they're spoiling. They spoiled the water too. They spoiled the land." The hall was quiet now. "I just hope the government listens to us," he said, and pushed back his chair. "So, this is all I wanted to say."

Harry ought not to have stood up. He knew better. But he cradled his glasses in his left hand and went to the microphone. He'd expected somebody else to take issue with Eddy. Had they been uptown in the Elk's Hall, rather than here in Old Town, there would have been any number of businessmen and local politicians ready and eager to defend the pipeline. He had no intention of being pro-pipeline, but he felt he had to speak. "Judge Berger, I'm the white boss referred to earlier. I'm the manager of a radio station soon to be dwarfed by a television station. So as bosses go, I'm pretty small potatoes." He heard the door of the hall bang shut and wondered if that was Dido and Eddy leaving. "This isn't going to make me popular with my own bosses, but I feel I have to say it. I'm speaking for myself as a resident of the North, you understand. Here we have an inquiry about the effects of the pipeline, what you, sir, in your opening remarks called the most expensive project ever undertaken by private enterprise anywhere in the world. But Judge, let's say you're able to recommend ways of keeping the pipeline far away from the communities. Let's say you're able to do that," Harry said. "Then it could be argued that its impact will do less harm in the long run than television beamed in from the south. I don't mean to trivialize the pipeline. My real point is that some things we can't escape, television's one of them, the pipeline's probably another. But we can slow them down and we don't have to resort to violence to do it. An example. Last March the settlement of Igloolik rejected television in a referendum. They chose instead to have a radio station they control. In my view the best thing your inquiry is doing is waking everybody up so they're on guard against being rushed and pushed and bullied into things. For the record, I don't want the pipeline, and I don't want it because the native people don't want it. After all, we white people from the south are in the minority up here. We should stop trying to get our own way all the time." Harry thanked the judge, and returned to the back of the hall, hoping for what? Not Dido's semi-smile, her look of cool appraisal, if that's what it was. That's certainly what it felt like. Teresa touched his arm when he sat down. "Thank you, Harry."

Not long afterwards, as Harry was leaving to go home, a reporter from the local newspaper stopped him at the door, wanting to be sure he had his name and position right. Once he was home, Harry made a pot of coffee, and then he went for a long walk and came upon Gwen, in her fur coat, staring up at the northern lights.

"Aurora Borealis," he said. "Electrically charged particles in the solar wind collide with molecules in the Earth's upper atmosphere, and the collision gives off light."

"You should be in bed," said Gwen.

"The green is caused by oxygen and the violet by nitrogen."

They continued to stare at the colours in the sky, Harry recalling the moment last summer when Gwen had been decorated head and shoulders in blue damselflies. Here she was again, glad to be out in the elements. It made him feel better just to see her.

"I did something I shouldn't have tonight," he said.

"What was that?"

"I took a political position. I said where I stood."

"That's commendable."

"Not for the manager of a public radio station. We're supposed to be objective, not take sides, especially in a political climate as charged as this one."

It became known as the Harry Boyd incident, and it caused him more grief with his own newsroom than with head office. Head office merely rapped his knuckles and warned him not to do anything like it again. But Thwaite and Tupper were furious with him for making their own lives more difficult. Here they were trying to present themselves as unbiased, which they were, and their station manager had to run off at the mouth at a public meeting. They sent a letter of complaint to the head of the Northern Service in Ottawa. There would be a later letter, too, signed by others.

ONE DAY IN EARLY NOVEMBER, Dido came to work in dark glasses. That evening Gwen found her staring out the window of the empty office, lost in thought. She'd pushed her sunglasses to the top of her head, and Gwen saw the bruised and puffy left eye.

Between the two women there sprang up a momentary, unbridgeable silence. Dido's cool glance. Gwen's stock stillness. Dido hadn't turned on the overhead light. Except for one desk lamp, the room was dark. Fleetingly, Gwen remembered sitting in the shade of a plum tree after her mother's funeral. A neighbour, attending to his garden on the other side of the fence, scraped a trowel against a clay pot, and the earthy sound cut through all her troubles and made her aware of the grass and plums and birds.

"Dido?"

"I'm right here."

Gwen hesitated. Then she took a step forward. "We don't talk much any more. Something went wrong. I don't know when it all began."

Dido smiled a little. She was wearing a close-fitting leather jacket over a black top. Her hands were expressive and lean and white as she took her dark glasses off her head and folded them and set them on the desk in front of her. "I knew we'd end up talking about this."

"And you don't want to." Gwen had settled gingerly on a chair about eight feet away. There was the smell of old coffee. A dark purple iris on the calendar on the wall.

Dido smiled again. "You're hot and cold."

Gwen absorbed this, the surprise of it, the weight of it. "I don't think so," she said, puzzled. No one had ever said such a thing to her before. If anyone was hot and cold, it was Dido herself.

"I used to go home at night and slam the table and yell your name, I'd be so mad at you."

Gwen stared at her in amazement. "But what for?"

"For some slight during the day. I'd say something and you'd answer something back as if to say I was stupid."

"No." Gwen was shaking her head. She felt like a child caught doing wrong, cold and sick in her stomach.

"Yes. That's exactly what you do. You say by a look, or just your tone of voice, that the idea someone's talking about is ignorant. You can be so contemptuous."

"Dido, I don't feel *any* contempt for you. If I seem to, I'm sorry."

"Are you sure?"

Gwen sat there, dumbfounded. She scanned back through the past, trying to resurrect incidents, but she and Dido, working their separate shifts, hadn't seen each other much at all. She wanted to say, Are *you* sure you've got the right person?

She said, "I get nervous. I know that puts me in a bad mood. Usually I'm so uncertain about what I'm doing." She stopped. Then deliberately she quoted Dido back to herself.

"Some people know exactly how good they are. Some of us aren't like that at all."

But Dido didn't appear to catch the reference. "Well, you shouldn't make *me* suffer for it. I expect to be treated differently by you."

Gwen sat back in her chair. Dido was being unreasonable. She wanted to be treated with kid gloves. A queen. But she was a slipping queen. There she was with a black eye.

"Does it hurt?" Gwen asked. "How did it happen?"

Dido gave her a long look. "I don't feel I can trust you." She delivered her deadly verdict in an even voice. "Not with anything really important. You're too unpredictable."

"You can predict what I'm going to talk about," Gwen said carefully. "You knew we'd end up talking about this."

That's when Dido's face softened somewhat and she backed off. "I suppose you're right." She reached over and turned on another lamp.

In the additional light, Gwen saw how vulnerable she really looked. It was more than the black eye, it was her skin, which looked paper-thin instead of creamy, and the way she rubbed her thumb with the fingertips of the same hand, repeatedly, but seemed unaware she was doing it. The way she dug her teeth into her lower lip, leaving tooth marks.

For a while they talked about other things, but not about anything really important: not about Dido's black eye, for instance. What they talked about was work. Gwen had taken it upon herself to dramatize a series of northern legends about Raven, trickster and creator of the world, and she asked Dido to be the narrator, something she'd been meaning to ask for days. "That is, if you don't mind working with me."

"I don't mind," Dido replied. "If you treat me with respect."

"Dido, everyone respects you. Don't you know that?"

Although Dido didn't respond, Gwen could see by the way she swept her hair off her face — an old and confident gesture — that she was pleased, and Gwen felt almost forgiven.

Before Dido left for the night — leaving the station in Gwen's hands — she hugged her, then stood back and surveyed her wary, appeasing face. Then leaned forward and kissed her, for the second time, on the mouth.

"Don't be afraid," she said in response to the alarm in Gwen's eyes. "I won't rape you."

═══

In fairy tales there is the fairy who is not invited, the child who is not protected, the princess who is wooed by the wrong prince. These shocking moments are lifted whole into the light, drawn up out of a deep well, and there they hang, glistening and floundering, all exposed.

The first time Eddy and Dido got stoned together, Dido learned what *the body electric* meant: they were their own northern lights, murmured Eddy, who kept up an intoxicating riff of suggestive, explicit words as he made love to her slowly and expertly. Dido had walked away incredulous, then gone back for more. Eddy had a basement apartment on a street two blocks south of the radio station. His furnishings were meagre and provided by the landlord, but he kept it very clean. Once the weather turned cold, he'd stopped using his space in the warehouse in Old Town and moved all his transmitters and radio parts and cameras into the spare bedroom. He took photographs of Dido and developed them in the bathroom until a photographer at the local newspaper let him use their darkroom instead. He showed Dido his shots of her and pinned several to the wall. She didn't know about the other photographs he was taking, and when she did find out — and viewed them — she made the same excuses, offered the same rationale that Eddy would.

His place had no curtains and the light that came across their bed was like moonlight from outer space. Their bodies glimmered against the sheets. Then came the early morning when she wanted to leave and he wouldn't let her. He pinned her less than playfully to the bed. The next time he got rough with her, she got rough back, and that aroused her in a way that shook and sickened and excited her.

Dido's confusion deepened after an interview she did — a native linguist in his fifties remembered his experience in residential school. He began to tell her in a calm voice what happened.

His mother died when he was three, he said into the microphone, and for a while he was raised by his grandparents, but one day his grandfather put him on a horse-drawn wagon and said in their language, "You are going away." He was sent to Elkhorn, Manitoba, to a boarding school run by an Anglican mission. In school they were all warned not to speak their own language, but the day came when he had been caught too many times, and he was punished. The Anglican missionary slapped his face until his cheeks were red and hot, but he didn't cry. Then he was told to take off his clothing, his coveralls, and he was smacked on his bare behind, and then he cried. His hands were strapped behind his back, his ankles were tied, and he was put on a tall stool and left there until he fell off the stool and messed himself. Again, he was spanked. He was ordered to fill a basin with warm water, to stir a bar of soap, cut in half, into the water, then to wash his mouth with it. Soon his mouth was raw inside and he felt the most incredible thirst. Then he was put into an empty room. After a time the priest came back and brought out his penis, "but I was five, and I didn't know what he meant, so he shoved it into me, and I fainted."

The man's story of childhood horror triggered a personal memory – pulled from somewhere deep inside her – of a child spanking a younger child's bottom, and she was the child. She was five, the younger child was two or three. They were upstairs in her house, a group of them, playing. And what prompted it? All she remembered was pulling down the little one's panties and the suffusion of feeling that accompanied the application of her bare hand to that bare bottom. It rushed through her untrammelled, a sense of dirtiness, excitement, and guilt.

She'd forgotten, she'd forgotten, and now it flooded back. A five-year-old's upwelling sexuality. Maybe it wasn't untypical, she told herself, maybe it was something all but a few outgrew, all but a few celibate priests who got it off by spanking bare bottoms and more, the unutterable things the native linguist spoke of, until she said to him, "This is too hard to listen to."

"Yes," he agreed, and he stopped, and didn't seem to mind stopping.

She asked Harry what she should have done and what they should do next. Harry told her she'd done the right thing by listening until it was too painful to listen any more.

"I feel like a coward," said Dido.

The phone calls to the station were mostly from offended listeners who didn't believe the man. He'd come to Yellowknife to appear before Berger, testifying to the long destruction of native languages and what was likely to happen in that regard if the pipeline went through. Dido had known only that he was respected in his field (Ralph Cody had told her how highly regarded he was) and had asked him, innocently, about his background.

"What should I do in the way of follow-up?" she asked Harry, sounding at once agonized and prim, sounding quite unlike her old self.

Harry suggested she take it on as a project, not doing piecemeal interviews from time to time, but gathering information for a documentary about abuse. "It's time the schools and churches were held to account."

"I'm not sure I have the heart for it," she said.

Harry nodded. "I don't blame you."

＝

It happened bit by bit, over the weeks, as the nights grew longer. Dido's troubles gathered around her. She began to look seedy, sallow, unwashed. Beside her mouth pimples blossomed. Her voice had the same calm, thrilling energy on air, but in person she seemed distracted and people remarked on it. Is something the matter with Dido? Is she ill?

It was strange to see her briskness vanish and her confidence recede. At the dinner table, on the occasions when they ate together, Eleanor noticed how Dido's hands were always in restless motion: she would pick up both fork and knife and roll them endlessly between her fingers, or smooth both sides of the placemat repeatedly, giving the impression of agitated competence, of a newly spawned nervousness. At work, there were days when she had to force herself to pick up the phone and line up an interview. Dido, who had formerly brimmed with life, was not faring well with love.

Dido didn't confide in her any more, and so Eleanor was left to brood about the eloquent stillness that came over Lorna Dargabble's face when she saw Dido's black eye, and her quiet questions about Dido's personal life, not to be prying, she said, but out of concern. And then Lorna's words with Eddy, her little confrontation. Lorna was sitting beside the jade plant when Eddy appeared with his coat on, heading outside. She called to him and he stopped. "I've seen you half a dozen times and you haven't seen me," she said. His eyes narrowed. He studied her. "I'm on my break," he said.

"Your mother would be ashamed of you."

Eddy shoved his hands into his pockets. "I don't know what you're talking about."

Lorna followed Eddy's progress up the street by watching him through the big window, and Eleanor said, "What was *that* about? Lorna?"

"I've just made an enemy. But it can't be helped."

"Lorna?"

"I don't care for sneaky men who can't keep their hands to themselves."

One late November morning, Harry found Dido standing on the shore of Back Bay, looking across at the cemetery, chilled to the bone. She smiled at him when he approached and said she'd been thinking about her father.

"Have you heard his voice again?"

"I hear it very often. I should say, I remember hearing it. It keeps me sane."

"What's wrong, Dido?"

"Nothing. Nothing's wrong." But she couldn't stop shivering.

Harry took her home and wrapped her, fully dressed, in a blanket and set about making coffee. "I'd give you a fur coat if I could," he said.

"Would you?"

"In a minute."

After a pause, "Who do you suppose gave Gwen the fur coat?"

He glanced at her and didn't answer. Then busied himself putting out milk and sugar, forgetting for a moment that Dido drank her coffee black.

"Your mother must have had a fur coat, Harry. What happened to it?"

"She wears it," he replied. "Every winter."

He poured the coffee and she laced her fingers through the handle of the mug and stared down at it.

"Drink," he coaxed.

She lowered her head and sipped.

He looked at her pale face, her hair damp and pulled back as if she'd been swimming in the wrong season. "You're deeply loved," he heard himself say, but she didn't respond.

He pulled out a chair and sat next to her. "Leave him," he urged. "He's not right for you."

Her voice was quiet. "Why don't you like Eddy?"

"He has no soul." For a moment he held his own against her glittering eyes, but then he backed down. "Maybe I'm wrong."

"You *are* wrong."

Her face had colour again. That much he'd accomplished – putting the blood back in her cheeks.

"You deserve so much more," he said.

"Are you so much more?" She would punish him for pitying her. "Should I settle for you?"

Harry winced and rubbed the back of his neck. He stood up. "Let me run a bath for you," he said.

Ten minutes later, alone in the bathroom, she sank under the hot water, remembering how Eddy had once bathed her by hand, every limb, every inch of her.

That was the day Harry fed her hot drinks and hot food, made up the spare bed, tucked her in. She slept. When she woke up in the middle of the afternoon, feeling rested for the first time in weeks, she gazed around the peaceful room and heard Harry in the kitchen, talking to his dog. Suddenly, also for the first time in weeks, she felt safe. And she stayed.

To Dido's great surprise Harry was uninhibited and appreciative in bed. His vulnerability descended like a wave from his balding head to his yielding eyes and responsive mouth and down to a softly furred chest and belly, to sturdy hips and to a penis more narrow than wide – more O Henry bar than chocolate slab, more spring rhubarb than autumn gourd, more canoe than motor boat.

He appreciated everything Dido did. He responded to everything. He was animated, uncritical, and ardent.

For six weeks they lived together in Harry's house on Latham Island, the little white house he'd been renting and just recently had managed to buy. He planned a party for the new year, complete with champagne and roast caribou, to celebrate his new house and new life with Dido. But there would be no roast caribou, no champagne.

═══

Harry would remember Dido's big wristwatch, not least because she continued to wear it after he bought her a new one. At Eldonn Jewellery, in the first week of December, he selected an elegant watch with a narrow band that looked like beaten gold. But Dido put it away in a drawer and continued to wear the watch her father-in-law had found on the beach and slipped onto her wrist. Her large hand was always turning it, as someone else might turn a wedding band. It clicked against tabletops, including the one in the studio covered with baize for that very reason, to mute every rustle and thud. The green baize was like the winter footgear that muffled the sounds of your feet. Harry wore caribou-hide mukluks with felt liners, and the only time they failed to keep his feet warm was after he walked across the wet floors inside the doors of the Hudson's Bay Company store. Nothing else, not front hallways or vehicles or other stores, or even the floor of the Strange Range, had enough meltwater to soak through the hide-and-wool combination and interfere with his footwear's capacity to insulate. In a frozen world you dressed for the cold. Mukluks, snow pants, parka, parka shell, fur hat, fur-lined mitts. None of the barehanded, bare-headed going-without of southern Canada.

On the coldest days and nights, chimney smoke rose straight as a plumb line. One of those days was Dido's birth-day. She was twenty-nine on December 5, the date, she told Harry, when children in the Netherlands put a shoe beside the stove to be filled in the night with gifts from Sinterklaas. Dido put her hands on Harry's face and looked into his eyes. "I'll leave my shoe beside the stove tonight and you can put a gift into it. I don't want anything else."

"What about a cake?"

"I love cake."

He made her a glorious Black Forest cake. He started at eight o'clock in the evening, little realizing how much time he would need. Four layers, and his oven too small to hold more than two at a time. The last layers came out of the oven at mid-night. Dido was in bed, the dog curled up beside her. The bedroom door half open and the fragrance wafting in. Nothing could be cozier, she said, when he came in with a tray and on the tray the whipped cream beaters and the bowls, the cake itself too warm to assemble. They had a little picnic of tastes and lickings. The next morning she had a piece of triumphant cake with her coffee in bed.

"You would make a wonderful mother," she smiled.

He would, in fact, like to be a father. "Have you ever wanted children?" he asked.

"I can't seem to picture myself as a mother, Harry."

After the cake and coffee, she inspected her shoe and found the gold watch she said was too good to wear. He asked her if everyone in Holland set out their shoes for gifts, and she said, "The Netherlands, Harry. There are two provinces, north and south Holland, inside the Netherlands. And yes, we put a shoe by the stove or fireplace with hay and carrots in it for Sinterklaas's white horse. No, your ordinary sturdy leather shoe, and in the morning the hay and carrots are gone and there are the presents: toys, books, candy, chocolate letters. The initial D in thick Droste chocolate. I used to eat it between two slices of buttered homemade bread, and if it was raisin bread, even better. My mother made the best raisin bread. We never had to bicycle between the raisins, my father used to say."

Later that week, all-too-transparent Harry tried his hand at several loaves of raisin bread. He left work at noon, and when he returned at six o'clock to pick up Dido, he walked into the station carrying the smell of hot bread on his wintry clothes. Together they went out to his van and it was like stepping into a heavenly bakery. All the way home Dido breathed in the homey fragrance, touched by Harry's devotion, but impressed even more by the enduring nature of certain evanescent things. The sound of her father's voice. The taste of Christmas marzipan. The smell of Eddy's skin.

The air crackled whenever she and Eddy passed in the hall or were in the same room. As far as anyone could tell, Dido did not avoid him and he did not seek her out.

It was a source of considerable interest, this new pairing

of Dido and Harry, even as the man she'd left for Harry continued to work in master control. Eleanor and Teresa talked
about it more than once, Eleanor struck by the apparent civil-
ity amongst the three: Eddy's and Dido's work didn't appear
to suffer from their proximity, and their proximity continued
without incident, day after day. Harry, she said, looked ten
years younger.

"You mean," laughed Teresa, "that instead of looking as
old as I do, he finally looks his age. The man tells me he's only
forty-two."

Another time, Eleanor said, "I underestimated Eddy. I
never imagined he'd let Dido go so easily."

"Just wait," Teresa said. "They haven't reached shore yet."

Teresa had some experience in this line, she said, having
watched her sister leave her husband several times. Audrey
had come to her during their separations and Teresa could
almost time the stages. Her sister would have a short period
of determination and peace of mind, followed by a bout of
waiting for the phone to ring, followed by a third phase when
she tried not to phone her husband, but did. Audrey was
addicted to him, perhaps they were addicted to each other, and
there was nothing she could do except be there to pick up the
pieces. "I wonder how long Dido will hold out against Eddy."

Eleanor cocked her head. "Eddy's manipulative. I've
known that for quite a while."

"She might be too," Teresa said.

On the shortest day of the year, a mother of young children
told Dido on the air that she was able to see the sun rise and

set outside her small kitchen window. Her window faced south, she said, the sun came up on the left and went down on the right, staying well within the window view all the while, and taking four hours to complete its journey. The poor woman was trying to set up a mothers' co-op in a church basement to give kids a place to run around screaming and mothers a place to talk with someone over the age of six. Dido listened with sympathy. She recognized fraught nerves when she heard them. Her own life was calmer now, but only on the surface. Underneath, everything that mattered was unresolved. Eddy had closed himself off. He ignored her as completely as he had in the very beginning after she'd spurned his invitation to go with him to Prosperous Lake. She admired his steely self-assurance, of which he seemed to have an unlimited supply, but she felt sure he was hurting inside. One afternoon, moments after congratulating herself on having stayed away from him for three weeks, she walked into master control and touched his shoulder. How are you, Eddy? He turned around and looked at her – a look that told her everything she needed to know. He'd been suffering too. And so they were right back where they'd started, except that now Harry was in the picture.

Harry was so amazed to have Dido in his life that he'd stopped drinking in order to savour every moment. Last winter's habit of emerging on his nights off from overheated bars into temperatures that were thirty below Celsius, of standing drunkenly under a ravishing sky as his eyelashes froze together and the insides of his nose got seared by the desiccating air, of thump-thumping home in a van whose tires had frozen flat – all that belonged to the past. Now he stayed home every night to be with Dido, who was frequently pensive and restless, but also companionable and sometimes caressing. He left her only to take his dog for a walk on the frozen bay. Outside, the air had a certain smell, sweet, from wood smoke, and pure, from the cold. The snow, so dry and brittle underfoot, sounded like fingernails screeching on a blackboard, but rhythmic, evocative, fascinating: the most northern of sounds. *You're breaking my back, you're breaking my back* squealed the snow as he trod upon it. His parka hood rustled against his ears, the fur trim extended several inches beyond his head like a woman's hair blown forward in the wind.

One particular night would stay in his mind, for its eerie and unnerving quality. He and Ella were on the bay, and Ella had bounded ahead full of rapturous doggy-spirits. His own feet were playing a squeaky duet on the violin-snow, when for some reason he looked behind him and saw two huge dogs on shore. They stood perfectly still, watching him. He walked on and glanced back and there they were, gliding along, keeping pace. Uptown, there would have been a few cars on the road, taxis. Not here. He shouted to Ella and she bounded over and stayed close. He looked back a third time. The dogs were still keeping pace, tracking him, stalking him, and his blood ran cold. A few months later, a small boy would trip and fall directly in front of a chained-up husky and within seconds his head was torn open. A hundred stitches to close the wounds, his round scalp like a football laced with zippers. Harry looked back a fourth time, and the dogs were gone.

A few days before Christmas, Eleanor flew to Ottawa to spend the holiday with her mother. She hadn't ever looked for another roommate. She would have, but she'd suspected that one day Dido would need a place to come back to from Eddy. Instead, Dido had turned to Harry. But how long would that last? Only yesterday she'd seen Dido and Eddy walking down the street together, and Dido had a vibrancy about her, like a watered plant after a drought.

On the long flight home Eleanor thought about her and Eddy. About the evening when she'd come to appreciate his lethal but understated anger. Their northern support group had gathered in her trailer. She'd been the one to spot the ad in the local paper by the pro-pipeline group that had swiped their name, and she showed it to Eddy. He took a pair of scissors and clipped the ad, then laid it on the kitchen table and studied it, his right hand crumpling the rest of the newspaper until his knuckles were white. Dido sat away from the table, silent, while the others expressed outrage. But then Eddy began to talk. He said this wasn't a walk in the park. If they were going to play dirty, then so should we. That was the night their little group disbanded. Eddy was too scary, too contemptuous of the rest of them for not being radical enough. Only Dido seemed to agree with him. Eleanor pondered another moment too. She'd had a copy of *The Diary of Anne Frank* on her desk, and Eddy had picked it up and said, "Any teenager could have written this." His dismissiveness, his crassness. He enjoyed being inconsistent if it kept you off balance and made him look ahead of the game. But somehow Dido had fallen under his spell, the spell exerted by strong men through the centuries, perhaps.

By the time she reached Ottawa, Eleanor had decided that on Christmas Eve, when she took her mother to church, she would light a candle for Dido.

Christmas Eve in Yellowknife was warmer than usual, about twenty below Celsius, and snow was expected before morning. Gwen had persuaded Harry to be her special guest on air from midnight till one. *Christmas Eve with Stella Round.* He could use a pseudonym too, she told him. He could be Johnny Q.

She sat in master control, wearing headphones. Harry was on the other side of the glass, in the studio, and they were discussing favourite songs when he startled her by saying, "Let me demonstrate." Tilting the microphone towards the corner, he stood up and walked over to the piano, making a rapt listener of Gwen and of anyone who was tuned in at home. They heard his footsteps across the studio floor, the creak of the stool, the pause before he began to play, and the fumbling start. Then his pretty decent version of Irving Berlin's "What'll I Do?"

Gwen was completely charmed by Harry, by the song, by the surprise of hearing him at the piano. She hadn't even been aware that he knew how to play. The "liveness" of it transported her, and she wished that all radio could be so spontaneous and simple, that all nights could be like this one.

The rest of the hour unfolded in the same relaxed spirit of music and impromptu recollections, including hers of hearing Kathleen Ferrier sing Brahms over the car radio one summer when she and her parents were held up for nearly an hour at a lift bridge in Hamilton. His "Alto Rhapsody," or as the announcer called it, the "Rhapsody for Dark Voice." Harry responded by telling her that Kathleen Ferrier had been a telephone operator for a while, "Did you know that?"

"In England?"

"Can you imagine calling the switchboard for a number and getting Kathleen Ferrier on the other end? In northern England, while she studied music. She was only forty-one when she died, poor thing. Maybe you know this, in that rhapsody Brahms is pouring out his longing for two women, Clara Schumann and Clara Schumann's daughter, who's about to be married."

"I didn't know." And something occurred to Gwen that hadn't occurred to her before, except as foolishness. The real possibility of a man loving two women, first one, then both.

"Harry, how did you get that cauliflower ear? I ask, because I've been admiring it for months."

"You're after my secrets. Well, never play rugby if you value your ears."

"You can count on me," said Gwen.

Harry slipped out of the studio, returning a few minutes later with two cups of Maxwell House Instant spiked with Hudson's Bay overproof rum, which he'd liberated from his bottom desk drawer. Also a recording of Kathleen Ferrier singing nineteen songs. Gwen dedicated "Blow the Wind Southerly" to Lorna Dargabble, "my favourite hairdresser," who didn't call afterwards, as Gwen expected her to; but it was Christmas Eve, after all.

Gwen and Harry were in such good spirits themselves that they didn't sign off as required at one in the morning, but continued for another half hour. Gwen coaxed Harry back to the piano, where he played "Autumn Leaves" and sang the words, forgetting only a few, and afterwards remarked that the lyrics were good, especially about missing the girl's sunburned hands, but Johnny Mercer made a serious mistake about the weather, did you catch it? And Gwen said yes. Days grow shorter as the leaves fall, they don't grow long. "They're growing longer *now*," she added. "Today we gain seven more minutes of daylight."

After they finished for the night, Harry phoned Dido to say he was on his way, he'd be home in a few minutes. "I thought she'd be asleep," said Gwen, suddenly forlorn in the doorway.

"Not Dido. She's making a cheese fondue."

Harry helped her on with her fur coat, looking her up and down, she thought, with all the romance of a sales clerk. He got his parka from his office and drove her home through the falling snow. It came down gently, fine, dry, and in surprising quantities.

That night, Lorna Dargabble went for a walk and didn't come back. Her husband reported her missing on Christmas Day, but her disappearance didn't become common knowledge until two days later when it was broadcast on the news. Eleanor returned from Ottawa that evening to all the speculation.

Her husband reported that she'd gone for a walk, she was always going for long, solitary walks late at night. She didn't take her purse. It was on the table in the hallway. Her coat was gone, her boots were gone. She'd left behind her hat, but no note of any kind; he had looked. Irving Dargabble was a handsome man in his ruddy, white-haired, thick-tongued way. He'd been a foreman at one of the mines and he was a heavy drinker. Anyone acquainted with him suspected he was in the habit of roughing up his wife. The police knew it for a fact, having been called to the house more than once. They brought him in for questioning. Then for lack of any evidence to hold him, he was let go. They questioned the neighbours on either side. They appealed on the radio for anyone who knew anything about the missing woman's movements that night to come forward.

The search for Lorna took in the areas her husband suggested, places where she usually walked, and extended beyond them to School Draw, to the other side of Frame Lake, to the area known as Tin Can Hill, to the shoreline. But the Christmas snowfall had been followed by another, a day later, and this one was also undisturbed by wind. Whatever tracks Lorna had made had been covered over and wherever she might have gone lay hidden by snow.

AT ELEANOR'S KITCHEN TABLE at the end of December, Gwen was making a circle with her fingertip, gathering up crumbs.

"She was so unhappy," said Gwen. "I keep wondering if it was suicide. I think it was."

Eleanor didn't reply. She was remembering how Lorna had confronted Eddy, and wished she'd asked more questions while she had the chance. It seemed to her the frail, old woman must be dead, if the husband was to be believed, and even if he wasn't. There was talk that she might have gone back to Boston, slipped away on a plane without anybody knowing. But how could she have gone without her purse? There was talk about the husband, too.

Gwen said, "I keep seeing all those boxes in her basement full of papers and receipts. She was so worried about money."

"It might have been foul play," Eleanor said.

"The husband, you mean?"

"I guess so."

Across the table Gwen rubbed her hands free of crumbs. She sat back in her chair, then leaned forward and started again on the irresistible toast crumbs, gathering them off the table with her fingertip. "One of her neighbours thinks she went to Edmonton, just because it's the nearest big city. That's what he told the police. But I don't think so. I think she went for a walk, like her husband said, like she always did."

"Well, it wouldn't be hard to get lost at night if you turned the wrong way."

"Or if you went too far. I mean, she was old. She might have fallen, I suppose. Or just become tired. It might not have been deliberate," said Gwen, but she sounded unconvinced, especially to herself.

Then she added, "I knew something was wrong when she didn't phone me after I played Kathleen Ferrier for her."

On New Year's Eve, Gwen was alone at the station doing the late shift as usual. Shortly after nine o'clock she went into the record library, and minutes later she heard voices and footsteps. A whiff of patchouli, pungent, exotic, weird; a nasty smell, she thought. She crossed the hall to the editing cubicle and saw them at two removes: Eddy and Dido in master control. The mystery couple, mysteriously together.

What she saw next reminded her of scenes from the romantic comic strip she'd loved so much as a girl. Though comic was hardly the word – a saddie rather than a funnie. They had their coats on, they looked to be quarrelling. Dido wheeled around to leave and Eddy grabbed her by the wrist, jerked her back to him with a hard twist of the arm and she retaliated by slapping his head. Gwen stood rooted to the spot. Dido's perfume was still in her nostrils and it made her feel queasy, sickened and not herself, as she watched Eddy take

Dido's head between his hands, and tipping her head back, kiss her mouth with such incredible tenderness that Gwen thought *nobody will ever love me like that*. She felt doubly returned to girlhood. An almost shameful sorrow for her undeveloped self.

She retreated to the record library across the hall and stayed among the records until just before the hourly station break, when she went down the hall into the announce booth and did the thirty-second ID and weather, and saw that master control was empty. She went out to the front, to the reception area. They weren't there either. Poor Harry, she thought. I wonder if he knows.

There would be a light, firm tread on Harry's front steps and a knock on the door. Dido recognized the footsteps and felt herself cave in, a landslide of feeling that left her barely able to stand. Eddy knew her hours, he knew Harry's whereabouts, he wanted her to come away with him and she was making him wait.

In Eddy she saw a fine recklessness based on having nothing to lose. He came through the door as if she were his, and it was the nerve of it that appealed to them both. Partly the nerve, partly the secretiveness, mostly the physical pleasure. She led him, not to Harry's bed but to the spare room, which had the advantage of anonymity spiked with risk.

Every day Harry thought of Dido lying in his bed at night — the feel of her skin, the curve of her bottom, those dark, tanned-looking nipples erect against creamy skin – never less than incredulous at his good fortune and never unaware of her tolerance. She was sexually knowing and relaxed, she knew what pleased her, she could direct him, and she could turn away. Sometimes she turned away. He would run his hand down her back and she would move perceptibly away, as if to say *I don't like to be touched there.*

And it was this that held him. Her little bit of physical disgust with him that made her, yes, the love of his life.

One night there were his usual jokes in bed and even though he was exhausted – amorousness; but so short-lived this time, so train through a tunnel, that Dido went still with disappointment. Harry felt her lying there, slipping out of his hands.

"Don't leave me," he begged, and she was touched and repelled. "What are you thinking?" he asked, and a sad half-laugh reached his ears.

She was thinking that she didn't know what to think. Eddy was on her mind, he always was. She wondered why he was willing to share her with another man for even a minute.

"I used to know what I wanted," she said. "I never thought I'd be like this."

"You're perfect."

"I'm fucked up, Harry." Her voice was flat and distant. He'd almost never heard her swear.

"We're all fucked up," he replied. He was remembering a tape he'd heard years ago, Japanese, of course, of female orgasms from around the world, and the cries of Western women seemed forced and overdone, while Asian women were quiet and intense and finally uncontrolled. And as he lay beside her he knew he wouldn't be able to hold on to her. Peter Peter Pumpkin Eater. Had a wife and couldn't keep her.

She said, "I don't like myself very much at the moment, Harry."

Towards the middle of January, Harry and Dido were in the penthouse of the only high-rise in town. It looked like a waiting room for Air France, dark leather chairs, a kind of airless faux luxury. From some of the windows you could see Con Mine's property, a desolate wasteland of rocks and stumpy trees that extended a long, snowy distance to the shoreline of Yellowknife Bay. Harry, looking out the window, remembered years ago having a picnic with an old sweetheart on a bit of a cliff right along the water's edge. He told Dido that he would take her there in the summer, and she smiled. "I'd like that," she said.

The occasion was a territorial government reception, and Dido had come hoping to meet Tom Berger, but he wasn't there. Laid out were wine, cheese, arctic char. Harry was speaking to the vice-commissioner when Dido came up to him and said she had to leave.

He accompanied her to the elevator. She was wearing a yellow sweater draped over her shoulders; her parka was over her arm. She got into the elevator and took his breath away by saying very quietly, before the doors closed, *I love you*. The doors began to close and she mouthed the words a second time. *I love you.*

Harry stood there, watching Dido say she loved him, and then down she went – into the underworld, he thought later, since when he got home, she was gone, she and Eddy too, as he found out later.

HARRY WAS ALONE NOW in his little house. The inside surface of the front door and the doorknob itself were feathered with frost. The windows had a thick buildup of ice on the inside. He was drinking and in his muddled mind it occurred to him that he should have given Dido flowers. But a woman friend once confided that the worse things got, the more European her husband's gestures became. Dozens of roses, she said, rolling her eyes.

He had given her a gold watch instead, which he'd found in her bedside table along with a key chain and a letter. The letter was addressed to Dido at Box 853, Yellowknife. It had a Halifax return address with the last name Moir and a December postmark. Harry held it, suddenly aware of what he'd picked up. The slim envelope came alive in his hand. He hesitated, then drew from it the single page of notepaper. His eyes flicked from salutation to signature, from *Dear Dido* to *Daniel*. Then he read the letter itself – a bold, tidy script saying that his new wooden skiff had lovely lines, that his grandson was turning into a sailor in his own right, that apart from these two pleasures he found things as they were intolerable, but he saw no way forward at the moment. He thought of her constantly and loved her.

Harry could see that Dido's father-in-law wasn't about to "walk through that door" any time soon, but he still wondered why she'd left the letter behind.

On a Sunday in late January, two weeks after Dido had left him, the police came to his house not once but twice.

Around noon, there was such insistent knocking on his front door that his heart leapt. But it was a Dene fellow wavering on his doorstep. He'd been shot in the foot by somebody who was in the house across the road, and another guy had been clubbed on the head with a rifle butt, and would Harry help him out and call the police?

Harry brought the man into his kitchen. His name was Arthur, he said. And that's when Harry recognized him. He was the one who'd complained at the inquiry about getting a parking ticket on Dene land. Harry drew out a chair for him, then went to the phone, and in the time it took him to make the call, a pool of blood had formed around one of Arthur's leather boots.

Harry poured a glass of orange juice for him and gave him an ashtray. Then he hushed Ella, who was growling, sent her off into the living room and told her to stay, and saw out the window the other man stumbling past Louise's shack next door, holding his head in his hands as he lurched forward through the snow.

He put on the kettle for coffee and the police arrived before it boiled. They showed up in three cruisers with bullhorns and rifles. They made a show of loading their rifles, but it wasn't necessary. Four men and two women trooped out of the house in question and stood passively at the side of the road, no longer arguing or drinking. Harry went out to help. The man with the wounded head was now in the back seat of one of the cruisers, and when the ambulance arrived Harry helped him onto a stretcher, helped lift the stretcher into the ambulance. There was a lot of blood, and the poor guy was crying.

After that Harry led the police into his kitchen. The kettle was boiling away, the juice in Arthur's glass was gone. Two policemen lifted Arthur off the chair and half-carried him outside, a third took the cigarette from between his fingers and dropped it in the sink on his way by. Harry would find it there, soggy, later when he went to do the dishes. After the police were gone, he cleaned up the glutinous puddle on the floor and discovered what congealing powers blood has. Only then did he feel sick, quite sick and shaken. They'll have to cut Arthur's boot off his foot, he thought, his brand new leather boot with the high heel.

Later that day, the police were at his door again. Not about Arthur, it turned out. About Eddy. They were following up a complaint and they wanted to talk to Harry as Eddy's employer.

Harry listened to what they had to say.

"I don't believe it," he said.

After they left, he sat still for a while. The police were investigating something sordid. Men giving Indian girls booze for sex in a motel on the road to the airport. One of the girls had wandered outside and nearly frozen to death.

He'd told them they were barking up the wrong tree. Eddy didn't drink, for one thing. For another, he wasn't that kind of guy. For a third, he'd left town before the incident occurred. Harry wanted to know who'd fingered Eddy, but the police wouldn't say.

He stood and went over to the window. Outside, it was thirty-one below. The willows between his house and the bay were full of ptarmigan, feathery plops of white balanced on slender branches. He remembered Eddy saying we're too soft; fucking Eddy running his hands through his wiry red hair and boasting that he slept with a window open all winter. So where did fucking Eddy do all his fucking?

On the lake the ice was green, the snow lavender. On the far shore the gold mine nestled into the bay. Smoke flapped out of chimneys.

He thought of a phrase, something he'd read in one of Ralph's northern books: *to have felt snow and ice forever, and nothing forever but ice and snow.*

The cold gathered. It was just beyond his window. He could feel it pressing in. All the cold from all over the Arctic pressing against that pane of glass.

⸻

At work, Harry leaned against Eleanor's desk, idly lifted a few papers, then looked into her face.

"I haven't heard a thing from her," she said quietly. "Nobody has."

Harry had instituted Monday morning story meetings for everyone on staff. Just once a week, he said, to keep one another generally informed of what we're doing. And still he met with sullen resistance from the newsroom. If anything, they were more openly mutinous. Bill Thwaite attended against his will. "What have you got this week?" Harry would ask. And Bill would fold his arms and answer, "Not a thing."

They were in the studio, gathered around the big table. Harry peeled an orange over the metal wastebasket, the scent reminding him of lost Dido. The explosive fragrance. After she'd left him, his private drinking spree had cost him a week of work and earned him another black mark on the list of sins that would be used against him before long. Gwen watched his hands, fascinated by the way his fingers dug under the skin of the orange and ever so neatly peeled it back.

She had been brought in from the night shift to take over for Dido, a casual had been hired to do the night shift in her place, another was rapidly being trained by Andrew McNab to be a technician.

Harry looked around for Jim Murphy. But Jim, it would seem, couldn't be bothered to show up.

He turned to reliable Gwen. She mentioned having lined up an interview with a bush pilot who'd discovered the remains of a beer keg on one of the high arctic islands, probably left behind in the 1800s by a search party looking for Franklin, and Bill laid into her for poaching on his territory: That's *news*, he said, jabbing his ink-stained finger at her.

Turf wars, thought Harry. Inside the station, and out. "This is why we have story meetings," he said wearily, "to coordinate current affairs and news. If you want a clip of Gwen's interview for the newscast, all you have to do is ask.

And Gwen, you won't air the full interview until after Bill's run the clip. Okay?"

He turned to Teresa. Teresa had in front of her the newspaper story that related the case of a young Dene woman wandering naked and blind-drunk in the street after being locked out of a motel room; two men who worked at one of the mines stood accused of rape. She tapped the paper with her finger and said she wanted to do a series on violence against women. She had in mind an on-air manual in English and Dogrib of anecdotes, advice, information – what women faced, what they could do, who they could turn to. Gwen expressed immediate interest and they agreed to work on it together.

Before the meeting ended, Gwen asked Bill if he'd heard anything more about Lorna Dargabble. What were the police doing, anyway?

"They're doing their job," he said. Then, a little less grudgingly, he added, "I'm guessing we'll learn what happened in the spring, after the snow's gone."

In the background, providing a wealth of material for Gwen and Teresa, were quietly impassioned witnesses at the Berger Inquiry presenting what amounted to a catalogue of northern pathologies. Anthropologists outlined the history of prospectors, traders, whalers, and miners pouring into the North with their diseases, their alcohol, their licentiousness. Medical experts and social workers methodically outlined what happens when the traditional pattern of life breaks down and individuals, families, whole communities lose their way. They described the particular burden for women, their isolated and vulnerable lives during the long northern winters. And in the Dene communities, witness after witness told Berger about a close-knit culture increasingly fragmented by the white frontier mentality. Everyone, Dene and white, agreed that booze was the single most destructive force in the unravelling of lives that ended either in the slow violence of apathy and despair, or in the sudden violence of death by accident, homicide, poisoning, suicide.

THIS WAS THE WINTER, the winter of 1976, that Gwen would remember in part for the three unlucky things that happened to Harry, three months in a row. January robbed him of Dido. February brought a second loss, which unfolded far from town. March would have its own misfortunes.

On a Saturday in late February, Harry and Ralph went ice fishing. They took Harry's van and drove an hour to Prelude Lake, Harry's dog riding in the back with the gear. Normally, Ella rode up front with him, leaning into his side "like a hot date," in Ralph's amused estimation.

They parked at Powder Point, skied across the tip of the snow-covered lake to a small rapids and followed the portage around them, then skied across a stretch of frozen river before climbing a steep hill, crossing a small lake and following another portage into Hidden Lake. From the edge of the lake rose rocky outcrops dusted with snow. Slender birch trees and taller spruce had footholds near the shore and more haphazardly on ridges and between rocky hills farther back. Every so often a raven spoke to them, cr-awk, cr-awk, and flew from one tree to another.

Ralph took note. The raven's call had a little pop or pong sound, it seemed to him, an oval-shaped noise more appropriate for a mouth than a beak. He'd helped Gwen assemble and dramatize her program of Raven tales, lending her his books and doing much of the writing of the trilingual scripts, since he knew a basic, uninhibited Inuktitut from his days of teaching in the eastern Arctic. From Teresa he was now learning some basic phrases in Dogrib — Teresa had written and delivered the Dogrib repartee for the Raven tales, as natural an actor, as uninhibited and relaxed, as she was a broadcaster. The beautiful Dido had narrated, but she hadn't stuck around to hear the broadcast.

Long ago, went the central tale, man and the wild animals lived in utter darkness, for the great Chief hoarded the light. Raven, inspired by his own dark cunning, devised a plan to steal it. He turned himself into a pine needle, set himself afloat on water, and was swallowed by the Chief's daughter, who became pregnant, giving birth to a boy. The boy grew up playing with his grandfather's bags of light, biding his time, until finally he was old enough to fly up through the smoke hole and with a triumphant squawk empty the bags into the sky, thus giving light to the world.

A book of northern legends weighed down one of Ralph's pockets, a flask of whisky weighed down another.

Ella, in her glory, bounded along beside them, darting off into the bush, darting back. Such easy travelling, wind and bug free (unlike last summer on the same lake when Ralph applied his hand to the back of his head and felt about twenty little bodies smear into his scalp; this he'd done every few seconds, it seemed, with unvarying results). In a sheltered cove, they used an auger to cut through the three-foot depth of ice, making four holes about half a foot in diameter each.

They dropped in lines baited with the small fresh-water herring called cisco. Each line was attached to a short stick propped up in the snow: when the stick fell over they had either a bite or a trout. To keep warm, they built a fire on shore and made tea and ate Ralph's ham sandwiches. Once, Ella broke through the thin ice that covered a fast-running stream. The dunking soaked her fur, which froze immediately, making her look like a four-legged wraith. But her spirits were undampened.

With bare hands Harry and Ralph pulled up their lines, landing a total of five fat trout. They warmed themselves at the fire and talked about the summer expedition they were planning to the Thelon River. The trip was rapidly taking shape. A group of four was best, Ralph believed. More than that would be cumbersome. Fewer would be risky. "You say Eleanor is keen to go," he said.

"She's motivated," nodded Harry. "And steady. I've never seen her lose her cool."

"I like her," smiled Ralph. "She puts up with me."

"There's Gwen. She's avid to go too, even though it means two weeks without pay."

"But I wonder if she's got enough muscle," said Ralph, "enough heft."

"She's wiry. She's a worker. You'd get your money's worth, I think."

"She's got physical courage," Ralph admitted. "It's not a mean feat, driving by herself all the way from Ontario."

"There's holiday time for her to work out. Eleanor, too. Six weeks is a long stretch."

"Can *you* get away?" asked Ralph.

"I'm the boss," said Harry with a mock swagger.

"Shall I tell them we're on then? Or will you do the honours?"

"I'll leave that to you," said Harry.

The conversation turned to Eddy. Harry had told Ralph when it happened about being visited by the police. But there was no reason for Eddy to be mixed up in that kind of thing, he said again, still puzzled, still disturbed. He was a strange guy, but if he had anything it was a sense of morals.

"No reason you can think of." Ralph rubbed his hands together close to the fire. He remembered Gwen's view that Eddy had a problem with women. "Why I wonder did he and Dido take off so suddenly."

"I don't know. I don't know."

About three o'clock they headed back to the van. Under the overcast sky, they had trouble seeing any contours until they were upon them, the snow deceptively flat in the fractional light. Harry kept a concerned eye out for leg-hold traps, having seen snowmobile tracks leading across the lake and knowing that trappers were about. He kept his dog close to him. But within sight of the road Ella bounded far ahead, suddenly stopped, then went after something.

Harry, coming alongside, shouted at her until he saw that it wasn't a trap, just some dark indecipherable thing sitting above the snow. Not a body, animal or otherwise, but a piece of meat or skin. He called Ella away, she refused to come.

He skied on, paused, called her again. This time she came, but reluctantly.

They stowed their skis and packs, took swigs from Ralph's flask, surveyed the dim sky. They were about to get into the van when the dog began to act strangely. She let out a whimper, turned in circles, then fell to the ground and lay writhing. Harry knelt beside her, his hands on her jerking head, until she quieted, then he lifted her into his arms. The dark something must have been baited with poison and left in the open for wolves, probably, or foxes. A trapper hunting fur with poison.

Harry gave the keys to Ralph. In the passenger seat he held his nearly spent dog in his lap, while Ralph stepped hard on the accelerator. After about ten minutes, the second fit took hold, her limbs kicking, her whole body convulsing. Again, she quieted. Harry spoke to her, soothed her, stroked her.

Ralph kept the accelerator to the floor, but after a while Harry said what Ralph already knew, that there was no need to speed any more.

In the weeks that followed, watching Harry's sadness, Eleanor found herself talking to Dido in her head, *You left somebody in the lurch, you know.* She wondered if she would ever get the chance to say it, face to face.

It was Eleanor's fourth winter in Yellowknife. For the duration of it, all eight months, she missed the tiny flowers and richly coloured lichens that dotted the rocky outcrops, but she wasn't sorry not to see the quantities of garbage that surfaced everywhere in the spring. She missed the long grass that shone whitish-gold with a purple tinge in the setting sun; the wild, small, misshapen raspberries sufficient for a modest pie; the occasions when half a dozen Dene children tore up and down the street, tumbling about at midnight, having a loud and happy time. But at the same time she was glad not to have to look at the cowering, cringing, beaten dogs that spent the summers chained to willows and covered with flies.

One afternoon, when she and Gwen were in the Gold Range café talking about how to prepare for the summer expedition, Gwen said to her, "Sometimes I see Lorna out of the corner of my eye. At night I catch glimpses of her grey fur coat. It's never her, of course."

Eleanor didn't answer. She felt a helpless anger about Lorna and her sad life and no doubt sadder end. About Dido she felt a different sort of anger. Cavalier Dido, who'd also left suddenly, without saying goodbye, then chosen to inform the station she was gone by calling at around seven in the morning, when she knew Jim Murphy would be the only one there. She'd told him that she and Eddy were in Hay River already, and they wouldn't be coming back.

Suddenly Gwen looked up and asked, "Do you think I'm hot and cold? Too unpredictable to be trustworthy?"

"I wouldn't be going on a canoe trip with you if I did."

Later that afternoon, Harry came to Eleanor's trailer, having offered to mend the worn patches on her kitchen floor with some leftover linoleum he had in his house – a pattern of black and white squares that he measured and cut, showing more dexterity than she'd given him credit for. His grandfather had been good with his hands, he explained, passing on the information that the old man had been a furrier in Winnipeg. In Eleanor's mind something clicked.

"Did *you* give Gwen the fur coat?"

He looked up from where he was kneeling on the floor. For a moment he was silent. "It was my grandmother's," he

admitted. "Gwen looked to be the same size." He shrugged.
"It's a loaded gift, a fur coat, that's why I don't want her
to know."

"You thought she might take it the wrong way."

He bent to his task.

"You're an unusual man, Harry Boyd. How did you
happen to have your grandmother's fur coat?"

"I had my mother put it in the mail."

"That's a lot of trouble to take," she said quietly.

"She didn't mind. It didn't fit her. The coat was going to
waste."

"I mean a lot of trouble for *you* to take."

Harry knew what she meant. A trace of a smile crossed his
face. "It was an act of charity. I know Gwen. She'd never
spend money on a good parka."

"I'll say it again, Harry. You're an unusual man."

He ran his eyes from corner to corner of the black and
white linoleum. In a quarter of an hour he'd be finished
and have to return to his own house, for which he no longer
had the slightest enthusiasm.

Eleanor poured him a Scotch when he was done. "You
signed the card 'your secret admirer.'"

"Did I? I suppose I wanted to put her off the scent."

He took his drink and went to look out the window.
Eleanor came over and stood beside him. No one was outside.
Nothing flew by. Or moved.

"One of these days," said Eleanor, "this winter's going to
end."

"Right. Why should love last when nothing else does?"

"Poor wretch," she said, and put her arm around him. She

said there was a beautiful ode by Horace to that effect. It made
the very point that earthly love turns with the seasons, and
there's nothing we can do about it.

"The seasons return, though," she said after a moment,
"and so can love."

"It didn't for Horace," he said.

At the end of March, when Harry was thinking that only one
month of winter was left, his third stroke of bad luck occurred.
It was a bright and sunny Tuesday. He sat at his desk going
through the mail.

A bit later, when he saw Gwen pass by the door of his
office, he called her to come in. He had his feet on his desk and
a letter in his hands. His glasses were on his desk, too, beside
the phone.

"You didn't sign this," he said, waving the letter.

She looked mystified, and he said, "I thought so. You
didn't know about it."

"About what."

He handed her the letter and she read it, then sat down and
read it again. It was dated March 18, 1976. It was addressed to
the head of the Northern Service in Ottawa and it was signed
by George Tupper, Bill Thwaite, Jim Murphy, and Andrew
McNab. Calling themselves the most senior employees at the
station, they said they'd heard that Harry Boyd was going to
be appointed permanent manager and they wanted to express
their views about his unsuitability before it was too late. Then
followed a list of Harry's sins and errors in judgment: his
autocratic style, his anti-news bias in favour of current affairs,

his inappropriate public statements, his infringement of union rules that prohibited management touching the equipment, his negative attitude towards television, his trouble with the bottle. It would be a grave mistake, they said, to appoint to the job someone who didn't understand the role of manager or the future of the CBC in the North.

Gwen looked up. Harry was watching her. He pointed at the letter, and said it was a copy of the original; his buddy in head office had sent it to him so that he'd know what he was up against.

His eyes looked old and worked over. He ran his hand slowly down the side of his jaw. "I wouldn't have taken the job anyway, not that I think they were about to offer it to me."

"Harry, I'm sorry."

"It just makes it awkward as hell."

"Let *them* feel awkward. They don't know what they're talking about."

He smiled. "That's my girl."

"But you'll stay on."

He looked out the window. "I just called Ottawa. I made them swear they'd have my replacement here by the first of June. Not a day later." The sun was shining and he squinted his eyes. "Whoever takes over, it won't be me." Still looking out the window, still squinting, "Anyway," he said, "this makes three."

She understood. Dido, his dog, his job. It had to be the end of his run of bad luck.

BY LATE APRIL, the long hours of light were back. In town all the snow was gone, and all the garbage, so thinly but effectively disguised, had resurfaced, soft and soggy and in unbelievable amounts. It was the time of year when winter secrets got revealed.

The foursome who would be canoeing the Thelon River were already in harness, walking miles in the early morning or in the evening with brick-filled packs on their backs. They were meeting regularly to plan the expedition, the maps, supplies, equipment, freeze-dried foods, mosquito nets, new tents, extra-warm sleeping bags, life preservers, extra paddles. Firearms, given the likelihood of grizzly bears. But none of them knew how to use a gun, and they agreed that having one along would endanger them more than a grizzly would. They read books on canoeing skills. Only Ralph had done extensive trips with whitewater – he had special paddles he was attached to, his favourite one having been made by a native wood carver in eastern Ontario from a single piece of cedar. But all of them had paddled, Harry and Gwen since childhood, and Eleanor since her early twenties. Ralph, with his customary relish, became the chief organizer. Had they ever formally chosen a trip leader, had they ever agreed that it would be Ralph, then some of their initial difficulties might never have arisen. They were going forward with a kind of informed innocence, with the naive faith that they had the physical and mental resources to make the journey and come back unharmed.

Teresa couldn't resist ribbing them. Only you white people, she said, approach the land like it's some great undertaking. You have to do fifty miles a day with your maps and your compasses. You have to count up the miles. Are you sure you don't need a guide? she smiled. Babes in the Barrens, she called them. At least take a gun, she advised. I'm serious.

They were gathered at Harry's house one evening when Ralph Cody arrived late. They heard him before they saw him, his familiar, humour-filled voice talking loudly to itself as he came up the driveway.

"Ralph!" Gwen called from the front door.

He saw her waving.

"I feel like Odysseus," he yelled.

He came striding in, jacket unbuttoned, beret in hand. He had walked to Frame Lake and back, a distance of several miles, and this after jogging five miles earlier in the day. Even Harry was lifting weights, though he had no small view of his own strength, being stocky and able to lift heavy things with ease. Quietly, he'd cut back on his drinking.

That evening Gwen took one look at Ralph's tentative list of supplies – the thirty salamis, the forty bars of chocolate, the forty-two rolls of toilet paper – and accused him of going wild. How much liquor was he planning to bring? A case?

Ralph called her a cheap Scotswoman.

Her retort was brisk. An aunt of hers used to write down

all the things she wanted and couldn't afford, and then burn the list. It was very effective.

Eleanor agreed. She had used the same method for losing weight: write down all the foods you want to eat on a sheet of paper, then burn it.

Ralph accused them of being female missionaries to his bold adventurer, and Eleanor promised not to sing "Jesus Loves Me," just to think it.

Gwen's thoughtful, emboldened eyes remained on Eleanor. "That's what you really believe." It was almost a challenge.

Eleanor smiled and didn't take the bait, and Ralph saw and approved. Harry was right. Eleanor had the necessary temperament for a trip like this. Even-keeled, unruffled, steady.

The two women had spoken privately about what it would mean to spend six weeks in Ralph's and Harry's company. Gwen had wondered aloud what sort of lover Ralph might be, and Eleanor surprised her by saying she thought he might be rather good.

"He eats so fast," Gwen said thoughtfully. "That's never a good sign."

"He would *enjoy* sex."

"But would I?"

Eleanor smiled. "What about Harry?"

A cloud came over Gwen's face. "Fast, furious, drunken," she guessed.

"That's not what Dido implied," said Eleanor.

Harry read books about the Barrens to take his thoughts off Dido. Whenever he stopped reading, she floated into his mind — the sandal markings on her swinging bare foot, the winter imprint of a knitted sock, the memory of thinking that nothing wants to be forgotten. Summer doesn't. The sock doesn't. I don't.

One day his eyes rested on Gwen and she understood his bleak expression perfectly, she thought. He was thinking about Dido. Wishing she were Dido.

He had a book under his arm and a fresh mug of coffee in his hand. They were in the announcers' office and he said to her, "Silence is an incredible weapon."

Gwen had suspected as much: Harry hadn't heard a word from the fugitive pair. She'd thought of asking him once or twice if he'd had any news, but it would have been cruel if it turned out he hadn't.

"I'll show you," he said.

They took facing chairs. He fastened her with an intent look, then pulled a question out of the air. "Why do you hate your father?"

She lifted her hands and shrank back in her chair. A long pause, and then she struggled to say something.

"I suppose because he preferred my brother to me. And because he never asked me a thing about myself. And because he wasn't too kind to my mother."

"See? Silence is an interviewer's greatest asset. All you have to do is wait, and the person feels obliged to fill the vacuum with a serious answer."

But it didn't seem entirely fair, what she'd said. Certainly it wasn't the whole story.

"Why do you love Dido?" she asked.

Harry glared at her, but she held his glance. Fair is fair.

"That's a dirty question."

"So was yours."

Slowly, Harry's face gave way, and Gwen felt gratified and sorry, fascinated and pained.

He said, "I think I loved her before I ever saw her. I loved her voice, first of all. Then I loved the way she looks. Then I loved the way she entered a room –" He stopped. "I don't need to teach you a thing."

In the beginning Dido didn't change when she entered a room, that's what Gwen remembered. She didn't gulp for air and something to say. There had been a smoothness to her entries and exits. Rather than the winter of shyness and the summer of over-effort, she was all of a piece and natural. But then she did change. Her personality darkened and shifted before Gwen's eyes, and reminded her of Ralph's grasses moving under water, of words dissolving on a page.

Gwen didn't miss her, or Eddy. The station was easier without them. She had even read the news a few times, on days when Jim Murphy couldn't, and the usual hadn't happened; she hadn't stiffened; her brain hadn't slammed into the hard, cold fender of nervousness. But it was wrong to say Dido and Eddy had left. They were here, she thought, present in every sad ounce of Harry's body.

In his office Harry was reading about John Hornby. There were nights when he didn't bother to go home. In a grim and sardonic act of defiance, he'd had a La-Z-Boy installed. His successor would have the chair removed in a month's time, and would discover on the floor, gathering dust, a multitude of balled-up memos about television and the impending new building.

There were two ways of looking at Hornby, thought Harry. If you took his life as a series of disasters in rapid succession, if you saw him as a distillation of his shortcomings, then you'd call him a loser, feckless, under-prepared, dangerous. If you saw him, instead, in all his complexity, in the fullness of his extraordinary life, then he was no less irresponsible, but he was also astonishingly vivid, driven, solitary, intense, endearing. Harry was all for seeing people in their complexity and having them return the favour. But what spoke to him most was the duality of the man – his courage and his foolishness, his loyalty and his carelessness, his shyness and his poetic, almost erotic attachment to the land. Also the size of his mistakes, and the way death spared him from having to live with the consequences.

Harry set aside Whalley's biography, and thought about what lay ahead. Ralph, he suspected, wanted to prove himself – prove that at sixty-one he was still youthful. And Eleanor had indicated that she and the Barrens might be a good spiritual fit. And Gwen had the young person's all-consuming desire to see a place for the first time, especially since it would complete a story that had captured her imagination as a child; she would see with her own eyes where its final chapter unfolded. As for himself, he was looking forward to a clean break from old dissatisfactions, a summer that would help him forget his winter.

A week later, as it happened, George Whalley's daughter brought her father in to see him, as she'd promised to do when he came to visit. Harry chatted with George Whalley, only a little surprised by the mid-Atlantic accent, neither Canadian nor English but cultured, the sort of voice that used to be the only voice on CBC Radio. Whalley looked to be in his fifties, tall and grey-haired, forthcoming yet reserved, a professor poet. He told Harry how he'd first read Edgar Christian's diary in 1938, soon after it was published in England, where it caught everyone's imagination to the extent that it was reprinted several times. Like many other readers, he couldn't forget the events it recorded. He'd thought of writing something at the time, but it took fifteen years before he saw how to do it, making a radio version of Edgar Christian's diary, a broadcast that was then heard by people who'd known Hornby and got in touch with him to fill out the picture. What followed was the seven years of research and writing that produced the full-length biography, *The Legend of John Hornby*. Harry listened and thought of his own life, his years in Toronto when things had gone from bad to worse to bizarre to desolate, until the moment his old friend Max Berns stumbled upon him and put his hand on his shoulder and said *Harry? Harry?* and he'd snorted awake into what he knew was a rescue. How much better, he thought, to have encountered something as a young man, to have been ignited as Whalley had, and to have remained on fire ever since.

Harry asked him if he was willing to be interviewed. Later, listening to Whalley's dialogue with Gwen, what struck him most was how the professor responded to the question of whether he and Hornby were alike. He hesitated, then said he supposed he shared with Hornby a tendency to approach life "crabwise," meaning sideways and backwards rather than head-on. The man was gentle, serious, fascinating. Gwen fell for him instantly, he could hear it in her voice, and Harry took heart from Whalley's own view of himself. The man wasn't on a forced march, but rather on a wandering route notable for its "digressions and divagations," as the old explorers liked to say. A route of the soul, perhaps.

Judge Berger wasn't moving in lockstep either. Back in March, the news had reported that he was under pressure from the federal government to complete his inquiry by June and have his report ready for them in September. But Berger wouldn't be pushed. He was planning to take his inquiry south, to big urban centres like Vancouver and Winnipeg, and involve the larger Canadian public in the debate about the competing claims of the indigenous peoples and the pipeline companies to the same land. He wanted everyone to ask themselves seriously what gave them the right to exploit the North, to subject its shifting terrain of sea coast, tundra, boreal forest, rocky hills and marshy plains, permanently frozen ground and discontinuous permafrost to a development project that scientists were saying couldn't be completed without ugly consequences, certainly not in the time allotted and at the cost predicted. According to one soil scientist, as soon as they started to dig into soil that was held together by ice, it would melt, like ice cream.

Berger had spoken of the arctic wilderness as "the last of North America, the eighth wonder of the world." This was after he'd flown by helicopter along the arctic coast and seen migrating caribou, three grizzlies and several wolves, and dozens of seals on the sea ice. Harry knew that where they were going on their canoe trip was even more remote, in the sense of less settled, less visited, less on the human map, than where Berger had been.

IN THE MIDDLE OF MAY, a young woman in braids, walking her dog near Con Mine, stumbled upon a body. She was on an old road the mine hadn't used for years. Every winter it got snowed over, and in the spring two or three dog walkers usually trod out a path. The young woman's dog had wandered off, fifty yards, and was making his way through trees and low brush when he began to bark. He didn't stop barking until she came over to investigate, tripping over tree roots, sinking into a remaining patch of snow.

The evening news said that after almost five months, the mysterious disappearance of Lorna Dargabble had apparently ended with the discovery of a woman's body on Con Mine's property. Police said they were almost certain the body was that of Mrs. Dargabble, who was last seen in Yellowknife on Christmas Eve and was reported missing Christmas Day. The body had been found by a city resident. It would be flown to Edmonton for lab and X-ray tests. At present there were no indications of foul play. The body had been found spread-eagled on the ground, with one arm above the head, clothed in a fur coat and slacks similar to those worn by Mrs. Dargabble when she was last seen.

After the newscast, Gwen stood in the doorway of the newsroom, looking at Bill Thwaite. He was frowning over a page in his typewriter. "What does 'spread-eagled' mean?" she asked. "Was she facing up or was she face down?"

His eyes went to her. He leaned back in his chair. "Facing up," he said.

All day a rumour had flown about the station, and so Gwen asked, "And was there a liquor bottle beside her or is that just talk?"

He didn't answer for a moment. Sudden death changes everyone, at least for an hour or two. He didn't send Gwen packing as he might have done.

He said to her, "If you put what I'm about to tell you on the air, I'll skin you alive."

"I'm not going to say anything on air."

Bill scratched the back of his neck. He'd seen Lorna Dargabble many times, bending Eleanor's ear and Gwen's ear, and he'd thought of her as a pest, a nuisance. She was easy to ridicule. The husband he knew by sight, well enough to say hello to. A hard drinker, always in the bars. He and his buddies liked to sit at a table and make vicious fun of women's lib. He'd heard Irving Dargabble refer to his old lady as a perfect punching bag. He said, "She had something in her hand but it wasn't a bottle."

Gwen came all the way into his office. She moved some newspapers off a chair and sat down. She waited.

He held up his open hand and closed it. "A hank of somebody's hair," he said.

Gwen stared at him. She tried to picture the hair in

Lorna Dargabble's old fist. "What *colour* was the hair?"

Bill rubbed his nose and looked at her closely. "You sound as if you think you know."

"White," she said, thinking of the onion-husband.

"Try again."

She looked into his sly, shrewd eyes. "I can't. I don't know."

"About the colour of your hair. Light brown."

The local newspaper had a gentler account of the discovery. Eleanor read the article several times, especially the final paragraph. "Lorna Dargabble was known to take long, solitary walks. Her body was found to be in a peaceful, reposing position as if she had laid down to rest."

As if she had laid down to rest, she repeated to herself, "*like a lost wave* finding *a forgotten shore.*" She was back in Rockcliffe Park, listening to the wind move through the canopy of trees, hearing her father utter a quotation she'd never been able to identify, and thinking that we only ever get *part* of the story. By its very nature Lorna's death would always be a mystery. More searching might provide more parts, but never the whole. Though, of course, that was part of the whole – this partialness. On Sunday she went to church and found herself weeping for Lorna Dargabble. The phrase "the kingdom of God" had come to have enormous meaning for her, though. It summoned up a wide and widening realm.

That night Eleanor's phone rang, and it was Dido.

She was calling from California and her voice was buoyant, jarring. "We're here among the orange groves."

"Dido." And Eleanor sounded sharper than she intended, but perhaps no sharper than she actually felt.

"Don't be angry."

Eleanor pictured the glow and weight of southern fruit, she pictured Dido and Eddy bronzed and unaware. "You left somebody high and dry," she said.

"How is Harry?"

"He's well enough. He's busy. We all are." A pause. "I'm glad to hear from you, Dido. I really am. But I'm curious to know why you're calling me now after all these months."

"I meant to call a long time ago. I should have called."

"You should have, you're right." Then, struck by a possibility, "Is Eddy behaving himself?"

"Eddy's being a very good boy."

Boy. As if Dido were his mother. Just possibly, thought Eleanor, Dido and Eddy deserved each other.

"Don't be angry," Dido said again. "I didn't intend to hurt anybody. Certainly not you."

With these last words Eleanor felt seen through and silenced. But after a moment she asked, "So why did you take off the way you did? In the middle of the night?"

"It wasn't the middle of the night."

"It might as well have been."

Eleanor heard Dido take a deep breath before answering. "I suppose it was a test, to see if I loved him enough to go with him. An old friend of his called and said there was work down here. Eddy wanted to go and he wouldn't leave without me."

"It felt like you ran away from something." There was no response at the other end. "Dido?"

"No. We just wanted to get away from all the complications and to be together."

Eleanor reached for a chair. She dragged it close to the phone and sat down. "So what am I supposed to tell Harry? You took off, you left him in the lurch, you left the station in the lurch. What am I supposed to tell him?"

"He doesn't have to know I called. I just wanted to hear your voice and to find out how you are. To find out what's new."

"Well, I'll tell him you're all right. It's simple kindness," Eleanor said.

"You can tell him I'm sorry."

"No. That's something you would have to tell him yourself." Eleanor studied the kitchen floor, Harry's handiwork. Then said, "They found Lorna Dargabble's body last week near Con Mine. I haven't been able to think about much else."

A certain stillness came down the line. And in the same way that a phone call bearing bad tidings has a different ring, a slightly more urgent tone, this silence felt charged.

Yet Dido's voice, when she spoke, was unaltered. "Was she murdered?"

"We don't know. We won't know till after the autopsy." Eleanor paused. She weighed her words. "Lorna and Eddy didn't care for each other, did they?"

Dido replied easily. "I don't think Eddy knew who she was."

If you say so, thought Eleanor. "You haven't told me what you're doing with yourselves down there."

They were learning about film, Dido said, both of them were. Eddy was spending time with his little niece, but making contacts too. Also organizing a show of photographs he'd taken in Yellowknife. She herself had found work as a script assistant. This last caused Eleanor a moment of déjà vu. That's what Gwen had wanted, she remembered. To be in the background.

Eleanor said, "I wasn't aware that Eddy took any photographs, let alone enough for a show."

"He didn't make a big deal of it. They're very political, very disturbing. Hard to describe, really."

Then Dido asked what else was new, and Eleanor told her about their imminent canoe trip, which was three weeks away now. Dido's response startled her. "Have you got room for me?" she asked.

Eleanor didn't know what to say. She heard Dido's tone of voice, plaintive, flirtatious, knowing, sad. As if the trip were something she didn't deserve, yet knew no one could deny her if she chose to come along.

Dido said, "The trip will probably change your life."

Eleanor absorbed the yearning behind Dido's words. A car went by and children were yelling in the distance. "You sound sad."

"I am sad sometimes."

Then, in a different tone, as if returning to safer ground, Dido said, "I have something I'm going to send you. A little something to take along on your trip. That way," said Dido, "you'll remember me."

"Did you think I would ever forget?"

Eleanor stepped into Harry's office the next day and closed the door. He hadn't begun to clear out his desk, even though this was his final week. On his last day, Eleanor would bring in a cake and round up the willing and the unwilling in a farewell gesture that was notable for its awkward brevity and for Harry's parting shot. "When it comes to television," he would say, "listen to radio, and when it comes to managers, don't listen at all."

But now Eleanor leaned her back against his door and hesitated a moment, taking in his defenceless morning face, then told him Dido had phoned. "Last night. She's fine. She's with Eddy. They're in California."

Harry took off his glasses and leaned back. "She's well, you say."

"As far as I could tell. They seem to have jobs in film. I should have asked more questions. She gave me her phone number, though."

Harry heard what she'd said, but all he could think was that Dido had phoned Eleanor, not him. Apparently, she hadn't even asked about him, or Eleanor would be telling him.

To Eleanor he looked so defeated suddenly, and so hurt, that she was afraid he might collapse into dust — as in the fairy tales. She almost said, Dido asked me to tell you she's sorry, but then held back, knowing how empty it would sound.

She said instead, "Maybe I shouldn't have mentioned it. But I thought you'd want to know."

Harry looked up. "Of course, I want to know. Of course, you should have told me."

"Good. That's what I thought."

He said firmly, a flicker of anger in his eyes, "There's nothing worse than being in the dark."

===

Eleanor and Gwen arranged a gathering in Lorna Dargabble's memory. They wanted to somehow commemorate Lorna's passing, given that no funeral seemed to be in the offing. They ran a note on the community announcements: anyone who would like to remember Lorna Dargabble's life would be welcome to come to Eleanor Dew's mobile home in Forrest Park on Sunday, June 6 between two and five in the afternoon. They had no expectation that the husband would come, and he didn't. Others came, however. Lorna hadn't had a wide circle of friends, by any means, yet she was well known, and Eleanor's home barely held everyone. The memorial was never meant to be anything but simple. There was wine and tea and coffee and pastries. Mortality in the air. And not that much talk, at first.

Almost everyone was grey-haired, veterans of the magic five years — it being thought that if you lasted that long in Yellowknife, you might stay for decades. They'd known Lorna from her previous, happy life, with her first husband. They'd known that in her second marriage she was abjectly miserable. One woman spoke about Irving Dargabble as a horrible drunken lout, and said she knew Lorna had been "holding it together," just barely, for years. Another older woman, wearing a bright red vest, said she suspected Lorna just wandered off into the night "which is so easy to do up here." She herself had been in Igloolik one time, she said, and started to walk back to the hotel and thought if she turned right instead of left, she'd never be found. "The vastness really hit me," she said with feeling.

There was a young woman who came, too, a young woman in braids. She turned out to be the one who'd stumbled upon Lorna's body. "Actually, it was my dog who found her. He deserves the credit." She had tied him up outside before coming into the trailer and pointed to him now out the window, a big brown and black dog named Stan, she said. The young woman joined in the conversation about wandering off and getting lost. She'd heard about blizzards in the eastern Arctic where the wind blows for three days, then stops, and you can be fooled into going outside, only for the wind to swing around from the opposite direction and disorient you totally. Ralph recalled stepping outside into a blizzard in Fort Simpson, and not being able to breathe; the wind sucked his breath out of his mouth. Everyone agreed, however, that on Christmas Eve, when Lorna went missing, conditions were peaceful. A gentler night, Lorna's last night. No wind at all. But cold, certainly cold.

Gwen listened, haunted by the unexplained light brown hair Lorna was holding in her hand. A chilling detail that wasn't common knowledge. She'd mentioned it to the others, though, to Harry and Ralph and Eleanor, thereby learning about Eleanor's lingering suspicion of Eddy, even as she put it to rest.

In the middle of June, just days before they left for the Barrens, the local coroner issued his long-awaited news release. There would not be an inquest into Lorna Dargabble's death, after all. As reasons, he gave the following: there was no evidence of wounds, injuries, poison, or disease on the body; the pathologist in Edmonton had given the cause of death as exposure to the cold; and the investigation by the police clearly absolved all individuals who might have had something to gain by her death. He concluded that there was absolutely no suspicion of wrongdoing or complicity on the part of any person.

The four canoeists were in Harry's house, re-packing, rearranging, jettisoning a few things (like the hip waders Ralph had intended to use when he fished in the rapids for trout, like the second bottle of Scotch Harry had planned to bring along). Now that they were within forty-eight hours of having to hoist everything onto their backs, they were being realistic. The evening light poured into the living room as Harry packed an extra sweater and woollen socks. So suicide then. Lorna had walked out on Christmas Eve and consigned herself to the elements. As for the hair clenched in her hand — the investigation had shown it was a lock of hair, cut from somebody's head, not torn out by the roots. It could have been anybody's light brown hair. She was a hairdresser, after all. But whose hair? he had to wonder. And why had she taken it with her that night?

He continued to organize his supplies. The day after tomorrow they would fly to the eastern arm of Great Slave Lake, and in a few weeks they would reach the Thelon River and view the remains of John Hornby's cabin, the spot where his body had lain undiscovered for more than a year in that wooded oasis in the Barrens. Harry heard Ralph across the room remark that the western sky looked clear, promising, but he felt too preoccupied to respond. The fact of Dido's phone call had stirred up more unanswered questions, which worked on his mind. At times, the thought of her father-in-law's letter was consoling. She'd left behind two loves, he thought. His and Daniel's. Possibly she was saying, It's not just you, Harry. I'm leaving everything behind. He could feel almost reconciled then, able to carry what he felt for her and carry it easily; he would hear from her in time, he would see her again. But then he would picture her with Eddy – think of her leaving without a word – think of her phoning, finally, but not phoning him – and his reaction was so intense it stopped him in his tracks. And so it went, back and forth, between feelings of love and feelings of anguish.

Just days ago something else had brought her back in an unexpected way. A small package from California had arrived in the mail for Eleanor, who'd shown him and the others what it contained. A Saint Christopher medallion on a chain. Eleanor was wearing it now. It fell forward as she leaned over her impossibly heavy knapsack. *Saint Christopher, protect us.*

ON THE MORNING OF JUNE 17, they loaded their canoes and packs into a float plane and took off from Yellowknife Bay. The pilot flew them to the rugged, uninhabited eastern end of Great Slave Lake. They planned to camp there for two nights, on Charlton Bay, breaking themselves in slowly. Then, following in Hornby's footsteps, they would undertake the classic route of Pike's Portage into Artillery Lake, and from there continue on to the Thelon River.

By afternoon they were on a rocky sunlit point of land in Charlton Bay, setting up their tents, judging which spots were warmest and most sheltered by the depth of the moss and lichen. They were alone now. About three hundred miles below the Arctic Circle in almost continuous daylight, facing six weeks in the wilderness.

Chunks of ice floated by. Candled ice, the long vertical ice crystals that form when meltwater on a frozen lake works its trickling way down to the water below, had bunched against the shore. The candles tinkled and chimed, and Gwen taped the sound. Ralph headed off in his canoe, eager to test his muscles and to take his first photographs. Harry gathered wood for a fire, and Eleanor listed birds in her notebook. Lapland longspurs, gone from Yellowknife two weeks ago, were with them here, where it was colder. The little birds let her walk noisily over stones to within two feet of them, before they hopped away. Twice, Hornby had overwintered nearby, building himself a little cabin, and nearly died both times.

Although they had what seemed like all the space in the world and all the time, they were committed to a definite destination: the Twin Otter would come back for them on July 27 at Beverly Lake, five hundred miles from here. And so time and space were in potential conflict.

The next day, their first full day, they deliberately took it easy, exploring the site of old Fort Reliance near the mouth of the Lockhart River. They paddled to the ruins after breakfast and discovered a site of great loveliness. It was like a park of white and green moss and lichen, with spruce trees arranged as though planted. They followed a path, and then a wider one, almost a driveway though the natural park. The trees had tiny buds. They were heading backwards, they realized, into a much later spring of lingering ice, and fresh snow on the hills in the morning, melted by early afternoon. Eleanor said she could picture Jane Austen walking here it looked so civilized, so groomed. There were three perfectly shaped birches and two graves, fenced with weathered slats, one a child or infant's grave, tiny, the other larger.

"The past is as close," Eleanor said to Ralph, "as I am to you."

Ralph, a man of books and pockets, and pockets stretched out of shape by books, opened George Whalley and read the quotation from J.W. Tyrrell, the land surveyor and mapmaker who had stood in this spot in 1900 and sung its praises. "Five stone chimneys only now remain of what were 66 years ago three substantial buildings . . . situated on a lovely level green terrace about twenty feet above the harbour, and two hundred feet from the shore." Back's Chimneys they were called, after Captain George Back, who came through in 1833 and used the fort as his winter quarters. He and his men were a relief party on the trail of Sir John Ross, who was on the trail of the North-West Passage (*to have felt snow and ice forever, and nothing forever but snow and ice*), though in the end Ross, unlike so many, needed no rescuing.

That afternoon Ralph pulled Gwen up the sandbank laughing, and a few minutes later Harry accused him of taking his cup.

"That's my cup you're drinking out of."

"No. It's mine." Ralph's voice was even, easy.

"No, it's not," he growled back.

"I brought it up with me from the canoe."

"No." And Harry was about to battle on when he saw his own cup sitting a few feet away on the moss. He reached for it, attempted a laugh, and turned to see Eleanor eyeing him critically.

She said, "Watch you don't slip a cog."

Afterwards, he asked her to repeat that expression, the one she'd castigated him with.

Slip a cog. "Poor Ralph was sitting there quietly and I knew it was his cup because I saw him bring it out of the canoe."

"I don't feel as cantankerous as I sound." He managed an apologetic smile.

"Well, it's good you can laugh about it now."

He felt reproved and childish and he wasn't laughing. The mosquitoes were fast. Wilder, or it was just earlier in the year; they escaped before he could slap them.

Pike's Portage was twenty-five miles long, a series of small lakes and trails that led to Artillery Lake, itself fifty miles long. An Indian route from time immemorial. Its first leg (to Harry Lake, of all places) was brutal, as they knew from trip reports by other canoeists, three miles long with a climb of five hundred and ninety feet, rocky and wooded, when their packs were heaviest and they were least in shape.

The feeling of release once Harry reached the end and sank to the ground and extricated himself from the eighty pounds of torture on his back, was like sprouting wings and floating up to heaven. But the feat had to be repeated three times, first with one pack, then with another, then with a seventy-pound canoe on his shoulders. He portaged one canoe, Ralph the other. Five trips, if you counted the there and back, and more taxing than anything he had ever done before or ever imagined. The only thing that kept him going was stubborn pride. Arms at his sides, fingers swelling up like stubby sausages, he trudged along under his burden, listening for Ralph behind him and trying to keep ahead, or at least not fall behind. He heard footsteps and after a minute Eleanor appeared around the bend, on her way back for another load. Then Gwen. The women had to carry packs that weighed sixty pounds or more. He'd hoisted Gwen's pack onto her back and she had swayed and he'd steadied her, and then she'd stepped forward – all five foot three of her and 120 pounds – Hornby's size, he thought – and started up the trail. Now here she was going back for the second round. Eleanor was a bigger woman, taller, heftier, but they shared the same look of exhausted, dazed determination. The women disappeared and he stopped for a moment, and still he heard the thumping of feet, then realized it was the blood pounding in his head. Mosquitoes abounded. He felt something on his tongue, explored with his finger, and came out with a drowned mosquito. At the end, his legs gave out. Going into the little hollow and across to the rocks, where he could ford the last stream, he felt them go rubbery and only just managed to totter to the finish line of open water, where he let the canoe fall from shoulder height into a cradle of willow bushes. Again, the sweet release.

At the end, after everything had been transported, they bathed in the warm evening sun, their bodies bone white, stone white at the water's edge, scooping aching cold Harry Lake over their heads.

The next day, June 20, the fourth day of their trip, Harry had an early-morning dream about Gwen. Of coming into her house through the back door and she was in her dressing gown, having called him for help. A stalled car? She went upstairs to change and after an interval he followed and entered her bedroom through the half-open door. She was sitting on the edge of her bed, still undressed, except for panties that were in tatters (her drastic underwear he would see set out to dry on the arctic willows, waist pulling away from elastic, saggy brassiere) but no brassiere in the dream, her breasts round and warm as she turned an undershirt right side out, her eyes concentrating on the cat's cradle of what had become a lacy camisole — the undershirt had become pretty in the dream — and all of her alert, attractive, attracted, naked. Was he not about to reach for her breasts and she about to respond when he woke up?

Harry couldn't recall ever dreaming about Dido, which surprised him. Perhaps if all of your waking thoughts are taken up with someone, then your sleeping mind has to catch up. He found himself carrying the dream about Gwen through his arduous day.

But it was Ralph, who would bury his face in the tundra heather and say he wanted tundra tweeds, a full suit made of the stuff and bearing its array of muted colours and its smoky, subtle smell, it was garrulous, poetic Ralph who would score.

They moved across the wilderness like a ragged troupe of toiling actors, it seemed to Harry, transporting sections of a colourful banner, namely the tents and canoes and packs. Ralph the gentleman duke. Eleanor the wise Queen. Gwen the moody princess. And he, the blistered and bitten and disgruntled fool. After a mere four days, he was so stiff that to get up he had to roll on his side and push with his aching arms. He took the huge blisters on his heels to Eleanor, who bandaged them. Took his aching shoulders to Gwen, who pressed and rubbed and kneaded. Gwen he began to call Kate, "Kate like the hazel twig," since against the backdrop of so much immensity her small body seemed not fragile but intensely delicate, her eyelids like petals, her small ears astonishing.

On the fifth night, he assumed a new identity, haughty chef Rodrigo. "Pork chops Rodrigo" became the first of many such dishes. "Grayling Rodrigo" and "trout Béarnaise" and "boeuf ha ha ha," all served with flourishes of theatrical bad temper. "My kingdom for a garlic press," he would snarl. Or, with a snap of his fingers, "The Great Rodrigo must have curry." And he would rummage in his pack and pull out the unexpected spice, earning genuine applause for his gastric foresight.

Gwen burned her mouth on his bedtime cocoa. "That's the point of cocoa," he told her. "I've lost half my taste buds!" she said. "You have far too many taste buds anyway," he told her.

Ralph had brought along Farley Mowat's *Tundra*, a fine collection of excerpts from the accounts of great arctic travellers, and that night he passed it to Harry, suggesting he read them to sleep. Harry's voice recounting the adventures of Samuel Hearne (who coined the phrase *the Barren Ground* for the arctic expanse of treeless plains that he toiled across between 1769 and 1772), Harry's voice carried from their tent to the women's tent a dozen feet away. *From the 20th to the 23rd of June, we walked nearly twenty miles a day without any subsistence other than a pipe of tobacco and a drink of water when we pleased. Early on the 23rd we saw three muskoxen, and the Indians soon killed them. But to our great mortification it rained before we got them skinned, and the moss could not be made to burn to make a fire. This was poor comfort for people who had not broken their fast for three or four days . . . The weather remained so bad, with rain, snow, and sleet, that by the time we were again able to make a fire of moss, we had eaten the amount of one muskox quite raw. I must confess that now my spirits began to fail me a little. Indeed our other misfortunes were greatly aggravated by the weather, which was cold and so very wet that for three days and nights I had not one dry thread on me. But when the fine weather returned, and we had dried our clothing by a fire of moss, I endeavoured, like a sailor after a storm, to forget past misfortunes.*

From above, in the never-ending light, their canoes and tents looked like separate fruits on a flat tree espaliered against a grey stone wall. Gwen's orange tent, shared with Eleanor; Harry's, lemon-yellow, shared with Ralph; Harry's red canoe; Ralph's silver canoe. Aircraft, or anyone at a distance, would have spotted them easily, which was the point, and became the point.

They were proceeding from lake to lake in the string of eight lakes that comprised Pike's Portage into Artillery Lake. Harry Lake then French Lake then Acres. "This is where we can get lost," said Ralph, examining their map repeatedly. Then Kipling Lake.

By now they were moving into the Barrens. The north-facing side of Kipling Lake had stunted trees or none at all, and any leaves they saw were tiny. It should have occurred to them then what lay ahead, but by day it was so warm. Their faces and hands burned, their fingers and lips cracked and split. They tied the canoes together in the middle of the lake for lunch, catching the wind which kept away the mosquitoes, and drifted gently to shore, where they finished their salami, cheese, bannock, peanut butter.

After Kipling came Burr Lake, large and surrounded by round hills, all of a height and bare, except for a few boulders sitting on top, dropped by a retreating glacier eight thousand years ago. In the simplified landscape you could see a very long distance. It was rather like a kept golf course, thought Harry. Beautiful lines, beautiful details — silver-grey lichen, tiny pink flowers. Easy to walk on, the growth ankle-high.

That evening he watched Gwen wash her hair. She knelt on a rock and bent her head forward, exposing the tender ring around her neck formed by the chafing collar of her wool shirt. She dipped her head into the aching-cold lake, quickly swept water over her head with one hand, rubbed in shampoo, rinsed, lowered her head into the lake again, again swept water over it. "Still soapy," he called to her, and with both hands she scooped water and splashed it more vigorously over her hair, then grabbed a towel and wrapped it around her head, achieving sweet and immediate relief as he could tell from the relaxation of her shoulders, which were bare, her upper body clad in a faded blue undershirt, soft from use.

Birds sang in the background, white-crowned sparrows. One called nearby, a long summer call, another answered faintly on the other side of the hill, declaring its territory.

"My little trout," smiled Ralph when he looked up from the fire and saw Gwen.

"Quasimodo," grinned Harry, thinking of her hunched shoulders at the edge of the freezing lake, and wanting to be contrary and humorous and remembered.

It wasn't the change of scene that was making things easier, thought Harry, or the hard labour, or the distraction of sore shoulders and a sore knee. It was being removed from all possible contact. No mail, no phone.

On their sixth day they reached Artillery Lake, only to experience what would be the first in a series of shocks ending in something far worse. The lake, fifty miles long, turned out to be covered in ice.

They were at the southern end, a narrow fjord of open water that turned an ominous white in the near distance. Ralph climbed a ridge with his binoculars and didn't return for some time. When he came back he was subdued and would only mutter, "a lot of ice."

They had moved still farther back in time to pre-leaf catkins, red-tipped, on the dwarf willows, and to the first subtle blush of green on the miniature birches and alders. Yet it was June 22.

At nine-thirty in the evening, Harry retreated to his tent, away from flies and light and consciousness, away from people and things to do, away from Ralph's indefatigable drive. Already they were crossing swords about how early to get up each morning and when to pack it in each day. He heard more birds and a stream in the distance. Then Gwen boasting about the dessert she was cooking. "Come and look." He didn't stir. He wanted a drink, not a bloody dessert. But his bottle of Scotch, wrapped with care in a sweater, and siphoned little by little into his hip flask, was going to have to last the whole trip. He held off.

With fiendish energy Gwen had made a version of strawberry shortcake: sweet bannock scones topped with freeze-dried strawberries boiled and sweetened and thickened with cornstarch, and topped in turn with thick cream from a can. She brought him his portion on a plate and he had to admit it wasn't bad. He lay in a corner of his tent, by himself, out of harm's way, licking his fingers.

But Gwen's achievement was a direct challenge to The Great Rodrigo, and so he redoubled his efforts, concocting in the morning a deluxe porridge to seduce her, the confirmed porridge-hater. A bowl of oatmeal topped with freeze-dried peaches, brown sugar, a dab of butter, his own special cream of powdered milk and Coffee-mate, a sprinkle of cinnamon. She ate his "porridge à la crème pêche" out of kindness and wouldn't be coaxed a second time.

The next day, their seventh day out, they took as a day of rest, exploring and photographing, napping and reading. Eleanor sat quietly, waiting for creatures to appear, fingering the Saint Christopher medallion, cool to the touch, and shaking herself every so often to keep away the flies, like a cow in a lichen pasture, she thought. She and Gwen had pitched their tent on a flat bed of lichen. When she crawled inside, the floor of the tent scrunched like wrapping paper. She lay on her thin mattress of insulite, away from bothersome mosquitoes, and listened. Harry and Gwen were drinking coffee by the fire, washing dishes, talking. She heard an intimacy beneath the banter, and saw without closing her eyes the landscape they'd been looking at for days – rocky slopes covered with all manner of lichens, silver-grey, mustard, lime-green, soft-green; the exquisite balance of boulders left perching thousands of years ago; tiny leaves, gold, red; and pink flowers in clumps, scattered, as were

antlers left to bleach on the side of the hill, and animal drop-
pings. The air holding the warmth.

She'd been so very tired yesterday, especially around
supper time, trying to drive tent stakes deep enough into the
ground – quite a wind then; but now the air was perfectly still,
and a second wind was inside her. Lying on the ground, being
reshaped, was like lying awake beside a new husband. Inside
the orange tent the light was eternal sunshine no matter the
hour, her burned face and hands gave off rays of heat. She
closed her eyes. Pink flowers against lichen flashed in a near
irritation of feeling, an over-arousal; the wedding bed again.

At first, they stayed in the narrow leads of open water between
ice and shore, making progress of a sort. Sometimes the leads
turned into wider channels and they paddled in smooth water
under a hot sun. Where the ice was tight against the shore,
they portaged, or if the ice happened to be smooth, they
pushed their loaded canoes across it, but carefully, wary of
falling through. Whenever they could, they lined the canoes,
guiding them forward with ropes through shallow water until
they got caught up in rocks, and then once again they were
carrying everything on their backs over uneven ground.

Impatience made them bolder. Instead of hugging the
shore, they began to push their canoes over long frozen
stretches of Artillery Lake farther away from land. Ice-
canoeing, they called it: one foot in the canoe, the other on
the half-rotted ice, they scooted forward, ready to hop into the
canoe if the ice gave way, and once it did. Harry and Eleanor,

who always paddled together, managed to hop aboard in the nick of time. But then they were wedged in place, surrounded and pinned on all sides by ice. Eleanor leant forward, she was so tired, and cried for a moment. They got free, finally, by pushing and rocking and breaking up the ice around them until they reached a portion that was solid enough to take their weight. Then off they went again, pushing forward with one foot, like Scott and Shackleton and all the other polar lunatics.

Deep water below, and ptarmigan off to the right – in three hours the only sign of life. By late afternoon, they were exhausted.

In Harry and Ralph's tent, the larger of the two, all of them huddled in awkward silence, since ten minutes earlier Harry had pointed a finger at Commander Ralph and told him to fuck off.

"Harry, *do* something," Ralph had barked when he saw Harry standing immobilized. The rain starting to fall, their packs uncovered, Ralph busy with tarps and with stones to weigh the tarps down. "Do *something*."

Harry pointed his finger. "You, fuck off."

And so it was ice, rain, headwind, bad temper. Harry's felt hat, beaten about by the weather, no longer looked quite so dapper. Yet when they walked across certain patches of sun-warmed ground, they inhaled the perfume of small pink flowers and it was the lightest, most papery, most northern of scents. Harry stopped and breathed it in, burying his troubled mind in a tree full of apple blossoms. A fragrance as different from patchouli as anything he could think of. If it came to that. And it did. It was a sudden thought.

Inside the tent, out of the wind and rain, they risked making tea on their little butane stove, and Eleanor took a restorative sip.

"'Sweet are the uses of adversity,'" she murmured into the tension-filled air.

"'Which, like the toad, ugly and venomous,'" continued Ralph, "'wears yet a precious jewel in his head.'"

Earning himself a wide and appreciative smile. He had picked up and finished the quote, just as her father would have done.

═

Although they were locked in ice, the air flowed – the bright, bitter light of June. For two days they stayed put on Artillery Lake, hoping the ice would loosen and move away from shore. It was too cold for flies, that was the blessing. Rain fell, then slowed to a drizzle, then turned into low cloud, then lifted.

Harry climbed a butte and saw goshawks and cliff swallows, a hill covered in purple flowers, and through the binoculars endless ice. Eleanor knelt next to a rock to be out of the wind and pulled out her flower book: the purple was Lapland rosebay, while around her blossomed low white clusters of small-leaved Labrador tea. Gwen made doughnuts, her arm coming floury out of the bannock bag, her face delighted by the boisterous encouragement from all sides, the cries for jelly filling and chocolate icing. She rolled the sweetened dough between her palms, formed rings and fried them, several at a time, in melted lard, then rolled the hot doughnuts in a mixture of cinnamon and sugar, and Harry offered up his joke. "So a guy goes into a restaurant and orders a hamburger. The waiter brings it to him and the guy takes a bite and pulls a long hair out of his mouth: 'Hey, what's *this?*' So the waiter takes him back to the kitchen and there's the cook pressing meat patties in his armpits. 'That's *disgusting!*' You think that's disgusting? says the waiter. You should see how he makes doughnuts."

They gave up waiting for the ice to improve and on June 28, they set off again, battling their way down Artillery Lake, skirting ice, or hauling themselves up and across it, or paddling in any open leads. Harry boiled over at the incessant headwind and slammed his paddle on the ice, almost breaking it, and he didn't care.

"I almost broke my paddle," he stormed.

Eleanor looked around from the bow of their canoe. "Slam your head into the ice instead, not something we depend on."

He refused to go on. They were considerably behind the other two, in what would become their standard pattern, but he beached the canoe and stood next to a rock. Eleanor stood beside him. He said, "I'm not going any farther till the wind dies down."

She felt an involuntary smile come up on her face, so she bent her head and walked to the canoe.

"Say something," he said.

"I will. I'm just thinking."

She said it might take a long time for the wind to die down. They hadn't moved for two days. They all wanted to get ahead.

He didn't answer, and they went on.

At Crystal Island the treeline cut diagonally across Artillery Lake as visibly as a long dark pencil mark on a blank page. They passed over the line into a world without walls, a land of rolling plains as exposed as the open sea. Their backs were sudden trees. Their hats were leaves the mosquitoes rested upon. Birds flew past their shoulders, like familiars. And at night their quiet talk around the little bannock fire was similar to the voices of the trees that spooked the early Eskimos, who ventured down in search of wood for their sled runners, but never stayed longer than ten days among the whispering, groaning wood spirits.

That evening they fell into recalling their first memories. Hers, said Eleanor, was of being blamed unfairly by other kids for breaking the eggs in a robin's nest, and this was an English robin, smaller than Canadian robins, with bluer eggs. That might be why a recent thought had taken the particular form it took: the robin in the egg doesn't know the robin's egg is blue.

"Meaning what?" asked Gwen.

"Meaning that we're blind to our own blind spots."

Gwen nodded slowly, picturing the robin inside the blue egg and herself inside her small world. "Like my blind spot about religion."

"If you want. Or like being in love with someone and not knowing it."

A pause. "Who are you talking about?" asked Gwen.

But Eleanor wasn't prepared to say, and then Ralph was confessing a first memory so personal and out of the ordinary that her point got lost for a while. Ralph's first memory was taking the dry little turds out of his diaper and lining them up in a careful row on the windowsill. "I had a collector's eye even then," he laughed.

"But what was your mother feeding you?" cried Eleanor.

Gwen remembered a piece of white satin fluttering in her grandmother's mahogany wardrobe, though it might have been a dream, she wasn't sure. Eleanor suggested that perhaps she was seeing the future. Her own grandmother was a little girl when she dreamt about a soldier's cap, then years later she saw the cap on her daddy's head as he lay in his coffin.

They were carrying wood with them, having left the trees behind. Gathering up whatever driftwood they could find, keeping an eye peeled for any dry sticks. Gwen, Harry noticed, looked like a young girl in her red wind jacket and running shoes, one pant leg turned up, bending over the fire or gathering wood. One evening she sat on a rocky outcrop above Ralph, who was fishing from shore. Ralph set down his fishing rod, turned around, and began to pelt her with snowballs. She giggled and shrieked, hands in front of her face, then scooped up the same snow and fired it back at his head. Soon afterwards he gave up fishing and went over to the fire. Gwen came down off the rock innocently: Ralph? Want any help? No, he was just letting the fire burn down to have coals for bannock. Then a blood-curdling yell as he felt snow shoved down the back of his shirt and rubbed against his bare skin.

From his perch several yards away, Harry lit another cigarette. The spit spit of tobacco off his tongue. He heard
Gwen offer to tend the bannock so that Ralph could take his
evening hike. Ralph leapt at the chance and Eleanor went
with him. Then it was Gwen and Harry by the fire. Every
evening one of them made bannock, a thick, wide, pancake-
biscuit of flour, salt, baking powder, powdered milk and
water. They cooked it slowly, patiently, in melted lard in a
frypan, providing themselves with a ready-made and speedy
lunch for the following day.

Old worries had followed her into the Barrens, Gwen
confided to Harry, lifting the bannock with a flipper to make
sure it wasn't getting scorched. Being all alone on the tundra —
as exposed to the weather as she'd been exposed on the air —
made her brood about certain things, like the flimsy shelter of
personality. She was beset by radio dreams, she told him. She
would be on a bus leaving town, for instance, and suddenly
remember she'd forgotten all about preparing her program
and she'd have to phone the station in a panic and tell them to
play music.

"There was another dream," she said. "About Dido."

Harry lifted his head. "What about her?"

Gwen didn't answer. She looked down at the soft-green
lichens adhering to the rock, impervious to any wind, at the
little twigs clinging to her wool pants. She was seeing the two
loons that swam ahead of them earlier in the day. Most elegant
red-eyed birds. Dressed in black stockings, it seemed to her,
soot-black, pulled over their heads and down their long necks.
And the white of their breasts, where breast met water, so
white they might have been pushing snowbanks ahead of them.

Immaculate, until they opened their beaks and sounded like nothing else you'd ever heard. Sorrowful calls that reached to the horizon. Or rippling, demented laughs.

"What about Dido?" pressed Harry.

"Just that she'd taken all my stuff out of the filing cabinet and replaced it with her own things." It sounded pathetic. She gave her shoulders a shake.

"She can't take what you have," Harry said quietly, "unless you let her."

Such a lot to unpack from that slender gift of a sentence. Harry was on her side, but only if she was on her own side, and there were no sides, really, unless she chose to look at it that way. But Harry understood the dream and didn't blame her, which was a comfort.

The contrast between comfort and discomfort was their daily bread – the pain of portaging and the bliss of lying in the evening sun, warm, fed, rested. A slight wind to keep the flies somewhat at bay.

But the sun wasn't shining, and hadn't been for days.

And then it was. On June 30 the sky turned blue and a canal as wide as a wide gateway (three canoes wide) opened in the ice on Artillery Lake. They paddled forward and it seemed biblical, blessed and childlike all at once. A pathway opened up through life. Winds couldn't trouble them here, where there wasn't enough open water to allow for any waves. For one enchanted hour the lake was less ice-infested than ice-enriched. On the bottom of the lake were stones so clear to the eye they could count every one of them, on either side was the endless surrendering ice, beyond them the canal snaked around the very corner that would take them where they wanted to go, while above, in the blue-blue sky, one low and narrow cloud hung close to the horizon, a soft repetition of the ice on either side.

Cool air came off the ice and mixed with warm winds offshore, a combination that recalled for Gwen a summer job sorting strawberries inside a refrigerated truck.

Pieces of loose ice crunched under the canoe.

And then they were beyond the ice. The colour of the water changed – deep blue, violet, green – platinum where it was shallow over sand. The two canoes pulled apart. Gwen and Ralph, always in the lead, continued at the same pace, while Harry and Eleanor fell far behind. Bewitched by the bright shore of white sand, they stopped to photograph a line of small green clumps of moss on which tiny pink flowers described a pattern. Pale-lilac, and Eleanor identified them as moss campion, a cushion plant. "Look how it protects itself from the wind. So clever," she said. "So persevering." She looked up and smiled at Harry with such affection that he felt restored.

They paddled on. The open water was calm and shiny, the mosquitoes abundant again; in the bow Eleanor felt like a splattered windshield from all the bugs knocking into her. Gazing into the clear water she and Harry spotted a big trout with a silver lure hanging from its mouth. Also, a goose walking across the ice – walking, walking. Was it hurt?

By evening the two of them were at the far end of Artillery Lake, looking for the exit. Rain clouds had blown in. They could see where it was pouring to the left and right.

Around them the country was the same as it had been for some time, low and flat, except now they were working their way through back channels, and they were lost.

They'd last seen Ralph and Gwen quite a while ago, and the maps were in Ralph's canoe. Ralph had misplaced his camera bag a few days back, setting it down on undifferentiated ground as he stalked a ptarmigan; it had taken half an hour of searching by all of them to find it. And to her chagrin, Eleanor had forgotten Dido's medallion while bathing one morning. She'd removed the chain from around her neck so it wouldn't slap against her skin, then not thought of it again until lunchtime when they were miles beyond where she'd bathed. She tried not to see the lapse as a bad omen.

They'd come too far. Or so they thought. They turned back and retraced their route and became even more confused and alarmed. Harry confessed he had no sense of direction. He told Eleanor about the infamous night in Toronto when he went to play poker at a buddy's house for the umpteenth time, but walked into another house entirely, on a different block. "I was hanging up my coat when the owner came out of the kitchen. I figured he had to be the new poker player. So I said, 'Where's the booze?'"

Eleanor took the compass out of his hand and studied it herself. But it seemed wisest to stay put and let themselves be found. She suggested they pitch his tent in order to make themselves more visible. They did that, and the bright yellow material fluttering in the air reminded her of what Ralph had said the other night about the frailty of arctic explorers. Dehydration was the biggest danger, the desiccating winds. If they lay down, said Ralph, it was "bye-bye butterfly."

A raven croaked as it flew overhead. Eleanor was grateful for the company. She asked, "Why is it that ravens don't turn white in the winter like ptarmigans?"

"Ptarmigans are like us," said Harry. "They need all the help they can get."

An hour passed and a grim fear worked its way into his bones. He pulled his flask out of his jacket pocket, unscrewed the lid, and handed it to Eleanor.

"Your secret supply," she said.

He told her about hearing a scientist say that cold, in the form of snow and ice, can be stored, but heat cannot. "He forgot about this," he said. Taking it back from her. "To our wives and sweethearts. May they never meet."

The liquor felt wonderful in every part of him.

Eleanor wrapped her arms around her knees. They were completely alone, apart from that passing raven. "My father told me his hair turned white when he was fourteen," she said. "But I hadn't the wit or the curiosity to ask why."

Harry said the same thing happened to Amundsen when he was twenty-one. He spent a winter on a whaling ship in Antarctica and the experience was so appalling, all those months of darkness, that his hair turned white.

"So his white hair was a source of light," said Eleanor.

Another hour passed. Beside him, Eleanor was quiet. "Are you praying?" he asked.

"Yes."

Good, thought Harry.

The flask was empty. In an act that would ensure his entry into heaven, he had given her the last swallow.

"They're waiting for us to show up," she said.

"How long will they wait, do you suppose?"

"I wonder."

Her prayer was ongoing and free form. At the moment she was talking to her father. She was saying to him, I've never asked for anything before, and now I am.

Aloud she said, "Maybe this is what happened to Hornby. Maybe he got lost. Maybe that's why they took so long to get to the Thelon." Then she said, "That goose wasn't hurt. The one we saw walking? It's moulting, that's all. Moulting geese can't fly."

Harry put his arm around her. He hadn't forgotten his boyish sense of a world filled with a divine presence and with many lesser spirits, especially in the woods, especially in the dark; he still believed that just because we can't see something doesn't mean it isn't there, or – more to the point – just because something *is* there doesn't mean it's seen. Here they were, he and Eleanor, completely exposed, pathetically visible, but unseen, lost. "We're like Adam and Eve," he said, and with those words he began to laugh, for an old limerick had lit up his mind. *In the Garden of Eden lay Adam*, he recited, *Complacently stroking his madam, And great was his mirth, For on all of the earth, There were only two balls – and he had 'em.*

Later still, they made a fire with what sticks they could find, and went on watching the water and a sky that normally was too light for sunsets. But tonight, the prolonged colours of sun under dark cloud echoed the shades of the tiny pink and white flowers near at hand. There grew in Eleanor the sense that no matter what happened it was a privilege to be here, to see this vast tundra landscape that produced one-inch flowers and immeasurable skies. She thought of the Japanese artists who stood out in the weather for hours, simply observing, then went back inside to make their prints of the floating world. We're being visited by the possibility of utter disaster, she thought, but what swept through her was a sense of joy: of dependence on a great personal Being somewhere far off yet nearby, and *our lives are in Your hands*, she thought.

Then Harry started to whistle, and suddenly she shivered and rubbed her arms through the sleeves of her heavy woollen shirt. "What's the coldest you've ever been?" she asked him.

He knew the answer without even thinking. Saturday afternoons, bicycling home from playing hockey on the duck pond, his hands on the icy handlebars. His mother would tell him to run cold water from the kitchen tap over his cold hands. Frozen feet too, jumping from foot to foot. The air around the electric light all blue and rainbowy, his eyes so cold. His mother would give him a cup of scalding cocoa and nine times out of ten it took the roof off the top of his mouth. "Nothing holds the heat like cocoa does," he said, "but it doesn't *store* heat the way ice stores cold."

Eleanor said she had a theory that there's something about heat that actually reinforces memory. She broke off, and Harry waited for her to go on. "When I was about sixteen," she went on, "my friend Jill and I went to a Saturday matinée and when we came out it was dark and freezing cold and the bus didn't come. Ottawa in January. So I decided to walk home and Jill was positive I was going the wrong way. She refused to come with me, she held on to a parking meter with both hands, *no no no*. That was the coldest I've ever been. And all I remember is plodding home and Jill dragging her feet behind me and me trying not to think or feel *anything*. The movie, on the other hand, I remember every detail of, because I was inside and warm."

"*Were* you going the wrong way?"

"No, it was the right way."

"You'd better do the navigating from now on."

She was about to tell him which movie it was when a sound – a cough – made them turn around. Impossible to say how long he'd been squatting there, twenty yards away. Unkempt, dark-haired, unsmiling. Cradling a gun in his arms.

Harry stood up, but Eleanor stayed where she was, her arms around her knees. Where on earth had he come from?

The stranger stood up too and came down the barren slope, and Eleanor thought of Eddy, because the man didn't smile and he looked dangerous. The movie on the coldest night of her life was *Teahouse of the August Moon*, for which Brando starved himself in order to play the Japanese interpreter Sakini. Now, in one of those uncanny coincidences that guide us through life, if we let them, their wild-looking saviour turned out to be Japanese.

His name sounded like Ee-zay and he was travelling "solo," he said.

By means of a map and some English and a good deal of gesturing, he told them he was coming from Snowdrift on Great Slave Lake and heading to Chantrey Inlet on the arctic coast by way of the Back River. Through his binoculars he'd seen their tent, which stood out, being in such an unlikely place. Wanting to stretch his legs, wanting to be sure they were all right, he had hiked the low ridge behind them. His own canoe was out of sight around a bend.

A Saint Christopher medallion hung around his neck. Eleanor pointed to it in some surprise and his face lit up. "Is your?" he asked, and undid the fastener and handed it to her.

After that, Eleanor couldn't stop smiling. You never know how help will come, she thought, or in what form. She felt protected, rather like the Thelon River wildlife sanctuary to which they were headed. *Nothing bad is going to happen to us.* The idea was like a crystal-clear hallucination, the product of a wild coincidence in a wild place.

Tonight Ee-zay would paddle and portage until he reached – he pointed at the map – Ptarmigan Lake, which was their destination too, not that they would get there as soon as this solitary adventurer. He liked to travel all night, he told them, when it wasn't so windy, then sleep during the day, then take off again. They could follow him, he indicated, and they would probably find their companions. By now it was after midnight and the silver lichen had a sheen rising off it like the wavery heat rising from a toaster.

They struck Harry's tent and packed their canoe and the three of them paddled until they reached Ee-zay's canoe. Then he led the way out of the back channel in which they'd been lost, and canoeing towards them came the search party of Gwen and Ralph. With that, the lonely Barrens turned into a place of domestic ease and multiple embraces. They beached their canoes and suddenly there was chocolate, dried fruit, conversation, laughter, repeated avowals of never letting you out of my sight. Ralph offered Eleanor morsels of chocolate on his fingertips, and in leaning towards him she caught an old childhood smell of Christmas: nicotine and chocolate and raisins — it was her father at the foot of her bed filling her stocking after he thought she was fast asleep.

They made tea, having a Barren Lands tea ceremony at one in the morning, boiling the water in a billy can, then dropping a bag of black tea into the water and serving it with sugar to their impressive Japanese traveller. Gwen got her tape recorder out of its brown canvas bag and their wild angel talked into it; he had a delightful way of saying pee-nuts ba-ta-, which seemed to be his mainstay along with any fish he caught. They gave him some of their supply of chocolate and dried apricots, then they all returned to their canoes and paddled to the entrance of the Lockhart River, where Gwen and Ralph had set up camp on an island. Ee-zay kept going and they watched his progress into what he called "the big of Ca-na-da."

Watching him disappear, Harry had a sudden intuition and felt somebody walk over his grave. Doug Palliser, Lorna Dargabble's first husband, who had drowned making a trek to the Arctic Ocean, had light brown hair. Lorna, he said to the others, must have gone out into the arctic night, holding in her hand a lock of her dead husband's hair.

THE NEXT MORNING they woke up on their island in the Lockhart River to fierce winds. The stillness of the night before now seemed like a mirage. This pattern of a golden evening followed by its opposite, of silence as the precursor to violent gusts of wind, wouldn't register in all its significance until it was too late.

What registered instead was the need to ignore bad weather. From Ralph, Eleanor was learning how it ought to be handled, not as reason for melancholy but as material for rough humour; he was always girding his loins and sallying forth "to be bloody, bold and resolute," treating as a romp the weather that made Harry so morose. Before breakfast Ralph had been out filling their canoes with rocks to prevent the wind from lifting them and tumbling them hundreds of feet down the shore.

Now it was late morning. Eleanor was in her tent, writing up the events of the day before and describing the terrible noise of unimpeded winds tearing at the nylon, the ropes, the poles on either side. *We pass our days in beauty and in drudgery,* she wrote, *like Cinderella.*

Gwen was beside her, stretched out in her sleeping bag, reading Eleanor's Bible.

"I'm too resistant," she said, putting it down after a few minutes.

"What are you afraid of?" Eleanor asked gently, looking up from her notebook.

Gwen was staring at the orange ceiling three feet above her head. "I'm afraid of being taken over," she said at last. "Of having to give up too much."

"Do you have so much?"

"I don't have much at all. But what I have is me."

"You wouldn't be less you, that's what I've discovered. You'd be more you."

"Oh, I'm as much of me as I can stand."

This conversation, once begun, threaded its way through the next little while with Eleanor saying to Gwen that her fear of being effaced was natural, but didn't she realize that her fears already effaced her? "I'm not trying to convert you when I say that Christ saved me from that sort of narrowness."

But there were certain words Gwen detested, among them: Christ, goodness, salvation, sin, saviour.

Gwen tried to figure herself out as the tent billowed sideways in the wind and the sound of flapping worked on her nerves. Earlier Ralph had said the wind sometimes blew steady for weeks, it blew for thirty days straight one year in Baker Lake. He'd pointed to willows so tiny they sat an inch or so above the ground, the wood tough and fibrous and lateral. He said it could take a hundred years for one of those roots to reach the size of a thumb. Now Gwen heard a bird call, only one, in the wind. Later, she would hear the sound of a door banging shut, and recognize it as the sound of her own deep longing for permanent shelter. It must have been a rock falling, she thought.

"Eleanor?"

"Yes?"

"What did you mean when you were talking about blind spots? I mean, being in love and not knowing it?"

"Have you noticed the way Harry looks at you?"

Gwen frowned. "That doesn't mean anything. He's in love with Dido."

"That's what he thinks too. Poor wretch."

On the second wind-bound morning on their island, Gwen picked up Eleanor's *Varieties of Religious Experience* and in the soft orange light of the tent became engrossed in William James. He certainly was a very good writer, she thought to herself, and there was something in his spiritual case histories that thrilled her. What she loved were all the outer details that clothed inner change. You knew a change was coming, you even knew what form it would take, but the details varied, the struggle varied, the language varied. One woman said, "I did lie down in the stream of life and let it flow over me."

Gwen closed the book and let herself feel the same marvellous thing.

Harry was beside the fire. He was thinking of Dido's *I love you* as the elevator closed, of the lingering look on her face. He was thinking of her voice, the way she pronounced *Harry* as if it were a problem she couldn't fix.

After she'd gone, there had been a lot of mail from listeners who missed her, who wanted to know what had become of her. One listener wrote that Dido was the first intelligent woman he'd heard on the radio. "Her voice was a balm." And Harry wrote back to say that Dido Paris had gone on to greener fields. The word *balm* had stayed with him as a perfect description of her sound. Only a few voices, he thought, were so expressive. And he remembered an old poet he'd heard on the radio once.

"Something's bothering you." Those blue eyes, bluer than ever, searched his face. "What are you thinking about?"

He poked the fire with a stick and Gwen noticed his broken fingernails, his banged-up knuckles. Then he looked up, and discovered an exit from his mood in her sunburnt, teaseable face.

"I was thinking about an old poet I heard reminiscing on the radio years ago. He said he was looking out the window when lightning struck the tree in his garden, and it threw off its bark, he said, 'like a girl flinging off her clothes.'"

Gwen laughed. "*That* I'd like to see. But not as much as you would, I think."

After lunch the wind dropped, and they scrambled to take advantage. They left their island and paddled up the Lockhart River. By evening they'd reached the rapids below Ptarmigan Lake and camped. July 3. Harry made a supper of "beef stew isolé" and Ralph headed up a hill with his binoculars, only to come back with "the foul, dank and dreadful news" that Ptarmigan Lake was also covered in ice.

The next day they moved one mile – over the portage to Ptarmigan Lake and back into a frozen world.

"'O me, my heart, my rising heart,'" groaned Ralph.

But then he put on his sneakers, stepped into the ribbon of icy water at the rocky edge, and began to muscle his canoe forward. The others followed, sliding, slipping, falling, cursing, until they came to a sheltered bay, where they set up camp in a thicket of small willows.

In the morning they woke to what they thought was rain falling on their tents. But it sounded odd until they realized it was snow. Snow falls more lightly than rain, and, if anything, it's wetter, the way it clings and melts. July 5.

In their willow thicket, their little rabbit warren, everything they did soaked them through – brushing against wet bushes to gather wet wood, breaking wet branches, cooking with wet dishes. The snow fell like wet feathers into the pot heating on the fire, it cruised down, thought Harry, knowing from Dido that *cruise* comes from *kruizen* for the zigzag motion of boats evading pirate attacks at sea. He looked up and for one brief moment saw a bush full of roses, orangey-red roses. But it was Gwen's tent in the snow.

Ralph was saying, "A day like today makes me appreciate a day like yesterday." He meant coming to a standstill made him appreciate a day of hard slogging.

"Twenty-two more days," grumbled Harry, "and the fifth day this week we've been weather-bound. Two hours to make bannock."

"An hour and a half," said Ralph.

Harry leaned back. Ralph seemed to be getting younger and fitter with each passing day. He was having the time of his life. He was even sleeping well, as Harry knew from having to endure his freight train of snores every night. "You've always got something to say. I say two hours. You say an hour and a half."

"That's making conversation, Harry. Most people want a response when they say something."

Gwen turned, grabbed Harry's foot. Tugged it. "You really want to know the difference between you two?"

"No."

"I'll tell you anyway."

"I'm sure you will," he said acidly.

But she held her tongue. She turned her face away.

Curious, Eleanor asked her, "What's really the difference?"

"No. Harry doesn't want to know."

A few hours later, when they found themselves alone, Gwen said to Harry, "You don't want to be here."

"You're right. I'd give anything for a plane to come and get me right now. Would you come with me? Would you run away with me, Gwen?"

She gave him a look meant to squelch his nonsense, but not entirely. Not entirely.

Eleanor examined her hands and said they'd aged thirty years in three weeks, they were the hands of an old fisherman. She held them out and they were large and cracked, red and rough in patches, swollen and scraped from sun and weather, from cold and wet. She said her father came to Canada and never wore gloves in the winter, they don't in England, and his hands were the mottled blue and red and purple of old books on shelves.

They all glanced at their sore hands with a certain amount of wonder and pity, and Gwen asked if they'd ever had their palms read.

No one had, except Gwen herself. She rolled her eyes. "The fortune teller told me I was a natural healer under a great deal of stress. I almost asked for my money back."

Harry grinned. "You were hoping for fame and glory?"

"At least."

The talk of colours and turns in fortune had Ralph thumbing through his copy of Farley Mowat, looking for and finding an excerpt from *Glimpses of the Barren Lands* by Thierry Mallet, a fur trader with Revillon Frères, who published his little book in 1930. One day Mallet came upon two little Eskimo girls helping their blind grandmother gather willow twigs. "'*Their faces were round and healthy, the skin sunburned to a dark copper colour, but their cheeks showed a tinge of blood which gave them, under the tan, a peculiar complexion like the colour of a ripe plum. Their little hands were bare and black, the scratches caused by the dead twigs showing plainly in white, while their fingers seemed cramped with the cold.*'

"What a painting," Ralph exclaimed.

He read on and the story was unforgettable. Mallet encountered a small band of inland Eskimos fishing through the ice one winter. Like Hornby, they had missed the herds of caribou in the fall and they were starving. Mallet and his guide gave them some of their food – the Eskimos were courteous to a fault – and learned their intentions: if the fishing didn't improve they would head for a lake twelve-days' walk to the northwest in the hope of finding muskoxen. In the spring, Mallet's guide and three others returned to the spot. Finding the camp deserted, they headed northwest and soon came upon the end of the story. First, a bunch of traps. Then caribou blankets. Then a child's grave, followed over the course of several days by a fish spear, a telescope, an axe, a snow knife, pairs of boots, then bodies, alone, or side by side.

They knew there were seventeen people in the band and three rifles. The old leader appeared to have fallen last, but he had no rifle beside him, and only sixteen Eskimos were accounted for. And so they kept on the trail. Five hours later they came upon the last body, a girl of twelve, who had continued on by herself, carrying the rifle, *with nothing but a sense of direction inherited from the old chief.*

How quiet they were when Ralph finished the account. After a bit, Harry joked huskily that they don't make kids like that any more, they won't leave home without a wallet full of travellers' cheques. And Gwen reached for the book and said "Thierry Mallet" slowly, as if memorizing the name, and Eleanor very gently corrected her pronunciation. "Tee-ay-ree, I think it is."

On the Barrens something happened to their sense of time. They were living every second of bad weather in a land that was barely out of the ice age, a place no different from how it had been a hundred years or a thousand years ago. They were seeing what Hornby and Samuel Hearne had seen, what aboriginal hunters had seen when they hunted here, far back. And so seconds ticked forwards and years swept backwards, and they got used to thinking of time passing in tiny increments and huge leaps.

Ralph would say that the long wait for the wind to die down – another two days of being wind-bound and ice-bound – made him think of Agamemnon waiting to set sail from Aulis. The north winds kept blowing day after day until they sacrificed Iphigenia, poor girl; then the winds fell away, the thousand ships set sail for Troy, and one thing led to another, until Aeneas fled his burning city and fetched up on the shores of Carthage, "where he broke poor Dido's heart," said Ralph, throwing Harry a sympathetic look.

With tender timing Eleanor and Gwen then compared the bruises on their legs, rolling up their pants and exposing shins that looked as if they had been beaten with sticks, but it was the ice they'd fallen against and battled through. The bruises filled Harry's mind with memories of his life with Dido. She'd been like a stray, a waif that he'd found by the shore and brought home. During those six weeks, she'd never talked very much. Never really confided in him. The black eye had been her fault, she'd said. And the bruise he saw on her arm happened from banging into a cupboard. He had to suppose that when she was with him she was just resting, recovering, biding her time until she was ready to leave.

Finally, at one in the morning, the sky began to clear. They could make out four or five ptarmigans in the meadow beyond the willows. Through binoculars they studied the male, its red markings above the eyes, its plumage a mottled brown until it flew up, and then its wings flashed white.

"What does ptarmigan taste like, I wonder," murmured Gwen.

281

"Ptough," said Ralph.

Eleanor remarked that seeing ptarmigans on Ptarmigan Lake was rather like seeing Harry on Harry Lake.

"You mean I washed myself in Harry?" cried Gwen.

"How lovely," said Harry.

———

It was noon of the next day. They were almost out of Ptarmigan Lake, having broken free of their snow-locked, weather-bound state by throwing caution to the winds. In the morning they'd hauled their canoes with ropes across the middle of the frozen lake, making several miles of progress. Gwen managed to tape the sound by hanging her tape recorder around her neck and holding the microphone between her teeth; Harry snapped a picture for what he called broadcasting posterity.

They skirted the blackest ice, the last stretch so rotten his feet did a little dance as he sped across. And then they were in open water. July 7.

In the early afternoon, a line of light blue appeared at the lower edge of the sky and in the distance something moved. A palomino boulder was swimming slowly across the lake. They paddled towards it and saw their first caribou, large and handsome, like a heavily built deer with a rack of dark antlers.

By evening the sky was clear. The light luminous and rich. Not brilliant as in the Mediterranean (where Harry once removed a splinter from a woman's finger on the streets of Sète in light that acted like a magnifying glass). Gentler. Almost autumnal. The hills didn't have light on them, they were in light, the way something is in water.

To Harry it seemed the Barrens relaxed. *One day something relaxed inside and I saw things in a new way.* The words came from an old book about an old botanist, and he felt the truth of them as they left behind frozen lakes and entered a land of flowing rivers. On July 8 they were on the Hanbury River, skimming along with the current, running two rapids and making three portages and completing a total of twenty-three miles. A grand day. That night they reached Sifton Lake and it too was melted, the next night they took advantage of an evening with almost no wind to keep paddling, hour after hour, in the pure golden light.

At midnight they beached their canoes and were about to make camp on an invitingly grassy bank when they saw, just across a small cove, something move.

They slipped back into their canoes and paddled closer. The grizzly was smaller than they'd imagined and very curious. It came to the water's edge, then waded into the water, climbing atop a rock several feet from shore. From there it stood watching them for fifteen minutes, brownish-blond, face like a wide dish, close-set eyes. At a distance of fifty yards, or less, they took pictures in the evening light. Then the bear turned around, waded back to shore, and ambled up onto a grass-covered knoll, where it lay down and went to sleep. They had no firearms, having failed to take Teresa's advice, and Harry suspected they'd been far too trusting, but the charmed evening had emboldened them. Even so, they paddled a full hour before they set up camp.

Several days after that, on July 13, a muskox in the afternoon. The bizarre beast appeared suddenly after miles of nothing. Dark massive head, down-curved horns, a fur coat like a chocolate-brown kilt, except along the uppermost part of the animal's back where it was lighter in colour as if faded by the sun. In the 1920s, said Ralph, after the decimation of the buffalo, muskox furs were in such demand for carriage robes that only protective legislation, inspired in no small part by John Hornby's observations and recommendations, saved them from being wiped off the face of the earth. This fellow stood on the riverbank with the blue sky behind him and sparse leafiness around his feet. After a few minutes he lumbered off into the distance, Ralph in careful pursuit with his camera, Eleanor calling after him to be careful: *Ralph!*

The next day, a group of three muskoxen. The animals thundered off and the humans inherited their flies. At supper mosquitoes plunged into the soup, kamikaze pilots in love with soggy death. Harry's emptied bowl had a dozen dead mosquitoes in the bottom. Eleanor took the bowl, turned it three times, and read the mosquitoes like tea leaves.

"I see a boy stung by bees," she said to Harry. "Six bee stings. No seven."

"Not a girl stripping off her clothes?" cracked Gwen, handing her own bowl to gypsy Eleanor, who turned it three times and said she saw a sudden change of course followed by a wedding.

Ralph instructed Eleanor to see money in his mosquito-leaves, huge sacks of it, mountains of it. But Eleanor saw, instead, a great expanse of water and suggested to Ralph that he might be going overseas.

By now Gwen's hair was sun-streaked and her face ruddy. "'As brown in hue as hazel nuts and sweeter than the kernels,'" remarked Harry, addressing her with a gleam in his eye.

She blushed and raised her hands, which were too dried and cracked to close. "They feel like baseball mitts," she said.

Harry surprised her by taking one of her hands in his. "I have just the thing."

From his pack he produced a tin of udder balm for chapped and swollen teats, then proceeded to work the ointment into her skin, especially her split fingertips. "What about your feet? Take off your boots," he said.

"What is the smoothest part of Gwen?" He reached for her bare foot, only to exclaim, "Not the heel!" His eyes widened. "You could do permanent damage with this heel."

Gwen's heels had never been so in the limelight, her rough, raspy heels. Harry would see them again when her tent blew down and she was out flying around in the middle of the night in bare legs and white heels and nightie, trying to re-stake and prop it up, while Eleanor held it down from inside. From his tent door Harry shouted at her to lay it flat and bring their sleeping bags in here, and Gwen shouted something back that he couldn't make out, for in the wind their voices tore like fabric.

Gwen later admitted she had seriously underestimated the importance of good shelter by bringing "that shitty tent," which sagged like a soft berry picked by the weather and man-handled between its fingers.

That night they lay across the floor of Harry's tent like four slumbering sardines.

WHERE THE DARRELL RIVER met the Hanbury River, they passed into the Thelon Game Sanctuary. It wasn't a definite shape but a continuation of what they'd seen, yet it took on the shape in Harry's mind of a garden, a garden in the wilderness. Now there were scattered trees again, more and more trees. On a single day, July 15, they portaged around Macdonald Falls, Dickson Canyon, and Ford Falls, about three and a quarter miles in all. Between the first and second carry, they walked back along the edge of Dickson Canyon and saw rough-legged hawks above, and churning water below, as well as three large pools to one side fed by the rapids, each pool feeding the one below, deep green water in which grayling swam. On a hill Harry noticed muskox hair caught in the willows and low trees, the soft wool called *qiviut*, so Eleanor informed him when she came alongside. She picked tufts of it off the twigs and slipped them into her pocket, reminded of poor Absalom caught by his beautiful hair in the branches of the biblical oak, and of Lorna holding that tuft of hair in her dead hand, and of the first Dido whose spirit wouldn't leave her dying body, Virgil said, until Iris descended and cut off a tress of her hair.

When finally they came to a halt that day, Harry soaked his head and feet and sore knee in the Hanbury River. They were on a beautiful sand dune – white sand beyond their tents, white snow above the sand. Fox and caribou tracks in evidence. And Gwen washing her hair.

"Always washing your hair," Harry said to her.

"Always watching me wash my hair," she said back.

She got him to stand behind her and wave away the flies and he felt like a painter with "Woman Shampooing Hair" on his easel.

"Your face is thinner," he told her when she turned around, her head wrapped in a towel. "You've developed cheekbones."

Eleanor looked up and watched the two of them for a long moment. The out-of-doors as beautician, she thought. Tanning Gwen's skin, lightening her hair, lengthening it (hair grows three times as fast in the summer she'd learned from Lorna Dargabble, as do toenails). Gwen's shirt was bone-coloured, bleached by the long light. And now the animals were appearing and the story was coming to an end, the story her father was reading to her when he died, since that would have been what happened: the ostracized, runaway girl would have been helped by the animals in the forest, and then some admirer would have come along, perhaps a secret admirer who had always appreciated her without knowing he was in love. And wouldn't the girl be looking the wrong way at the time, since isn't it the hardest lesson in the world, learning to appreciate people if you've never felt appreciated?

They were finding things, one after the other. A black thread hanging from a low willow. A weathered orange pip on a rock. A lantern base of heavy glass, and some fox traps left behind at the foot of a portage. A handmade sled runner, or so it appeared to Ralph, who pronounced it made in Captain Back's time. The 1830s. In the absence of trees that shed their leaves in autumn, objects could sit in the open for decades, centuries.

One night Harry caught a sizable grayling, a fish that was dull-brown in the water but vivid out of its element – in its death throes it went through a troubled array of colours from purply blue-black on its body to brilliant red spots on its large dorsal fin. Harry knelt to clean and fillet the pretty fish. He cut across the backbone, but left the tail in place in order to have something to hold on to when he skinned it. The carcass he threw into the river, having first shown Gwen what the fish had been eating: smaller fish, partially digested, the colour and consistency of grey glue. Gwen had her cassette recorder over her shoulder and she taped the sounds of scraping, eviscerating, slicing, rinsing.

This was the night, July 17, Eleanor elected not to go to bed at all in order to experience the brief middle-of-the-night twilight with its profusion of violet clouds directly overhead and its yellow gleam in the northern sky. Dressed in wool pants, wool jacket, gloves, with bug repellant smeared on her face and neck, she lay on her back on the warm, mattressy tundra whose thick growth held on to the day's heat. Tweedy smells rose from the soft tangle straight into her nostrils. The colours and textures at eye level, the russets, browns, blacks, reds, formed an embrace so gently erotic she dozed off with a smile on her lips, only to come awake when a ptarmigan whirred by, or a snowy owl flew down and sat on a big stone twenty feet away, or loons cried in the distance. The loon's long call seemed to her like a statement of the hour, a horizontal sound that tapered off into the horizon, while its laughter was vertical, high, flashy, rippling. The Barrens themselves were horizontal, but vertical, too, she thought. A vertical world of air: a country of clouds, an abundance of wind.

"You were the only sleepers," she said in the morning. "Everything else was awake."

The air, she claimed, was ten degrees warmer in among the plants than a foot above, and several degrees warmer still inside the actual blossoms. Ralph, wanting proof, knelt beside her and felt the warm air swell up from the heated plants, the tundra less a riot of colour, he said, to her everlasting delight, than a peaceful demonstration. She thought of the cool air that blows over your skin when you meet someone. Then with some few you feel warmer, as it was warmer by these vivid ten degrees close to Ralph, and close to the arctic ground, to the tussocks of moss and low cushion plants and ground-hugging berries and spreading mats of grasses and flowers and such.

Together they examined the tiny complete world at their fingertips. Over the last few weeks she'd identified flowers like yellow arnica, white-petalled arctic dryad with its look of wild roses, yellow and violet oxytrope and wild sweet pea, pressing them into her pocket-sized notebook and making sketches and lists: of the chickweeds or starworts with their little white starlike flowers, the violet and yellow louseworts rising up out of the moss, the pink arctic fireweed, yellow arctic poppy, twiggy Labrador tea with its neat, round clusters of white flowers and narrow rolled-under leaves, the buttercups, milk-vetch, white and purple saxifrage, the small, white bells of the arctic heather, the red-violet clusters of Lapland rosebay like miniature rhododendrons, the dwarf pink azalea.

When she and Ralph stood up, their eyes took in the full extent of the boundless northern wastes. Every foot of evenly rising plains and worn-away hills was as detailed as the small bit they were standing on.

A long-tailed jaeger flew overhead, its tail like a dark, slender, beautiful paintbrush. Sometimes, said Ralph, the canny suitor, he felt life ripple through him, connecting him to every other living thing, and his own existence was the least of it and the most of it. Yes, she said.

They came down off the tundra as if hand in hand, and joined Harry and Gwen at the water's edge. The river and the landscape it ran through stretched in immensity on either side – what vastness they had dropped in to visit – yet in each other's company, this fellowship of four souls, they felt light-headedly secure.

The next evening Eleanor came upon Harry sitting by himself on a knoll not far from the campsite, smoking a cigarette. She sat beside him and without looking at her he reached over and took her hand. The tundra rolled away into the distance, the undulating barren hills, the immense light.

"I want to know something," he said to her. "When Dido phoned you, did she even mention my name?"

Eleanor didn't answer for a moment. "Do you mean, did she say she wanted to see you or talk to you? No, Harry. She didn't."

Harry nodded. With a bitterness he wished he could rise above, he said, "I can't figure out what she sees in Eddy."

Eleanor reflected. "Maybe he makes her feel good about being bad."

Harry let out a short laugh.

"There's Gwen," said Eleanor.

They saw her heading off on her own, walking towards a ridge of land a short distance away. Her head was down. Her tape recorder was around her neck and she steadied it with one hand. She waved flies away with the other.

"What will become of her, do you think?" asked Eleanor.

"Eddy's going to ruin her life."

"I meant Gwen."

"Ah," said Harry.

Gwen had shortened the shoulder strap on her cassette recorder and hung it low enough on her chest to see the levels on the VU meter; easier to walk this way too. She looked down, alert to sounds, but otherwise lost in what Harry would have called a brown study; she was thinking about his soft, swollen ear and about his other appendages, wondering about them idly, not so idly, as the look of the scruffy heath imprinted itself on her eyes.

At the sound of loons, she automatically pressed record and stood listening to birds that mated for life, their beautiful mad laughter. What held her eye, however, was the look of her hand on the microphone. So weathered and chapped compared to the silver-metallic stem she was holding carefully, no rings on her fingers to click against the metal and transfer to the dark spool of tape, her equipment solid and unchanging and Japanese, her veins purply under the roughened, reddish-brown skin. She saw her hand on a doorknob, pushing open a bedroom door, and the phrase "inquiry without walls" came into her head, the Barrens like Berger's commission: you learned a great deal, more than you wanted to know sometimes, more than you knew what to do with. Could there be a more primitive, naked, intimate sound than the heavy breathing, the solitary moan and whimper she'd heard from inside Harry's tent an hour ago? The physical side of life, which stretched in utter loneliness and tenderness all around her.

A WOLF, WHITE, OLD, MANGY, ARTHRITIC, slowly stretched and yawned on the riverbank as they paddled by. A harbinger, had they but known. By now it was July 20 and they were on the wide, smooth, east-flowing Thelon River, seven days from the end.

Ralph spotted shapes moving in the distance. Gwen thought they must be geese, they were used to geese running along the shore. They drew closer and the scales fell from their eyes. A group of fifteen caribou were crossing the river ahead of them, antlers like high heels rising from their heads.

They paddled to the south side of the river, as did Harry and Eleanor, and waited with thumping hearts for the caribou to come towards them along the shore, but the animals clambered out of the water and went the other way. Then another smaller group swam across the river and they too went up the sloping bank through low willows and spruce, then up over the rocky ridge and out of sight.

They had lunch on the rise of land above the river and realized they were on the edge of a large herd. Caribou in the hundreds were all around them, in the distance and moving slowly, or not moving at all, blending in like boulders on the open tundra of grass and heath and rounded hills. What they'd been hoping for was finally happening.

La foule. The word came unbidden to Ralph from accounts of the great migrations of the past. It was like witnessing the arrival of a myth: the caribou emerged from the land and belonged to it, tentative, purposeful, graceful, shy, their colours buff, brown, grey, pale, Gwen's colours when she first arrived at the station. What they were seeing was the mass arrival of something beautifully recessive and fleeting. They could have missed it just as easily, a few hours one way or the other.

Ralph nestled against the lip of a low hill and looked through long grass at the large herd on the other side. Eleanor was close to him. Not far away was Gwen, her cassette recorder around her neck, her microphone in her hand, when a cow and calf came thundering right up to them, unaware of their presence, then ran off a bit, then came closer again. Soon several caribou were eating willow leaves just twenty feet below them. Gwen taped the sounds of their soft lips pulling off small leaves, the quiet sounds of chewing. A male reached around and scratched his back leg with his antlers. Dark, velvet, bone.

Black antlers above the greenery, the willows, the water. The look of heavy mascara around their eyes. The ripples of movement that occurred when one animal started and the rest followed. They were like camels in the sand dunes, beautiful on the blond hills, moving and gathering, arranging themselves in small, elegant groups around the willows, like a series of almost still-lifes.

Harry called softly. A group of ten was coming down the shore towards their canoes. The others followed him and stood very still under the high-pitched hum of clouds of gnats, watching intently and with enormous excitement. Gwen taped the sound of hooves splashing at the water's edge. Loud, their coming and going, yet subdued, and soon over. The large numbers that gathered on their side of the river all afternoon were spooked about seven in the evening. Having filed down to the water and along it, maybe five hundred, seven hundred animals, they suddenly drew back up over the bank and over the hill and out of sight across the tundra.

"I think we're in a thin place," Ralph murmured, remembering his father's passion for the Celts. "Where seen and unseen meet."

That being the very definition of this ancient caribou crossing, where the river narrowed and offered passage to the other side. The animals were every bit as sensitive as the witnesses at the Berger Inquiry had claimed, and this wasn't even their most skittish time. The calving and post-calving had occurred farther north, and now, less urgently, they were engaged in the long return to the timberline.

So quiet, whispered Eleanor. So easily not seen, and then so easily lost. She and Ralph stood together watching straggling cows with their calves, and solitary calves. On the opposite shore a bull and a calf entered the water and began to swim across, a twosome. But halfway, the calf dropped out of sight and didn't resurface, no matter how long they kept looking.

They were alone again "in the land of feast and famine." Nothing for so long, and then abundance, and then nothing again, but a nothing haunted by the previous abundance.

That night, thumbing backwards through Whalley's book, Ralph came upon Edgar, raw-boned and white in his photograph. Parted hair and ears sticking out. Then Hornby's emaciated face after one of his starving winters near Fort Reliance. The sunken, glittering eyes. The amiable smile. The head of hair still dark and thick. In 1925, the year before his last journey, Hornby was travelling with James Critchell-Bullock, an ex-army officer turned traveller-photographer-collector. After a squalid winter near Artillery Lake, holed up in a collapsing cave dug into the side of a sand esker, they were making their miserable way to Hudson Bay. On the evening of July 23, they sighted "a large group of caribou moving southwest on the south shore: about two thousand animals, mostly females, 'moving all over the hills making a tremendous noise calling to one another . . . a beautiful sight on the sand hills with the gold of the sunshine reflected on the water.'" Another sixty miles and the two men came to the sharp double bend in the river that took Hornby's fancy and sealed his fate, for on the north side rose a fine stand of white spruce that inspired thoughts of building a house and overwintering.

Ralph set down the book, understanding an aspect of Hornby for the first time: he had been seduced by the idea of a well-built home instead of a filthy cave or soggy tent or crummy tarp. The tiny, extraordinarily tough, self-destructive Englishman had actually been seeking a wild kind of comfort.

In himself something similar was going on. He felt a growing desire to be attached, not to a place but to a person.

For years he'd made a habit of keeping his options open, of not letting himself be pinned down, an approach to life that seemed almost juvenile to him now. They'd come such a long distance already, he and Eleanor and the others. They were two-thirds of the way there, two-thirds of the way home, and he felt more sure of his next step than he'd ever felt about anything. Eleanor wasn't even forty and he was sixty-one, but on the last night of their trip he would ask her to marry him.

The next day they paddled on. The air was calm. The mosquitoes ferocious, almost as plentiful as the caribou hair in the bushes and at the water's edge, white, brittle, hollow hairs and some finer fluff, a floating mattress of hair. The shore, formerly flat and hard, was churned up by hooves.

Clumps of Labrador tea among the rocks. A few terns overhead. Ashes from their small tea fire blown about by a sudden gust of wind. And the need to make twenty-two, twenty-three miles a day if they were to reach Beverly Lake on time.

And again they were among the caribou. Thousands of them were crossing the river that afternoon. In their canoes they drifted with the current while the caribou circled around them and continued swimming to shore, then climbed the bank, their dark antlers magnificent amidst the greenery in this paradise of leafiness and sky. Clumps of trees thickened into woods on the hills, hair covered the water, the shore, the grass. Grunting, so many of them now, like pigs rooting, mud and grass churned up. A heavy manure smell in the air. And Gwen recording.

More and more came, the hillside emptied and filled again. Caribou filed across the horizon on a high ridge, then down the steep slope to the water, a line of strolling players with the sky behind them and a wolf invariably bringing up the rear. The effect was joyous and spellbinding and sobering. Over supper Eleanor said she felt like giving thanks for Judge Berger, who would see to it that these vanishing herds were protected.

"The government must rue the day they appointed him," chuckled Ralph.

"He's a special man," Eleanor said, fingering the medallion's chain around her neck. "I can't imagine anyone else in the part."

No one disagreed. For five minutes.

Then Gwen wondered aloud if he wasn't too gullible. He gave the impression of believing every word every native witness said, but weren't they as human as anyone else, as capable of self-interest and poetical exaggeration? She wondered if the bond they felt with the land and the animals was as genuine now as in the past, before they had high-powered rifles and snowmobiles.

Harry said she had a point, but insisting on purity wasn't fair. The natives felt a connection to the land, he said, that was almost incomprehensible to us. He said he had the sense of miraculous brakes being applied. He was betting on Berger, betting he would manage to delay for a considerable time the onslaught of development. "And if that's possible, what isn't?"

The next afternoon they were looking at John Hornby's grave in the sun. Three simple, weathered, wooden crosses shored up by rocks piled at the base of each one. EC. JH. HA. The ruined cabin just to the left, its bottom logs still in place, but the roof fallen in, and the walls. Some caribou antlers inside the cabin and more just outside the door. It was July 22.

They had come 350 miles, from old Fort Reliance to this beautiful spot, an open bank rising up steeply on the north side of the river to the famous stand of spruce. Late afternoon, the warm sun shining, and after an hour of looking and taking photographs, they decided to stay for the night. Gwen wandered around the little makeshift cemetery, the remains of the cabin, and then she headed off on her own, her brown canvas tape recorder bag over her shoulder.

Harry was making supper. He was saying to Eleanor that young Edgar's fate reminded him of what happened to the Eskimo girl in the Thierry Mallet story. The last one left alive carries on.

He'd borrowed Ralph's copy of Whalley's biography and read the final pages that described Edgar letting the fire in the stove die out. Edgar placed his companions' papers and his own diary in the cool ashes, then lay down on his bunk and pulled the blankets up and over his head. Whalley imagined the sounds he might have heard, perhaps "the faint sound of ptarmigan feeding outside," and the effect of the silence, "like wings folding about him."

What Harry admired so much was Whalley's restraint in telling the story. Whalley was like Berger in that way. He didn't pick on people. He didn't ridicule Hornby for his mistakes, or excoriate him. He could have so easily. A journalist would have.

He added another stick to the fire and saw Ralph coming up from the river, but he didn't see Gwen. And then he heard her.

Gwen had climbed the wooded slope that rose gently behind the cabin, looking for signs of Hornby and finding them in the axe cuts in old stumps that she'd read about. She had her eyes down to negotiate the branch-littered ground, the thick ground cover. A little farther and she thought she might get a fine view of the river below. In the northwest corner of this fringe of trees between cabin and open Barrens, she expected to find the windbreak of stones Hornby had erected from which they watched for caribou. In her mind she was with Hornby and Edgar and Harold Adlard as they made the same ascent, alone or together, early on when they were healthy and strong, and then later when they were desperate. Once, they saw thirty caribou in the distance and thought salvation was at hand, but the animals disappeared before they could get close to them. She turned to look south towards the river, but the twisted, slow-growing trees, some of them at least four hundred years old, still blocked the view. She turned back and saw something blondish-brown out of the corner of her eye. Fifty feet away? They aren't huge animals. They don't have to be huge. It lifted its nose and sniffed.

Experts say to avoid eye contact. To back away quietly. Not to turn and run.

Gwen's scream coincided with her seeing a set of small, black, gleaming eyes. She turned and ran.

It was like going full tilt down a flight of stairs covered in books. She felt her feet go out from under her even as she tumbled forward, and instinctively she grabbed at the nearest tree and slowed her descent at the expense of her arm. Her right shoulder wrenched out of its socket. Then she was lying in a small heap, the pain so intense she couldn't make a sound.

Her head slid forward to rest on the ground and she bit down on the dead branch that offered itself, aware in a flickering part of her brain of an age when biting down on wood offered the only consolation in moments of physical agony. Her shoulder wasn't there, nauseatingly not there, but her heart was bouncing her off the ground. She heard the bear behind her, then beside her. She heard its heavy breathing. She felt it nose her left leg and she bit harder into the wood. It nosed her leg a second time and she closed her eyes, lay completely still, apart from her thumping, cartoonish heart. She smelled the animal. Heard the saliva bubbling in its mouth. Kept as quiet as she always had at the dining-room table when a wave of fury would darken her father's face. She braced herself for more pain, and heard the bear moving, and realized it was moving away.

When they found her, she was coming slowly towards them like a shell-shocked survivor of the trenches or the highway. She saw them and sank to her knees.

Harry was beside her.

"Shoulder," she managed.

She felt his hands on her shoulder, and with a slight, subtle adjustment her arm was amazingly back in place.

"I thought you were proposing," he would say later, bringing a weak smile to her face.

He helped her to her feet and she breathed out, "We're not camping here."

The next morning, before the others were up, Harry went down to the water. They had paddled two hours beyond Hornby Point (he and Eleanor taking more of the load in their canoe so that Ralph could paddle alone as Gwen rested her shoulder, to say nothing of her mind) and they'd camped on a steep bank on the opposite side of the river, to be extra sure. Harry hadn't slept much, thinking about Gwen and the grizzly, wondering if they were travelling under a lucky star or if their luck had run out. He would never forget the sight of her coming down the slope. She looked damaged, lopsided, wrong. They had to brush twigs and leaves off her cheeks and forehead, but the imprint remained for hours.

They'd talked at length about how long it lasted, her encounter with the bear. Not as long as she thought, he was sure of that; a second with a grizzly is an eternity by any measure. He'd heard her terrifying scream, they all had, and they'd come charging up the hill and through the trees, but she hadn't heard them. They were downwind for one thing. In Gwen's mind there was only the noise of the bear's breathing, a kind of huffing, a moist huffing, and the powerful reek of animal, and the memory of small, cold eyes. It nosed her leg "like a teacher tapping your shoulder in the hall," she said, and she'd tapped Harry's shoulder to demonstrate, not hard: sending a chill down his spine. *Detention, young man.*

Now, as he came down to the water, he saw a tiny calf, its side ripped open, resting under a tree. It struggled to its feet upon seeing him and ran desperately into the water, then tottered back to shore, then back into the water and back to shore, where it collapsed, "all tuckered out," he would tell the others at breakfast. Using the biggest stick he could find, he put the little chap out of its misery with three hard blows. Then he reached for his knife. It took him a long time to dress the meat; he was reminded as he worked of his grandfather, of all the furriers and trappers and woodsmen who constituted a dwindling breed of their own. Often they were the most soft-hearted of men, and it had to do with being on the land so much, something the anti-trappers would never understand. That night they had caribou veal and it was certainly his most delicious and most poignant culinary dish.

Eleanor told them about her father speaking very fondly of a dinner he'd had at the Waldorf Hotel in New York. Green turtle soup, double breast of grey partridge, and strawberry mousse. This meal was just as memorable, "but I wonder if I'll talk about it quite so much."

"Gwen?" Harry offered her seconds.

She was hungry, as hungry as someone who's just escaped the firing squad, and she held out her plate. She'd done every-thing wrong, she knew, fleeing when she should have stood her ground, turning herself into prey. Yet here she was, still alive. The world around her tingled with life.

Gwen saw admiration in Harry's eyes, and in Ralph's and Eleanor's too, and she basked in it. But when they told her how brave she was, she shook her head. "You should hear me when I get a paper cut."

Later, she would say the bear's eyes were like Eddy's, small and mean. Harry would turn his hand into a micro-phone, "Now tell us how you *really* feel." And Gwen would smile, until he dropped his microphone-hand back into his lap.

Then suddenly she remembered the shoulder bag containing her tape recorder and tapes. Back there, back where she'd fallen. Back being pawed by the grizzly bear. Thus occurred their first irretrievable loss.

Gwen sat disconsolate on a flat stone and the trip ran like a reel through her mind, erasing itself as it went along. The tinkling ice on Charlton Bay, the songbirds on Pike's Portage, the sounds of paddling, straining, cursing, of crackling fires and roaring rapids and wriggling fish, of mosquitoes being slapped and long tent zippers being opened and more rapidly shut, of gargantuan snores, of footsteps among the ankle-turning stones and the whish-y tread of boots on tundra. Of Ee-zay saying pee-nuts ba-ta. Of ice-hauling accompanied by the tap of her teeth on the microphone. Most prized of all, the tapes of the Barren-ground caribou, their clicking hooves and strenuous swimming and muted eating, since who had ever recorded them before?

Harry's efforts were good-hearted, if clumsy. He suggested she could recreate what she'd lost, using sound effects and words. Gwen let out a despairing groan, but he was patient. He told her what mattered more than sound effects was the effect of sound. He liked remembering car tires going through puddles and over melting snow on the street outside school, blue jays in the woods, squirrels high in the trees — sounds that evoked the soft days when winter was turning to spring and long summer holidays were around the corner. We had a bell in the Town Hall, he said. Tom Finnegan rang it every day at noon and at five in the afternoon. If it rang hard and successively, it meant fire. Train whistles were wonderful too, and dogs barking in the distance. And the radio. I always loved the sound of the radio. "What's the first sound you remember?" She shook her head. "Come on, Lippy." And she gave in and laughed a little.

"Maybe it was the rain," she said.

"And what about the first thing you heard on the radio?"

"'Blue Suede Shoes.' I was four years old."

That set Harry off. His first piece on air was a movie review he recorded in a bedroom closet because he couldn't stand his roommate hearing him read the script. A month later he was hosting a program, and two years afterwards he was working in Toronto. "That's how quickly fortunes can turn," he said, thinking as much of what had come after as what had gone before.

This was the evening they saw a strangely beautiful group of caribou emerge from the water and slowly approach, their pattern governed by hunger and available food – by the arrangement of leaves on willows fifty feet away. No matter how they moved around the low trees, reaching up or down or forward or around, the animals seemed exquisitely placed, as if by an Old Master.

Their little group of four was also being reconfigured. In the mornings Ralph took Eleanor a cup of tea, unzipping the door of the tent she shared with Gwen, and singing snatches of songs to her when she arrived at the campfire. One evening he reached for her hand and they moved in three-four time across the widest dance floor in the world.

There were summers in Gwen's childhood when her father's favourite brother came to visit from the States, and the anticipation of his arrival, that keen pleasure, was like this one of watching Ralph and Eleanor together. To witness the two brothers greet each other, to gauge the level of their affection, to watch her sociable uncle take pleasure in her unsociable dad and her dad take pleasure in her uncle – all this was high, ardent drama. She wanted to see every moment of mutual delight and there was never quite enough to satisfy her. Did her uncle know – did he have any idea – how much her father loved him?

Something blossoms in an unlikely place. An oasis of trees miles above the treeline. An arctic river warmer than any other water they'd come upon. The four of them bathed in the waters of the Thelon, wading out into it, almost swimming. On shore they towelled themselves dry and dressed, and there was no feeling to equal the splendour of warm clothes on river-cold skin.

The next morning Ralph said to Eleanor within Gwen's hearing, "I was dreaming about you last night."

"What was I up to?"

"You were pointing with your finger at very specific places on your body that you wanted me to kiss, and I obliged you with pleasure."

Then no sooner had all of this closeness come about than it dispersed. That night Eleanor asked Harry what he was going to do with himself next, and he surprised them by saying he wanted to leave Canada behind for a while, not radio but Canada; his friend Max Berns knew people at Broadcasting House in London; he might well move to England.

In thinking it through over the past weeks, turning this way and that in his thoughts, he'd reminded himself of caribou at the river's edge. They retreated once, twice, three times. He'd never known before that migration wasn't one unbroken forward movement; it was sideways, backwards, forwards, a passage enlivened with indecision in the face of real and imagined danger. They came to the river, they shied away. He wasn't like Eleanor, he thought. He felt attuned not to the God within but to the uncertainty within. His connection was with the poor, dumb animals.

Eleanor had her own surprise. She'd been thinking about opening up a bookstore just down the street from the post office in Yellowknife, and she'd almost convinced Ralph to be her partner. Ralph grinned. "She wants my pretty coins," he said.

And once again Gwen's favourite uncle was back in the States and the first day of school was looming.

BY NOW IT WAS JULY 25 and they were making swift and easy progress to their final destination of Beverly Lake, and their last night on the Barrens. A strong current, almost no headwind. A wolf, perhaps the same one that raked open the side of the little calf, swam across the river ahead of them. A grizzly and her two cubs appeared on the riverbank; one of the cubs stood between its mother's hind legs and watched them as they paddled by. Passing an island on their left, they spotted a magnificent moose in a grassy marsh. Above them soared a golden eagle in the eggshell-blue sky.

They were seeing sunsets now. Mosquitoes became flecks of light in the evening. A rock in the water moved with flies when they approached.

The land continued hilly and pasture-green. They saw semipalmated plovers and low, protected blue flowers. The wind came back and the clouds and the rain.

That evening they boiled up a pot of soup and one of tea, a fire that would scar the tundra for years. Their effect, just passing through, wasn't insignificant. And the effect of the trip on them?

They paddled on. The woods thinned out. The sun shone. They were within reach of Beverly Lake now, and felt the swell of the lake reach up the river, waves high enough to splash Eleanor in the bow and chill her through.

They reached the lake on the afternoon of July 26. In time. The float plane would arrive in the early morning hours of the next day.

Their last campsite was on the north shore of a deep bay near the remains of two sod houses on the open tundra, little more than remarkable outlines, and the bushes around them full of muskox hair. The tundra wide, open, forever, the water calm and violet-blue, the light clear and the number of mosquitoes infinite. Eleanor pointed out a tern's nest – or egg, since the beach was the nest, a pretty egg, green and brown with some dark spots; the tern flew off as she approached.

Across the big lake, the rolling plains and undulating hills turned the horizon into a thick to thin line of dark ink. The four of them were the only moving parts in a landscape more remote from settlements of any kind than almost anywhere else in Canada.

At supper Ralph announced that he was going to shave and put on clean clothes. "No need to leave the bush looking like part of it," he said. After he reappeared, looking ten years younger, he asked Eleanor to go for a walk with him and they were gone a long time.

That evening it was perfectly still. Not a breath of wind.

Eleanor and Ralph were in the lee of a knoll on the tundra, lying together, listening to the silence, happy. Ralph told her a special memory of walking in an ancient rain forest and hearing music far away on a transistor radio, a party of geologists, he thought, and he headed towards it, curious, but the sound moved away like a bird. It was sound without a source, he said to her, reaching over to stroke her face and her hair, it was the sound of the forest itself. Here on the Barrens there wasn't music, but a hum, a vibration, the sound of the earth, he thought, and she agreed. In moments of silence, she'd heard it too. It reminded her of Buddhist singing bowls vibrating at their lowest octave.

She noticed crawling specks of light in Ralph's hair, even the mosquitoes were beautiful. She noticed how smooth his mouth was without whiskers, his lovely mouth, and how their bed was mostly white labrador tea.

The sun was low on the hills when Ralph thought of ending the trip as he began, with a last paddle, a last few pictures. Eleanor was asleep. He took off his clean shirt and arranged it gently over her face to keep away the flies. Then he went down to the shore, grabbed another shirt from his pack, took his paddle and his camera, his life vest, and slid his empty canoe into the water.

Harry saw Ralph's canoe far out on the glassy lake. He'd been walking on the tundra, and now his attention was diverted by a young caribou, perhaps a yearling, that came over the hill. It turned and skirted him. He stood still, while flies rained down upon his head and got into his eyes. He raised his hand to brush them away, by which time the caribou was some distance off. Despite the flies, he felt a tranquility on this piece of tundra that he'd hoped to feel more of the time and sooner. He headed back to shore and found Gwen sitting on a rock, tending her driftwood fire. He squatted beside her.

She'd made the fire inside a circle of stones, a little stone wall. She loved these outdoor kitchens, these uninhabited places suddenly inhabited – arranged for minimal comfort. Her brush with death was so recent, so vivid that she still felt marked, set apart from the others. It was Eleanor who'd suggested the bear might have been Hornby himself, guarding his bit of paradise, an idea that appealed, since it meant she'd been visited in a special way, visited and spared. But for what? "I've been wondering," she said to Harry, "if this trip has changed me."

He smiled.

"Has it changed *you*?" she asked. "I mean, besides drying you out."

"Wretch," he said, and to Gwen's ears he made the word sound like the most affectionate of endearments. "Ask me in five years."

"Let's meet in five years," she agreed eagerly. "We can be like Hornby and Critchell-Bullock planning to meet up years hence."

"Except they didn't meet up."

"I know," she said sadly.

"Time was so different then," said Harry, musing to himself. "Those were the days of long voyages, long visits, long courtships, long seductions. In some ways I envy Hornby. The man was so busy surviving he didn't have to learn how to live."

"Are you really going to England?"

"I think I might."

"But you belong *here*."

He put his arm around her as he laughed. Her small shoulders were rounded, dejected. In his view no one belonged to a place unless they were aboriginal. The rest of us were like the dust of the earth blown east, west, north, south.

"Gwen, do you realize we've travelled the last few weeks without setting eyes on another human soul?"

He was poking the fire now and she watched his hands fix, arrange, finesse. In her loneliness she felt her chest tighten, and remembered their world as it was just a few weeks ago, blocked with ice and impassable, as it would be again in several weeks' time.

"Oh, Harry," she said. "I wish I were a different kind of person."

He took off his glasses with one hand, a gesture she loved, and studied her. He was exposing himself to her gaze even as he was seeing her with his own eyes.

What kind of person, he wanted to know.

"Someone," she said slowly, "who truly loves life."

He was still looking at her, still cradling his glasses in his left hand. He said, "You're the kind of person who never stops trying."

She returned his honest gaze. He seemed to mean it. And so she let herself absorb this worthwhile compliment and her place in the world opened up. That's what she would be. The kind of person who never stops trying. And though this wasn't a moment of pure release, of the ice finally giving way, still, everything in her life would flow from this exchange.

On the water Ralph noticed the lake become a little wrinkled. He looked over his shoulder and saw Gwen and Harry, who

looked very small on shore. And then the wind hit – a soft blow
to the side of his head – an offshore wind out of nowhere, and
the canoe started to move. He set his camera on the floor of the
canoe and picked up his paddle. He looked over his shoulder
again and the wrinkle was a ripple moving towards him, darkened water, a disturbance of small waves racing in his direction.
The wind swung him around. It came out of the northwest and
he knew if he wasn't careful it would blow him out into the
middle of a lake two miles wide. He slid down onto his knees
and moved forward until his belly was against the middle
thwart and then he began to paddle hard, trying to swing the
canoe into the wind, trying to get back to shore, but his knees
slid around, he had nothing to lock his feet under, no way to
get a good bite with his paddle. He did his best, he worked
hard. There were little whitecaps now, but not too bad. He was
thinking he'd been lulled by the perfect stillness into coming
out too far, and it felt like a bad decision to be alone on a lake
this size. *Once a lake is ten miles long it might as well be an ocean.*
Some canoeist's voice from another trip years ago. The bow of
his empty seventeen-foot canoe was like a weather vane. The
wind kept taking it and pushing him farther out. His canoe
bounced on the waves, then started to bang, but the sounds
were carried off by the wind.

Eleanor didn't feel the wind come up, and neither did Gwen
or Harry, the one asleep, the others sheltered beside their fire.
They intended to bed down in the open air that night, since
the float plane was expected in the early morning. Had they

pitched their tents they would have been aware of the wind sooner, the slight flapping.

Half a mile out it's a different world.

The waves were eighteen inches high now, two feet high, it happened fast. Ralph was exerting all his energy trying to straighten out the canoe, but the errant wind was determined to blow him away. He no longer thought he was in control, but it took him a few moments to realize he was in trouble. The waves picked up his canoe and surfed it forward, and he felt the sweat pour down his back. Out of a clear sky he was thinking – a rogue wind like a mini-storm, a mini-hurricane, at least way out here. On shore, would they even notice?

The sun goes down so slowly, it hangs on the horizon and goes slowly down. A wave splashed over the back of his canoe, then another, and his knees were in two inches of water. He leaned out far, dug in extra-hard and the paddle gave way and he was in the water before he knew he was going over. In the water, holding the shaft of his cedar paddle in one hand, the blade gone. Gasping from the cold. He grabbed the canoe – it was wallowing upright – he grabbed it with his left hand, but he couldn't catch his breath, the water barely above freezing, and nothing mattered, except getting out of it. He heaved what was left of his paddle into the canoe and tried to climb in over the side and the canoe rolled over. He tried to pull himself up onto its bottom, but the bow went up and the stern went down under his weight and the canoe slid out from under him. He tried once more from the side and the canoe rolled over again and sat upright. Then he was just hanging on, hands on the gunwales, an iron grip, the shore endlessly far away.

Eleanor had slept for half an hour, perhaps. When she opened her eyes, she felt the warm shirt on her face and stood up and looked around for Ralph, and felt the wind. She walked back to their campsite holding the shirt in her hand, looking around her at the tundra, at the sky, then down at the uneven ground. When she came to some bushes, she stopped and gathered tufts of muskox hair off the twigs, slipped them into her pocket, a gift for Ralph. The sun was going down, it was ten o'clock by her watch, so she scrambled down to shore and saw Gwen and Harry talking by the fire.

She said, "Where's Ralph?"

Harry stood up and scanned the lake. He'd forgotten about him. The last he'd seen, Ralph was a long way out and the water was calm. Now he couldn't see the canoe at all and the lake was choppy. It was always worse out on the water than it looked from shore, he knew that. Maybe Ralph was behind that big island. Eleanor was reaching into her pack for her binoculars. The three stood gazing out at the lake, waiting for Ralph to come into view. While they watched, the sun went all the way down and the wind died away.

He had no idea how much time had passed, how much time he had left. So quiet now. So incongruous, he thought, to be fighting for his life when it was calm and peaceful.

Breathing is loud when there's no other sound. It reminded him he was alive. He rested his head against the side of the canoe and there was the astounding silence and his breathing. He was eating apple pie with his mother. He was looking at the wedding ring on her floury hand. Then he was back in the present, an old man with no feeling in his submerged body, agony in his arms, hands like stone claws from holding on. He was sorry, so profoundly sorry to be losing everything, and so sorry about the trouble he was going to cause. He called for help, unsure whether any sound would come out. It did, and he felt relieved. He was still alive. He called again. His mouth couldn't form a word, but his throat produced a sound. He heard it. He heard his breathing, and his breathing wasn't inside him any more, but outside, disembodied. He was lying with Eleanor on the tundra. The warmth, the ecstasy. He was seeing to the bottom of the lake and it was covered in beautiful stones. A camera lay among the stones, his last pictures of Eleanor in the camera, and the camera was so close, the water was so clear, that the metallic parts of it were shining, and he could touch them. He could reach down and touch his canoe, which was glinting too. He could touch the floating man in an orange vest bobbing in the water beside his canoe.

A one-hour blow, that's all it was. The wind died down as they watched, the water went flat, and they kept looking and Ralph didn't reappear. Maybe he was fine, probably he was fine.

They took Harry's canoe, he thought to throw in a jacket and a length of rope, and set off down the lake, staying fairly close to shore. Every few minutes Eleanor stopped paddling to raise her binoculars and scan the water. Gwen, with another pair of binoculars, walked the tundra above the shore. She had a whistle around her neck. She would blow the whistle if she saw anything, that was their agreement.

Alone on land, Gwen felt as she had on those Sunday nights when her parents drove her brother back to university and she spent several hours imagining the car accident that would leave her orphaned. Fourteen years old and the radio for company. She became aware that she wasn't looking for a silver canoe at all. She had her eyes trained on the red canoe, not willing to let them out of her sight, but at a certain point she couldn't see them any more.

Midnight, and it was perfectly still. The wind comes in the front door, it goes out the back door, and the house returns to a supernatural quiet.

Eleanor and Harry paddled and looked until their eyes hurt. The sun below the horizon, the light duskier, it was harder to see, and they lost track of time. "I'm not an artisan," Eleanor remembered Ralph joking once. "I don't make anything except commotion." Which wasn't true, but she loved him for saying it. This is too much commotion, she was saying to him. Please.

The landscape changed before her eyes. A movement here, a shadow over there, a hint of light, a shape that her eyes fastened on with such greed, such greedy longing. She was looking for Ralph and seeing nothing but ghosts. Her arms worked, her eyes were intact, but her soul was coming apart. And when she saw, finally, a spot of drifting orange that receded and shifted and came into being, she recognized that she was seeing her future, and it was a future of infinite sadness.

They were on their way back. Gwen saw how the canoe was lower in the water and how their paddling was automatic, deadened, slow. She headed back to their campsite, stumbling, running. She would make a fire, she thought, she would make tea, she would make them something to eat.

Her hands were shaking but she made a fire, she got water boiling. She rummaged in the packs for tea bags and packaged soup, then went to the water's edge. Eleanor stepped out of the canoe and dragged it up a little. Then Harry hauled it up the rest of the way.

It was the sound the canoe made on the gravelly shore that marked the end for Eleanor. She walked a few feet and sank to her knees.

Gwen drew her to the fire, helped her into dry clothes. Put a mug of tea into her shivering hands and remembered Eleanor saying once that nothing puts you together like a cup of tea. Eleanor lifted the mug. It hit her teeth. Gwen took it out of her hands and held it for her and Eleanor sipped. Gwen wrapped her arms around her friend, rocked her back and forth.

Later, Harry and Gwen lifted the body out of the canoe. Eleanor watched them lay Ralph on a stretch of sandy shore. She would never forget how they grew in stature before her eyes, head and shoulders above themselves. They took off Ralph's life vest and there he was in his old shirt, and she remembered his wedding shirt, the clean shirt he'd placed over her face, but she couldn't remember where she'd put it and couldn't rest until she remembered. Gwen found it for her, folded up, on a flat stone ten feet from the fire.

Harry went to get a nylon groundsheet. He came back and Eleanor was sitting beside the body. The sun wasn't up yet. She was examining Ralph's small hand in twilight that was bright enough to read by, if you had good eyes. A refrigerated hand. She stroked the back of it, turned it over, and studied the stiff fingers. They were asheny-blue, a little rough, still stained by nicotine.

Harry stood for a moment watching her. Her head looked like the heaviest of peonies after a rain, her body, tilted forward over Ralph's. And the thought came to him that it wasn't just one person who had died, but all the filaments of life connecting that person to everyone he'd ever known and to every place he'd ever been.

Eventually he persuaded Eleanor to leave Ralph's side. He led her up to the tundra to a makeshift bed he'd prepared – their thin insulite mattresses and sleeping bags. She crawled into hers. He and Gwen lay on either side of her, inside their bags and under a tarp. She began to talk then, wondering about Ralph's final minutes, how long he suffered, how much, and Harry said it would have been very quick, he would have drifted off in a stupor. If only I'd gone with him, she cried. She meant that if they'd been together, two in the canoe, it never would have happened. And what did happen? The wind came up, yes, and the lake was wide and long, but how had he over-turned? We'll never know, said Harry. He got into trouble, we'll never know exactly how. Don't blame yourself, he said. Nobody's to blame, said Gwen.

Harry and Gwen slept a little. Eleanor lay awake. After a while she eased herself out of her sleeping bag and went down to the water. It was wrong to leave him alone. He lay wrapped in Harry's groundsheet, a broken body, and she sat on the shore beside him. So cold to the touch when she pulled the nylon sheet away from his dear, lost, clean-shaven face. She found herself repeating the 23rd psalm and why it should give her comfort under the circumstances she couldn't quite fathom, since she felt real bitterness too. She'd lost her father too soon, she'd lost Ralph even sooner. But she murmured to herself the words about the valley of the shadow of death, the house of the Lord, and she felt situated in a larger place, so large it held every possible thing, including all the minutiae of every kind of pain.

The sun came up and with its warmth the mosquitoes came alive and Gwen stirred and Harry slept on. Gwen joined Eleanor and they walked together along the shore, listening, waiting for the Twin Otter to arrive. Around seven they heard it in the western sky. Gwen went to wake up Harry and found him folding the tarp, rolling up their sleeping bags. Then they went down to the shore and prepared themselves for the last part of their journey.

They noticed the wind, of course. The stillness of the previous night seemed hallucinatory now. It had been perfectly calm for how long? A few hours? Long enough to fool Ralph into going out alone and too far. Now they knew that the only reason it was calm was because the wind was shifting. The stillness fools you, because it's never really still. The stillness is the time before the change.

Grey clouds on all sides. Blue sky with cumulus clouds above.

And then the Barrens were far below them, glowing in the sun, all vast and distant and bronze. The body of Ralph was inside the body of the plane, which was bouncing over the body of the world, and Gwen reached for a motion sickness bag and quietly threw up. Ralph's canoe was in the plane too. The pilot – older, experienced – had brought reality of a different kind into their midst. He'd said they should find the missing canoe. He used the word *evidence*. There would be questions, because there had been a death. He and Harry had set off in the float plane and it hadn't taken very long to spot what the sun had already picked out. The glinting canoe had drifted almost to shore, not far from where they had found Ralph floating face down in the water.

WHERE THEY HAD BEEN WAS SO VAST, and Ralph's death so unforeseen, that their sense of the ordinary died with him. The normal grasses of life never quite grew back. On the day they returned from the Barrens, there was the official business of death. The police took Ralph's body to the hospital, where he was examined by the coroner. For the other three, there were questions by the police and statements to sign. There was Bill Thwaite with his microphone. By late afternoon they were so exhausted they returned separately to their homes, where each of them had a variation of the same almost surreal experience. Harry reached for a can of coffee on his kitchen shelf, then stood marvelling at this simplest of things, a wooden shelf at eye level. Gwen stood in her bathroom, enraptured by the dusky light emanating from the porcelain sink and the warm water flowing from the tap. Eleanor listened spellbound for a moment to the whispering slide of wood on wood when she opened and closed a dresser drawer.

Gwen, it was, who phoned Harry to say that no matter what Eleanor thought she wanted, they shouldn't leave her alone. They arrived at her door soon afterwards, only to find Teresa already there. Teresa, who had kidded them quite rightly about not knowing enough, knew exactly what to do.

She got them talking and their impromptu wake began, hours of stories about the trip, about Ralph. His foibles, his turns of phrase, his stamina, his passionate heart. Around midnight, half-crying, half-laughing, Eleanor said, "Some men will do anything to avoid a wedding."

After the others left, she got into bed and slept for twelve hours. When she woke, she went into her kitchen, discovered the fruit and cheese and bread and ham that Teresa had put in her refrigerator, made herself a small plate of food, and nibbled at it. Then went back to bed and slept four hours more. During that time she had a dream. She was in her father's study on the second floor at home, stuffing paper into a big hole in the wall. She was preparing to sell Ralph's books. She pulled forward a small table, moved the other furniture to one side, and felt a breeze, a cool lake breeze coming from somewhere. She went out to the hall landing, then headed downstairs, and on the stairs she felt the breeze even more. Suddenly the front door blew open and Ralph was there in the sort of detail that cannot be recaptured in waking life. She went to him and pressed her face against his neck and felt his whiskers. She could smell him and feel him. He wasn't big, but he had bulk, muscle. She didn't want to let him go, but she wanted to look at him. He was wearing a red and black flannel shirt, a T-shirt underneath it, his old baggy pants. His grey hair was mussed and plastered to his forehead, and his face was flushed from recent exertion. She told him how overjoyed she was to see him again, and his face brightened and he intimated that she shouldn't worry. Then he said something more, something important. He was passing on the secret of life and she began to realize she was dreaming. But that isn't what woke her up. She woke up because she was crying. For a while she lay in bed, going over the dream, struggling to remember what Ralph had said. But she couldn't.

The next day, as she reached for the hairbrush on her dresser, she experienced a visitation of a more mundane kind. She looked in the mirror and saw her mother.

You pass a photograph on the piano, she thought, a picture of a family member, a face utterly familiar, but bearing no relationship to your own. And then a stranger comes along and sees the resemblance you've overlooked. Staring in the mirror, she was her own stranger, noticing in her altered face something more recognizable than herself, the expression of worn-out grief she had seen on her mother after her father died.

Later, she sat down and wrote to her. I'm back from the trip I told you about, the trip Dad would have loved to make. But something happened. Four of us made the journey and only three of us returned. She related everything in detail. She wrote, I find myself thinking of you a great deal.

A week and a half later, she would read her mother's reply. "Something punishing has happened to you," her mother wrote, and Eleanor was struck by the aptness of the word. A single word balanced atop a mountain of feeling.

———

After the close-knit intensity of the trip, and the closer-knit shock of Ralph's death, Gwen settled back into herself, into work, and it felt wrong. It tasted off. Compared to Harry, the new young manager was a pipsqueak, she thought, who never looked you in the eye. His only interest was the new building, or so it seemed. Earlier in the summer, construction had started on a building site on the outskirts of town, far removed from the heart of Yellowknife. Things were well underway, and if plans went as scheduled, they would move out there next June. Everyone around her, it seemed to Gwen, was on edge, poised to see what openings television would bring, and how they might advance themselves.

At Ralph's funeral there had been hymns and old songs and they'd spoken to her in some way she didn't quite trust. They filled her with what she thought of as easy emotion, and made her feel vulnerable. The church they'd used for the service was Eleanor's church, and the pews were filled, not with Ralph's family, which was scattered and distant – he had an ex-wife and no children and only one surviving sister – but with his friends from the radio station and from town. "There is a Balm in Gilead." "Unto the Hills." She listened to Eleanor's quavery, thin voice, a little embarrassed for her, and ashamed of being embarrassed. But why should things be censored and simplified, she thought. Why should Ralph's death be softened, when it was shockingly hard, and sweetened by hymns, when he wasn't a religious man, not that she'd been aware of. For six weeks they'd shared a canoe and she'd come to know just how strong and stubborn he was, and how gentle and erudite. He knew more things by heart than anyone else she'd ever met. She pictured him now, wrapped in a groundsheet, hoisted like a gunny sack into the float plane.

The minister was a short man, clean-shaven, elderly. Without preamble he read a psalm and from the first words,

Lord, thou hast been our dwelling place in all generations, he made the hairs stand up on the back of Gwen's neck. His Bible was open in his hands, but he didn't once look down, speaking directly to them as a gifted radio actor might do. *Before the mountains were brought forth, or ever thou hadst formed the earth and the world*. And what struck Gwen full force was something she'd never really considered before, the idea of a spiritual dwelling place from the beginning of time. Not the idea of God, as such, but the idea of such a dwelling place, and such timelessness over time.

Gwen leaned over and whispered to Harry, "What psalm was that?"

And Harry, the minister's son, knew. "Ninety," he whispered back. "Nine-oh."

The psalm gave her the wider feeling she was after. It captured the sweep of past and present, reminding her of the immensity of the land they'd returned from just days before. The endless skies, the rolling tundra, and lakes the size of seas.

The following afternoon, as she was editing a tape, Dido's needling question suddenly echoed in her head. What time do you *want* it to be? And with the question came Dido's insinuation that she, Gwen, didn't know. That she was one of those people so out of touch with herself that she couldn't say or wouldn't admit what it was she wanted.

She could have said, What do you mean by *time?* She could have said, I want it to be bedtime. She could have said, I want you to stop giving me a hard time. But the answer she'd actually given still held, she thought, even if she wished her delivery had been lighter, less defensive. I want it to be the time it is. I want to be in the here and now.

A few days later, sitting at Eleanor's kitchen table, Harry observed, "You don't wear the St. Christopher medallion any more."

No. "It didn't quite do the job," she said. She'd put it away in a drawer.

"You have to eat," he told her. "Have you been eating?"

"Teresa feeds me. In fact, everybody feeds me." She opened her refrigerator door with a sad flourish. "Abundance," she said.

"Are you sleeping?" he asked her.

"Harry, you're a sweet man. I'm sleeping enough. I can't look any worse than you do."

She told him not to fret, she would be fine. That day she'd handed in her notice to his replacement at the radio station, the boyish-faced man with the small teeth and the nervous smile. She would fulfill her contractual obligation of a month's work, but that was all, for she was going to set in motion her plan to open a bookstore somehow. She hoped to sell new and used books, she told Harry, and she wanted to hang Ralph's photographs on the walls of the shop, his series of weeds floating on water, catching the light.

Harry said, "You're way ahead of me."

He still hadn't entirely unpacked from the trip, he admitted, although in his mind he was already weighing the next stage of his life and putting out feelers about work. He'd been mulling over what he would take with him when he left. He had to decide what to do with Dido's few things, the letter, the watch he'd given her, the key chain. Perhaps he'd use the key chain, throw away the letter, give the watch to a stranger.

The canoe trip had been medicine of a sort. Once the country opened up and they'd entered the flow of water and wildlife, he'd been taken past the Dido-wreck in his mind for continuous stretches of time. She receded for a while, several days, a week. But then she returned no less vividly and occupied his thoughts.

IN LATE AUGUST, three weeks after their return, Gwen was in the station when an older man came looking for Dido. His name was Daniel Moir. He was a close friend of Dido's, he said, and he was trying to find her.

Gwen told him yes, she used to work here, but she'd left, months ago. The man nodded and rubbed his lower lip with his knuckle. He was casually well-dressed, late fifties perhaps, tanned and fit, with a strong, successful face, what her mother would have called a fine-looking man. He stared out the window, and the next thing he said, he said to the window. "How many months ago?"

"In January."

"And she hasn't been in touch since."

"Not with me. But she's been in touch."

At this point Eleanor came back to her desk.

Gwen said to her, "This gentleman is looking for Dido."

Eleanor knew immediately who it was. Dido's description of the handsome father-in-law held true. He looked vigorous, capable, and disappointed. She told him that Dido was in California and had been since January, at least as far as she knew. They'd spoken in May, but hadn't spoken since.

He asked what had taken Dido to California. Eleanor replied that the person she'd gone with came from there.

"I see," he said. "My timing wasn't good."

Eleanor wondered if he was one of those worldly men who thinks timing is everything, as others believe everything is luck, when it seemed to her everything was fragile, that's all.

In the evening she saw Harry and said, "A man came to the station looking for Dido today. He said his name was Daniel Moir."

Harry raised his head. "The famous father-in-law."

"Yes." So Harry knew. "Poor Dido. But I wasn't sure how much to tell him. I almost gave him her phone number, but would she want that? I mean, if she wanted to be in touch with him, she'd be in touch with him, it seems to me."

"So what's he like?" asked Harry, grimly curious.

Eleanor, not to rub salt in the wound, said, "He's in good shape for his age."

Harry tracked him down at the Explorer Hotel. He wanted to meet the man for any number of reasons, the rival for Dido's affections, the fellow loser, the man who'd travelled so far on her account, the man who'd made Dido wait. *We just looked at each other, we just looked.* How had she gotten from A to Z, from this man's son to Eddy? He wanted to know something about the mysterious, self-destructive logic of Dido's love life.

On his way to the hotel, Harry'd felt unsettled, at odds with himself. But when he shook Daniel Moir's hand and looked into his eyes, he saw an old man, and his heart lightened.

"I'm Harry Boyd."

"Daniel Moir."

Harry explained that Eleanor Dew had mentioned he was here, and why. "I used to be Dido's boss," he said. "As well as a close friend."

"I'm Dido's father-in-law," said Daniel.

They went into the Snowshoe Lounge together and had a drink, and then another.

Daniel Moir looked rich, thought Harry. His hands had known weather, and immediate care afterwards. His way of holding a glass of Scotch in both hands, it was Dido's way of holding her coffee mug. No wedding band, but the white memory of one on his tanned ring finger.

"I was hoping she was still here," Daniel said. "I haven't had a letter in a long time."

Harry nodded. He could have told him he had a piece of their correspondence. "She spoke of you," he said.

Daniel glanced up, a sharp look. But he had enough self-control not to ask what it was that Dido had said about him.

She loved you, thought Harry. Later, he was sorry he hadn't said it. A person should know he's loved. "We missed her when she left," he said. "She was a natural on air – beautiful speaking voice, tremendous presence. She needed no training at all. She was born to it."

Daniel's face relaxed. "I find that easy to imagine." He asked what she'd done, wanting to know in detail, and listened intently.

Harry's lightness of heart subsided the longer he sat across from the man, whose features came into focus the more they talked. Press the Dido button, thought Harry, and the years drop away.

Daniel began to tell him about Dido's other abilities. She excelled as a student, he said. She and his son had studied together, that's how they met. She was one of the only girls in his philosophy class and unlike most of the other students she spoke out. "Well, she was a few years older. My son told us he'd met a girl who knew how to play chess. He was impressed, and so were we when he brought her home. His mother and I thought she was an extraordinary young woman."

"His mother and I." He was stating as a simple fact, thought Harry, something that had complicated his life beyond measure.

"What's he doing now, your son?" He didn't even know if they were divorced. He assumed not. She'd never said.

His son was in Toronto, studying law, said Daniel, and just recently he'd become engaged to a lovely girl, a registered nurse. "Someone a lot like his mother."

Harry pointed to the telltale evidence on Daniel's left hand. "You've parted company."

Daniel nodded. "A month ago." By now he was staring into his second Scotch. He began to talk about his grandson, his daughter's child. He hadn't foreseen how much pleasure having grandchildren would give him. He took the boy sailing, he said. He said he could count on one hand, less than one hand, the women he'd met who truly enjoyed sailing. Most women endured it for the sake of their husbands. But Dido had a real feel for it. She was terrific on the water.

Harry had the sudden suspicion that Daniel dreamt of sailing away with Dido. And on the third Scotch Daniel confessed to having done exactly that. He'd once taken her aboard his boat and hadn't brought her back for twenty-four hours. He'd been tempted not to bring her back at all. She'd joked that she was perfectly equipped for any eventuality. She was wearing pearl earrings. I'm dressed for any occasion, she'd told him.

His wife and son had been at a family reunion in Maine and never found out. Or perhaps they had. They knew something. Shortly after they returned, he and Dido went for a long walk on the beach, and then she left, moved away, came up here.

Daniel said, "I once thought my life held no surprises and I was content with that. I knew things might change, but I didn't think *I* would change. I pitied men who ran after younger women. But from the first moment I saw Dido," he said, then stopped. Then picked up again. "At the end of that first visit, she said goodbye and she put her arm across my back – I was sitting at the dining-room table – she put her hand on my shoulder and draped her arm over my back – and it was such a warm gesture. You can't understand it until it happens to you, what it's like to suddenly feel so much. It's a huge gift of feeling," he said slowly. "But I couldn't see my way clear until my son moved on in his life." He stared at his glass and shook his head. "I grow roots when I drink Scotch." Then he said, "Who's the man she's with now?"

Harry had been listening with interest, but no enjoyment as Daniel unburdened himself. "She ran off with the technician," he said.

Daniel eyed him. "Every man I've ever met falls for her."

"She doesn't fall for them, though."

"You're right about that."

"She likes men who are good at what they do," said Harry. He was remembering the drunken party at his house when only Dido remained awake and alert at the end, sitting on the floor in the lotus position, asking him if he thought Eddy was good at what he did. And he should have said, Other things matter more. Or as much. He said, "She likes men who are rough with her." Finally arriving at the heart of the matter.

Daniel didn't take his eyes off him. "How do you know that?"

"Not because *I* was rough."

They scrutinized each other. They'd finished their jockeying, satisfied their need to talk. They weren't ill-disposed towards each other.

Daniel said, "What are you telling me?"

"I was hoping you'd tell *me*. You know more about her than I do."

"Maybe. Or maybe I don't know as much as I thought." He looked away. "I gather she's in Los Angeles. I'm sure I could find her if I tried."

"Your son must be in touch with her. If he's getting married again." Divorce papers, Harry was thinking. He didn't let on that Eleanor had her phone number. He considered doing so, then decided not to push the man one way or the other. It was up to Daniel to figure out what he would do next.

At the end of August, the Berger Inquiry conducted its last community hearing. Over the course of 283 days of testimony, the inquiry had gathered 40,000 pages of transcripts presented by 1,700 witnesses. Now Berger faced the daunting challenge of completing a report in six months that would deliver on his promise "to tell the government and people of Canada what your concerns and thoughts are."

Harry had put his house up for sale. He sold it within a week, waterfront lots on Latham Island being highly prized. Then he began to organize the things he would take to England. He wanted to whittle his life down to its essentials, like Huck Finn, he thought to himself, and to that end he was confining himself to two suitcases. Everything else he was boxing up either for the church to give away, or for the dump.

One night, Eleanor and Gwen dropped by and found him surrounded by chaos. Help yourselves, he told them. Dig in. Take anything you can use. Then his tone changed, and he said he was looking for someone who might be able to use his canoe.

It was early September and the residue of the trip was gone from their faces and hands, even from their muscles — they had town faces, town thoughts, town dreams. The Barren Ground hadn't followed them into their sleep. It worked on them differently, more consciously, perhaps. It was a short, atypical chapter in their lives. They couldn't quite believe it had happened, even though afterwards nothing was the same.

"Are we ever going to see you again?" Gwen asked him.

"Ah, Gwen," Harry said. And wrapped her in a hug. He was drinking again, the sobriety of the canoe trip already a distant memory. "You're a sentimental soul."

"Can I hide in one of your suitcases?" she asked. She was ready to run off with him now, she said, ready to stow aboard.

Harry just smiled the comment away. His flirtatious banter of the canoe trip was a thing of the past, and she couldn't resurrect it, not even by telling him the radio station was unbearable without him. He'd moved on, it seemed to her. He'd already left.

She was right. Ralph's death had worked a change in him, turning his thoughts to Eleanor and her welfare, then to his own future.

Gwen stood in the living room as Harry wrapped up his life in Yellowknife. In one of those paradoxes she found hard to grasp, she felt more isolated in town than when she'd been on the Barrens with miles of emptiness around her. Just three months ago in this very room, they'd organized their supplies, full of excitement about leaving. How was it possible to feel safer in the wilderness – as safe as she'd felt almost until the end – and how was it possible to feel lonelier now?

A week before he was to leave Yellowknife, Harry opened *News of the North* and read a brief article about an exhibit of photographs in Los Angeles that was causing quite a stir. A series documenting young Dene women, unposed, half-naked, and looking as if they were high on something. Canadian Press had picked up the story. The report said viewers had responded with outrage and concern about the lives depicted, but with admiration for the political message and the artistic daring of the photographer. "The disconcerting intimacy of the pictures never feels exploitative," one reviewer said, and Eddy Fitzgerald was quoted. "I can't transform their lives, but I can show the truth of what's happening." He said he wanted to show the underside of life in a far northern town where whites were the majority, where they were racist, where they used and abused young native women. He wanted his pictures to be seen as a warning of what lay ahead if the pipeline went through. A book was in the works, he claimed, and all the proceeds would go to the Dene Nation. There was a small shot of Eddy, looking intense, unsmiling, and next to it one of his photographs: a young native girl sprawled on her side in what looked like a seedy motel room.

Harry realized with sudden and painful clarity that Eddy was going to make a name for himself, a thought that dismayed him almost as much as the pictures did. He couldn't tell from the article if the photos were true to life, or if Eddy had staged them for his own purposes. He didn't know if he should be impressed by what Eddy had done or appalled.

When he saw Teresa the next day in the Gold Range café, he asked if she'd seen the article.

"Jesus," she said. "What planet does Eddy live on?"

Harry felt relieved, and grateful for her straightforward reaction. "But it's all in a good cause, apparently," he said. Wanting her to elaborate, to clarify his own thinking. "Art in the service of politics."

"No," she said. "It's art and politics as a cover for – you know. His dick."

A response so unequivocal it blasted away the confusion in his jealous mind.

Eleanor was the only one of their foursome, except for Ralph, who would never leave the North. In early October, Harry moved to England, and not long after that Gwen began to apply to radio stations in the south for work. Vancouver, Toronto, Winnipeg, Ottawa. She wanted more experience, she told Eleanor, she wanted to learn from people who really knew what they were doing, and that meant going "outside," the northern term for anywhere south of the sixtieth parallel. By implication, the North, itself, was "inside." A distinction that first struck Gwen as an existential riddle, since how could this vast out-of-doors ever be construed as an interior? But then she experienced her first winter.

Now winter closed in again with frigid winds, icy roads, longer nights, and, yes, she was inside a place gripped by the cold. Ironically, now that she'd made up her mind to leave Yellowknife, she felt more bound to the place, eager to absorb everything she could. She intended to be gone before the station took up its new quarters the following summer. Under the present manager, she was back on nights. She preferred it. She saw less of the man, who, unlike Harry, had no interest in opening up broadcasting to women. Teresa didn't get on with him either. "But I've figured out how to handle him. He fires me, then I fire him," she laughed. "I've outlived bad bosses before," she added with a trace of bitterness.

They both kept tabs on Eleanor. She had made an arrangement with the owner of the stationery store to split the rent and devote her half of the space to books. One day Gwen helped her go through Ralph's photographs to select which ones to hang in the store. They discovered that he'd preceded his summer grasses with a series on grasses in winter that looked like Japanese calligraphy. The dry stalks were bent over like little sticks, pressed into shapes by weather, half buried under the snow. It was almost too much for Eleanor. Ralph had walked right back into their lives. She told Gwen then about the remarkable dream she'd had soon after he died, in which there was the sort of detail – sight, touch, smell – that an ordinary photograph doesn't have and neither does memory. But these photographs of what he'd bent down to look at so closely that he was inches away gave her the sense that she was looking through his eyes. This intimacy with him – so physical, yet intangible – came to her in a rush and made her feel his absence all the more.

As Gwen studied the snowy light in the black-and-white photographs, she was taken back to a winter's day seven years ago when she'd driven with her mother to Toronto to see an old friend, a painter named Marta, who'd rented an apartment in a high-rise overlooking Lake Ontario. There was just a bedroom, living room, small kitchen, not unlike my own apartment here, thought Gwen, except for one thing. Marta had a view. Large windows overlooked the lake below and winter sun poured in, such white, parched, unsparing sun-shine that everything seemed charged with unusual life. All the way home, driving with her mother through the bare countryside under the white winter sky, she'd felt Marta's aspirations working like sap running through her, and it wasn't the sap of spring, but the latent sap of winter. She hadn't ever forgotten, but neither had she known how to put the feeling into action. Now it occurred to her to use her kitchen table as a work space and try her hand drawing and sketching the things she remembered from her winter walks around town, like the hooded faces obscured by plumes of icy breath, and the makeshift log cabins and wood piles wrapped in ice fog, the skiers coming across the frozen lake, and the occasional dog team that surged over the snow, pulling a toboggan behind them like a snow boat, the dogs reaching to the side to swipe mouthfuls of snow.

At Christmas they received cards from Harry, who told them he was remarkably well for a man in his condition. He'd found a job at the BBC producing radio dramas.

That's *my* job, Gwen wrote to him. Eleanor replied too; she would be a faithful correspondent. Gwen wrote again in January when she was offered a job for the following July as a summer replacement at the CBC in Ottawa. Harry sent his congratulations, she wrote to him yet again, and when he didn't reply, she let it go.

In February, a hundred miles northeast of Inuvik, a young man working on an oil rig in the Mackenzie Delta was killed by a polar bear. His co-worker said that he'd left him alone, but only briefly, to warm up in a nearby trailer, and when he came out several minutes later, his partner was gone. He searched around and found a boot, a sock, and a polar bear paw print. The story ran on the news and inspired Gwen to write a radio reminiscence about her own encounter, and the little body of sound, her bag full of tapes, that lay on the slope above Hornby's quiet cabin. In response she heard from a retired Barren Lands trapper, Gus Daoust, who gave her his droll and terse assessment of the weather in that part of the world.

"Every wind is a headwind," he said. He also observed that around Yellowknife there were two periods in the year when everything seems to stop still. January and June. May, he said, was the month of sounds of all kinds.

Appropriate, then, that Berger released his final report in early May, since it generated so much talk. The report was more hard-hitting than anyone had expected. "No pipeline now," he recommended, "and no pipeline across the northern Yukon ever." He called for a moratorium of at least ten years on the Mackenzie Valley pipeline to allow for the settlement of native land claims. He recommended that measures be taken to protect critical wildlife habitat. He highlighted the need to preserve native culture and to foster the development of an economy based on renewable resources. "Ten Year Delay," trumpeted the headlines.

Copies of the report were flown to every settlement and waved in the air in triumph. Teresa personally delivered a copy to her grandmother in Fort Rae. Her grandmother couldn't read it, but that hardly mattered. There were many pictures, including one of herself smoking a pipe, her hair white, her eyes trained on the distance. She could turn the pages of photographs of the land and of the animals, and she did, repeatedly, until the binding gave way.

By the end of the summer it would be clear to everyone that a huge political shift had taken place. The inquiry and the report that followed had effectively stopped the pipeline. If it was resurrected, native peoples, empowered by their land claims settlements, would have a central voice in the process.

On her last night in Yellowknife, Gwen did her late show a final time. It was June, one of those brief nights we call long because the twilight is so extended. She was in the announce booth, in its very particular light, never more aware of the rest of the world than when she was so completely shut away from it. She opened her little sound-effects door wide for Sleepy John Estes, the blues guitarist, who used to recognize everyone's step, she said, so acutely did he absorb the sounds around him.

Shortly after one in the morning, Eleanor picked her up at the station and they drove to Old Town. The street lights were on and store signs were lit, but it wasn't dark. They rolled down their windows and the air smelled of the big lake. Harry's canoe was tied to a rack on the roof of the car. They were planning a long paddle on Yellowknife Bay.

They parked near the causeway to Latham Island. When they slid the canoe into the water, there was a slight breeze, but the air was so warm they only needed sweaters under their life vests. The last of the ice had been gone from the bay for just over a week.

They stayed close to shore. It was almost a year to the day since they'd set off for the Thelon River, and they hadn't been on the water since Ralph died. As they paddled, they passed Willow Flats on their right, Jolliffe Island on their left. They passed School Draw, and the shoreline turned wilder. Soon they made out the tower of Con Mine and more islands. Gwen assumed she would never see these things again and she wanted to say goodbye, to sign off, as it were.

After a while, they stopped and drifted. Eleanor in the stern, Gwen in the bow. The air had become perfectly still.

"I've been thinking you should have my fur coat," Gwen said. Everything else she'd packed or sold or given away, including the car and trailer she'd driven to Yellowknife two years ago. "Would you take it and wear it?"

"You'll need it in Ottawa," Eleanor said. "It's yours."

"It's not really mine at all. I've never thought of it as mine."

"It is yours. Harry gave it to you."

Gwen turned to look directly at her and saw that she was serious. "Why?" she asked. "Why did he do such a thing?" In her mind, besides the surprise, were the arresting words *from a secret admirer*.

"He said it wasn't being used and you needed a warm coat. It used to be his grandmother's, that's what he said." Eleanor smiled. "He wanted you to have a warm coat."

"What a kind and strange thing to do," said Gwen, adjusting herself to the kindness, the strangeness. *From a secret admirer*. Why those words, she wanted to ask. But she knew why. He wasn't being literal. His grandmother's coat, after all. A grandmother's coat isn't romantic.

"I'm spilling the beans," said Eleanor. "He didn't intend for you to know."

"I'm *glad* to know. It's been such a puzzle, wondering where it came from. Harry," she said, and laughed. "He didn't want the coat to go to waste. Or something."

"Or something," smiled Eleanor.

Gwen was remembering when they'd all been together a year ago, travelling into a second spring and a second winter. Last year's June had slid backwards into May and they'd heard all the sounds of breakup and renewal all over again. Lifting the needle, putting it back at the beginning instead of forward to the next song.

"You've changed," she said to Eleanor. Lifting the needle off herself. "When I first met you, you were biding your time. Not any more."

"We've come a long way together. But I think we're still recognizable."

Somewhere between three and four in the morning, as they were paddling back, they saw a world that Ralph might have photographed had he seen it, and that Gwen would later try to paint. But it wasn't possible to duplicate the colours except by closing her eyes. Then the islands in the distance became the right shade of jet black, and the sky and the water were an identical, intense, unblemished peach.

TOWARDS THE END OF A WARM SEPTEMBER, a full eight years later, Gwen heard Harry's voice again. She was in her kitchen with the radio on and she stopped what she was doing and stood transfixed. His relaxed, gravelly, conversational voice was so familiar that a decade of time dropped away and she was back in a place more vivid than the present. How rare it was, she thought, to hear someone on the radio who wasn't glib or pushy or out to impress you. Harry was talking to another man about the direction his life had taken, questioning him about the key turning point. They must be in a studio in Toronto, thought Gwen. The other man had been just thirteen, he told Harry, when he and his mother went to visit some elderly neighbours in a cottage and the couple brought out bread and beer. How can the boy grow if he doesn't drink beer? said the persuasive old neighbour, an amateur musician, it turned out, who then went to the piano and played a selection of musical warhorses – Beethoven's *Moonlight Sonata*, a waltz by Brahms, Mozart's *Eine Kleine Nachtmusik* – and the effect on the boy drinking his first glass of beer was electric. This is what he wanted to do with his life, he knew instantly. He wanted to study music. More than that, he wanted to arrange, rearrange, move around the notes.

The radio went from the man's voice to his music and it was Harry Somers, realized Gwen. The boy had grown up to be the composer Harry Somers.

Harry asked Somers about the Newfoundland folk songs he'd arranged that every child in a Canadian choir has at some time or another sung, and Somers answered that he was very drawn to them, that now, of course, they represented the memory of something rather than the thing itself, since that sort of life, the outport life, had disappeared or was disappearing. Then a choir began to sing "She's Like a Swallow" and Gwen's eyes filled with tears.

The phrase that came to her mind was "the long and sudden of it." We go on and on through the long months of our lives until we hit a sudden moment that stuns us. This was one such moment and soon there would be another. When the program ended, an announcer informed listeners that it had been recorded years ago; she'd been listening to a tape. Harry wasn't back in Canada, after all.

Gwen sat at her kitchen table, flooded less with memory than with feeling, as you sit flooded with feeling after a phone call tells you sad news about someone you love. Hearing Harry's voice had been like slipping on the soft tan glove of the past.

After a while, she stood up and switched off the radio, then went to the window. Autumn crocuses splayed wide in the garden below like mauve, over-the-hill mushrooms. Or birthday candles melted down into a soft, crazy tilt. From here she could see how candle-white the stems were. Autumn crocuses were something she'd never known about until she moved into this old house in Ottawa. The small, leggy flowers expired almost as soon as they appeared. At the window she became aware of unhappy crows, their racket outside. Then she saw somebody in what looked like a uniform at the foot of the garden, and somebody else, in the same kind of beige shirt and pants, run across the lawn and disappear around the side of the fence where the mint grew.

She went outside and her neighbour called over the high hedge, "There's a fox!"

"A fox?"

"With one leg missing. It was asleep in our yard and the crows went crazy. It's in your yard now."

Gwen went to the foot of the garden and saw the fugitive, its right back leg missing at the hip, trot leisurely from her garden into the alley. An extraordinary sight – a gaunt, grey veteran of the wild, moving at its own otherworldly pace.

The uniformed strangers were animal control officers and Gwen watched them corner the fox behind a neighbour's gas barbecue, then hook it around the neck with a wire noose on the end of a long pole, and hoist it into the air to hang limp, skinny, twisted, its eyes flat and expressionless, either too weak or too wise to struggle, before they dropped it into a cage. They carried the cage to their van and then drove away. For a few minutes, she remained outside. The crows had dispersed. The street was quiet. The fox had been too mangy, the control officers had said to her, potentially too dangerous to be allowed to continue on his way. By the battle-scarred look of him, he'd been fighting against the odds for a long while. There was a time when she would have brought out her tape recorder and taped the whole incident. Not any more. But sometimes she still thought about her lost tapes, imagined how another traveller might stumble over them, and listen to them later, only to be transported as she would have been back to that remote, animal-filled wilderness.

The fox had seemed magical to her. A creature from one world passing through another. But he didn't make it.

Saddened, she went back inside, and phoned Eleanor at the bookstore. She told her about the fox, told her he'd been minding his own business. And she got the sympathetic reaction she'd counted on. But was that really what prompted the call? "Another amazing thing happened today," she said. "I heard Harry on the radio."

"It must have been something he did for the BBC," Eleanor said. "He's still over there, I know. Holding the radio fort, tending the broadcasting fires, as he likes to say. You know Harry."

"No, it was a tape recorded years ago." Then she said, "I'm sorry. I should have asked if you were busy."

"It's all right. Things are quiet. How's David?"

"David's great. I've put another one of his masterpieces in the mail to you. We splash colour around when he gets home from daycare."

Eleanor said she was going to bring him some books on her next visit. She'd be flying down from Yellowknife in the week following Christmas to spend more time with her mother.

Good, said Gwen, she couldn't wait to see her, she missed her. "I didn't realize how much I missed Harry," Gwen said.

Early the next morning, having spent much of the night talking to Harry in her head, she phoned the BBC in London and they put her through. "Harry," she said when she reached him, "I spent an hour with you yesterday under the strangest circumstances."

"Gwen? Where are you?"

He sounded as pleased to hear from her as she'd hoped he would.

"Still in Ottawa. They replayed your interview with Harry Somers."

"It's so great to hear your voice," he said. Then, "You're up awfully early."

She was. It was six in the morning. She was the only one awake in her house. "Tell me about your life over there," she said. "Are you well?"

"No complaints. They've got me producing audio books now."

"They have you reading them on tape, you mean."

"No, no. We have actors do that. Proper professionals, not old radio hacks. This is Britain."

"But you would be great at it."

Harry chuckled. "I'll pass that on to them." Then he said, "I've been keeping track of you through Eleanor."

"What has she told you?"

"She tells me everything."

"Then she tells you more than she tells me."

Harry laughed. "I should be calling you a traitor for defecting from radio."

"Sometime over a drink, we'll talk. Do you ever come to Canada?"

"I do. Now and again, when I've got a good reason. I've been toying with the idea of showing up at Abe Lamont's retirement party just to give the old grump a surprise. It's in November," he said. "In Toronto, though."

And Gwen gathered from his tone that Ottawa wasn't in the cards. "When I heard your voice yesterday, I actually thought you were *in* Toronto. I thought you'd moved back."

There was no reply. Then, "Sorry, Gwen. Just had to hand something to a colleague. You're asking if I plan to move back to Toronto. Not really. I have things to keep me here."

His personal life, she thought. She'd been wondering about it. "Things besides work."

"As a matter of fact, yes. Mind you, I'm not as tied down as you are."

"No wife," she said. She heard him reach for an answer and assumed there was someone, but no one official, and intercepted slyly by asking, "Harry, you're not still relying on self-service, are you?"

There was a moment's silence. Then she heard a huge guffaw.

"You're very *forward*," he said.

They were both laughing, and Gwen felt more relaxed than she had in a long time.

He said, "So let's say I do go to Abe's party. Would it make any sense for me to take a side trip to Ottawa?"

She felt the smile broaden on her face. "It's only an hour's flight. We could have dinner together and catch up."

"Then I'll see what I can manage and keep you posted," he said. "I'm tremendously glad you called."

"I love your voice, Harry. It isn't like anyone else's."

Five weeks later, in the lobby of the Lord Elgin Hotel in Ottawa, Harry removed his glasses and looked at Gwen.

"I like the blue on blue," he said.

She glanced down at herself and recalled in the same moment her turquoise earrings. She touched her ears.

He said, "The blue blouse, the blue necklace, the blue earrings, and your blue eyes."

"Ah," with a smile.

She surveyed his face, adjusting to the changes of the intervening years. His eyes seemed smaller because his jaw was wider. His skin was ruddier, the cauliflower ear its fat, lumpy self. He was more solid yet more vulnerable. But aging made everyone that way, she thought, not that Harry was so old. By her calculation he was fifty-one or -two, and only somewhat better groomed than he used to be. A comfortable tweed jacket, decent trousers, scuffed brogues.

"What happened to your wrist?" he asked.

She glanced at the cast that encased her lower arm and extended beyond her sleeve. "I was making my way through the dark bedroom and I fell over my husband's shoes." She raised her eyebrows, smiled, then looked away. "I used to know that room by heart."

Harry had stepped into terra incognita, the state of a troubled marriage. He wasn't sure how to proceed. "You were going to tell me how you and radio parted ways," he said, slipping on his overcoat. "According to Eleanor, you got tired of asking people about things that were none of your business."

"Eleanor told you that? Well, that's certainly part of it."

"And the rest?"

"Let me show you where it happened," she said, buttoning up her coat. "It's on the way to the restaurant."

They walked over to Wellington Street, then made their way across the small bridge that spanned the canal and led to the Château Laurier Hotel.

One day about six years ago, she told him, when she was at work right up there, and she pointed to the top floor of the old hotel where CBC Radio had its studios, she looked out the window and saw that it was snowing, the first snowfall of the year. Around her everybody had their noses to the grindstone while outside huge, lazy flakes drifted down. One or two others noticed the weather and grunted and looked away. For a few minutes she stood by herself at the window watching the snow fall from the sky, and in those few minutes the light flurry of flakes, suspended in the air yet moving in all directions, became a thick squall, blotting out the buildings across the street, and then the snow was over. A big blue swath opened up in the sky. She thought how changeable and infinitely various the air is, and how she was being paid to cram it to the gills with talk, to bury it under endless information, and she couldn't do it any more. "Has that ever happened to you, Harry? Whatever you were doing you couldn't do it for another second, and you quit?"

"Getting fired was more my line." His tone and manner so wry that impulsively she put her arm around him, openly, easily fond. "Go on with the story of your life," he said to her, his voice a little gruff. "Eleanor told me you married a professor. How did you meet him?"

They'd met, she said, when she enrolled in social work and he taught her several courses. She hadn't finished the degree, though. She'd stayed home for a year after their son was born, then she'd volunteered at a hospice and found her calling. It was listening to people with real problems tell her their troubles. "It never tires me," she said. Now she was training to be a family counsellor who would work in palliative care, but she was doing it part-time, since David was only four. So there it is, she said. That brings you up to date.

They stopped at a corner and waited for the light to turn. "Your hair is different than I remembered. Shorter." He pushed it gently off the side of her face and touched the rim of her ear. It looked delicately chewed, as if by mice, he told her. "My good ear's the same," he said, the result of frostbite as a kid, those hours and hours of playing outside and walking to and from school. He told her he'd heard of Prairie kids who delivered newspapers and froze their fingers so badly that although otherwise their hands grew to normal size their fingers stayed stubby, the growth plates destroyed. "If you ever see someone with fingers like that," he told her, "you'll know the reason."

She fixed him with those eyes of hers. "I almost wore your fur coat today. I would have if it had been any colder."

"Then it hasn't fallen apart." He felt caught, but not displeased. "So Eleanor couldn't resist."

Gwen smiled. "The coat's still perfect," she said.

"Well, good. I just took pity on a poor girl who needed a warm coat."

"Thank you," she said. "Thank you, Harry Boyd."

He leaned forward with something in his manner that Gwen hadn't seen before, an almost beseeching gallantry, and planted a kiss on her ear.

They crossed the street and what came next might have seemed like a non sequitur, but it was far from that for them. "Last summer," she said, "my son stepped on a wasps' nest and got stung seven times."

Harry seemed to be wrapped up in looking at her.

"And I got stung twice when he ran into my arms."

"Last summer I was in New York," he said slowly. "I was walking in Central Park, when a woman touched my arm. She said, 'You don't recognize me.'"

From the change in his face, the way it widened in mystified sadness, Gwen guessed who it was. "It was Dido," she said, and her voice was flat.

He nodded.

Gwen turned her head and glanced at the traffic going by. "And what's she doing with herself now?"

"I'm not entirely sure. She has problems with her health. If I'd never seen her before," he said thoughtfully, "I might have mistaken her for a nun."

Gwen stopped and stared at him. In her mind she saw Dido in her pretty shoes. In a cashmere sweater and leather skirt. Slender, elegant, fresh from her time in L.A. "You could say many things about Dido, but comparing her to a nun isn't anything that ever would have occurred to me."

He smiled. "I don't mean she was wearing a habit. She looked very different, that's all. Thin. Not very happy. Eddy looked much the same as ever."

"So they're still together."

"He's got more work than he knows what to do with, he told me."

Gwen reflected. "I wonder if they have children."

"They didn't say so. I don't think they're even married."

Gwen was silent. Then she said, "Marriage is hard." She'd been about to tell Harry something more, about her own marriage, but the moment had passed.

—————

Harry had been walking in Central Park when he saw Dido after all those years. It was a late summer afternoon and the wide green spaces were full of light and movement. Runners, cyclists, the leaves stirring a little in the trees. To Harry, the park's gentle contours seemed incredibly inviting, and he stopped walking to take it all in, then felt a hand on his arm.

"You don't recognize me," she said. She'd leaned forward from her bench to get his attention. She had a book open in her lap.

The sight of her did something to his heart. He felt its exact location and entire size inside his chest.

She'd lost weight. She was wearing grey. A loose linen dress with long sleeves. He saw streaks of silver in her dark hair; a filigree of silver, he thought. No wedding band.

"The last time I saw you," he said, "you were wearing a yellow sweater."

She smiled. "We can't be feeling sorry for ourselves, Harry."

He sat beside her on the bench. "Why not?" he asked.

"How many years ago was that? Don't tell me." Her dark-light, buoyant-sad voice. "You were good to me. I haven't forgotten."

And what was he to make of that, he wondered. She hadn't forgotten, but she couldn't be bothered to explain.

"You disappeared without a word," he said. "I waited for you to come home. I almost called the police. Then I ransacked the house and realized you'd gone. Why the hell didn't you say anything?"

"Kill it before it dies," she said, and sighed. "I'm not saying I couldn't have done better by you. But at least you knew where you stood."

"What are you talking about? I didn't know a thing. You didn't *tell* me anything."

"You weren't listening. You're still not listening."

He shook his head at her, confounded.

"I'm not such a prize, Harry."

"That's not how I see it."

A boy on a skateboard zoomed by so close Harry drew in his feet, looked up, and a girl in jeans and a tank top glanced at them as she strode by. Then he saw himself, a middle-aged man with a hangdog look, sitting on a park bench with the woman who'd broken his heart. Snap out of it, he knew Dido was saying in her own way. Snap out of it, Harry.

She was rubbing the side of her face with her hand and *she doesn't look well*, he thought, pulled back into his concern for her. "Has life been good?" he asked.

"I've had better days," she said.

He pressed her with more questions and learned that she hadn't been able to work since June, a combination of exhaustion and depression; the doctors had suggested an extended leave might help, and NBC was being decent about it. Eddy

worked for both of them anyway, she said. He worked all
the time.

Listening to her talk, Harry wondered if Daniel Moir had
ever contacted her. He wanted to ask, but it was really none of
his business. If Moir had gone all the way to Yellowknife but no
farther, it wouldn't do Dido any good to know about it. And if
they had been in touch, it hadn't amounted to anything, obviously. Why meddle, he said to himself. Why open old wounds.

She and Eddy had been in New York for two years, she
was telling him. Eddy was directing a television series now, a
police show that was very popular. "But *you* wouldn't know
that," she said in a tone that had in it something of her old
manner, flirtatious, cutting. "Not being one for television."

"That doesn't sound like Eddy," he said, "a police series."

Dido shrugged as if she had no opinion on the matter, or
as if Harry's opinion was of no interest. She said Eddy had
other things on the go too. His photography for one.

"So." Harry lifted the cover of her book. "What are you
reading?"

"You won't know it," she said again, and she told him it
was an old volume by A.E. Coppard, one of the English books
her father had struggled with. He'd kept them in a row on a
shelf beside his bed, and she'd brought some of them back
with her after a recent visit to her mother. She'd been perus-
ing them to see what it was that had occupied her father for so
many hours. "This one's very old style. Not easy either. I
wonder how much my father understood. Shall I tell you what
it's about?"

There was something a little mocking in her voice, challenging, aggressive. "Sure," he said.

Well, she went on, it was about two women who go into the woods to gather dead branches for firewood, and while they work they reminisce about the same man. "The same long-lost man," she smiled. "Then the wind rises in the forest and they listen to it."

When she had come to that passage, a certain phrase had made her pause and read it a second time: the description of the wind in the treetops "as of some lost wave seeking a forgotten shore," and she'd become aware of the breeze in the trees around her and raised her eyes and there was Harry Boyd, large as life.

She raised her shoulders and let them drop. "Life is a bit of a joke," she said.

As if, thought Harry, he needed any more reminding that he didn't cut it as a long-lost man.

Then she sat forward, pushed up her sleeve to check the watch that fit her wrist exactly. "I have to meet Eddy in ten minutes." She stood up. "Why don't you come and say hello to him."

"Eddy doesn't want to say hello to *me*."

"You mean *you* don't. Come on, Harry. Keep me company."

The breezes had stopped and the air was heavy. Beads of sweat had gathered on his neck. They walked quickly through the park, Dido saying it wasn't far. A friend of theirs was having a show in a gallery and they'd been invited to the opening. Beside him, despite the heat, Dido looked cool, and quite at home in the city. They came to the address on West 57th and went up a flight of stairs and through a glass door into a sizable gallery. He saw Eddy at the back, talking to a younger man with a brush cut. Dido went to them and Harry followed in her wake. Eddy had a long, deep scratch on the top of his nose, red and recent.

Dido said, "Look who I found wandering around Central Park."

Eddy stared at him without a glimmer of recognition, it seemed to Harry.

Dido kissed the young artist on both cheeks. "You're a genius," she said. And introducing him to Harry, "He's going to be very famous one day."

Then she said, "Look at Eddy. The cat swiped him. Well, he deserved it."

"It's been a long time," Eddy said, shaking Harry's hand. "I can't remember half the things I've done since I left Yellowknife."

So he *does* know who I am, thought Harry. Eddy's eyes still looked absolutely neutral. It gave Harry the weirdest feeling.

"But I've always got more on the go than I can handle," Eddy said.

He wore black jeans and a black T-shirt, and he looked more substantial, Harry thought, more muscled. He'd been working out. His face had the old chiselled confidence. His haircut must have set him back a few bucks. "Dido tells me you're still taking pictures."

"Yeah. I might have a show here," he said, glancing around him. "It's not really my kind of space, though."

The gallery was filling up. Another admirer collared the artist and pulled him away, and for a moment, Harry and Dido and Eddy were their own little unit. Harry ventured to say he'd left Yellowknife not long after they had, but an older woman, wearing half her weight in gold jewellery, had approached Dido and begun to bend her ear, and Eddy excused himself and started to work the room. So Harry made his way around the gallery as best he could. It was hard to see the paintings for the people. The canvases were big, bold, abstract. He rather liked them. Once, in the early sixties, he'd flown into Resolute Bay in the Far North after a fresh snowfall, and the buildings around the airstrip were like these pure bands of orange and yellow. The people, however, were not his type at all. In some cases their clothes were so elegant and well-fitted he was tempted to say, "Who's your tailor?" He looked around for Dido, but the room was too crowded, he couldn't see her. And so he left, taking the stairs down to the street and stepping outside into the warm evening air. He turned east and walked for quite a while before it occurred to him that he was going the wrong way. He stood for a moment on a corner, trying to orient himself. Then he turned south and walked to the bar in his hotel.

====

Harry and Gwen located their restaurant near the market and took a table by the window. After they ordered glasses of wine, Gwen drew a snapshot out of her purse and showed him her son.

Harry studied the picture. "He's lucky," he said.

She laughed. "Because he doesn't look a bit like me."

He handed the picture back to her. "I was thinking of his father. He's a lucky man to have the two of you. Maybe he doesn't know how lucky he is."

Gwen's face was suddenly warm.

Harry asked her if she'd told her son about her time in Yellowknife and their trip on the Thelon River. "The delicious taste of Coffee-mate on porridge," he said, and smacked his lips. "And all the animals. The herds of caribou, the muskox, your encounter with the grizzly. Our slog across the ice when you held that microphone between your teeth. You wouldn't want him to grow up thinking city life is all there is."

"You seem just the same, Harry. Well, maybe a little balder."

"Wretch."

She laughed. He was easy to talk to, he always had been. And no, she'd neglected to tell her son stories about the North, but she would correct the oversight. She said she wondered if she could remember all the lakes on their long route, and began to list them. Artillery, Ptarmigan, Sifton. "Burr Lake," threw in Harry. French Lake, she continued. Kipling Lake. Harry Lake, she said with a smile. Beverly Lake, they didn't say, but knew each other was thinking. A look of understanding passed between them.

"You sound like a radio announcer," he said, "listing all the places the signal carries to." All the faraway towns, he thought, filled with listeners who are only half-listening, their minds on other things. *I used to know that bedroom by heart.*

He said, "You were saying that marriage is hard."

"Yes." She looked up. "I find it so." Here was the moment again. "But my mother-in-law is coaxing me to give it one more chance, for David's sake."

"So you're thinking it over."

"I'm thinking she's probably right."

"Yes," he said heavily.

When their food arrived, they occupied themselves with eating, hardly looking up. Then Harry thought to tell her about the special trip he'd made to Dover, to Edgar's school, to see the original red leather diary that lay inside a glass case in the headmaster's study, also the plaque to Edgar's memory in the school chapel. It felt profoundly circular, he said, that having stood in the very spot where the diary was written and then preserved in the cold ashes of a stove, he'd caught up with its final resting place. It made him wonder if the two places were separated — or if they were connected — by those several thousand miles.

Later, they walked back to Rideau Street. Harry offered to see her safely home. No need, she said, she'd grab a taxi, and she flagged one at the corner. She hugged Harry, then slid into the back seat as the light turned red, giving her a chance to watch him jaywalk across Sussex Drive, then continue up the slope past the Château Laurier. She had always loved the way he walked. Never in a rush, hands in his pockets turning a lighter or jiggling a few coins, shoulders square from having played rugby and from years in his father's church choir. His left foot a little pigeon-toed. She liked the outward curve of his left shin and she couldn't have said why, except that it seemed erotic.

A year passed before she phoned him again. This time she said, "Harry, when are you coming into my bed?"

ONE SUNDAY MORNING, during a long, wet spring, Harry opened the paper at the breakfast table and glancing through the obituaries almost missed Dido's. He read the short paragraph that summarized her life and early death, while the rain came down. It was almost tropical, the sound of the rain. All around them the steady beat, the full gurgle of water flowing off the roof, through the pipes, into the ground. Last night he'd heard voices outside at ten o'clock, laughter despite the weather and the hour, then a series of bangs that puzzled him until he remembered. He'd called to Gwen and she'd joined him at the bedroom window. Through a gap in the trees, they watched fireworks transform the rain-soaked sky into brighter and bigger cascades of colour until the final all-out volley and the sudden lights out. The twenty-fourth of May, the Queen's birthday. Always an occasion for firecrackers. A constant, he'd thought, since boyhood. A reassuring custom that knit together a whole span of years.

He passed the newspaper across the table to Gwen.

Her *oh!* then silence while she read about Dido's death "on May 17, after a long illness. Born 1947, in the Netherlands, only child of Johan and Griet. Cherished companion of producer and experimental photographer Edward Fitzgerald.

Adored aunt of Tracey, Erin, Joshua. Seven years at NBC. Filing cabinets filled with clippings about social justice, ideas for films, plays, screenplays, stories. Passion in search of a vehicle. An erratic, emotional, beautiful woman who never quite found herself."

Gradually the rain stopped, but the sky stayed heavy and grey. Everything brimmed – the rivers, the canal, the lakes. Harry threw open a window and they heard the trickling away of water and the birds.

In the afternoon, while David played next door, Gwen and Harry went out for a walk. At first they were silent, skirting puddles, occupied by their own thoughts. Gwen mulled over the words Eddy had chosen, perhaps self-serving in some way, but they had the ring of truth. An erratic, emotional energy – quick to leap and quick to subside. Dido's beauty had been the main event that summer when light made them tireless, like children playing outside till dark, but there was no dark.

"I'm astounded they stayed together," Harry said. "I never thought they would." He'd been remembering Dido in the art gallery, how she'd more than held her own.

"They must have loved each other," said Gwen.

Too pat, thought Harry. Too easy. It doesn't tell you anything. "Was it love, or something else," he said. Some unhealthy need, he was thinking.

"She was loyal to him, he was loyal to her," Gwen said simply. "They had a bond, call it what you will."

Harry nodded slowly, and for some reason the tangle in his heart let go a little. He felt his view of the pair, not reverse itself but widen – a bond, call it what you will. He slid his arm through Gwen's and they kept walking. They turned a corner and two boys were biking through puddles on Euclid Avenue. It began to spatter rain and they headed back.

That night, when she woke at three and couldn't sleep, Gwen did what she often did, she went north in her mind, into the summer air, down the road to Latham Island and out onto the pre-dawn waters. Usually Harry was sound asleep beside her, but now he spoke to her in the dark. The sound of his voice was the sound of that place, and it took her all the way back and brought everything forward. His voice was as dark as a plum, and the darkness in their room was the shade of a plum tree. He spoke to her again, and she felt held by his voice and taken under the wing of that faraway place.

In the morning, it was raining again. They heard it when they woke up, and Gwen murmured that they were lucky not to be in a tent. Or a boat, said Harry. The rain beat against the roof and slid down all the windows facing west. They felt vulnerable and protected, lying there, listening to the sounds the world makes in the month of May. How the earth could hold any more water they didn't know.

ACKNOWLEDGEMENTS

Always in the background as I wrote this novel was George Whalley's marvellous biography, *The Legend of John Hornby* (Macmillan of Canada, 1962), a book that has stayed with me since I first read it thirty years ago. The quotations from it, including "Garden of Desire" and "Country of the Mind," have been used with the kind permission of his widow, Elizabeth Whalley.

The quotations from George Whalley's radio drama, *Death in the Barren Ground: A Narrative of John Hornby's Last Journey*, broadcast on CBC Radio on April 10, 1966, have been used with the permission of CBC Radio and Elizabeth Whalley. To suit the chronology of my own narrative, in these pages the broadcast occurs five years earlier.

Ken Puley of CBC Radio Archives was unfailingly helpful in finding the material I needed. I thank him most gratefully.

The thought on page 260 that "the robin in the egg doesn't know that the robin's egg is blue" comes from